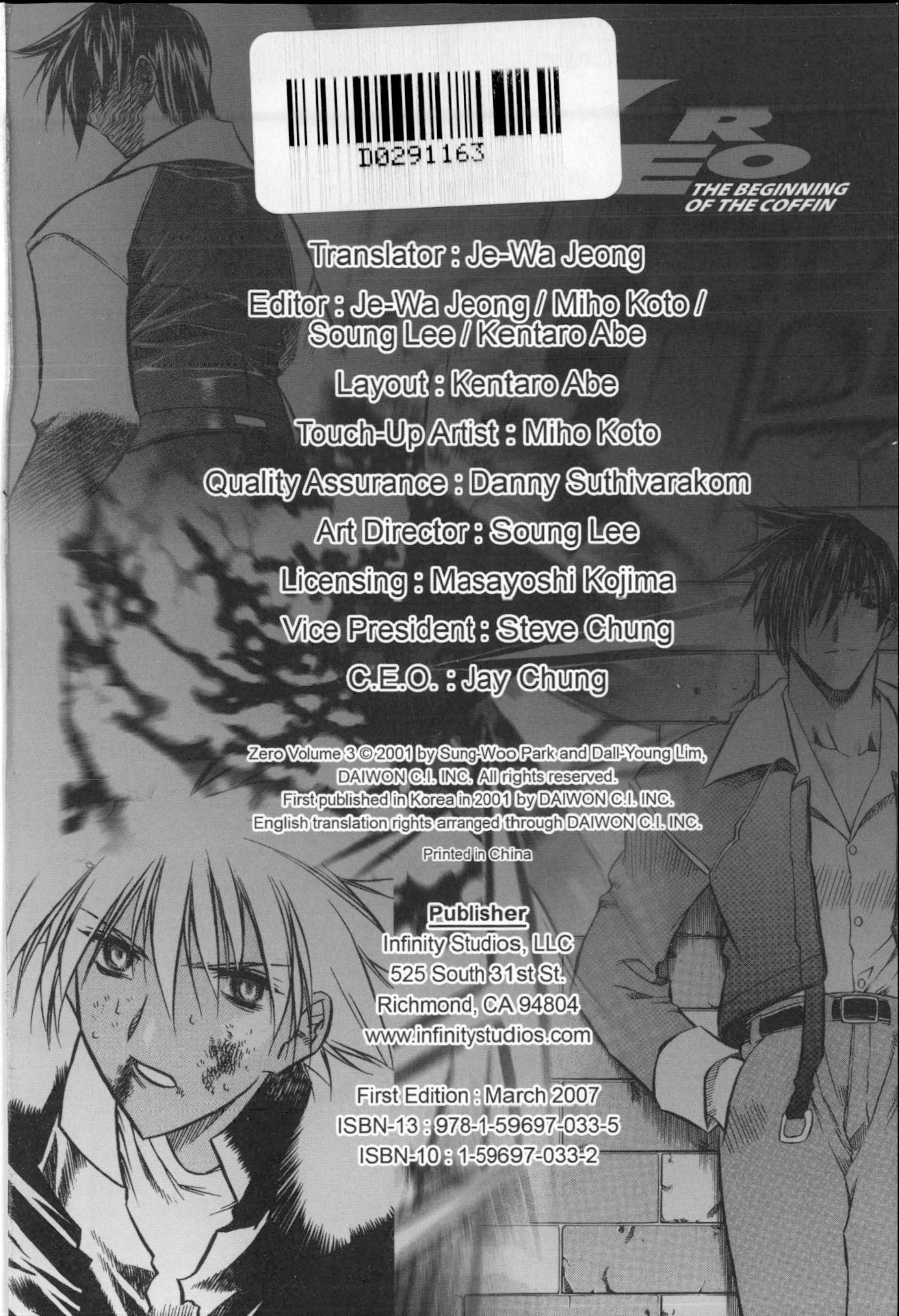

THE BEGINNING OF THE COFFIN

Translator : Je-Wa Jeong

Editor : Je-Wa Jeong / Miho Koto / Soung Lee / Kentaro Abe

Layout : Kentaro Abe

Touch-Up Artist : Miho Koto

Quality Assurance : Danny Suthivarakom

Art Director : Soung Lee

Licensing : Masayoshi Kojima

Vice President : Steve Chung

C.E.O. : Jay Chung

Printed in China

Publisher
Infinity Studios, LLC
525 South 31st St.
Richmond, CA 94804
www.infinitystudios.com

First Edition : March 2007
ISBN-13 : 978-1-59697-033-5
ISBN-10 : 1-59697-033-2

ZERO THE BEGINNING OF THE COFFIN

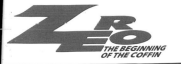

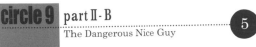

contents

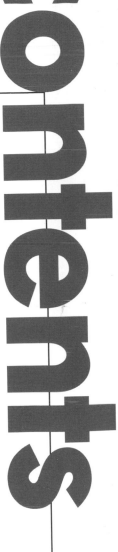

The Asakawa Family

Shuuichi, Katsumi, & Sumire Asakawa

Being the direct descendants of the original test subjects for the Zero project, they've spent much of their lives dreaming of escaping and hiding from everyone. Shuuichi is heir to his father's zero-type powers and Sumire has the ability to heal.

The story so far...

No one seems to understand the full extent and potential of Shuuichi's power... not even himself. When a gang of delinquents decides to pick a fight with him, they quickly learn they've made a big mistake. Even their combined Level C power levels are nowhere close to the tremendous power Shuuichi commands. As a result, the ECS feels the need to bring "M.O." out of hibernation to keep Shuuichi in check.

Classmates

| Harue Amano | Hayate Jonouchi | Shinichi Takayama | Akira Sendo | Ayaka Sendo |

Upon agreeing to the living arrangements with the ECS, Shuuichi reluctantly agrees to attend the special esper school. While on the most part, the students at this school are no different from most other schools, school yard fights can get out of hand due to the abilities & powers each student has.

ECS

Kenji Oshima   Natsuko Ishihara   Sachi Amamiya

M.O.

The ECS was originally a shadow organization funded by the government to research esper powers. During its earlier years, it ran unethical experiments on espers, but after a major incident involving Shuuichi's father, the ECS was disbanded and reformed as an aid organization to espers, providing both education and protection.

LEED

| Albert Bradley | Tohru Kanzaki | Yuuji Morigawa | ????? | Shizuka | Shira |

A secret group of powerful espers with unlimited economic & political powers and a clandestine objective. Their primary concern at the moment seems to be getting Shuuichi to join their organization by any means necessary.

ZERO

THE BEGINNING OF THE COFFIN

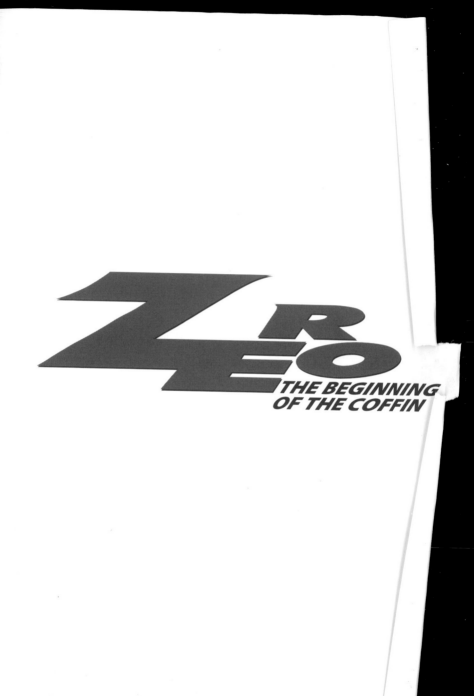

CIRCLE 9 part II
The Dangerous Nice Guy

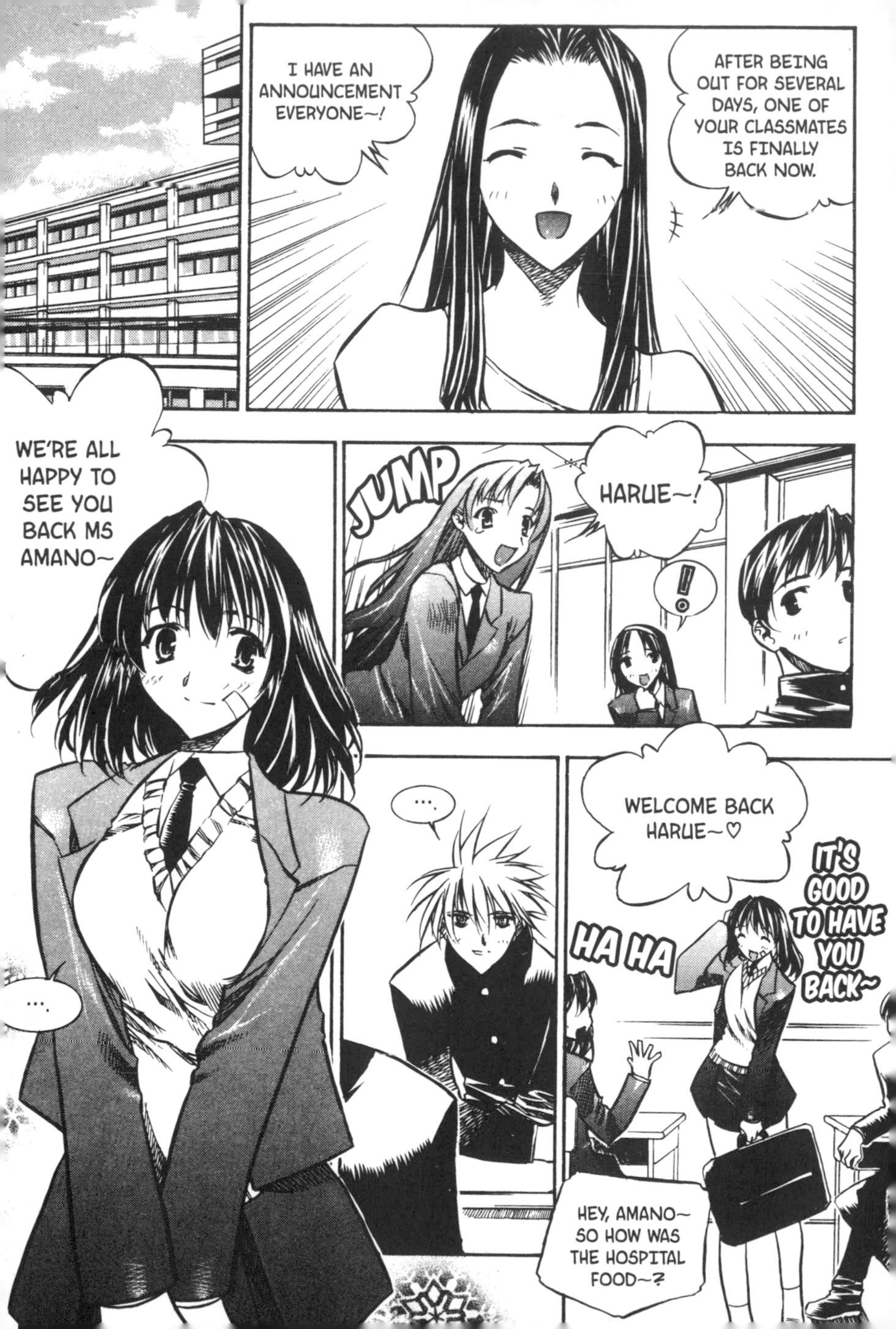

I HAVE AN ANNOUNCEMENT EVERYONE~!
AFTER BEING OUT FOR SEVERAL DAYS, ONE OF YOUR CLASSMATES IS FINALLY BACK NOW.
WE'RE ALL HAPPY TO SEE YOU BACK MS AMANO~
...
JUMP
HARUE~!
!
...
WELCOME BACK HARUE~♡
IT'S GOOD TO HAVE YOU BACK~
HA HA
HEY, AMANO~ SO HOW WAS THE HOSPITAL FOOD~?

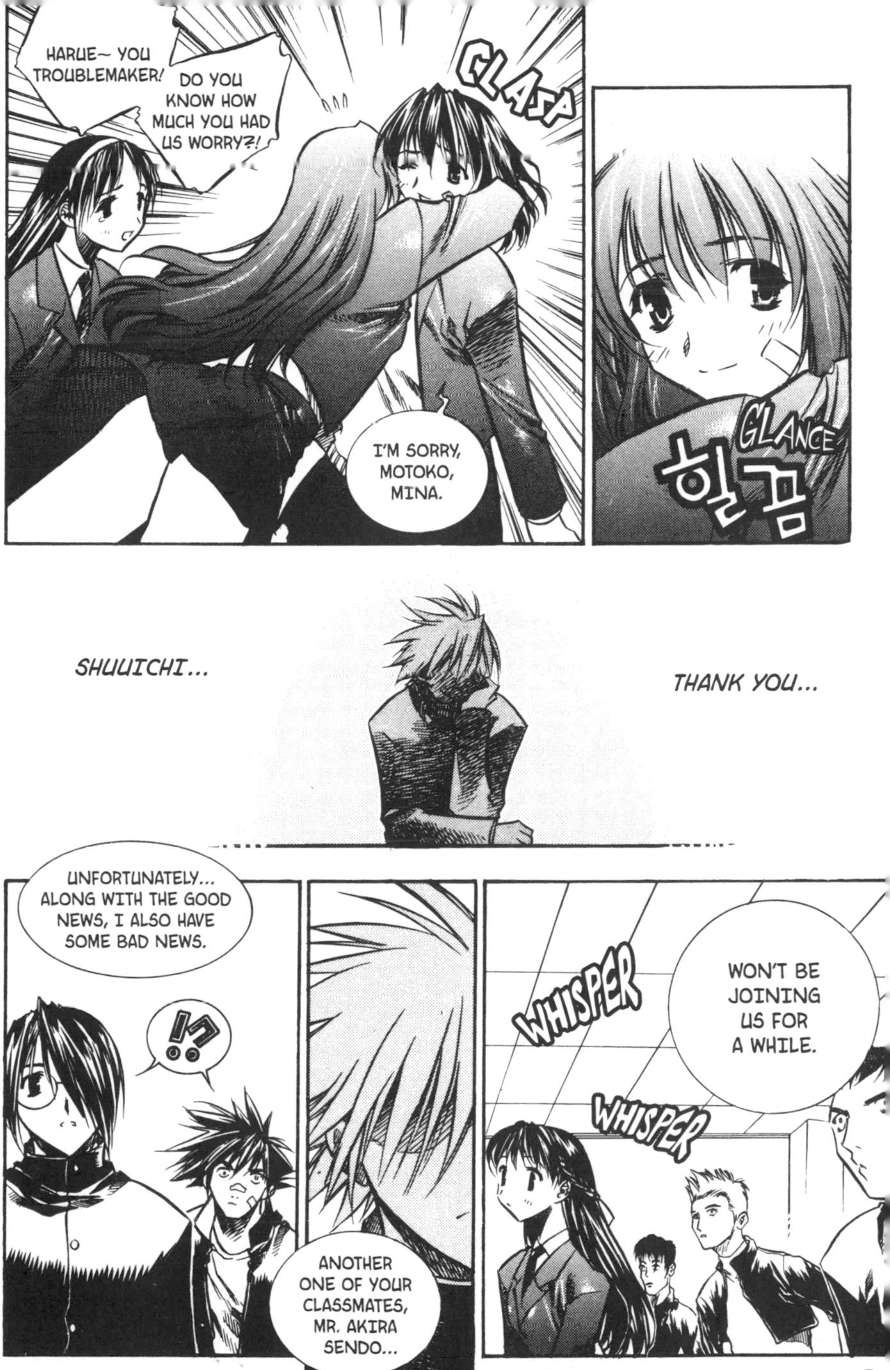
HARUE~ YOU TROUBLEMAKER!
DO YOU KNOW HOW MUCH YOU HAD US WORRY?!
CLASP
I'M SORRY, MOTOKO, MINA.
GLANCE
힐끔
SHUUICHI...
THANK YOU...
UNFORTUNATELY... ALONG WITH THE GOOD NEWS, I ALSO HAVE SOME BAD NEWS.
!?
ANOTHER ONE OF YOUR CLASSMATES, MR. AKIRA SENDO...
WHISPER
WHISPER
WON'T BE JOINING US FOR A WHILE.

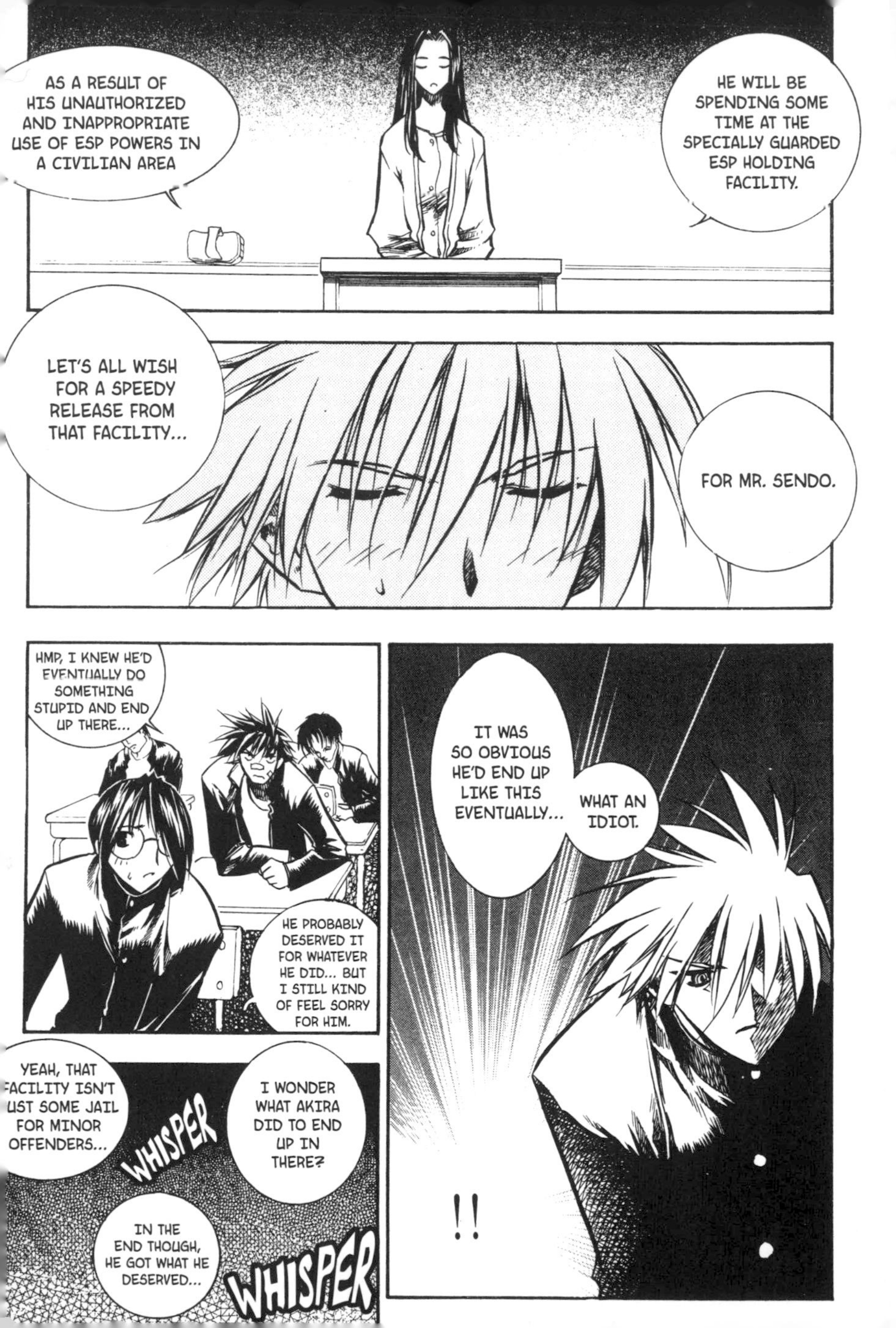
AS A RESULT OF HIS UNAUTHORIZED AND INAPPROPRIATE USE OF ESP POWERS IN A CIVILIAN AREA
HE WILL BE SPENDING SOME TIME AT THE SPECIALLY GUARDED ESP HOLDING FACILITY.
LET'S ALL WISH FOR A SPEEDY RELEASE FROM THAT FACILITY...
FOR MR. SENDO.
HMP, I KNEW HE'D EVENTUALLY DO SOMETHING STUPID AND END UP THERE...
HE PROBABLY DESERVED IT FOR WHATEVER HE DID... BUT I STILL KIND OF FEEL SORRY FOR HIM.
YEAH, THAT FACILITY ISN'T JUST SOME JAIL FOR MINOR OFFENDERS...
I WONDER WHAT AKIRA DID TO END UP IN THERE?
WHISPER
IN THE END THOUGH, HE GOT WHAT HE DESERVED...
WHISPER
IT WAS SO OBVIOUS HE'D END UP LIKE THIS EVENTUALLY...
WHAT AN IDIOT.
!!

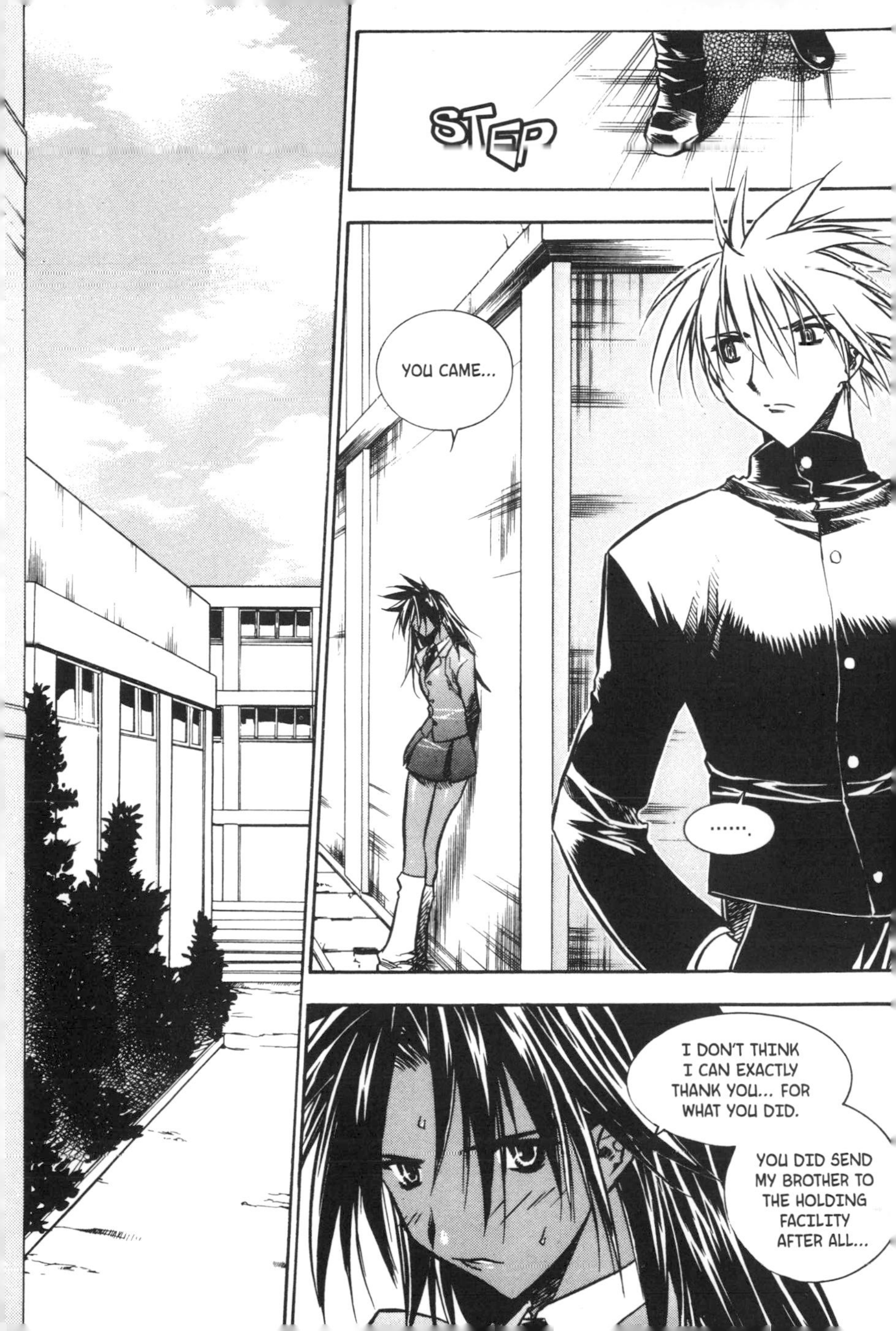
STEP
YOU CAME...
......
I DON'T THINK I CAN EXACTLY THANK YOU... FOR WHAT YOU DID.
YOU DID SEND MY BROTHER TO THE HOLDING FACILITY AFTER ALL...

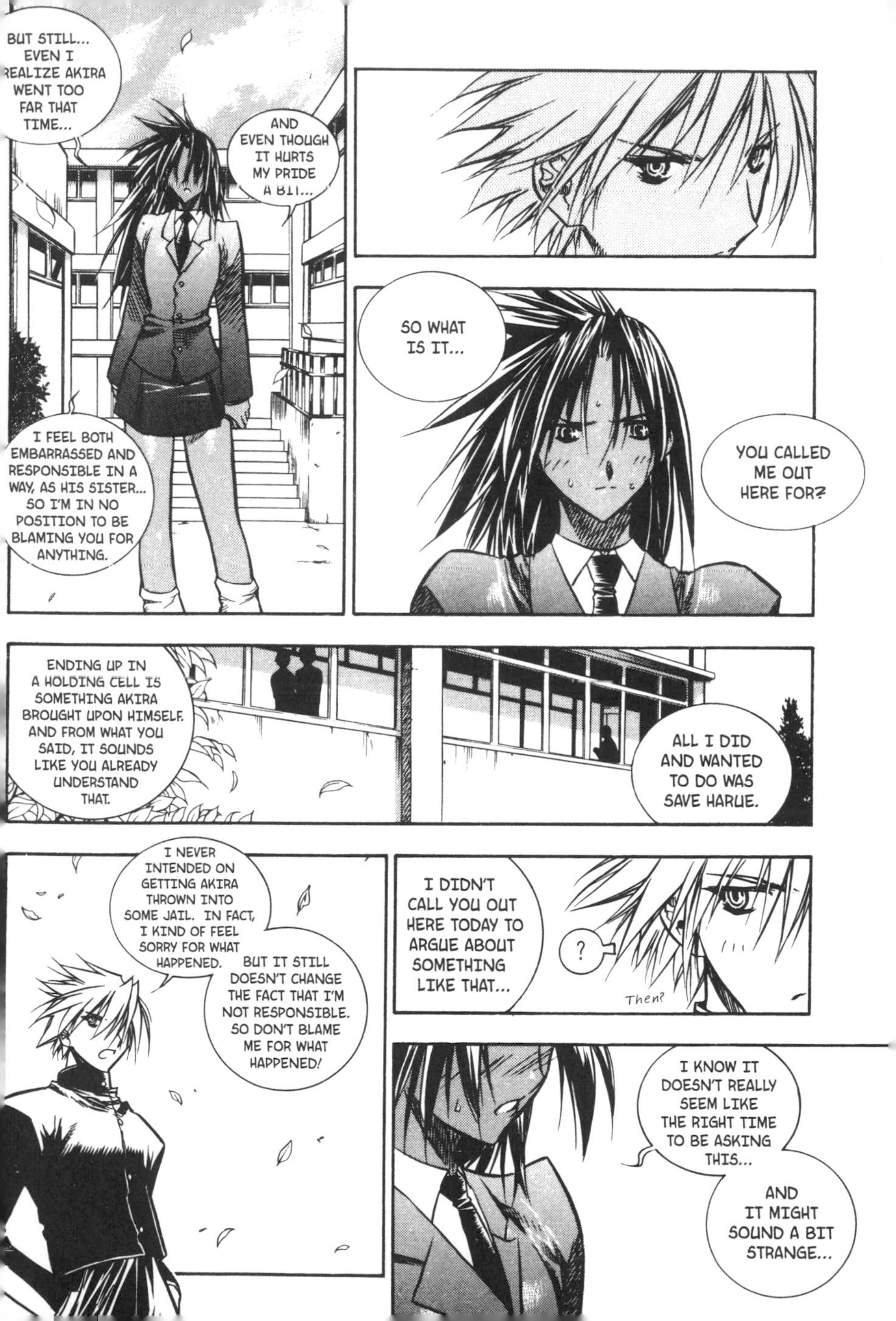
BUT STILL... EVEN I REALIZE AKIRA WENT TOO FAR THAT TIME...
AND EVEN THOUGH IT HURTS MY PRIDE A BIT...
I FEEL BOTH EMBARRASSED AND RESPONSIBLE IN A WAY, AS HIS SISTER... SO I'M IN NO POSITION TO BE BLAMING YOU FOR ANYTHING.
SO WHAT IS IT...
YOU CALLED ME OUT HERE FOR?
ENDING UP IN A HOLDING CELL IS SOMETHING AKIRA BROUGHT UPON HIMSELF. AND FROM WHAT YOU SAID, IT SOUNDS LIKE YOU ALREADY UNDERSTAND THAT.
ALL I DID AND WANTED TO DO WAS SAVE HARUE.
I NEVER INTENDED ON GETTING AKIRA THROWN INTO SOME JAIL. IN FACT, I KIND OF FEEL SORRY FOR WHAT HAPPENED.
BUT IT STILL DOESN'T CHANGE THE FACT THAT I'M NOT RESPONSIBLE. SO DON'T BLAME ME FOR WHAT HAPPENED!
I DIDN'T CALL YOU OUT HERE TODAY TO ARGUE ABOUT SOMETHING LIKE THAT...
?
Then?
I KNOW IT DOESN'T REALLY SEEM LIKE THE RIGHT TIME TO BE ASKING THIS...
AND IT MIGHT SOUND A BIT STRANGE...

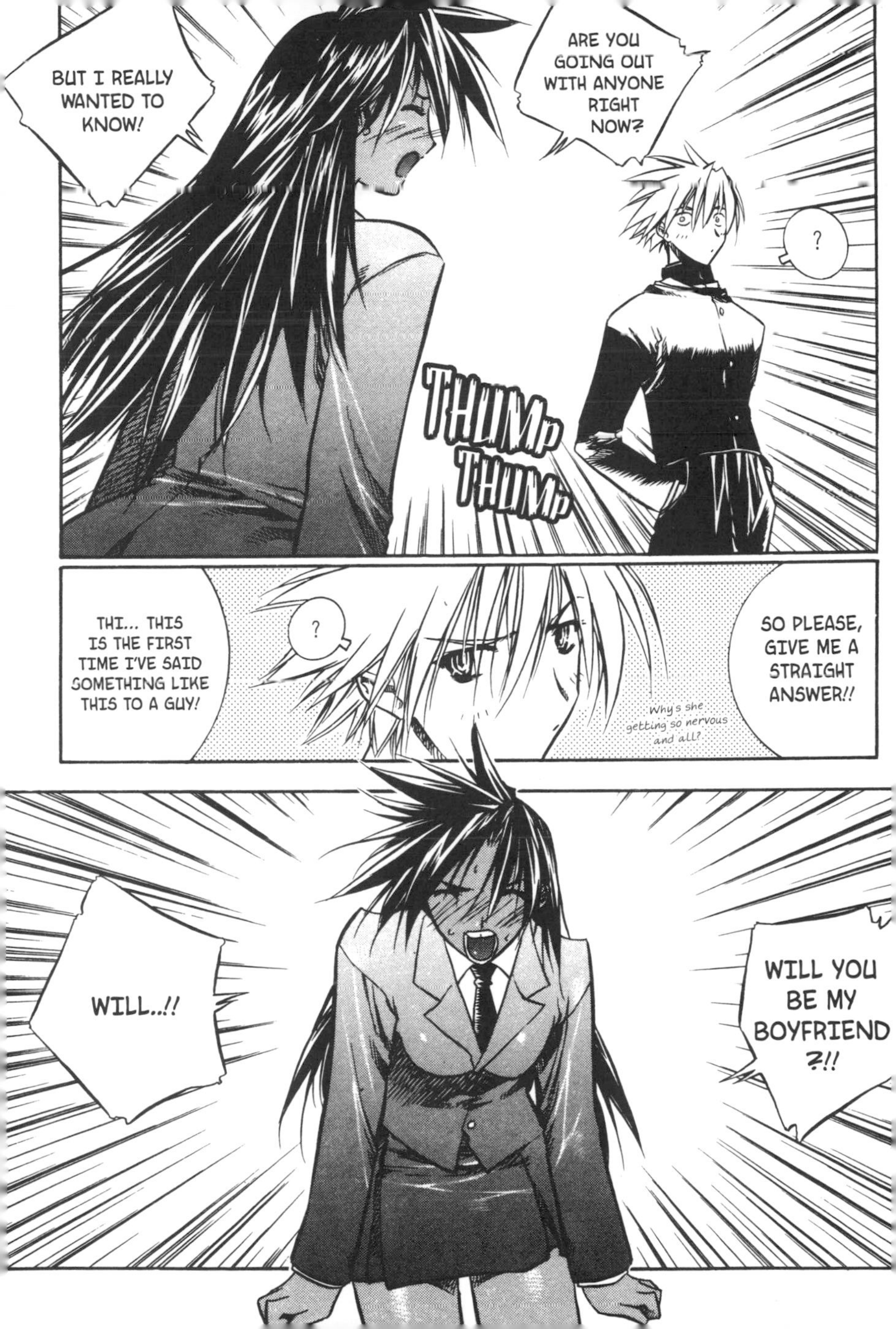
BUT I REALLY WANTED TO KNOW!
ARE YOU GOING OUT WITH ANYONE RIGHT NOW?
?
THUMP THUMP
THI... THIS IS THE FIRST TIME I'VE SAID SOMETHING LIKE THIS TO A GUY!
?
Why's she getting so nervous and all?
SO PLEASE, GIVE ME A STRAIGHT ANSWER!!
WILL..!!
WILL YOU BE MY BOYFRIEND ?!!

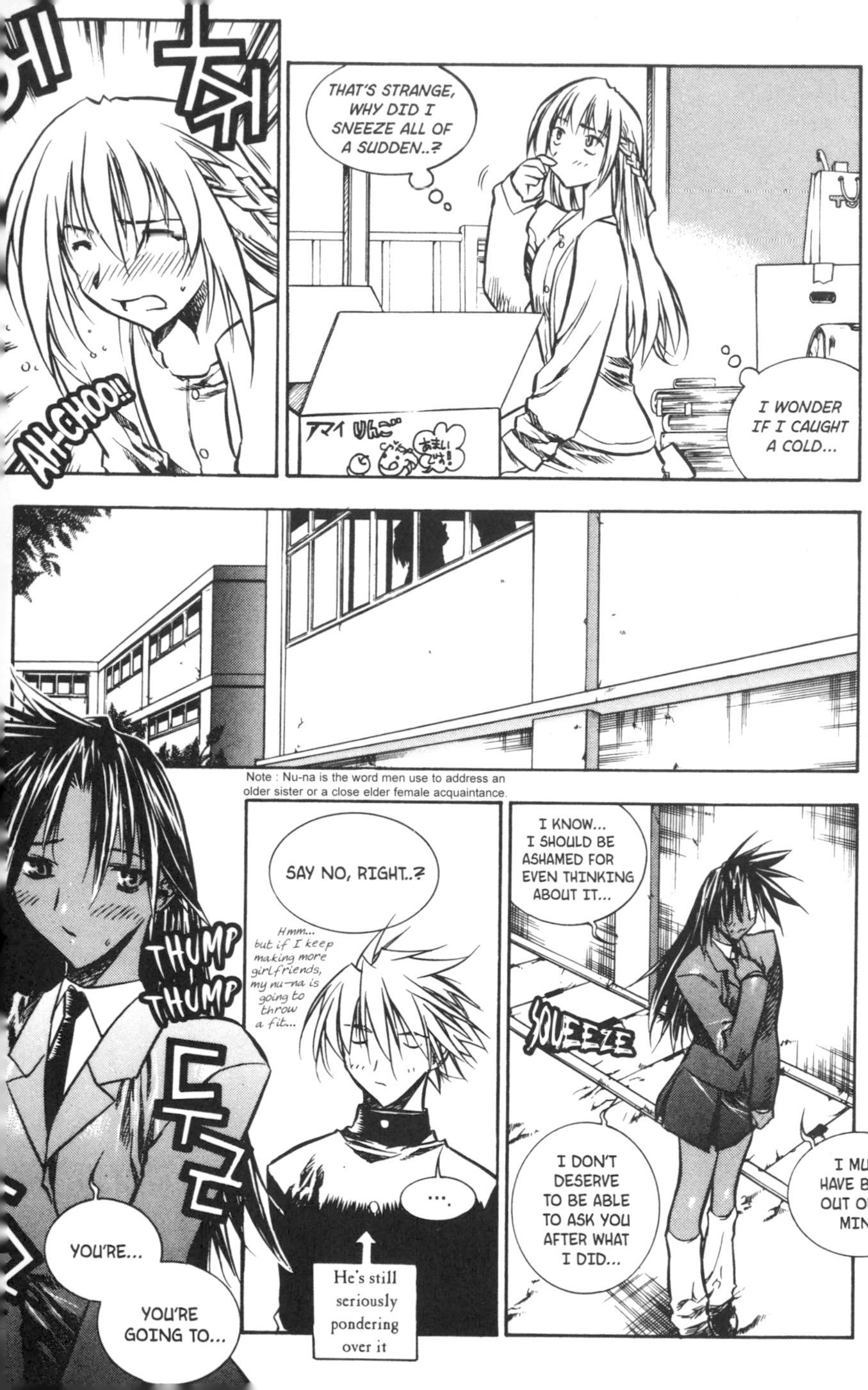
HATCH
AH-CHOO!!
THAT'S STRANGE, WHY DID I SNEEZE ALL OF A SUDDEN..?
I WONDER IF I CAUGHT A COLD...
Note : Nu-na is the word men use to address an older sister or a close elder female acquaintance.
THUMP THUMP
YOU'RE...
YOU'RE GOING TO...
SAY NO, RIGHT..?
Hmm... but if I keep making more girlfriends, my nu-na is going to throw a fit...
....
He's still seriously pondering over it
I KNOW... I SHOULD BE ASHAMED FOR EVEN THINKING ABOUT IT...
SQUEEZE
I DON'T DESERVE TO BE ABLE TO ASK YOU AFTER WHAT I DID...
I MUST HAVE BEEN OUT OF MY MIND...

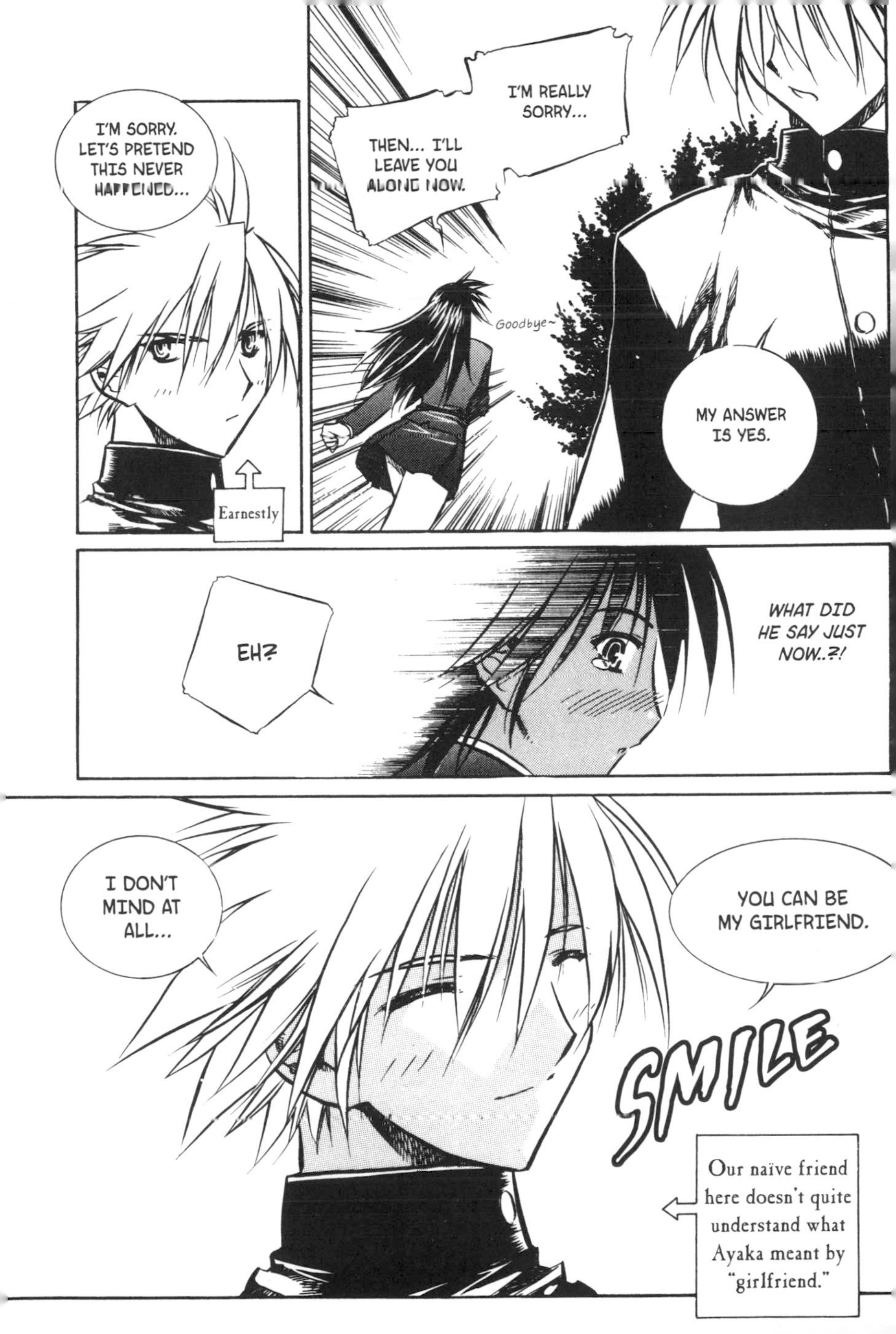
I'M SORRY. LET'S PRETEND THIS NEVER HAPPENED...
Earnestly
THEN... I'LL LEAVE YOU ALONE NOW.
I'M REALLY SORRY...
Goodbye~
MY ANSWER IS YES.
EH?
WHAT DID HE SAY JUST NOW..?!
I DON'T MIND AT ALL...
YOU CAN BE MY GIRLFRIEND.
SMILE
Our naïve friend here doesn't quite understand what Ayaka meant by "girlfriend."

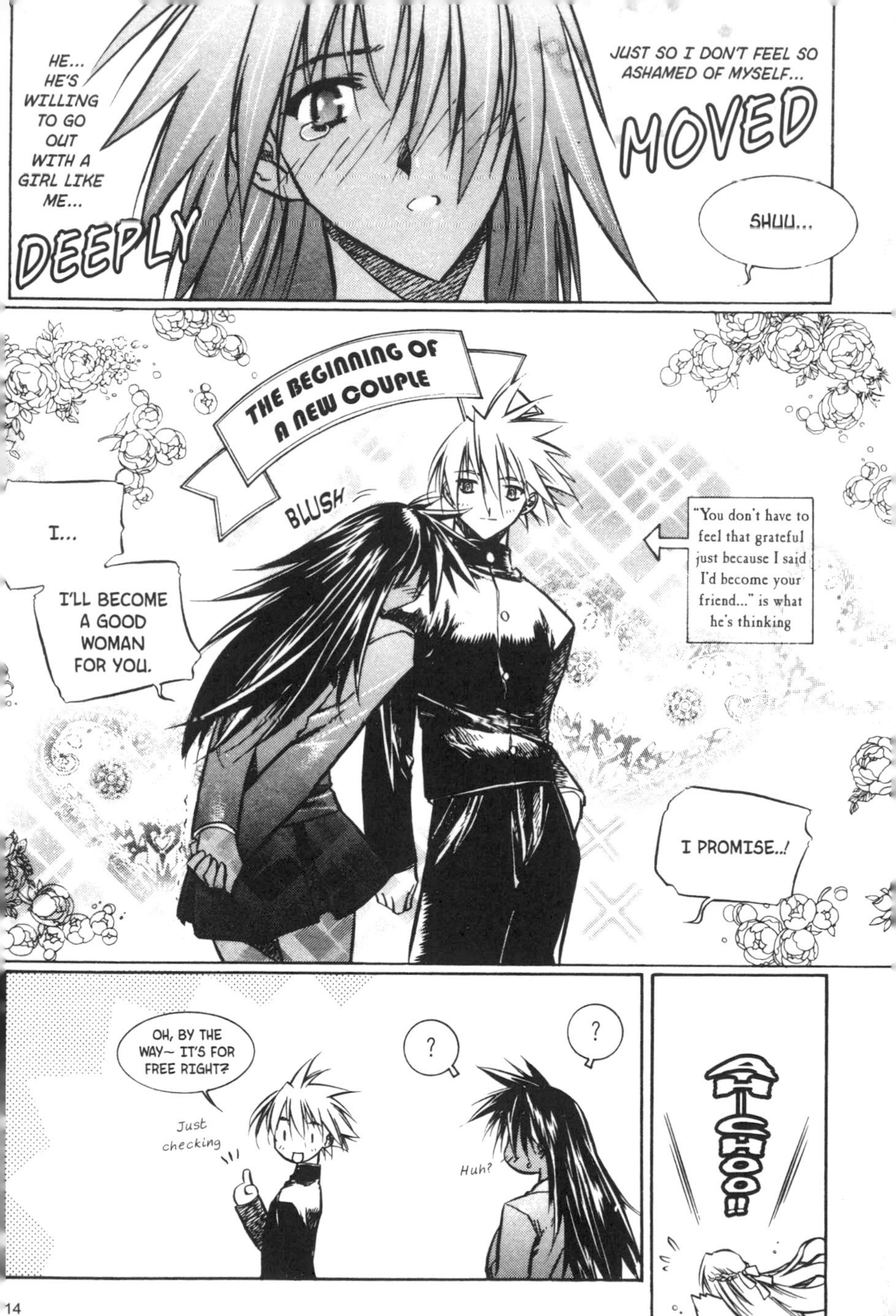
HE... HE'S WILLING TO GO OUT WITH A GIRL LIKE ME...
JUST SO I DON'T FEEL SO ASHAMED OF MYSELF...
DEEPLY
MOVED
SHUU...
THE BEGINNING OF A NEW COUPLE
BLUSH
I...
I'LL BECOME A GOOD WOMAN FOR YOU.
"You don't have to feel that grateful just because I said I'd become your friend..." is what he's thinking
I PROMISE..!
OH, BY THE WAY~ IT'S FOR FREE RIGHT?
Just checking
?
?
Huh?
A-CHOO!!

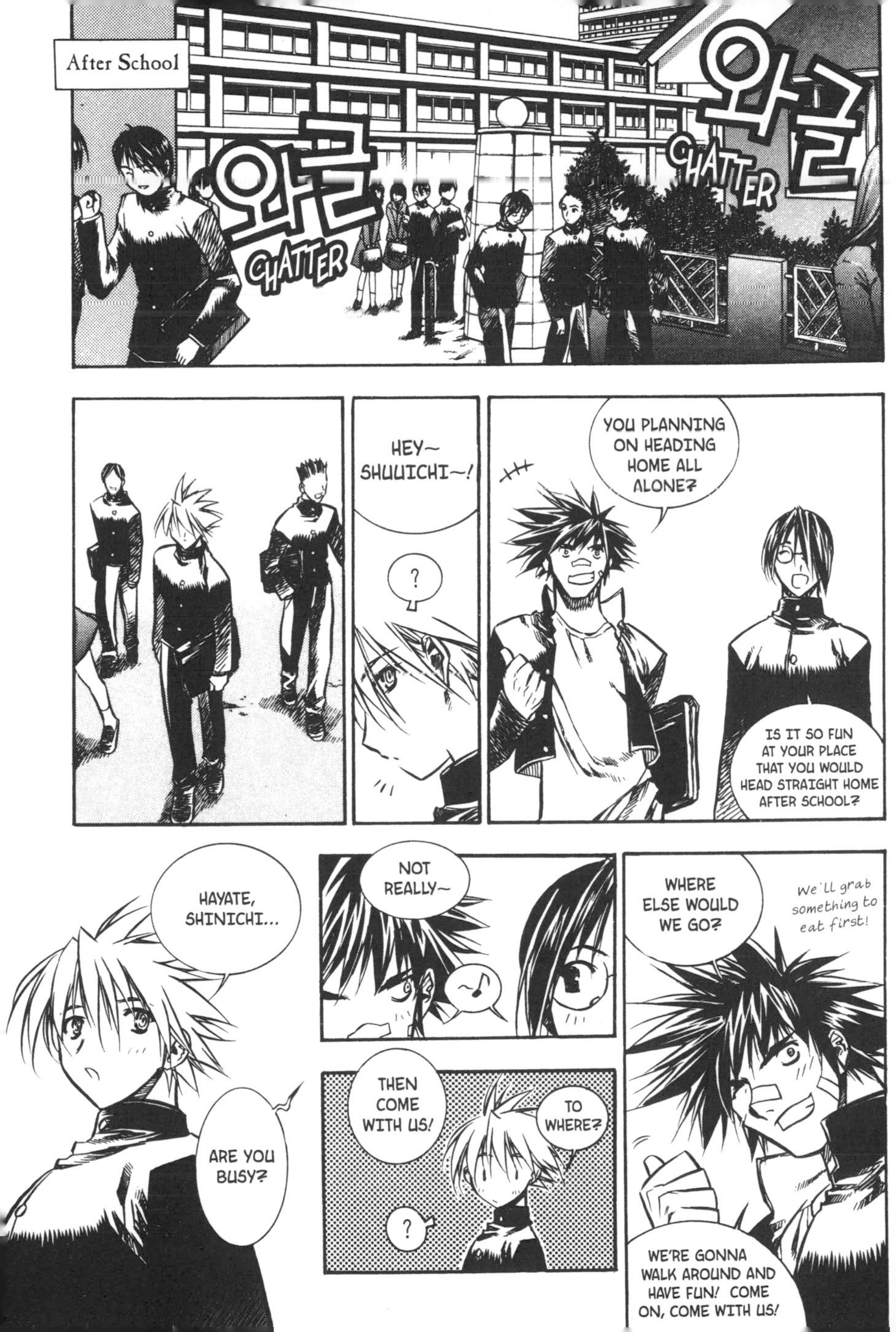
After School
와글
CHATTER
와글
CHATTER
HEY~ SHUUICHI~!
?
YOU PLANNING ON HEADING HOME ALL ALONE?
IS IT SO FUN AT YOUR PLACE THAT YOU WOULD HEAD STRAIGHT HOME AFTER SCHOOL?
HAYATE, SHINICHI...
ARE YOU BUSY?
NOT REALLY~
~♪
WHERE ELSE WOULD WE GO?
We'll grab something to eat first!
THEN COME WITH US!
TO WHERE?
?
WE'RE GONNA WALK AROUND AND HAVE FUN! COME ON, COME WITH US!

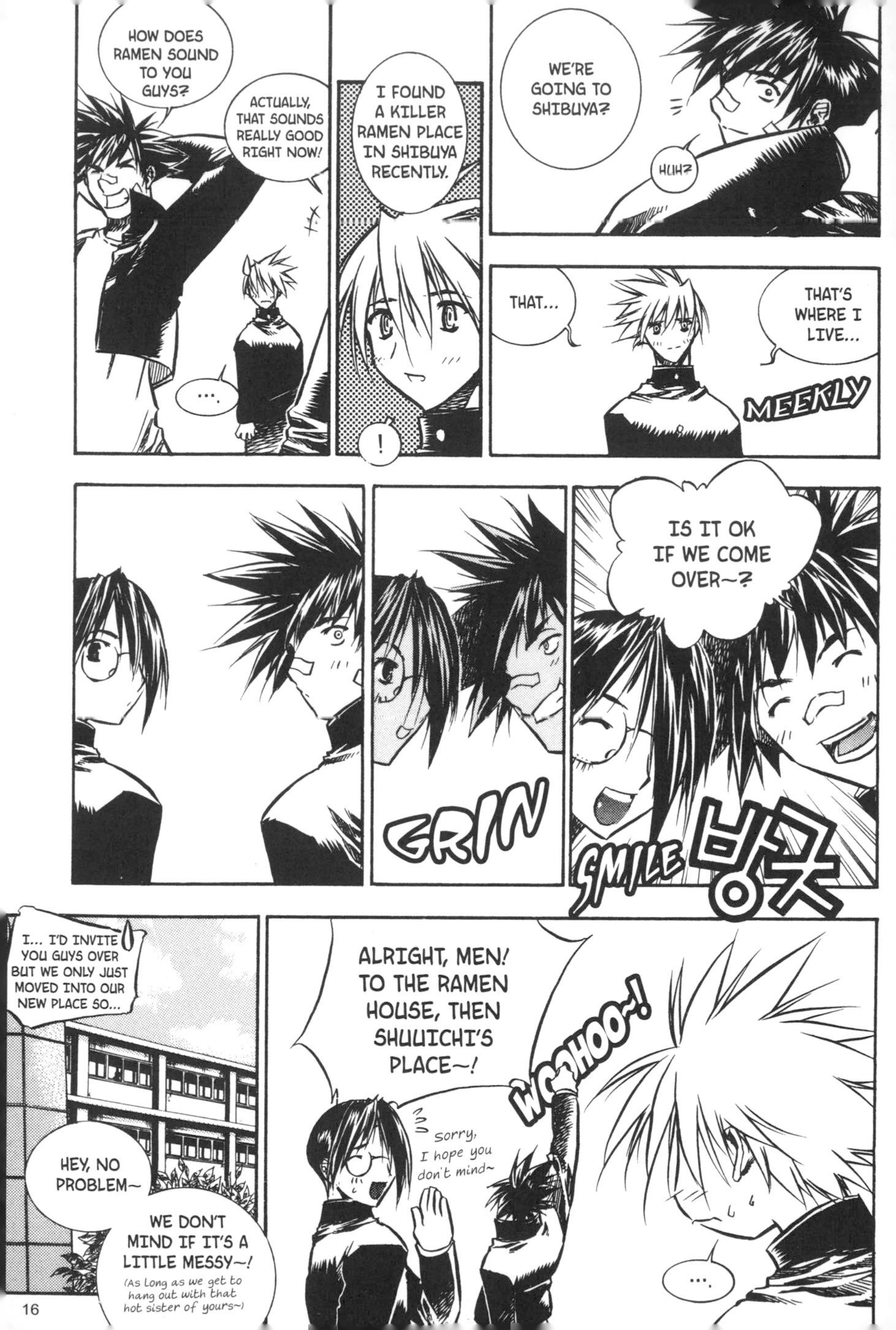
HOW DOES RAMEN SOUND TO YOU GUYS?
ACTUALLY, THAT SOUNDS REALLY GOOD RIGHT NOW!
...,
I FOUND A KILLER RAMEN PLACE IN SHIBUYA RECENTLY.
!
WE'RE GOING TO SHIBUYA?
HUH?
THAT...
THAT'S WHERE I LIVE...
MEEKLY
GRIN
IS IT OK IF WE COME OVER~?
SMILE 방긋
I... I'D INVITE YOU GUYS OVER BUT WE ONLY JUST MOVED INTO OUR NEW PLACE SO...
HEY, NO PROBLEM~
WE DON'T MIND IF IT'S A LITTLE MESSY~!
(As long as we get to hang out with that hot sister of yours~)
ALRIGHT, MEN! TO THE RAMEN HOUSE, THEN SHUUICHI'S PLACE~!
WOOHOO~!
sorry, I hope you don't mind~
...,

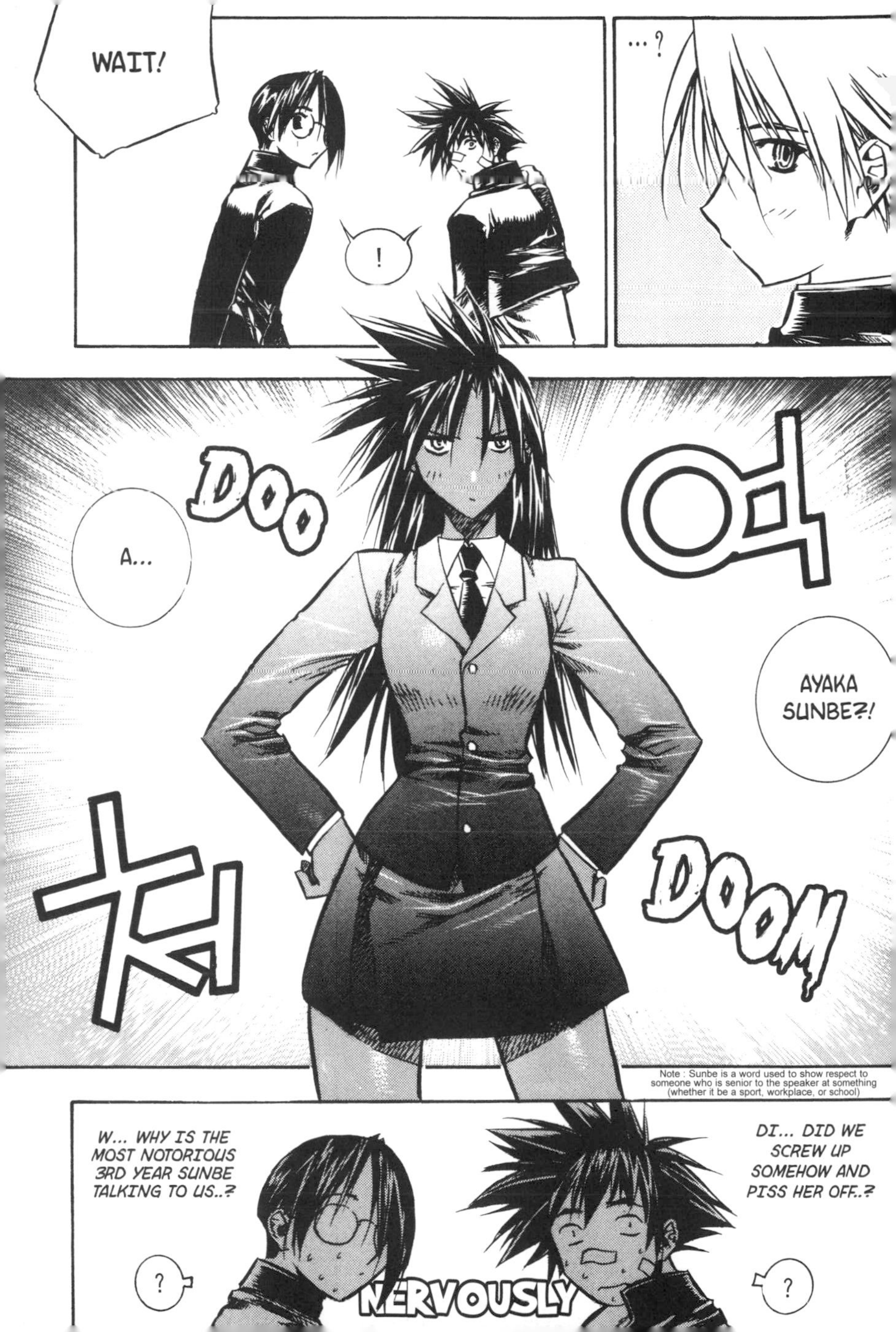
WAIT!
!
...?
DOO
A...
어
AYAKA SUNBE?!
DOOM
Note : Sunbe is a word used to show respect to someone who is senior to the speaker at something (whether it be a sport, workplace, or school)
W... WHY IS THE MOST NOTORIOUS 3RD YEAR SUNBE TALKING TO US..?
DI... DID WE SCREW UP SOMEHOW AND PISS HER OFF..?
?
?
NERVOUSLY

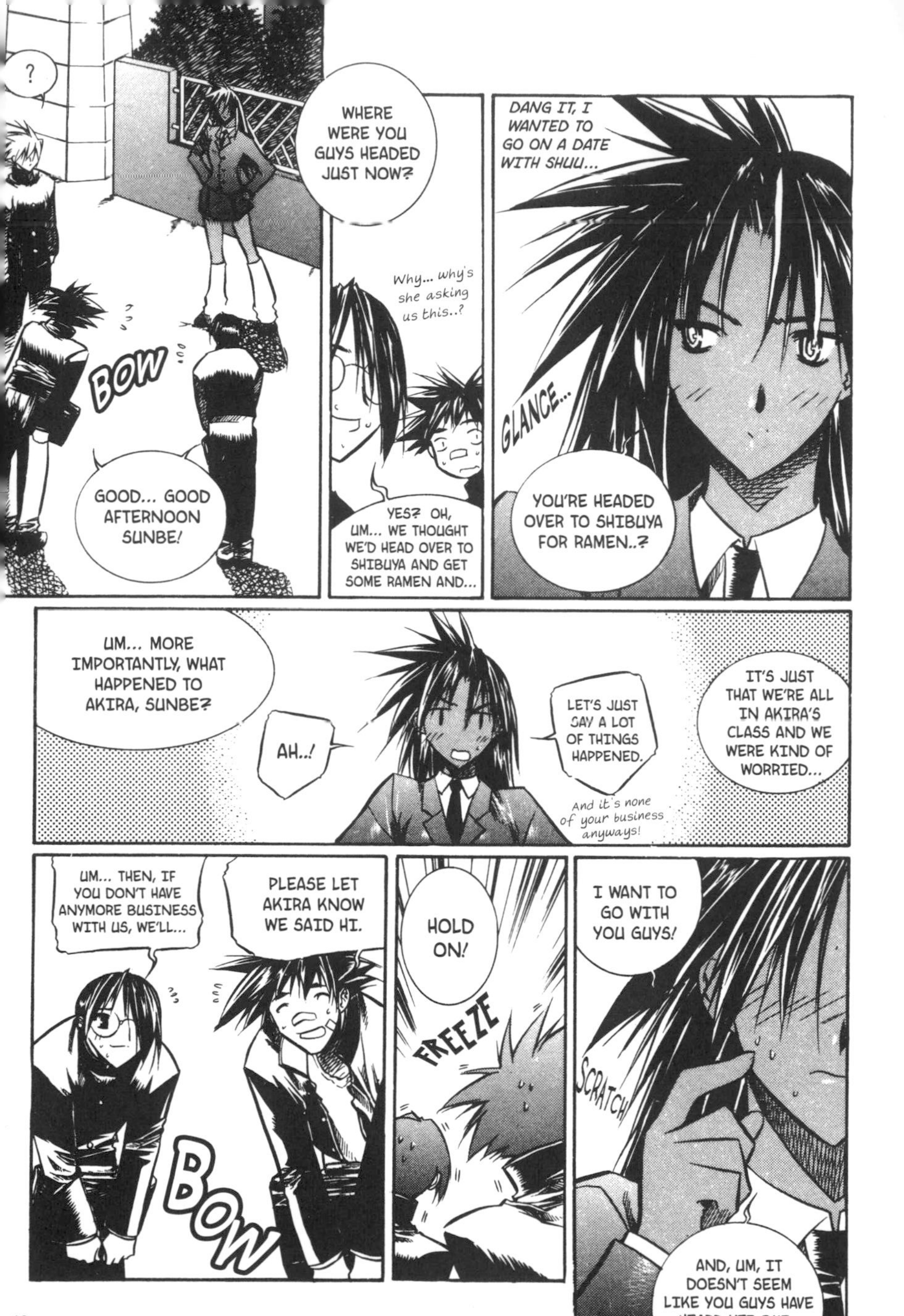
?
BOW
GOOD... GOOD AFTERNOON SUNBE!
WHERE WERE YOU GUYS HEADED JUST NOW?
Why... why's she asking us this..?
YES? OH, UM... WE THOUGHT WE'D HEAD OVER TO SHIBUYA AND GET SOME RAMEN AND...
DANG IT, I WANTED TO GO ON A DATE WITH SHUU...
GLANCE...
YOU'RE HEADED OVER TO SHIBUYA FOR RAMEN..?
UM... MORE IMPORTANTLY, WHAT HAPPENED TO AKIRA, SUNBE?
AH..!
LET'S JUST SAY A LOT OF THINGS HAPPENED.
And it's none of your business anyways!
IT'S JUST THAT WE'RE ALL IN AKIRA'S CLASS AND WE WERE KIND OF WORRIED...
UM... THEN, IF YOU DON'T HAVE ANYMORE BUSINESS WITH US, WE'LL...
PLEASE LET AKIRA KNOW WE SAID HI.
BOW
HOLD ON!
FREEZE
I WANT TO GO WITH YOU GUYS!
SCRATCH
AND, UM, IT DOESN'T SEEM LIKE YOU GUYS HAVE HEARD YET, BUT...

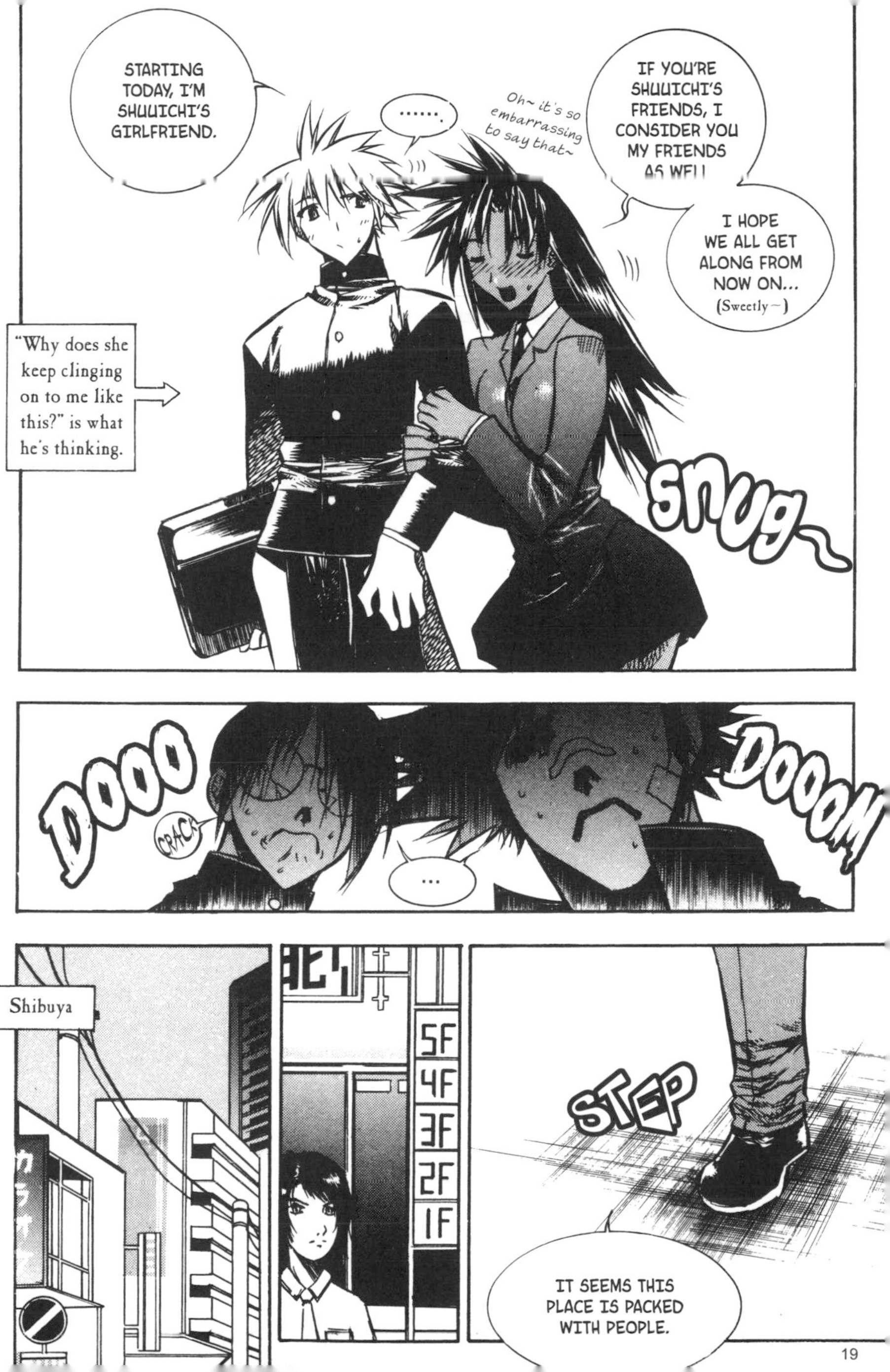

STARTING TODAY, I'M SHUUICHI'S GIRLFRIEND.
....
Oh~ it's so embarrassing to say that~
IF YOU'RE SHUUICHI'S FRIENDS, I CONSIDER YOU MY FRIENDS AS WELL.
I HOPE WE ALL GET ALONG FROM NOW ON...
(Sweetly~)
"Why does she keep clinging on to me like this?" is what he's thinking.
SNUG~
DOOO
CRACK
...
DOOOM
Shibuya
5F
4F
3F
2F
1F
STEP
IT SEEMS THIS PLACE IS PACKED WITH PEOPLE.

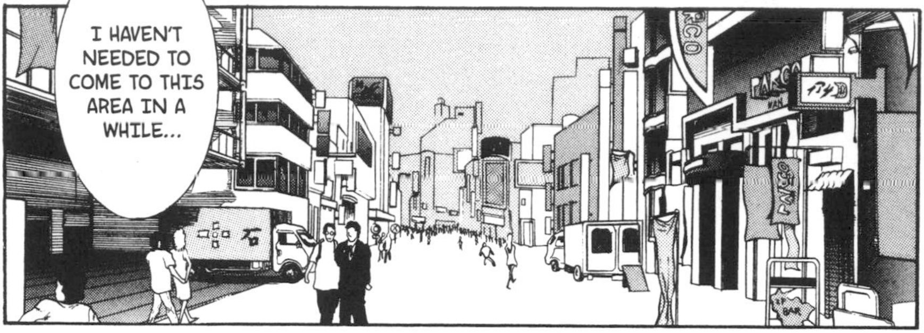
I HAVEN'T NEEDED TO COME TO THIS AREA IN A WHILE...

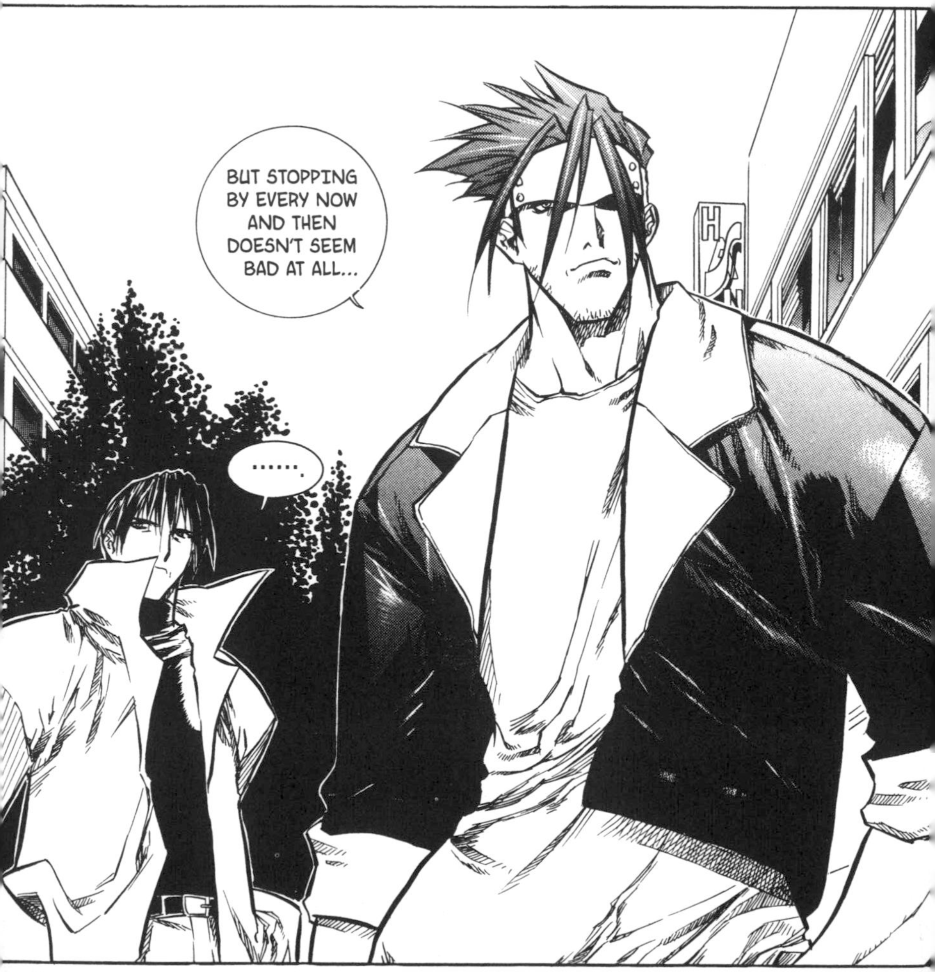
BUT STOPPING BY EVERY NOW AND THEN DOESN'T SEEM BAD AT ALL...
....

CIRCLE 9 part III - People of the Past
The Dangerous Nice Guy

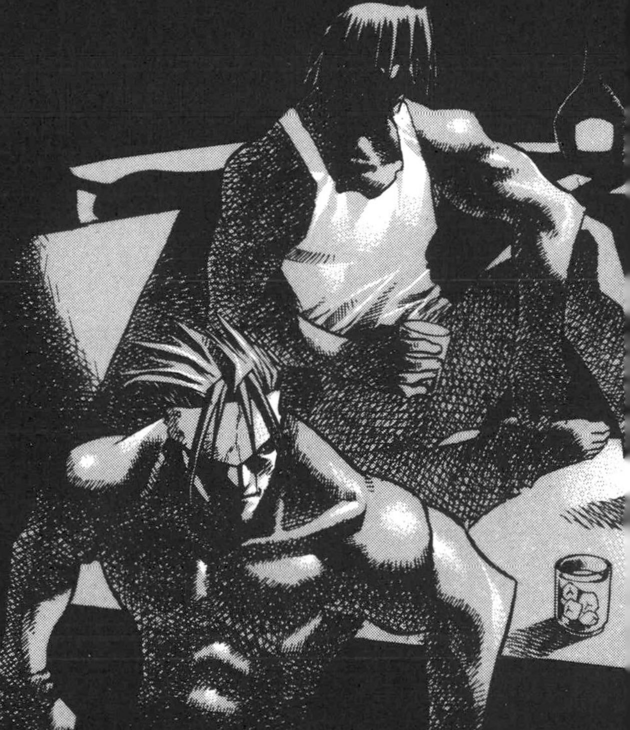

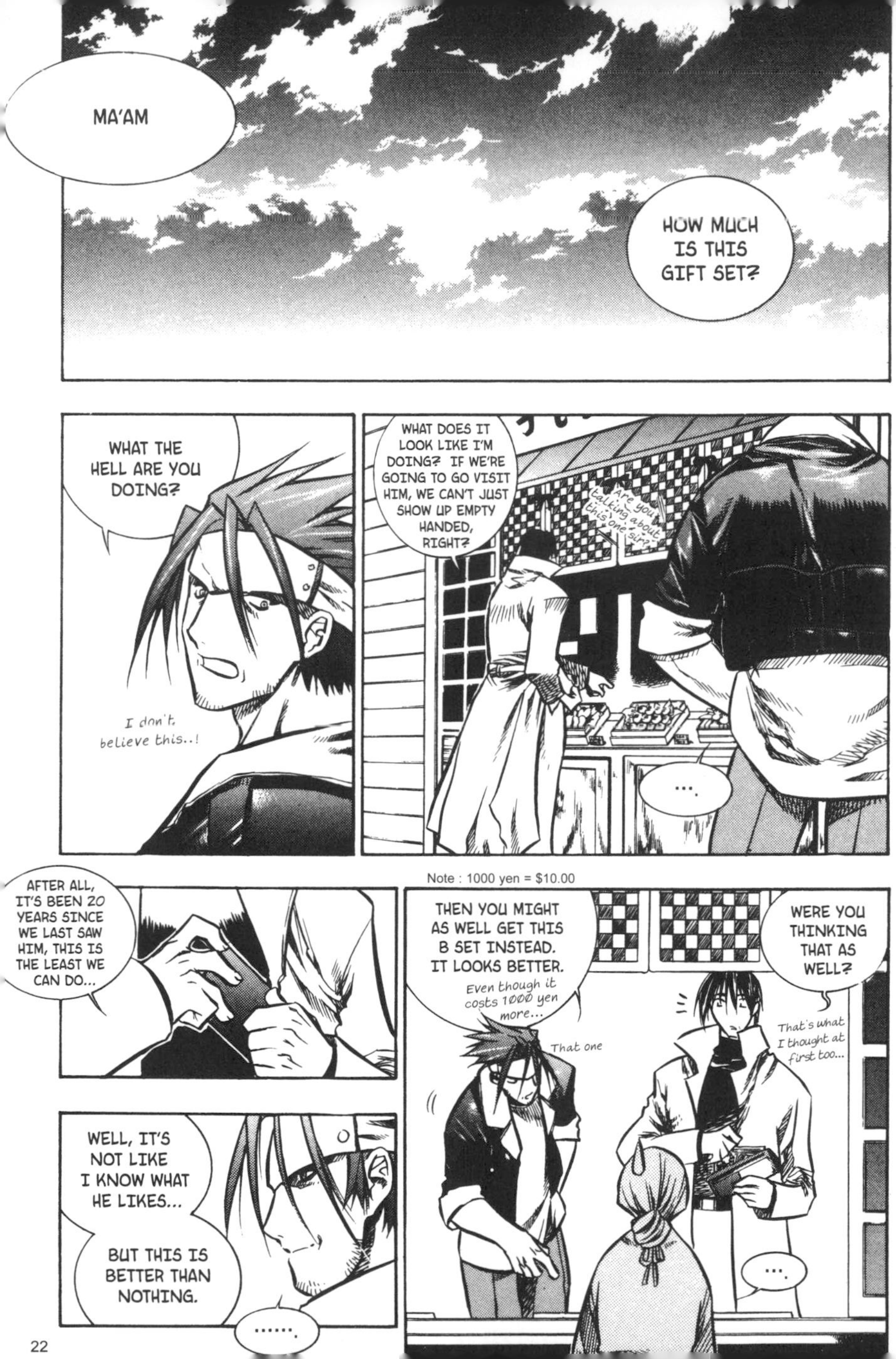
MA'AM
HOW MUCH IS THIS GIFT SET?
WHAT THE HELL ARE YOU DOING?
I don't believe this..!
WHAT DOES IT LOOK LIKE I'M DOING? IF WE'RE GOING TO GO VISIT HIM, WE CAN'T JUST SHOW UP EMPTY HANDED, RIGHT?
Are you talking about this one sir?
....
AFTER ALL, IT'S BEEN 20 YEARS SINCE WE LAST SAW HIM, THIS IS THE LEAST WE CAN DO...
WELL, IT'S NOT LIKE I KNOW WHAT HE LIKES...
BUT THIS IS BETTER THAN NOTHING.
....
THEN YOU MIGHT AS WELL GET THIS B SET INSTEAD. IT LOOKS BETTER.
Even though it costs 1000 yen more...
That one
WERE YOU THINKING THAT AS WELL?
That's what I thought at first too...
....

Note : 1000 yen = $10.00

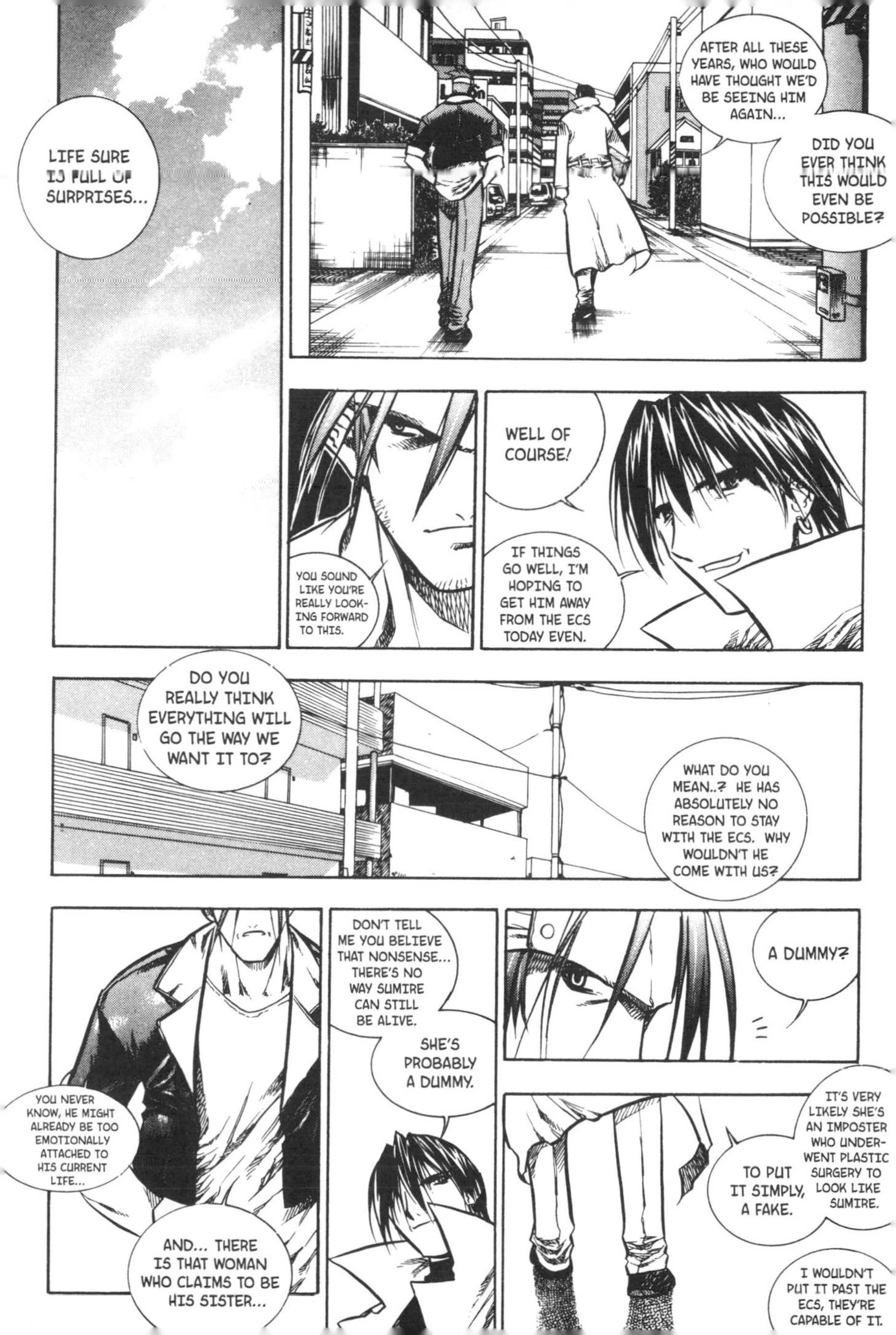
LIFE SURE IS FULL OF SURPRISES...
AFTER ALL THESE YEARS, WHO WOULD HAVE THOUGHT WE'D BE SEEING HIM AGAIN...
DID YOU EVER THINK THIS WOULD EVEN BE POSSIBLE?
WELL OF COURSE!
IF THINGS GO WELL, I'M HOPING TO GET HIM AWAY FROM THE ECS TODAY EVEN.
YOU SOUND LIKE YOU'RE REALLY LOOKING FORWARD TO THIS.
DO YOU REALLY THINK EVERYTHING WILL GO THE WAY WE WANT IT TO?
WHAT DO YOU MEAN..? HE HAS ABSOLUTELY NO REASON TO STAY WITH THE ECS. WHY WOULDN'T HE COME WITH US?
YOU NEVER KNOW, HE MIGHT ALREADY BE TOO EMOTIONALLY ATTACHED TO HIS CURRENT LIFE...
AND... THERE IS THAT WOMAN WHO CLAIMS TO BE HIS SISTER...
DON'T TELL ME YOU BELIEVE THAT NONSENSE... THERE'S NO WAY SUMIRE CAN STILL BE ALIVE.
SHE'S PROBABLY A DUMMY.
A DUMMY?
IT'S VERY LIKELY SHE'S AN IMPOSTER WHO UNDERWENT PLASTIC SURGERY TO LOOK LIKE SUMIRE.
TO PUT IT SIMPLY, A FAKE.
I WOULDN'T PUT IT PAST THE ECS, THEY'RE CAPABLE OF IT.

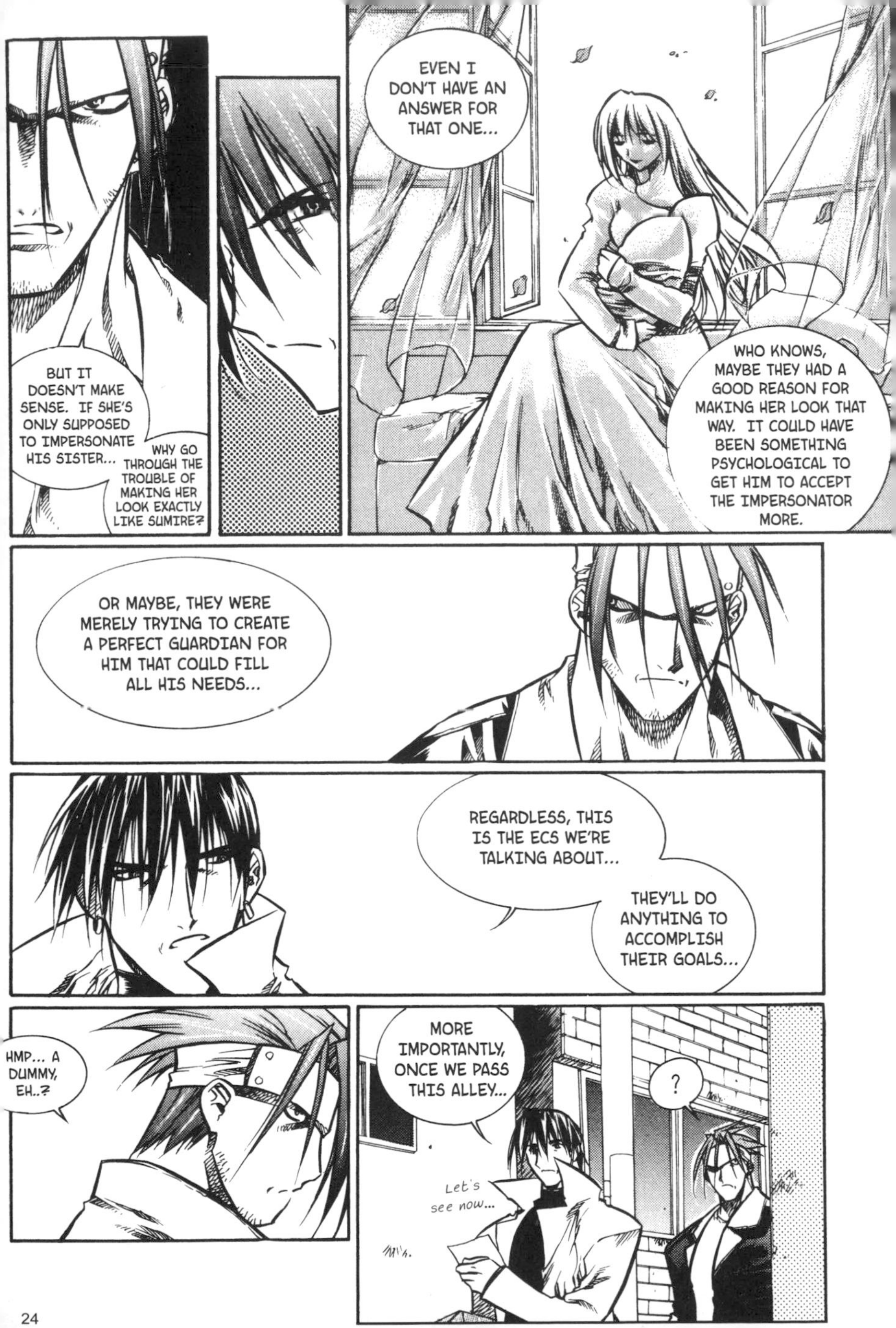
BUT IT DOESN'T MAKE SENSE. IF SHE'S ONLY SUPPOSED TO IMPERSONATE HIS SISTER...
WHY GO THROUGH THE TROUBLE OF MAKING HER LOOK EXACTLY LIKE SUMIRE?
EVEN I DON'T HAVE AN ANSWER FOR THAT ONE...
WHO KNOWS, MAYBE THEY HAD A GOOD REASON FOR MAKING HER LOOK THAT WAY. IT COULD HAVE BEEN SOMETHING PSYCHOLOGICAL TO GET HIM TO ACCEPT THE IMPERSONATOR MORE.
OR MAYBE, THEY WERE MERELY TRYING TO CREATE A PERFECT GUARDIAN FOR HIM THAT COULD FILL ALL HIS NEEDS...
REGARDLESS, THIS IS THE ECS WE'RE TALKING ABOUT...
THEY'LL DO ANYTHING TO ACCOMPLISH THEIR GOALS...
HMP... A DUMMY, EH..?
MORE IMPORTANTLY, ONCE WE PASS THIS ALLEY...
?
Let's see now...

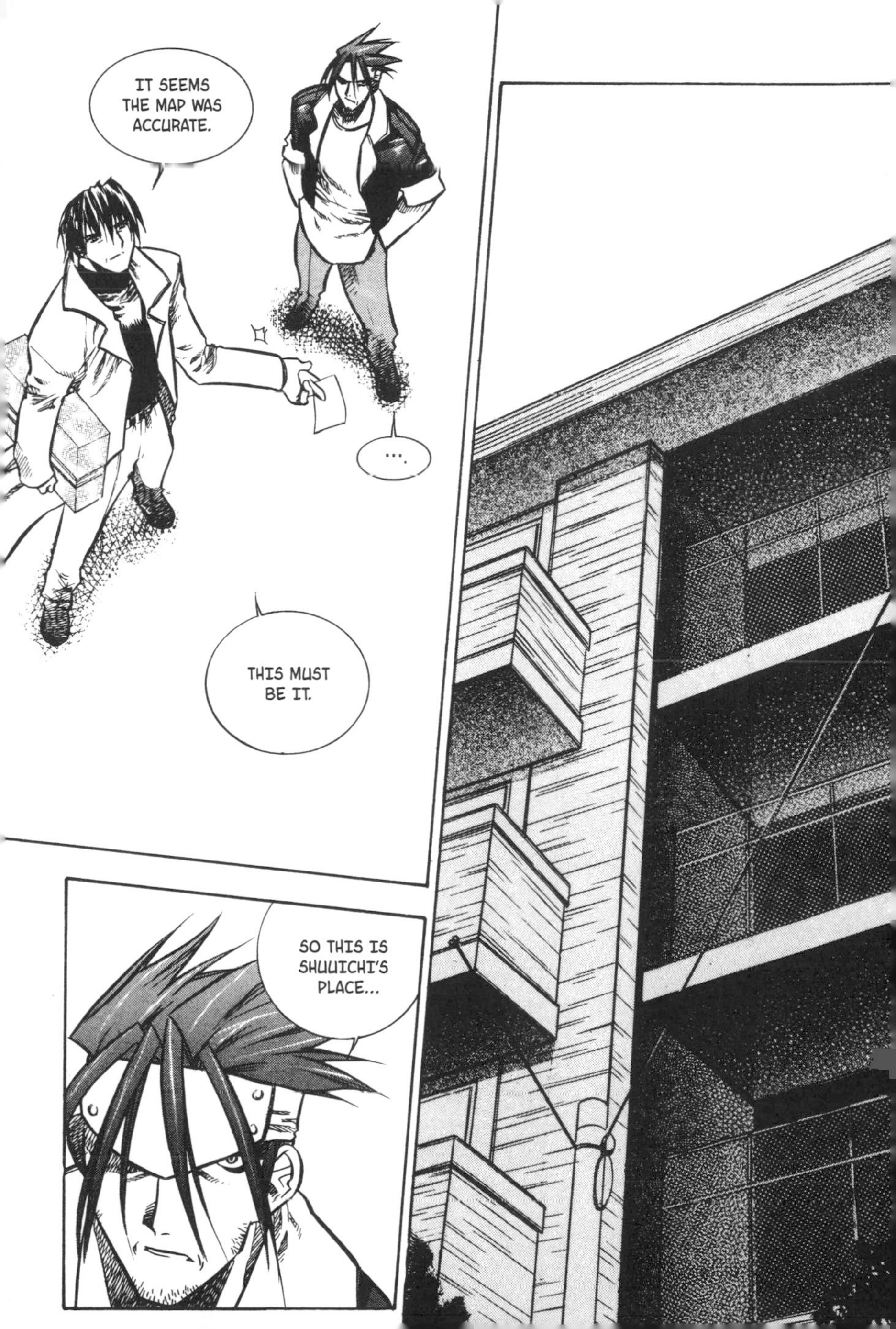
IT SEEMS THE MAP WAS ACCURATE.
...
THIS MUST BE IT.
SO THIS IS SHUUICHI'S PLACE...

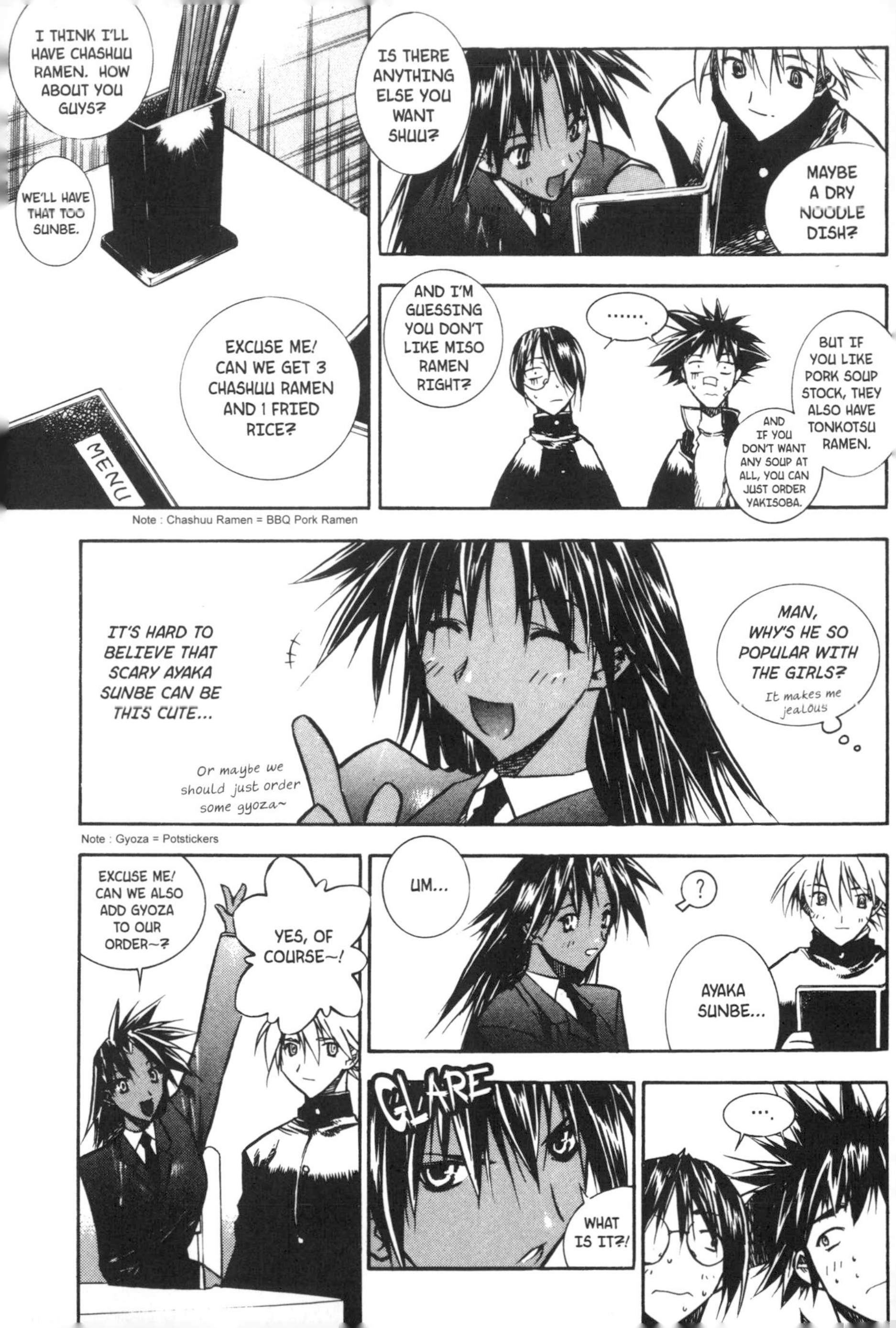
I THINK I'LL HAVE CHASHUU RAMEN. HOW ABOUT YOU GUYS?
WE'LL HAVE THAT TOO SUNBE.
EXCUSE ME! CAN WE GET 3 CHASHUU RAMEN AND 1 FRIED RICE?
MENU
IS THERE ANYTHING ELSE YOU WANT SHUU?
MAYBE A DRY NOODLE DISH?
AND I'M GUESSING YOU DON'T LIKE MISO RAMEN RIGHT?
......
BUT IF YOU LIKE PORK SOUP STOCK, THEY ALSO HAVE TONKOTSU RAMEN.
AND IF YOU DON'T WANT ANY SOUP AT ALL, YOU CAN JUST ORDER YAKISOBA.
IT'S HARD TO BELIEVE THAT SCARY AYAKA SUNBE CAN BE THIS CUTE...
Or maybe we should just order some gyoza~
MAN, WHY'S HE SO POPULAR WITH THE GIRLS?
It makes me jealous
EXCUSE ME! CAN WE ALSO ADD GYOZA TO OUR ORDER~?
YES, OF COURSE~!
UM...
?
AYAKA SUNBE...
GLARE
WHAT IS IT?!
...
Note : Chashuu Ramen = BBQ Pork Ramen

Note : Gyoza = Potstickers

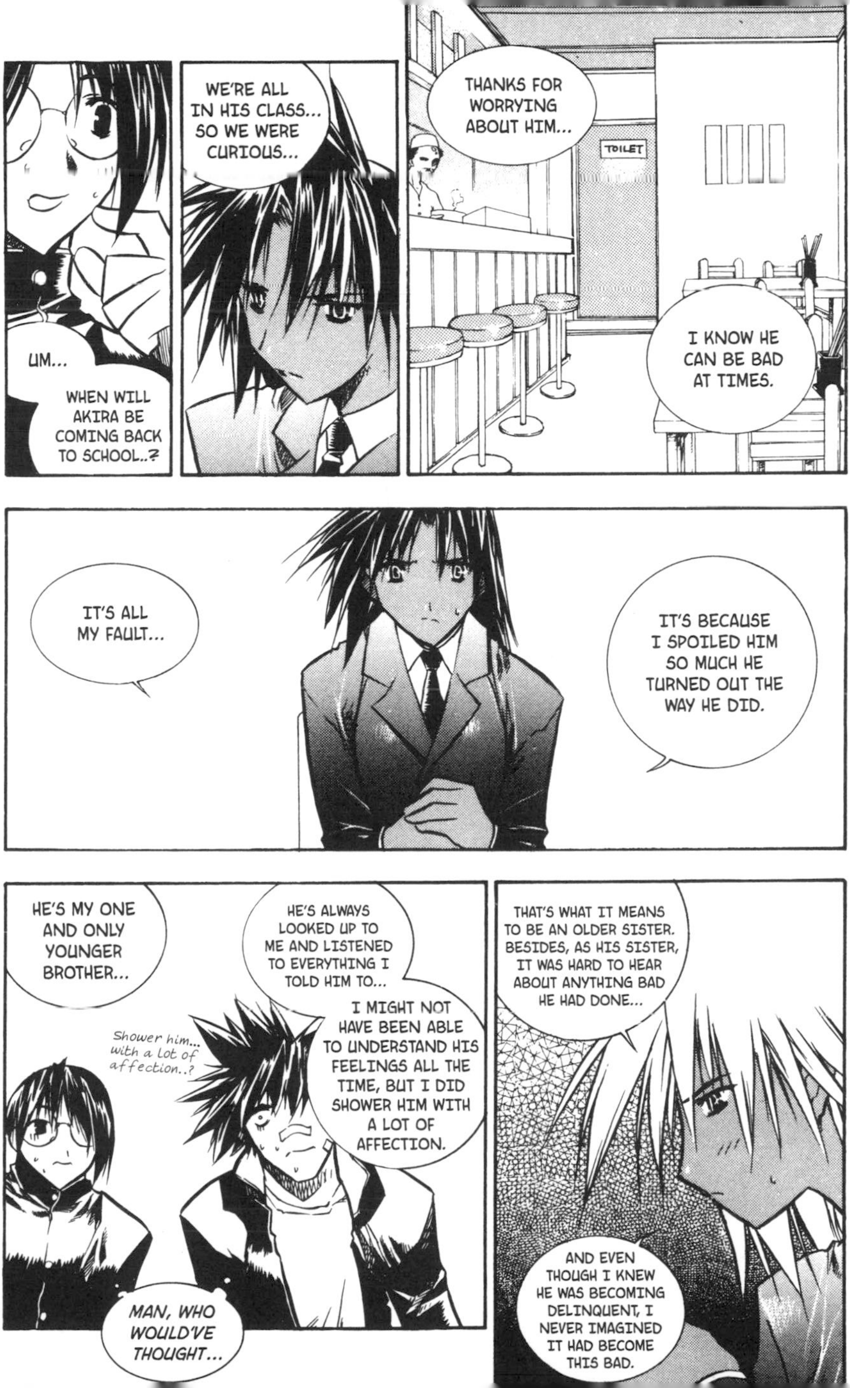
UM...
WHEN WILL AKIRA BE COMING BACK TO SCHOOL..?
WE'RE ALL IN HIS CLASS... SO WE WERE CURIOUS...
THANKS FOR WORRYING ABOUT HIM...
TOILET
I KNOW HE CAN BE BAD AT TIMES.
IT'S ALL MY FAULT...
IT'S BECAUSE I SPOILED HIM SO MUCH HE TURNED OUT THE WAY HE DID.
HE'S MY ONE AND ONLY YOUNGER BROTHER...
HE'S ALWAYS LOOKED UP TO ME AND LISTENED TO EVERYTHING I TOLD HIM TO...
I MIGHT NOT HAVE BEEN ABLE TO UNDERSTAND HIS FEELINGS ALL THE TIME, BUT I DID SHOWER HIM WITH A LOT OF AFFECTION.
Shower him... with a lot of affection..?
MAN, WHO WOULD'VE THOUGHT...
THAT'S WHAT IT MEANS TO BE AN OLDER SISTER. BESIDES, AS HIS SISTER, IT WAS HARD TO HEAR ABOUT ANYTHING BAD HE HAD DONE...
AND EVEN THOUGH I KNEW HE WAS BECOMING DELINQUENT, I NEVER IMAGINED IT HAD BECOME THIS BAD.

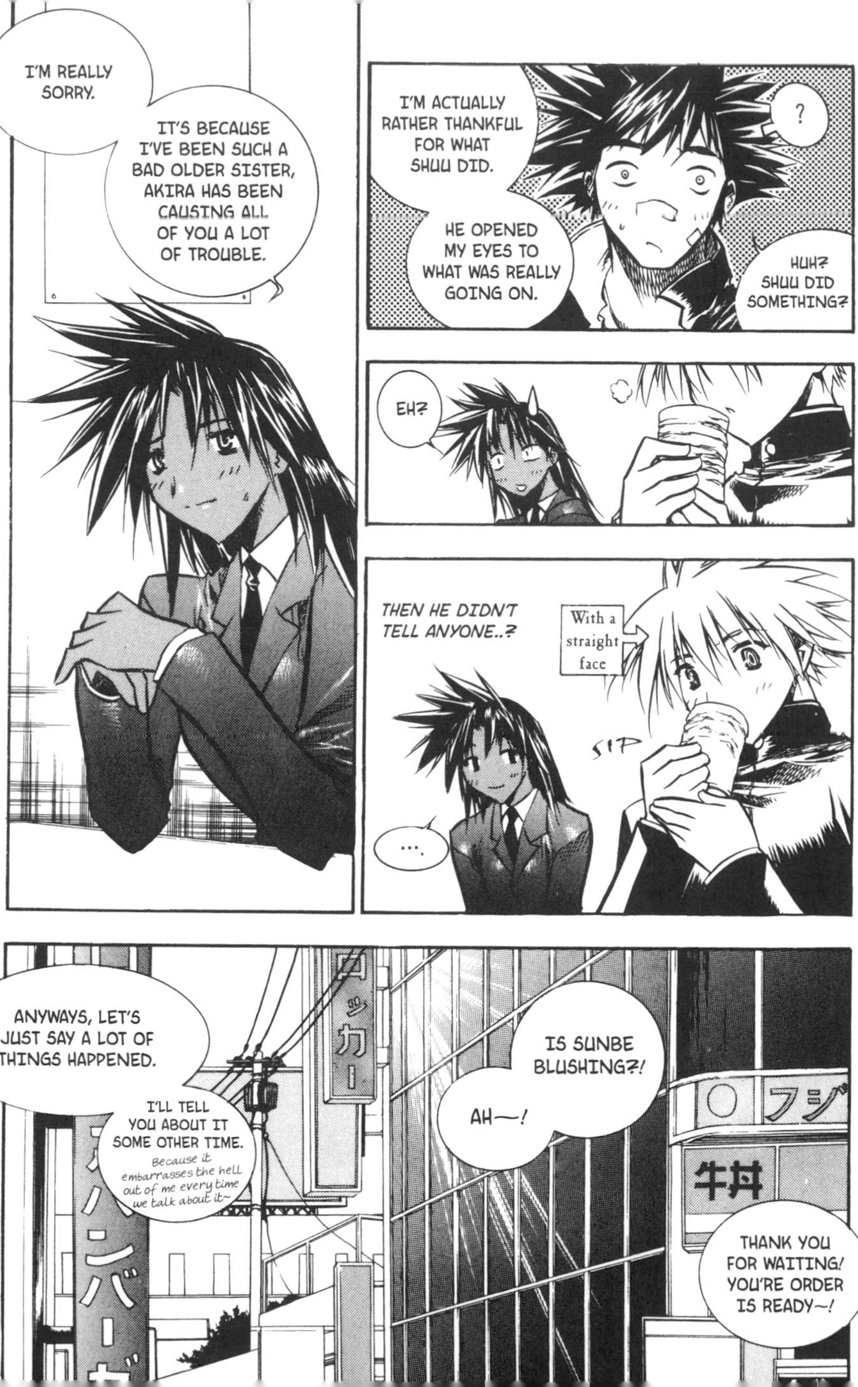

I'M REALLY SORRY.
IT'S BECAUSE I'VE BEEN SUCH A BAD OLDER SISTER, AKIRA HAS BEEN CAUSING ALL OF YOU A LOT OF TROUBLE.
I'M ACTUALLY RATHER THANKFUL FOR WHAT SHUU DID.
HE OPENED MY EYES TO WHAT WAS REALLY GOING ON.
?
HUH? SHUU DID SOMETHING?
EH?
THEN HE DIDN'T TELL ANYONE..?
With a straight face
SIP
....
ANYWAYS, LET'S JUST SAY A LOT OF THINGS HAPPENED.
I'LL TELL YOU ABOUT IT SOME OTHER TIME.
Because it embarrasses the hell out of me every time we talk about it~
AH~!
IS SUNBE BLUSHING?!
牛丼
THANK YOU FOR WAITING! YOU'RE ORDER IS READY~!

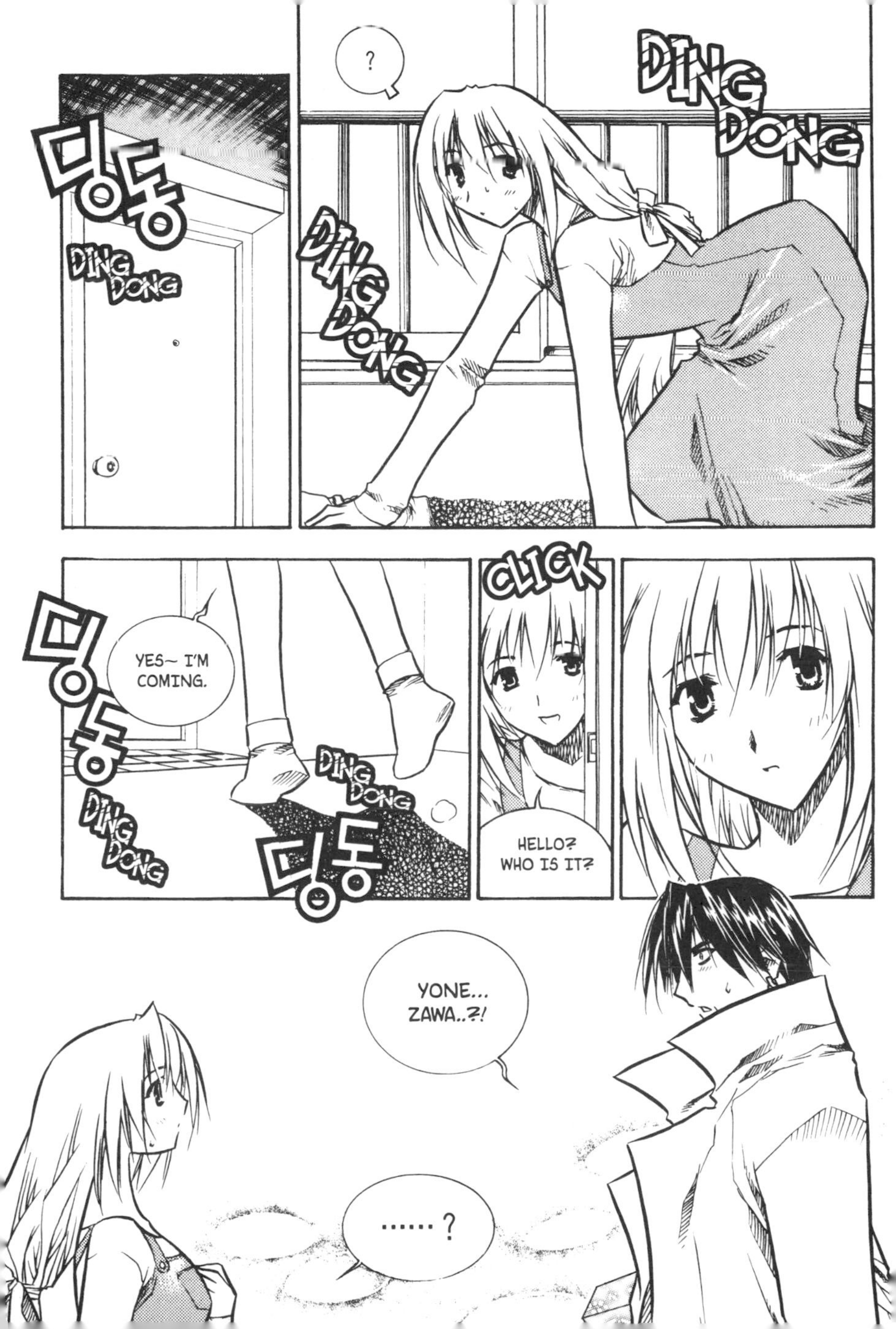
딩동
DING DONG
?
DING DONG
DING DONG
딩동
YES~ I'M COMING.
DING DONG
DING DONG
딩동
CLICK
HELLO? WHO IS IT?
YONE... ZAWA..?!
......?

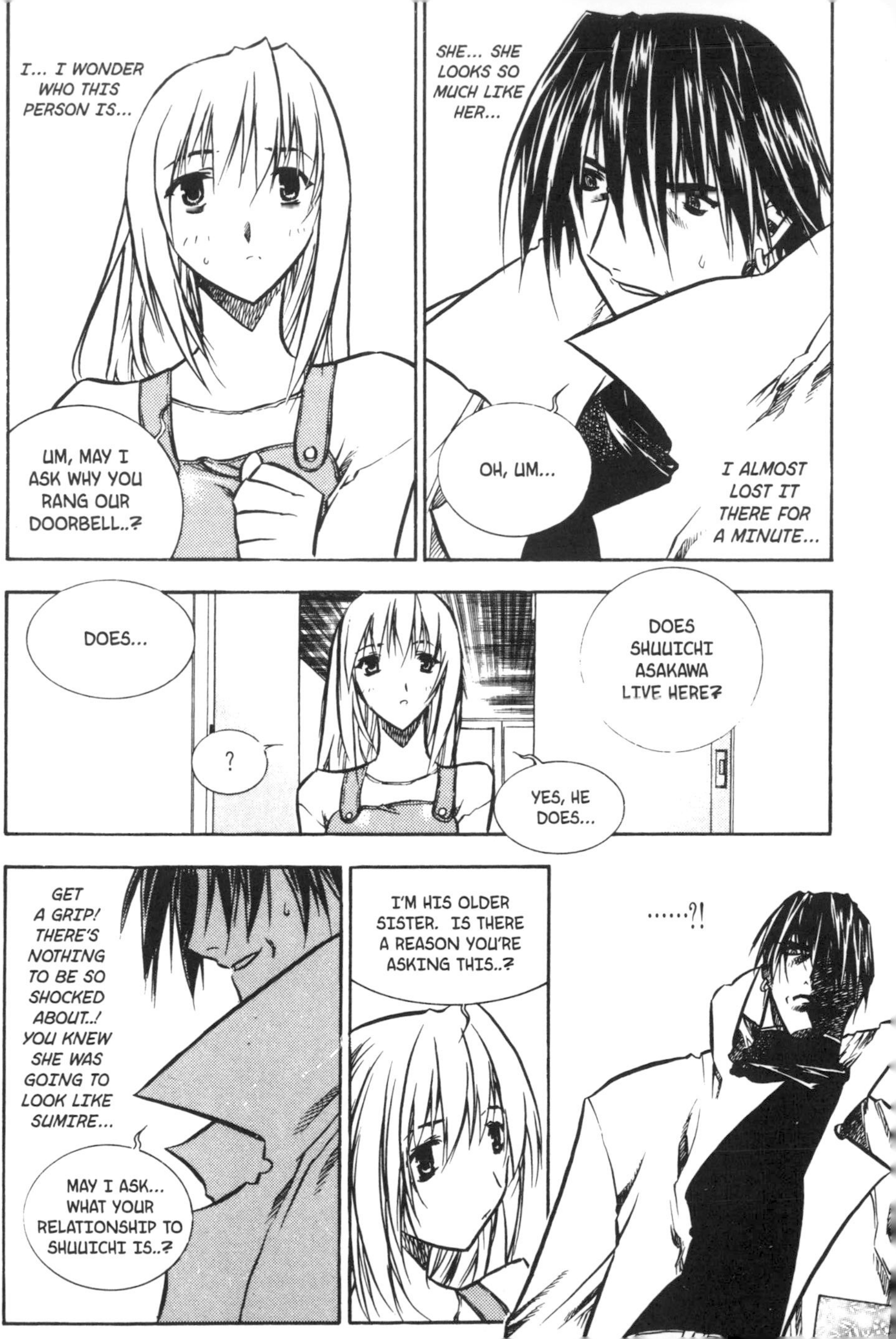
SHE... SHE LOOKS SO MUCH LIKE HER...
I ALMOST LOST IT THERE FOR A MINUTE...
OH, UM...
I... I WONDER WHO THIS PERSON IS...
UM, MAY I ASK WHY YOU RANG OUR DOORBELL..?
DOES SHUUICHI ASAKAWA LIVE HERE?
DOES...
YES, HE DOES...
?
......?!
I'M HIS OLDER SISTER. IS THERE A REASON YOU'RE ASKING THIS..?
GET A GRIP! THERE'S NOTHING TO BE SO SHOCKED ABOUT..! YOU KNEW SHE WAS GOING TO LOOK LIKE SUMIRE...
MAY I ASK... WHAT YOUR RELATIONSHIP TO SHUUICHI IS..?

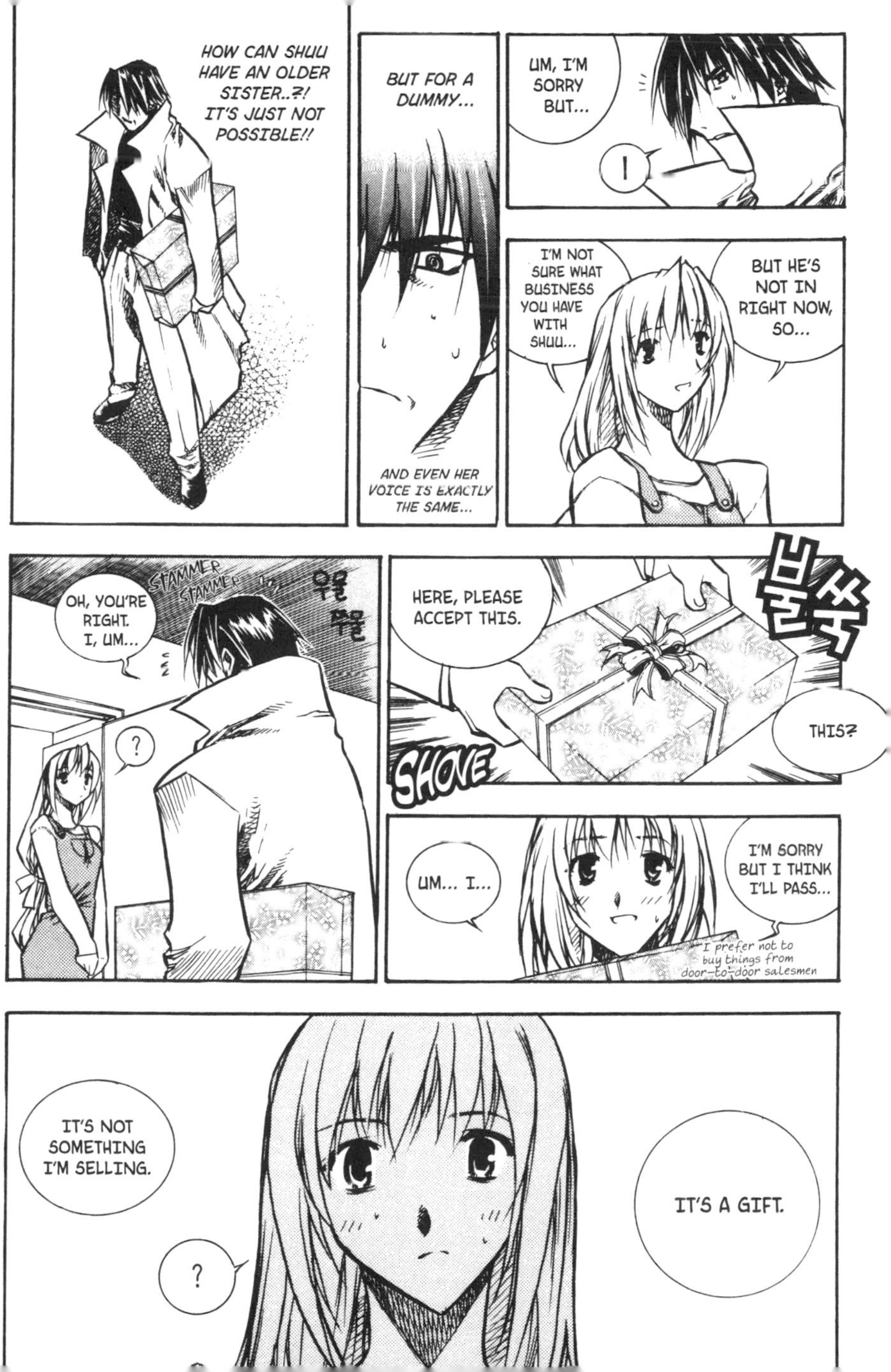
HOW CAN SHUU HAVE AN OLDER SISTER..?! IT'S JUST NOT POSSIBLE!!
BUT FOR A DUMMY...
AND EVEN HER VOICE IS EXACTLY THE SAME...
UM, I'M SORRY BUT...
!
I'M NOT SURE WHAT BUSINESS YOU HAVE WITH SHUU...
BUT HE'S NOT IN RIGHT NOW, SO...
STAMMER STAMMER
우물 쭈물
OH, YOU'RE RIGHT. I, UM...
?
HERE, PLEASE ACCEPT THIS.
불쑥
SHOVE
THIS?
UM... I...
I'M SORRY BUT I THINK I'LL PASS...
I prefer not to buy things from door-to-door salesmen
IT'S NOT SOMETHING I'M SELLING.
?
IT'S A GIFT.

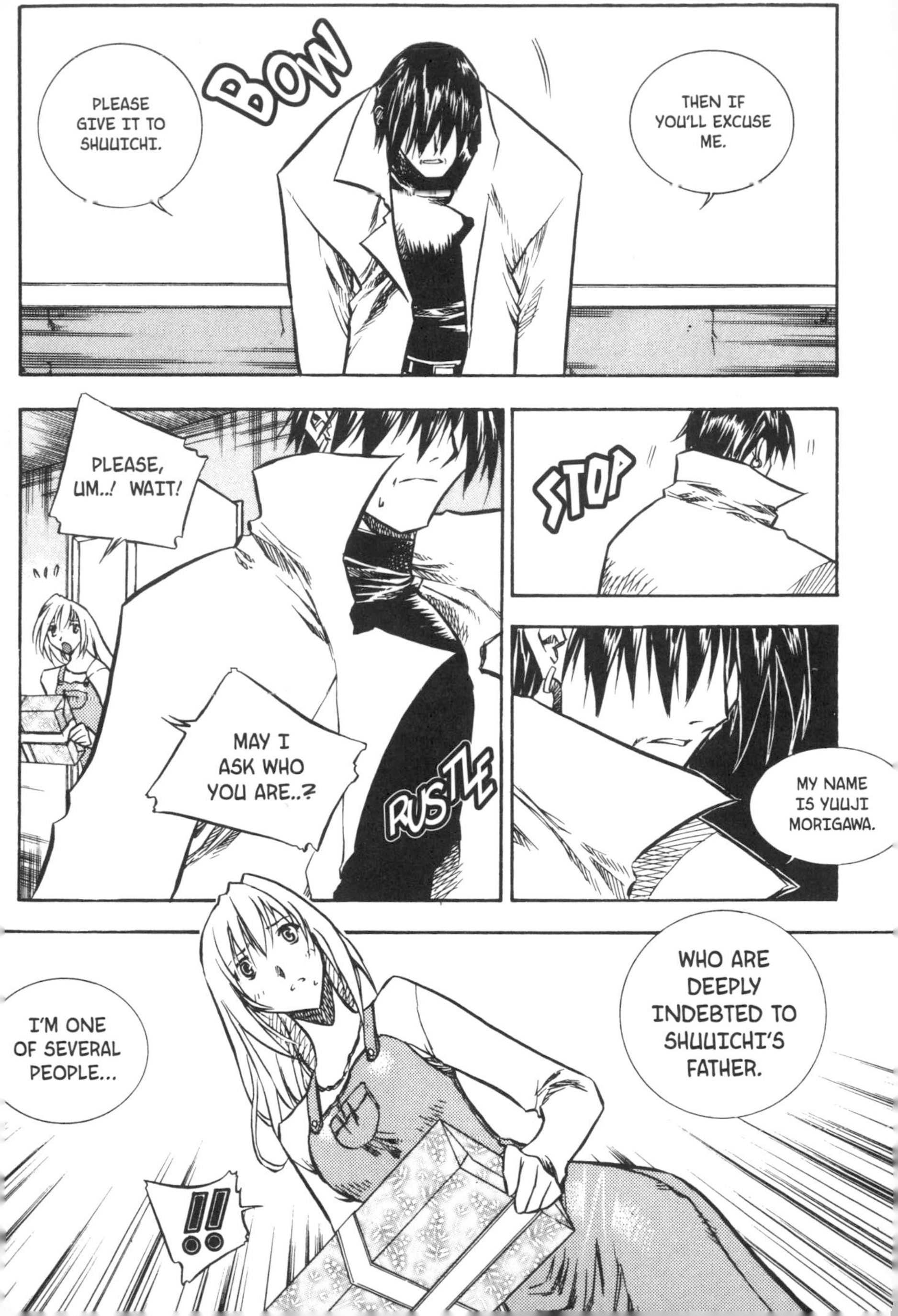

THEN IF YOU'LL EXCUSE ME.
BOW
PLEASE GIVE IT TO SHUUICHI.
STOP
PLEASE, UM..! WAIT!
MY NAME IS YUUJI MORIGAWA.
RUSTLE
MAY I ASK WHO YOU ARE..?
WHO ARE DEEPLY INDEBTED TO SHUUICHI'S FATHER.
I'M ONE OF SEVERAL PEOPLE...
!!

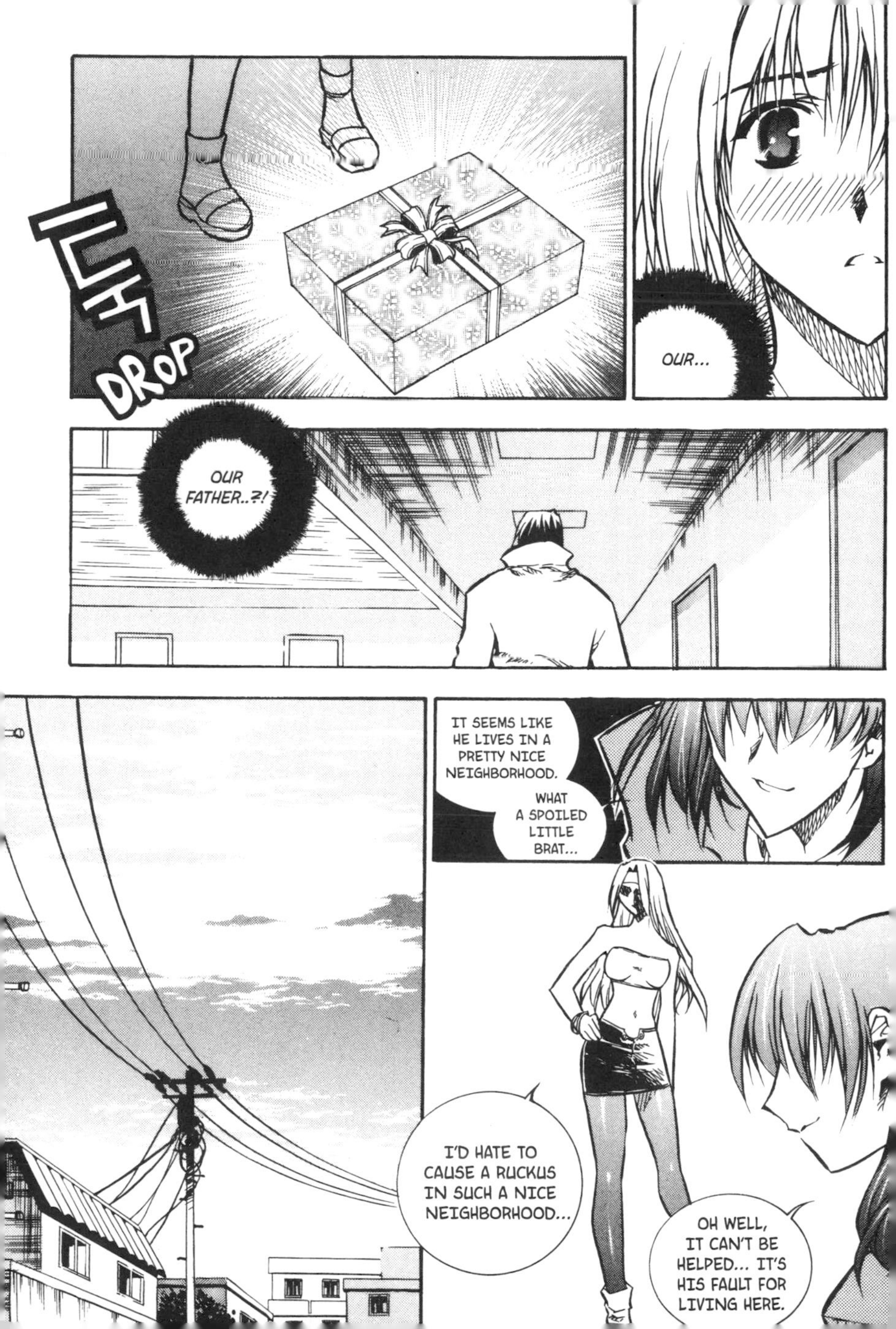

OUR...
DROP
OUR FATHER..?!
IT SEEMS LIKE HE LIVES IN A PRETTY NICE NEIGHBORHOOD.
WHAT A SPOILED LITTLE BRAT...
I'D HATE TO CAUSE A RUCKUS IN SUCH A NICE NEIGHBORHOOD...
OH WELL, IT CAN'T BE HELPED... IT'S HIS FAULT FOR LIVING HERE.

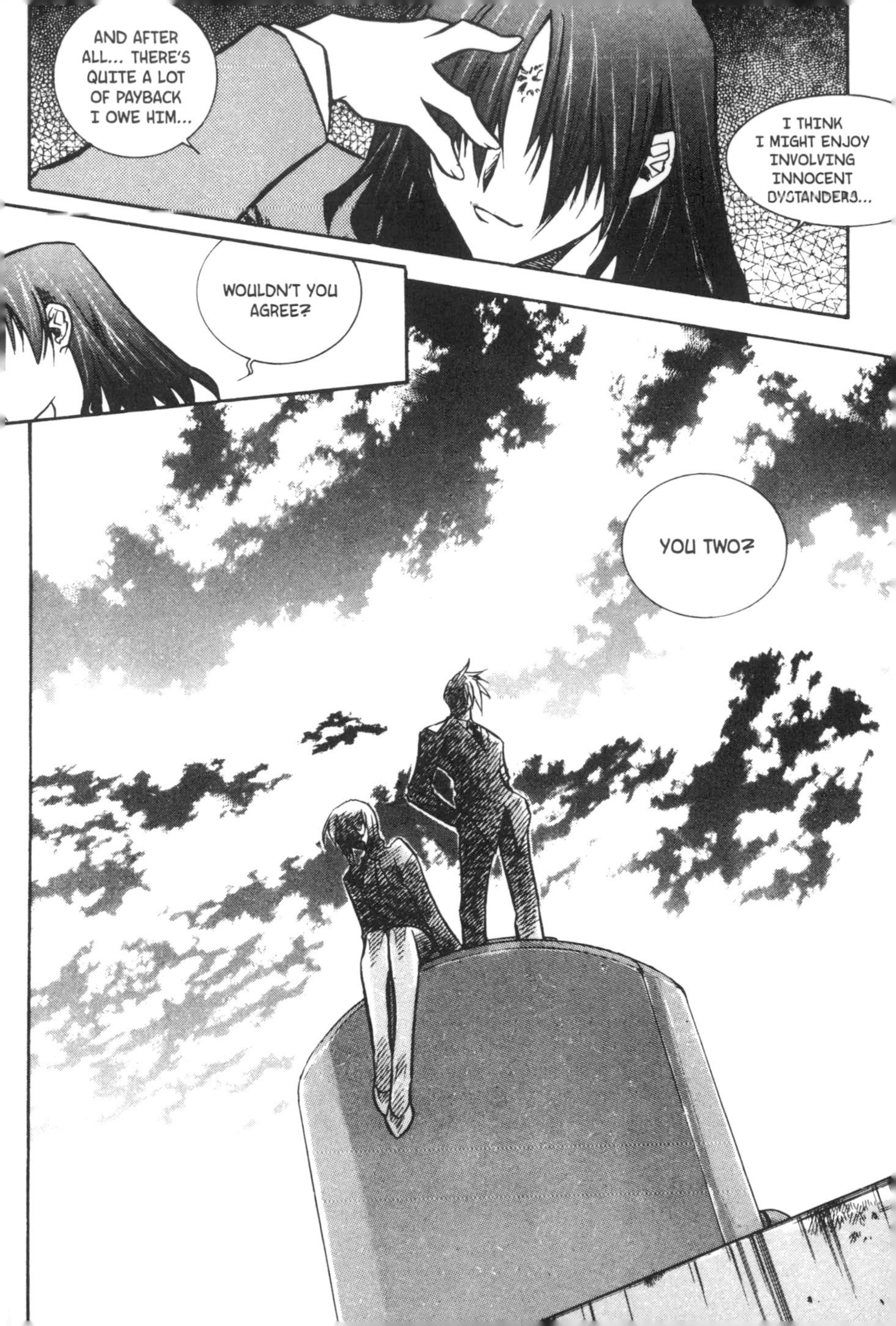
AND AFTER ALL... THERE'S QUITE A LOT OF PAYBACK I OWE HIM...
I THINK I MIGHT ENJOY INVOLVING INNOCENT BYSTANDERS...
WOULDN'T YOU AGREE?
YOU TWO?

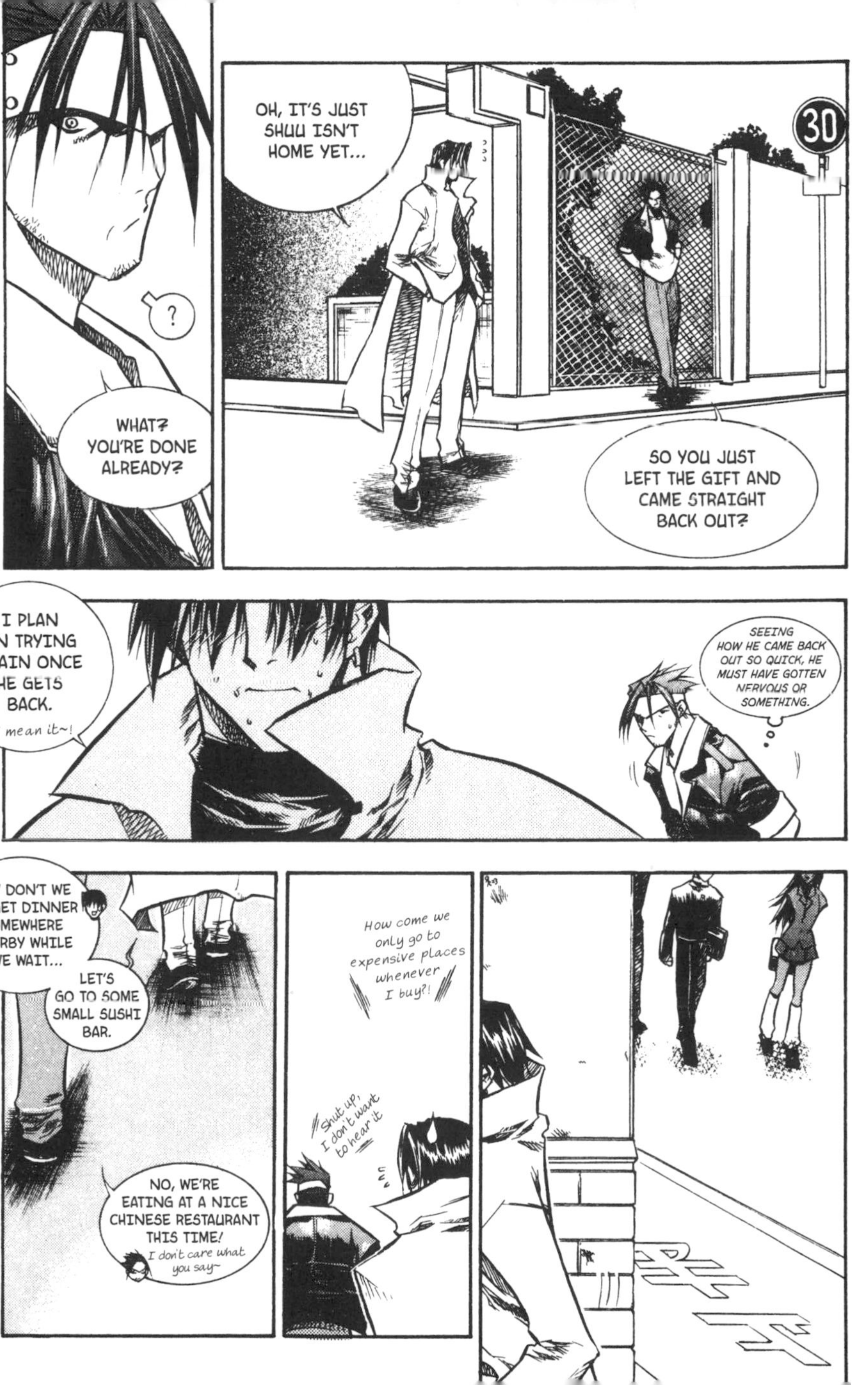

OH, IT'S JUST SHUU ISN'T HOME YET...
SO YOU JUST LEFT THE GIFT AND CAME STRAIGHT BACK OUT?
?
WHAT? YOU'RE DONE ALREADY?
30
SEEING HOW HE CAME BACK OUT SO QUICK, HE MUST HAVE GOTTEN NERVOUS OR SOMETHING.
I PLAN ON TRYING AGAIN ONCE HE GETS BACK.
I mean it~!
WHY DON'T WE GO GET DINNER SOMEWHERE NEARBY WHILE WE WAIT...
LET'S GO TO SOME SMALL SUSHI BAR.
NO, WE'RE EATING AT A NICE CHINESE RESTAURANT THIS TIME!
I don't care what you say~
How come we only go to expensive places whenever I buy?!
Shut up, I don't want to hear it

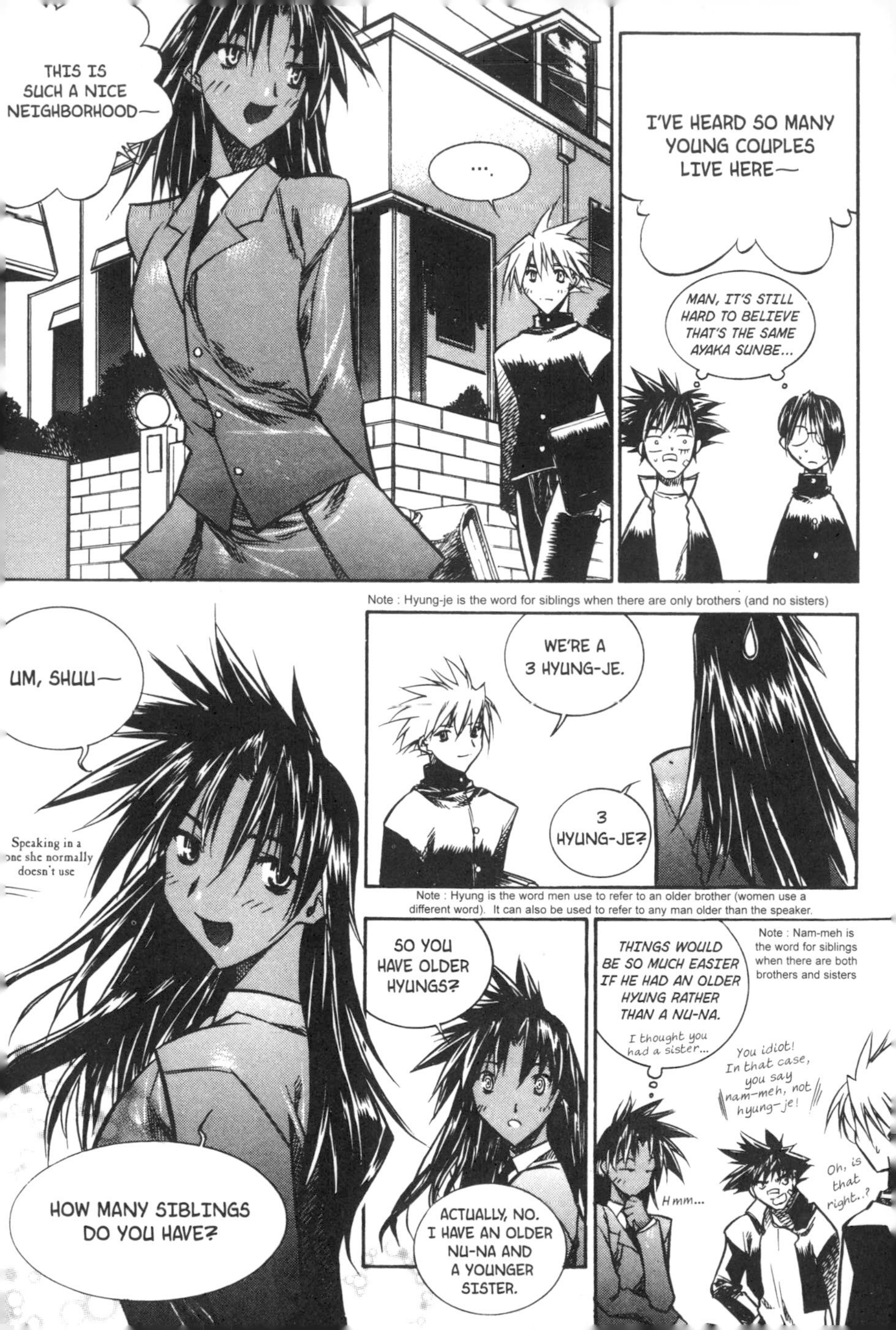
THIS IS SUCH A NICE NEIGHBORHOOD~
....
I'VE HEARD SO MANY YOUNG COUPLES LIVE HERE~
MAN, IT'S STILL HARD TO BELIEVE THAT'S THE SAME AYAKA SUNBE...
UM, SHUU~
Speaking in a
one she normally
doesn't use
HOW MANY SIBLINGS DO YOU HAVE?
Note : Hyung-je is the word for siblings when there are only brothers (and no sisters)
WE'RE A 3 HYUNG-JE.
3 HYUNG-JE?
Note : Hyung is the word men use to refer to an older brother (women use a different word). It can also be used to refer to any man older than the speaker.
SO YOU HAVE OLDER HYUNGS?
ACTUALLY, NO. I HAVE AN OLDER NU-NA AND A YOUNGER SISTER.
THINGS WOULD BE SO MUCH EASIER IF HE HAD AN OLDER HYUNG RATHER THAN A NU-NA.
Note : Nam-meh is the word for siblings when there are both brothers and sisters
I thought you had a sister...
You idiot! In that case, you say nam-meh, not hyung-je!
Hmm...
Oh, is that right..?

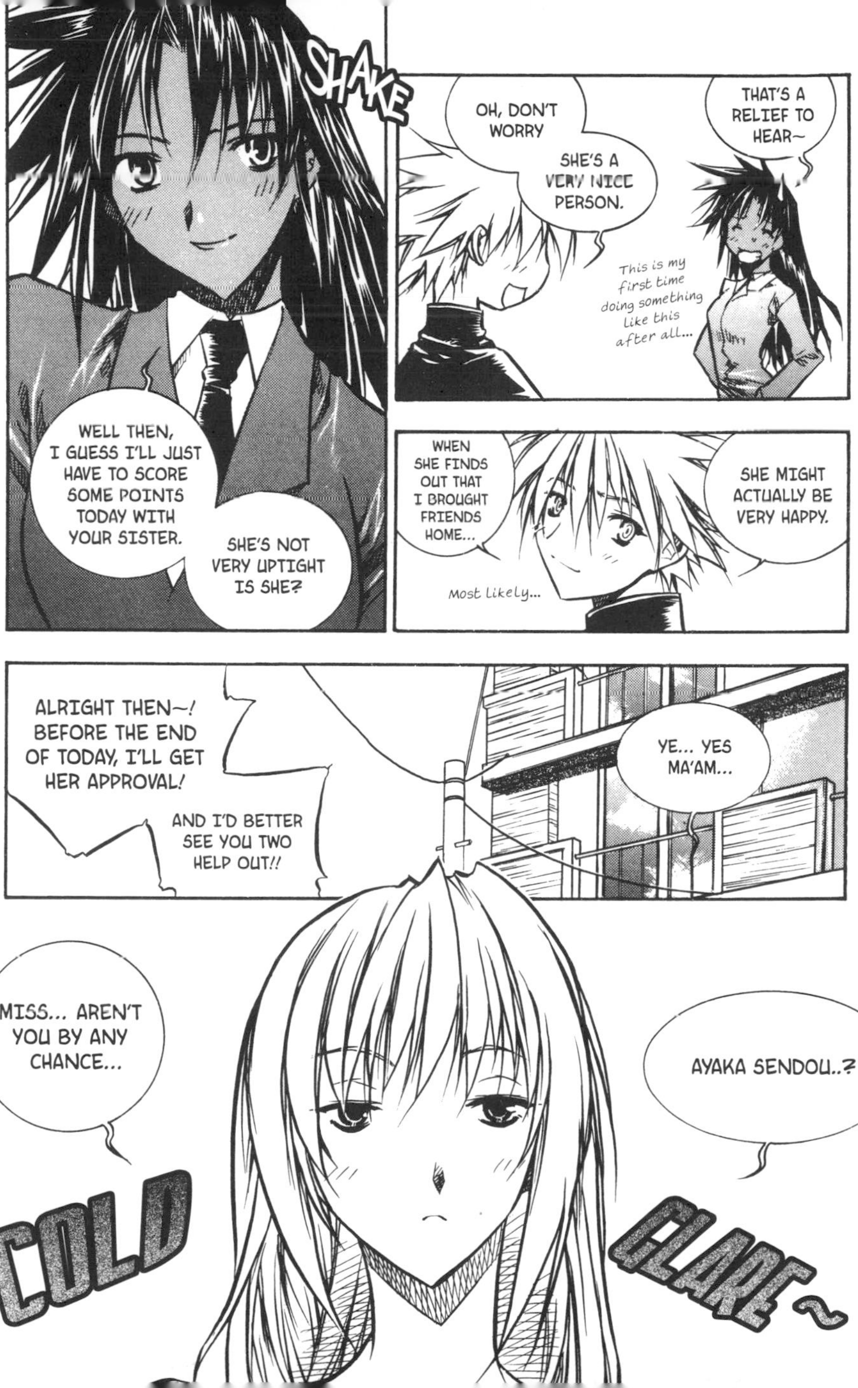
SHAKE
WELL THEN, I GUESS I'LL JUST HAVE TO SCORE SOME POINTS TODAY WITH YOUR SISTER.
SHE'S NOT VERY UPTIGHT IS SHE?
OH, DON'T WORRY
SHE'S A VERY NICE PERSON.
THAT'S A RELIEF TO HEAR~
This is my first time doing something like this after all...
WHEN SHE FINDS OUT THAT I BROUGHT FRIENDS HOME...
SHE MIGHT ACTUALLY BE VERY HAPPY.
Most likely...
ALRIGHT THEN~! BEFORE THE END OF TODAY, I'LL GET HER APPROVAL!
AND I'D BETTER SEE YOU TWO HELP OUT!!
YE... YES MA'AM...
MISS... AREN'T YOU BY ANY CHANCE...
AYAKA SENDOU..?
COLD
GLARE~

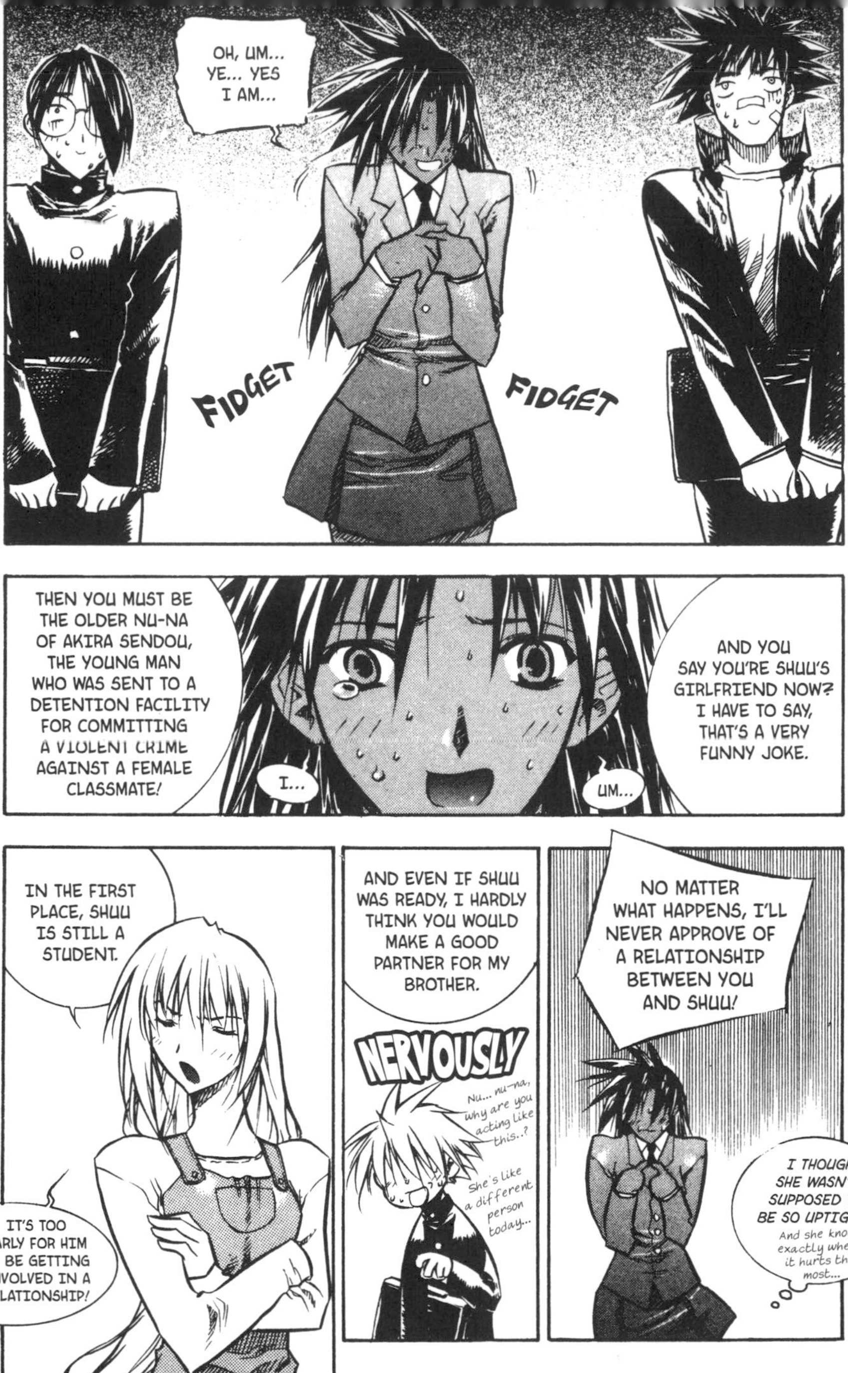

OH, UM... YE... YES I AM...
FIDGET
FIDGET
THEN YOU MUST BE THE OLDER NU-NA OF AKIRA SENDOU, THE YOUNG MAN WHO WAS SENT TO A DETENTION FACILITY FOR COMMITTING A VIOLENT CRIME AGAINST A FEMALE CLASSMATE!
I...
AND YOU SAY YOU'RE SHUU'S GIRLFRIEND NOW? I HAVE TO SAY, THAT'S A VERY FUNNY JOKE.
UM...
IN THE FIRST PLACE, SHUU IS STILL A STUDENT.
IT'S TOO EARLY FOR HIM TO BE GETTING INVOLVED IN A RELATIONSHIP!
AND EVEN IF SHUU WAS READY, I HARDLY THINK YOU WOULD MAKE A GOOD PARTNER FOR MY BROTHER.
NERVOUSLY
Nu... nu-na, why are you acting like this..?
She's like a different person today...
NO MATTER WHAT HAPPENS, I'LL NEVER APPROVE OF A RELATIONSHIP BETWEEN YOU AND SHUU!
I THOUGHT SHE WASN'T SUPPOSED TO BE SO UPTIGHT..!
And she knows exactly where it hurts the most...

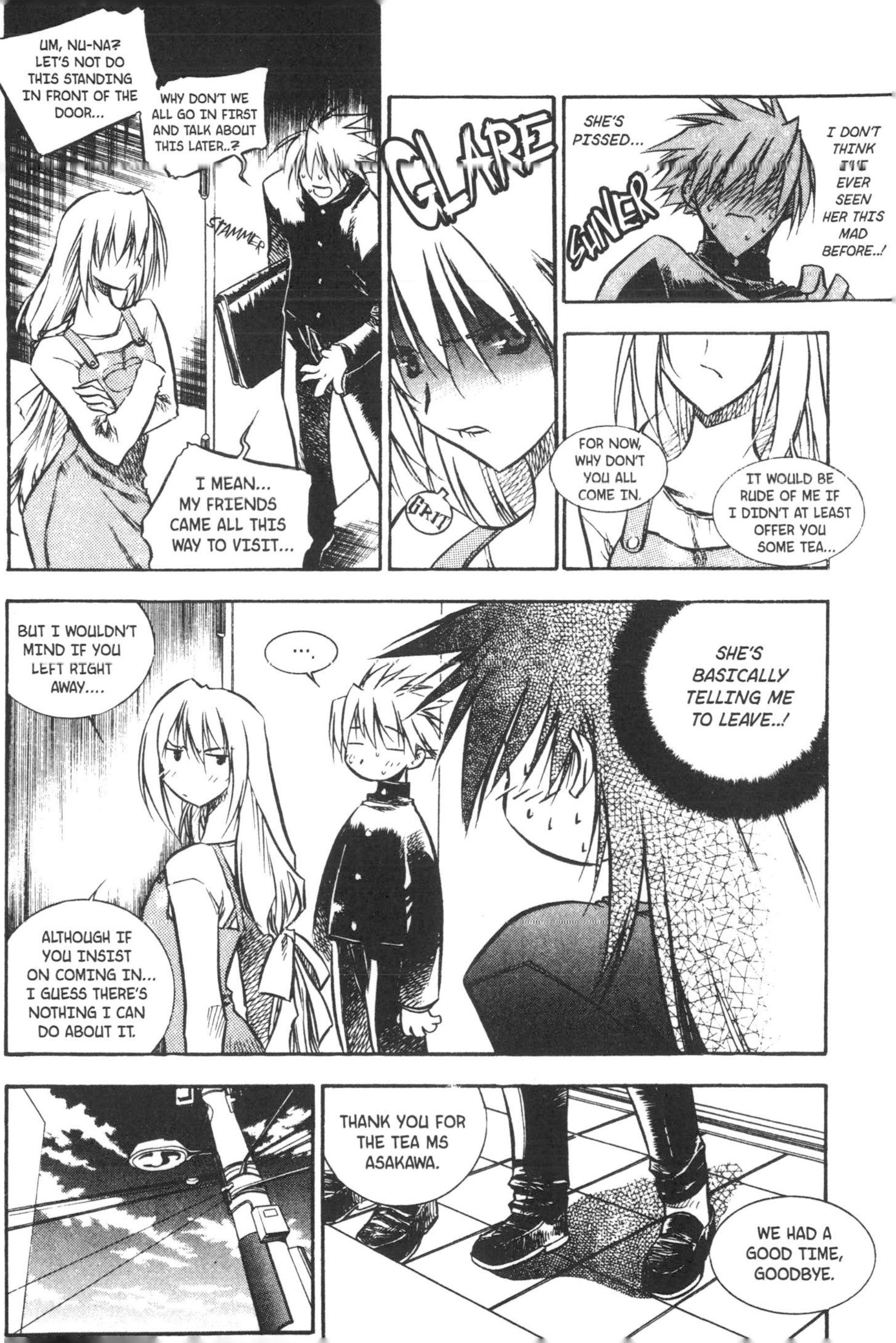

UM, NU-NA? LET'S NOT DO THIS STANDING IN FRONT OF THE DOOR...
WHY DON'T WE ALL GO IN FIRST AND TALK ABOUT THIS LATER..?
STAMMER
I MEAN... MY FRIENDS CAME ALL THIS WAY TO VISIT...
GLARE
GRIT
SHE'S PISSED...
SHIVER
I DON'T THINK
EVER SEEN HER THIS MAD BEFORE..!
FOR NOW, WHY DON'T YOU ALL COME IN.
IT WOULD BE RUDE OF ME IF I DIDN'T AT LEAST OFFER YOU SOME TEA...
BUT I WOULDN'T MIND IF YOU LEFT RIGHT AWAY....
...
SHE'S BASICALLY TELLING ME TO LEAVE..!
ALTHOUGH IF YOU INSIST ON COMING IN... I GUESS THERE'S NOTHING I CAN DO ABOUT IT.
THANK YOU FOR THE TEA MS ASAKAWA.
WE HAD A GOOD TIME, GOODBYE.

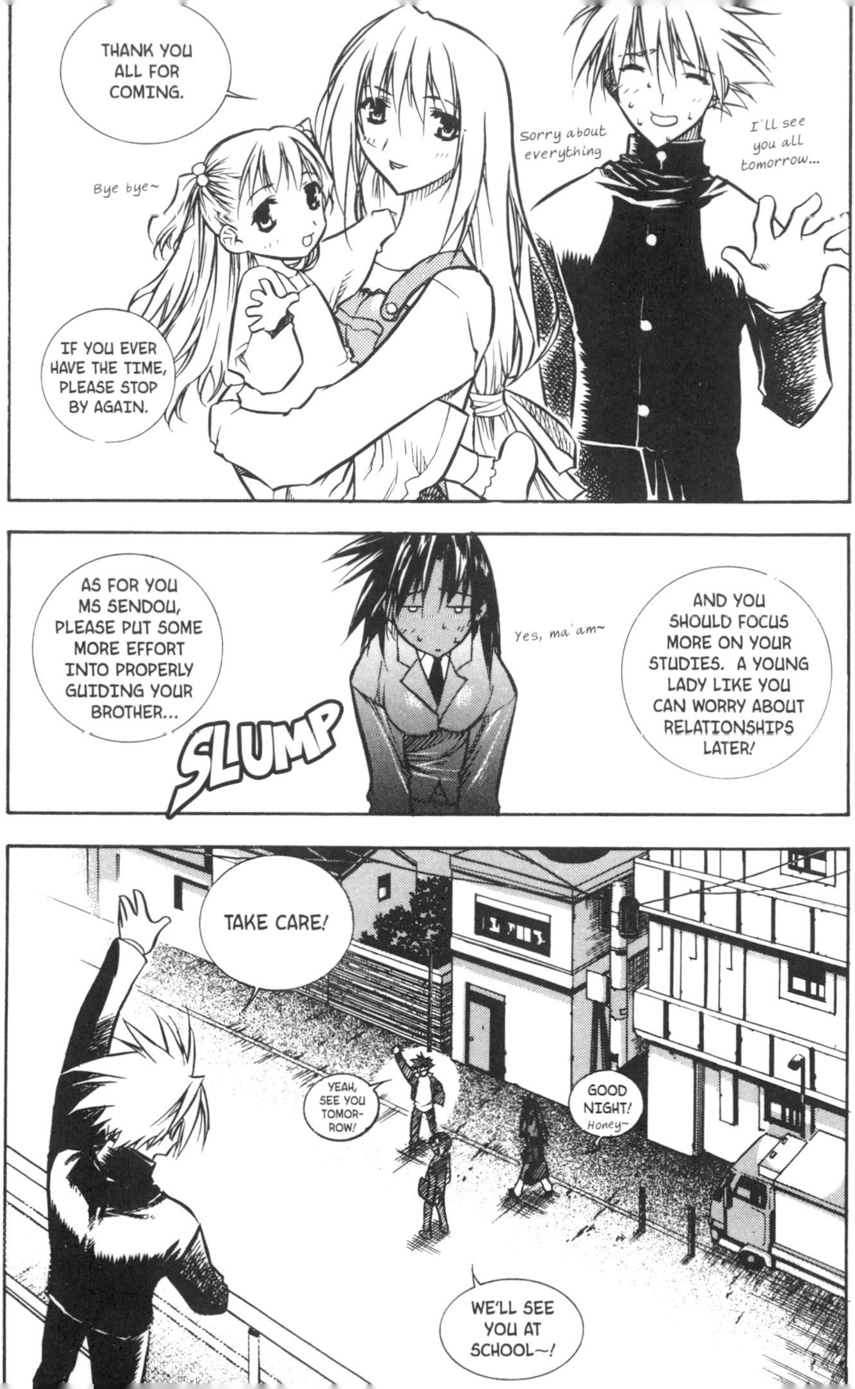

THANK YOU ALL FOR COMING.
Sorry about everything
I'll see you all tomorrow...
Bye bye~
IF YOU EVER HAVE THE TIME, PLEASE STOP BY AGAIN.
AS FOR YOU MS SENDOU, PLEASE PUT SOME MORE EFFORT INTO PROPERLY GUIDING YOUR BROTHER...
Yes, ma'am~
AND YOU SHOULD FOCUS MORE ON YOUR STUDIES. A YOUNG LADY LIKE YOU CAN WORRY ABOUT RELATIONSHIPS LATER!
SLUMP
TAKE CARE!
YEAH, SEE YOU TOMOR-ROW!
GOOD NIGHT! Honey~
WE'LL SEE YOU AT SCHOOL~!

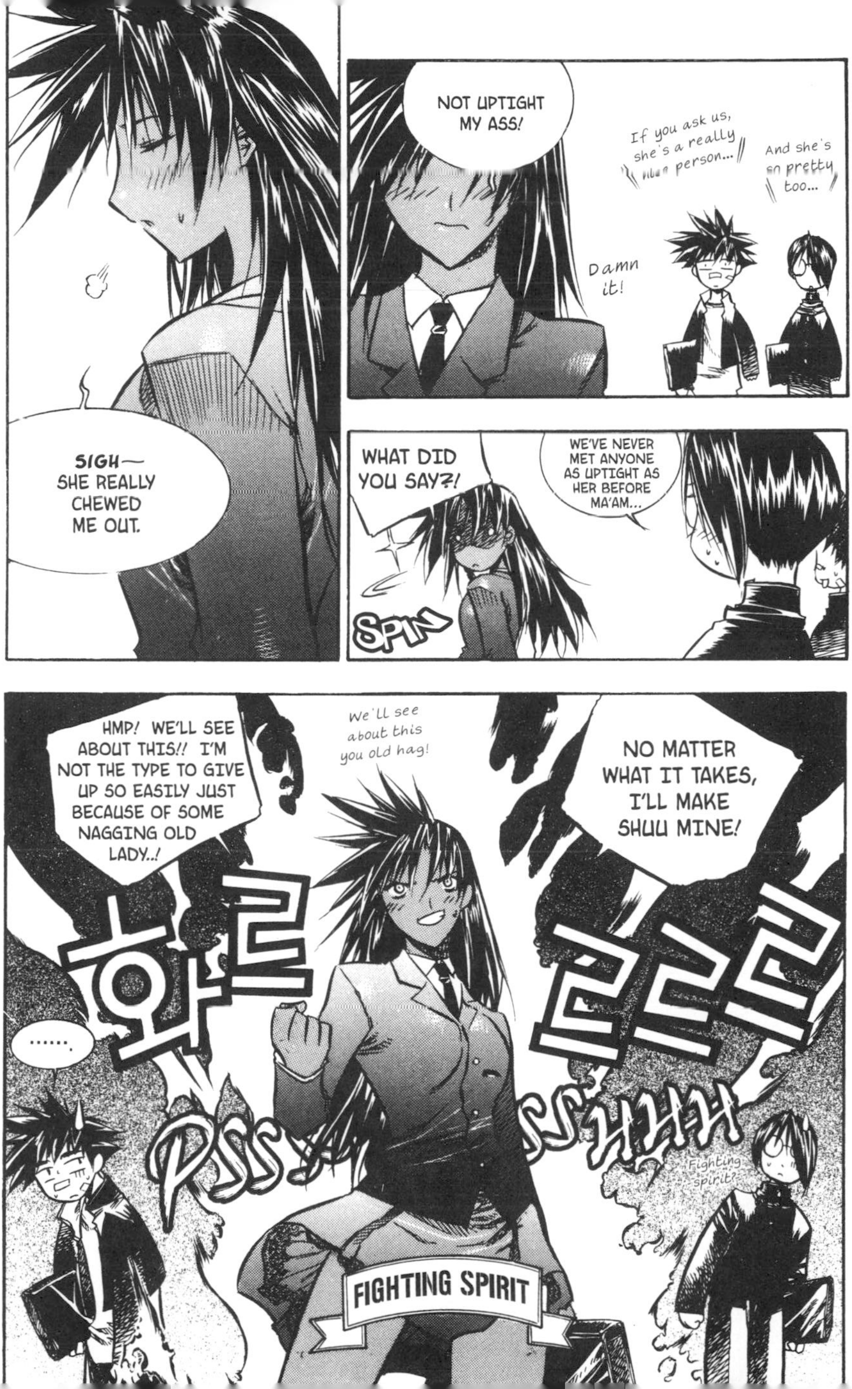
SIGH— SHE REALLY CHEWED ME OUT.
NOT UPTIGHT MY ASS!
If you ask us, she's a really
person...
And she's so pretty too...
Damn it!
WHAT DID YOU SAY?!
WE'VE NEVER MET ANYONE AS UPTIGHT AS HER BEFORE MA'AM...
SPIN
HMP! WE'LL SEE ABOUT THIS!! I'M NOT THE TYPE TO GIVE UP SO EASILY JUST BECAUSE OF SOME NAGGING OLD LADY..!
We'll see about this you old hag!
NO MATTER WHAT IT TAKES, I'LL MAKE SHUU MINE!
......
Fighting spirit?
FIGHTING SPIRIT

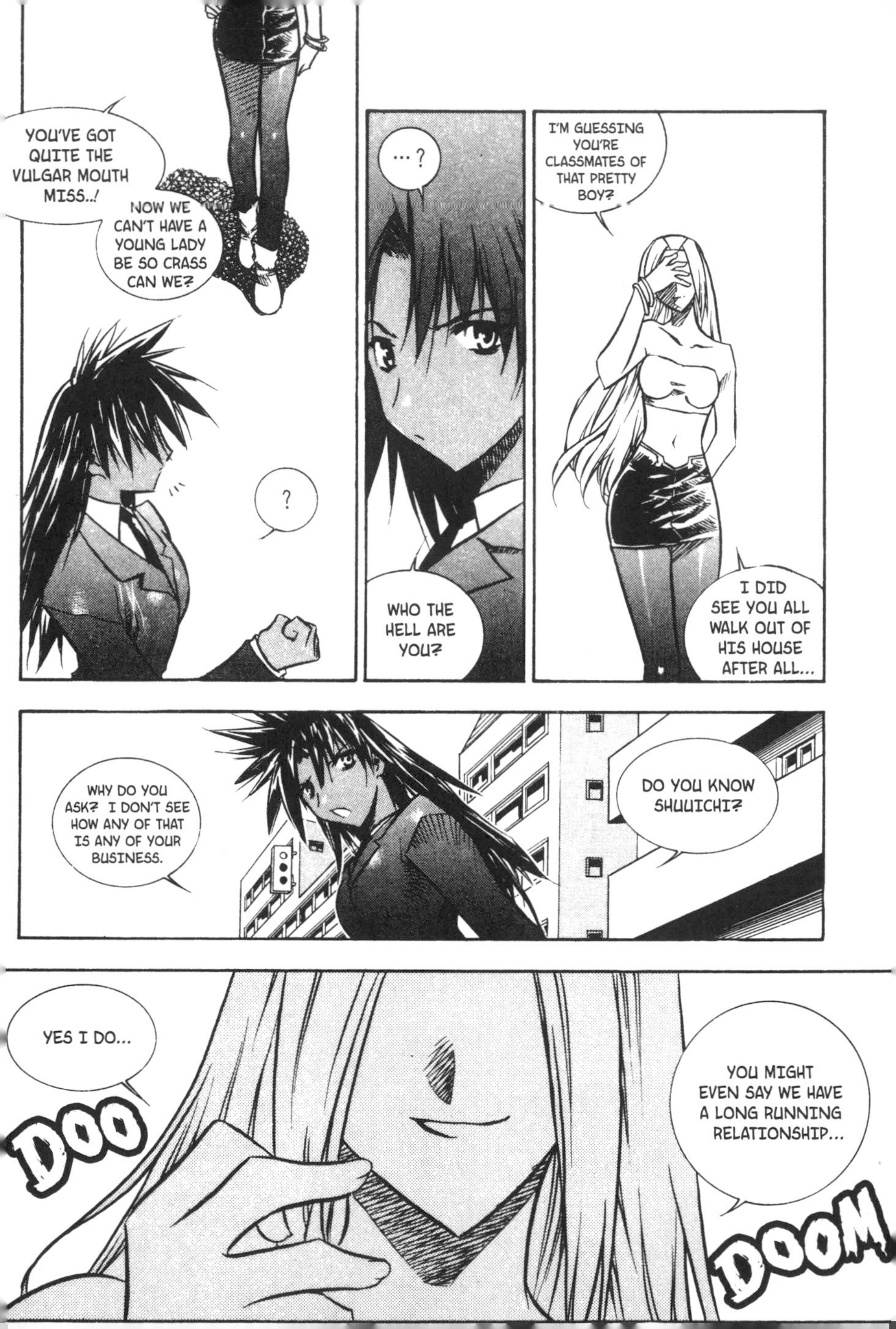

I'M GUESSING YOU'RE CLASSMATES OF THAT PRETTY BOY?
I DID SEE YOU ALL WALK OUT OF HIS HOUSE AFTER ALL...
...?
WHO THE HELL ARE YOU?
YOU'VE GOT QUITE THE VULGAR MOUTH MISS..!
NOW WE CAN'T HAVE A YOUNG LADY BE SO CRASS CAN WE?
?
DO YOU KNOW SHUUICHI?
WHY DO YOU ASK? I DON'T SEE HOW ANY OF THAT IS ANY OF YOUR BUSINESS.
YES I DO...
YOU MIGHT EVEN SAY WE HAVE A LONG RUNNING RELATIONSHIP...
DOO
DOOM

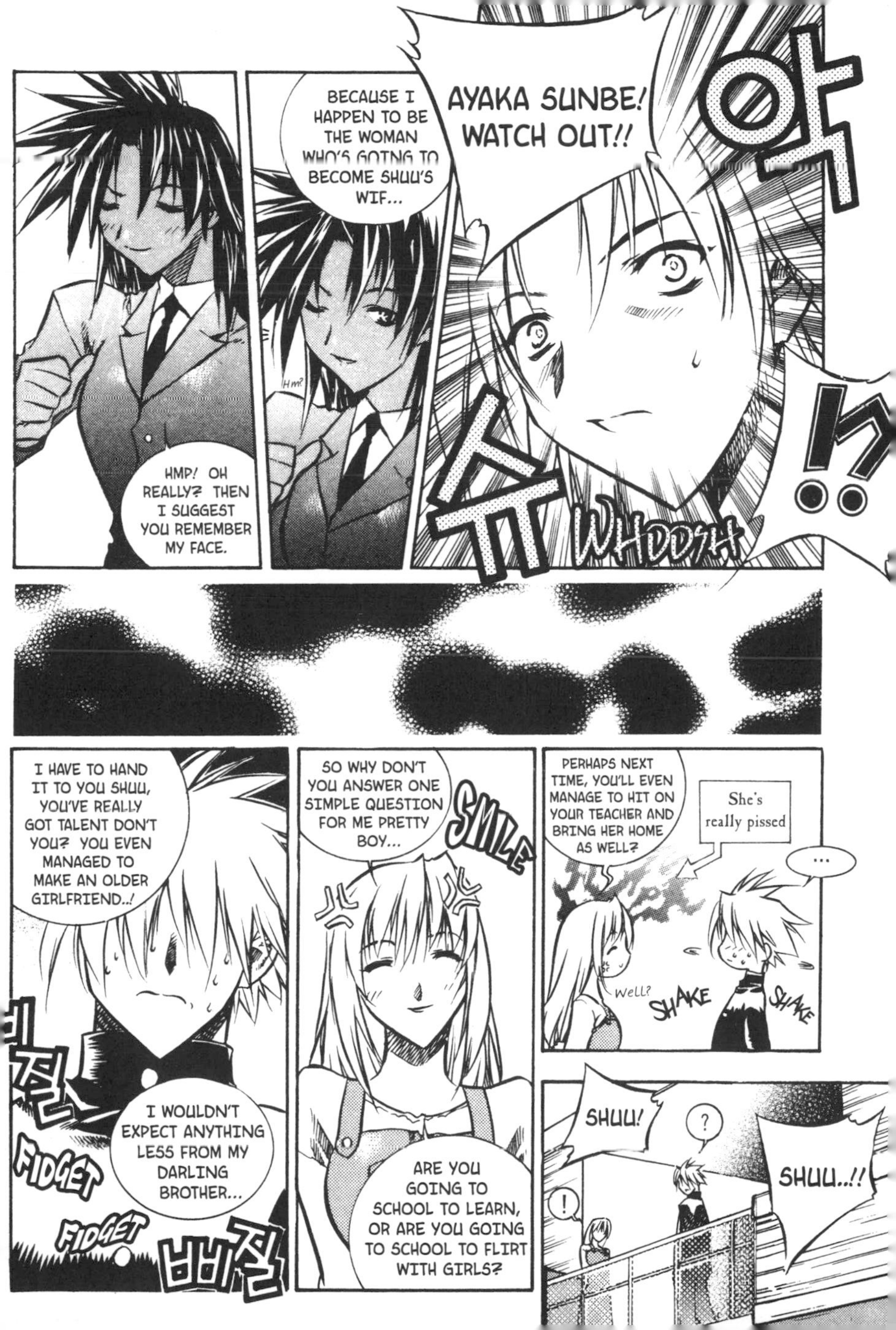
HMP! OH REALLY? THEN I SUGGEST YOU REMEMBER MY FACE.
Hm?
BECAUSE I HAPPEN TO BE THE WOMAN WHO'S GOING TO BECOME SHUU'S WIF...
AYAKA SUNBE! WATCH OUT!!
WHOOSH
I HAVE TO HAND IT TO YOU SHUU, YOU'VE REALLY GOT TALENT DON'T YOU? YOU EVEN MANAGED TO MAKE AN OLDER GIRLFRIEND..!
I WOULDN'T EXPECT ANYTHING LESS FROM MY DARLING BROTHER...
FIDGET
FIDGET
SO WHY DON'T YOU ANSWER ONE SIMPLE QUESTION FOR ME PRETTY BOY...
SMILE
ARE YOU GOING TO SCHOOL TO LEARN, OR ARE YOU GOING TO SCHOOL TO FLIRT WITH GIRLS?
PERHAPS NEXT TIME, YOU'LL EVEN MANAGE TO HIT ON YOUR TEACHER AND BRING HER HOME AS WELL?
She's really pissed
...
Well?
SHAKE
SHAKE
SHUU!
?
!
SHUU..!!

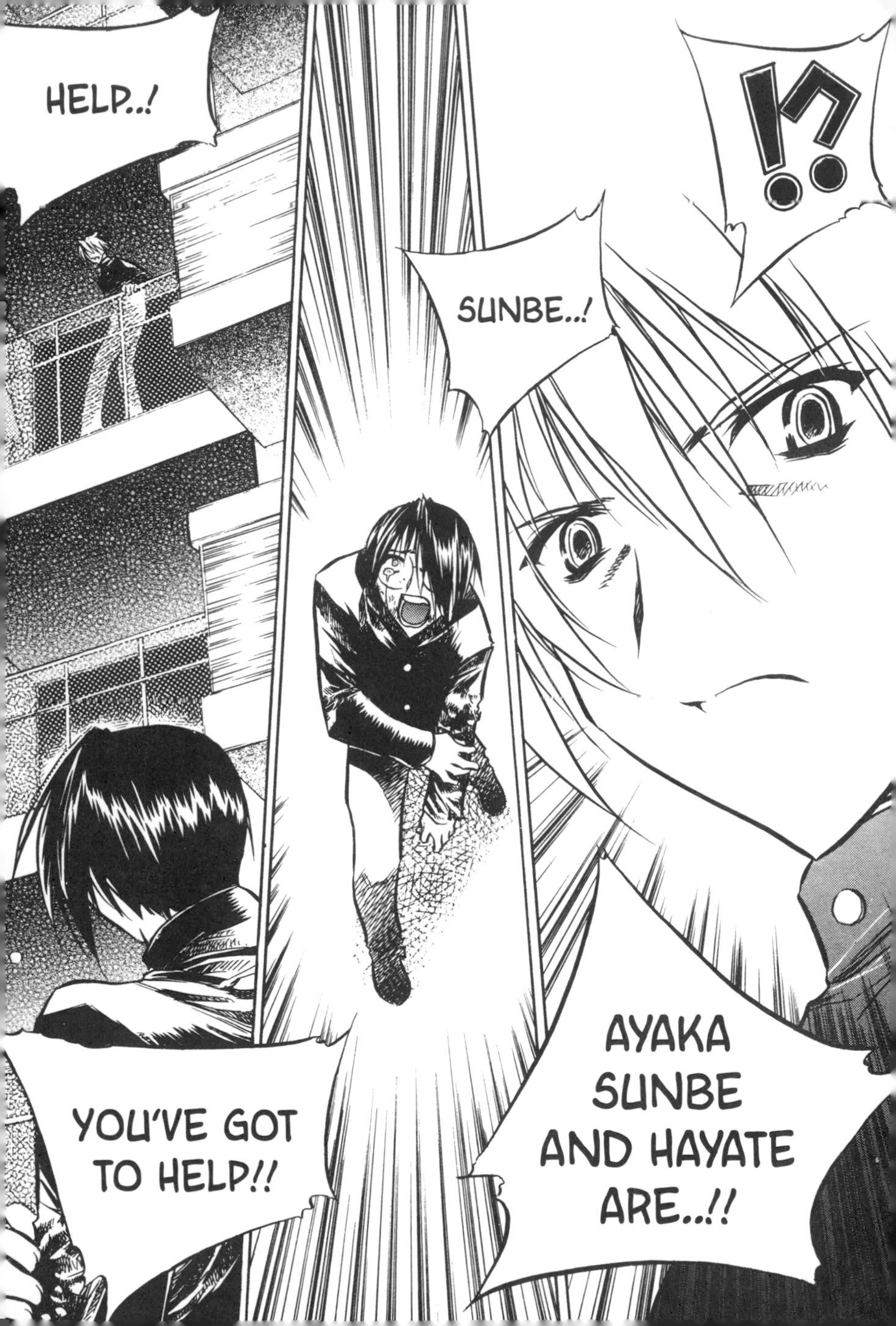
!?
SUNBE..!
HELP..!
AYAKA SUNBE AND HAYATE ARE..!!
YOU'VE GOT TO HELP!!

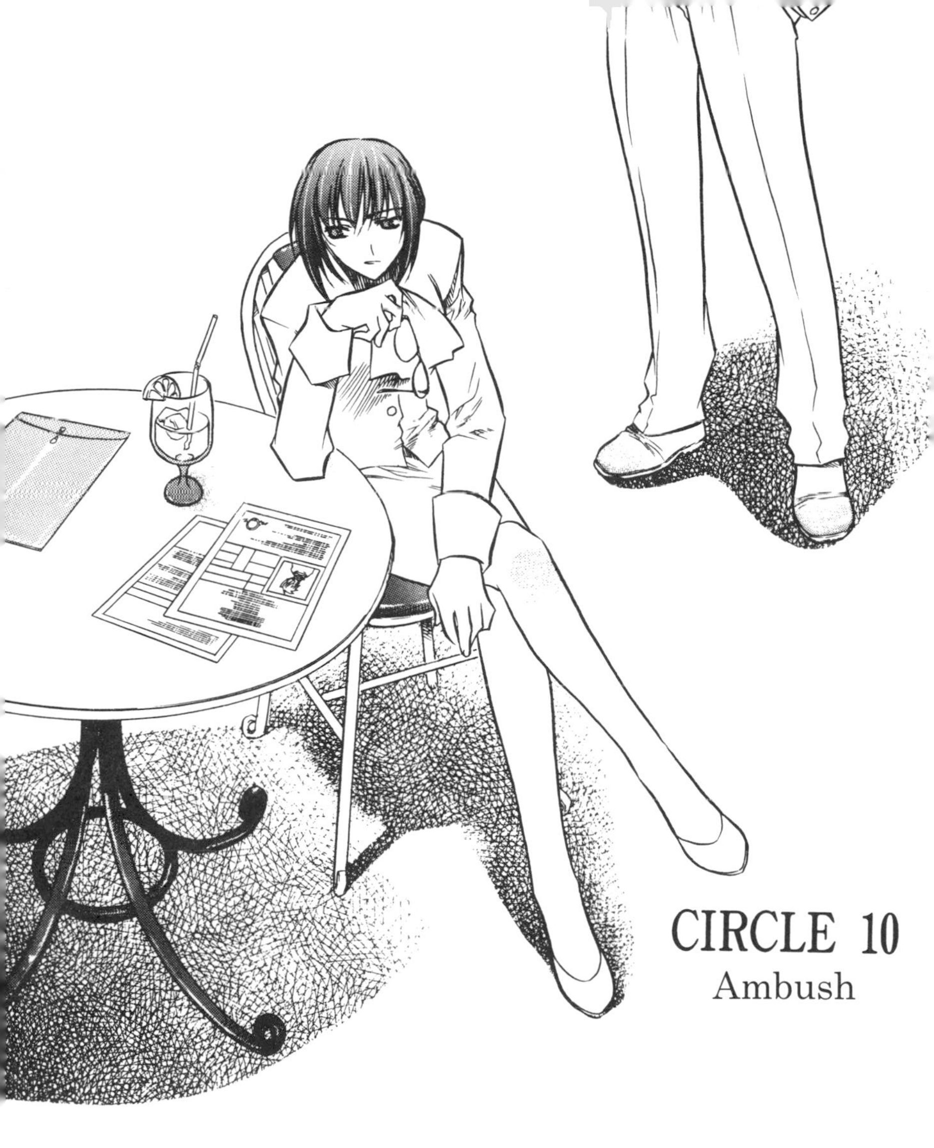

CIRCLE 10
Ambush

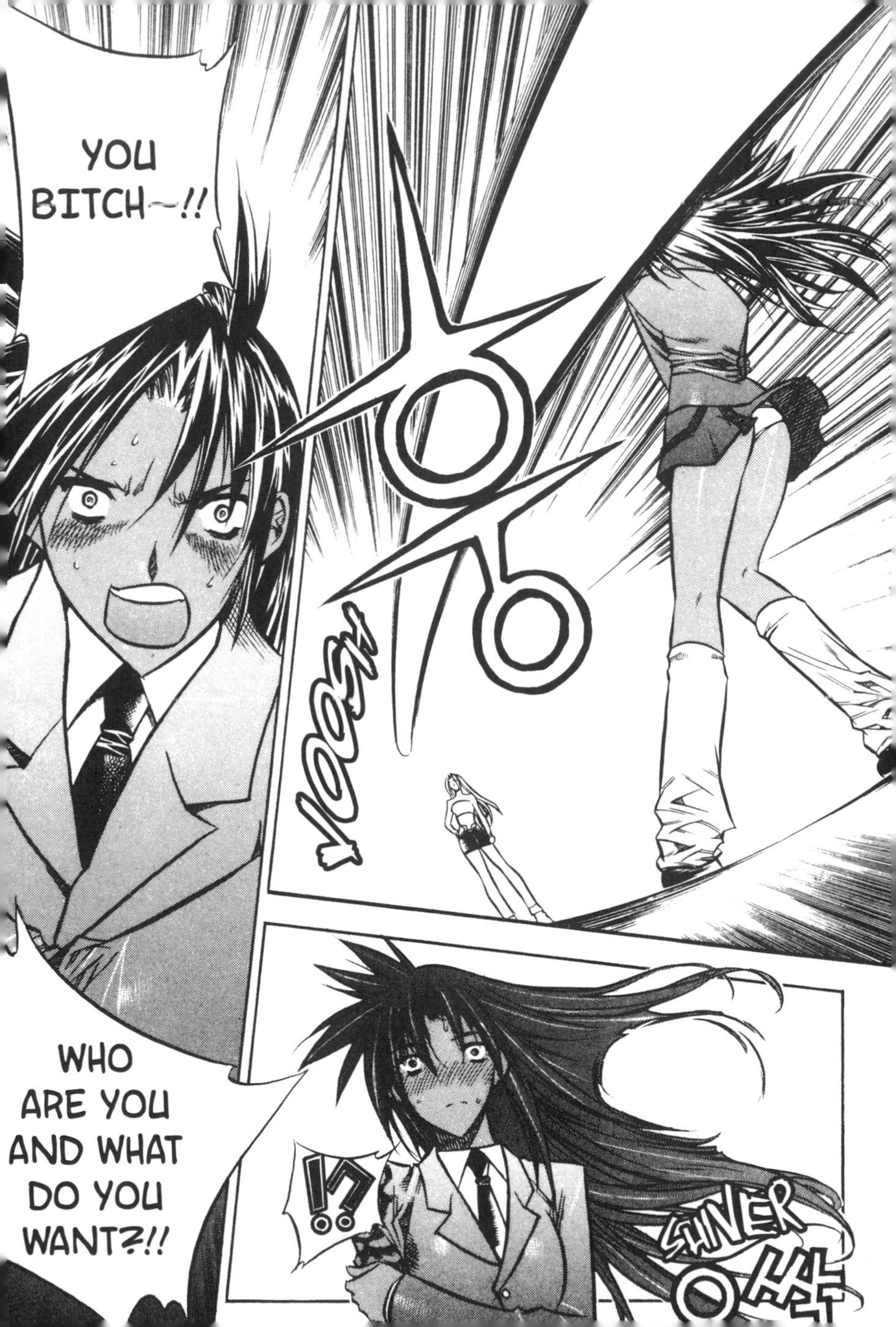
YOU BITCH--!!
VOOSH
WHO ARE YOU AND WHAT DO YOU WANT?!!
!?
SHIVER

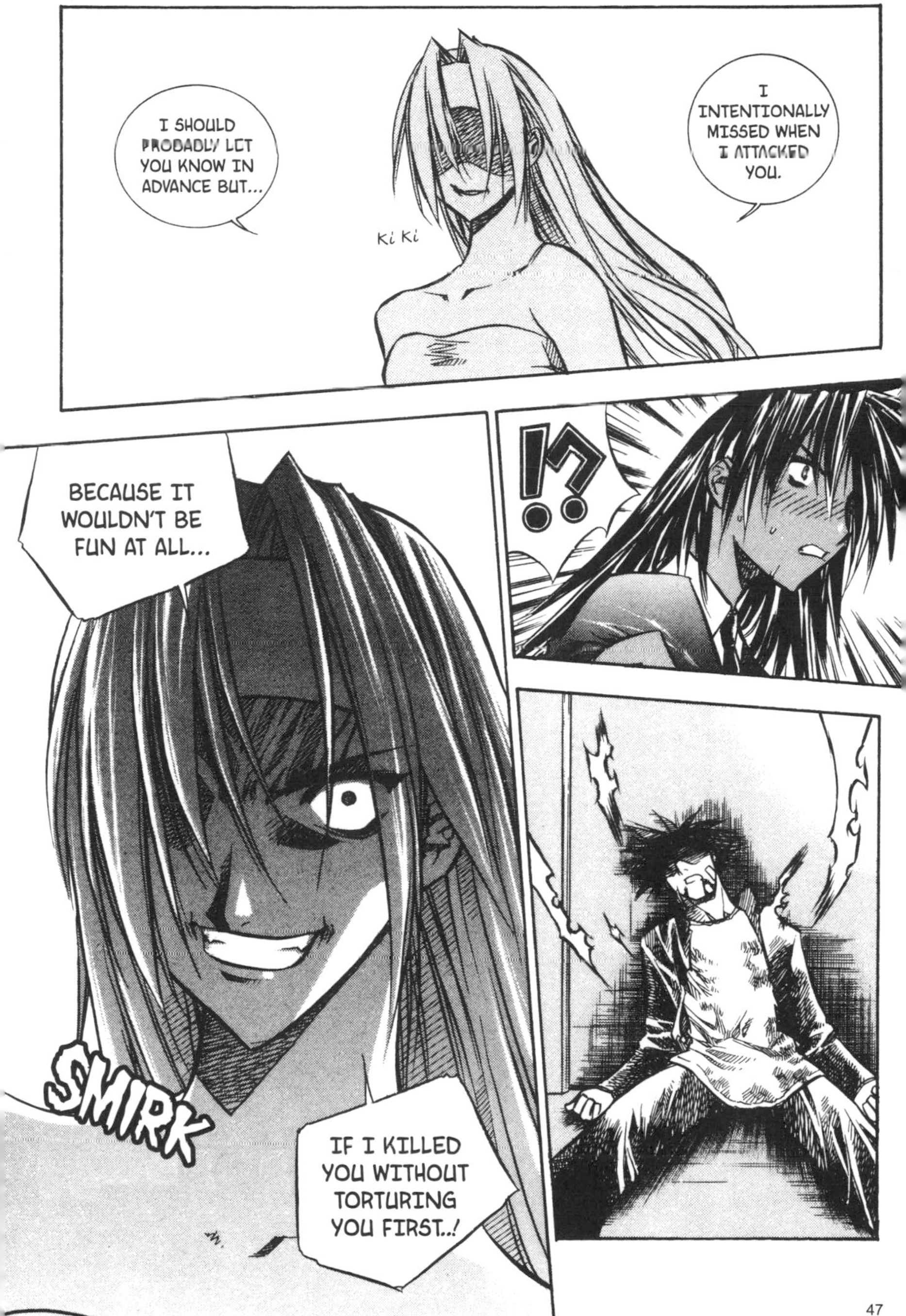
I SHOULD PROBABLY LET YOU KNOW IN ADVANCE BUT...
Ki Ki
I INTENTIONALLY MISSED WHEN I ATTACKED YOU.
BECAUSE IT WOULDN'T BE FUN AT ALL...
!?
SMIRK
IF I KILLED YOU WITHOUT TORTURING YOU FIRST..!

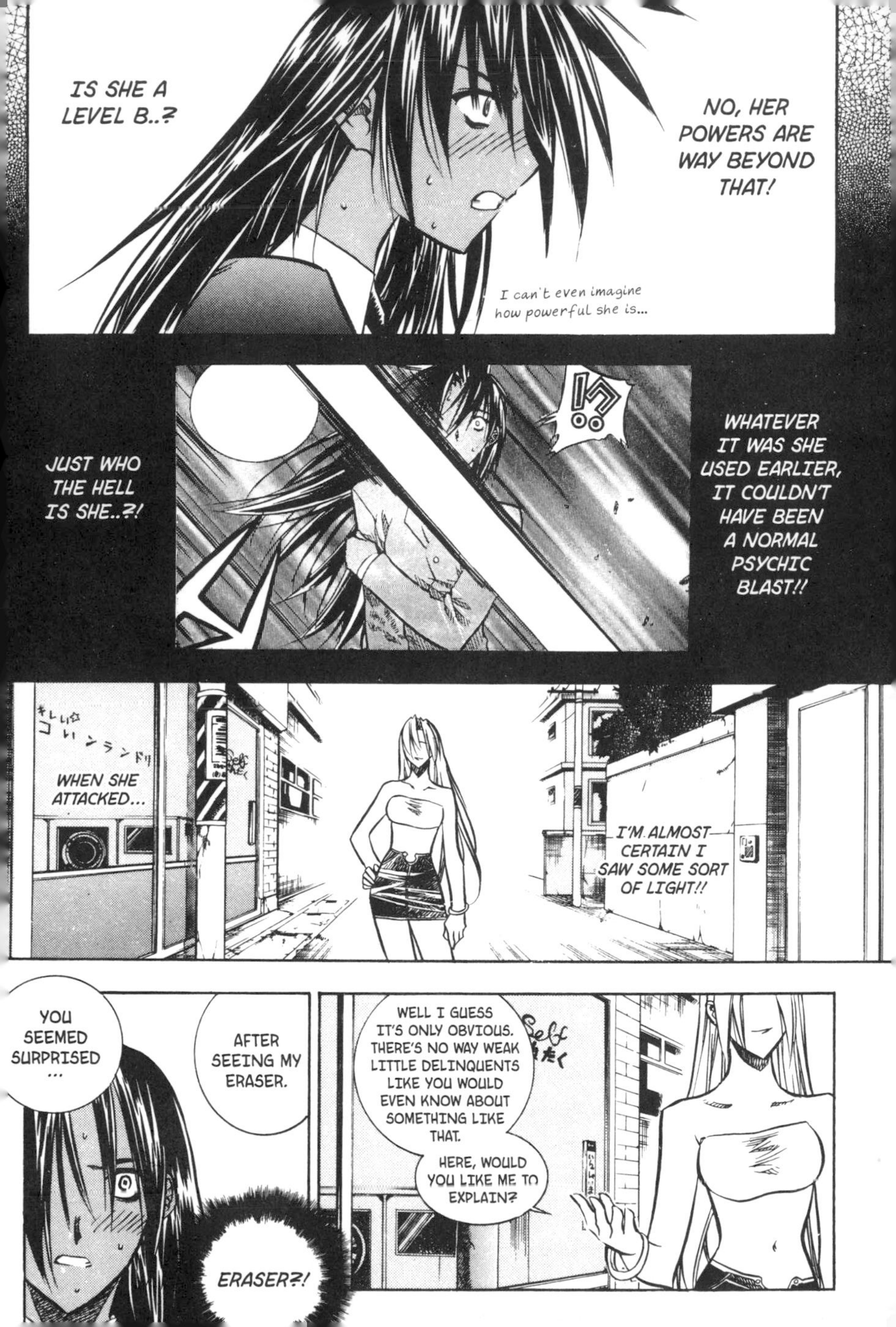
IS SHE A LEVEL B..?
NO, HER POWERS ARE WAY BEYOND THAT!
I can't even imagine how powerful she is...
JUST WHO THE HELL IS SHE..?!
WHATEVER IT WAS SHE USED EARLIER, IT COULDN'T HAVE BEEN A NORMAL PSYCHIC BLAST!!
WHEN SHE ATTACKED...
I'M ALMOST CERTAIN I SAW SOME SORT OF LIGHT!!
YOU SEEMED SURPRISED ...
AFTER SEEING MY ERASER.
WELL I GUESS IT'S ONLY OBVIOUS. THERE'S NO WAY WEAK LITTLE DELINQUENTS LIKE YOU WOULD EVEN KNOW ABOUT SOMETHING LIKE THAT.
HERE, WOULD YOU LIKE ME TO EXPLAIN?
ERASER?!

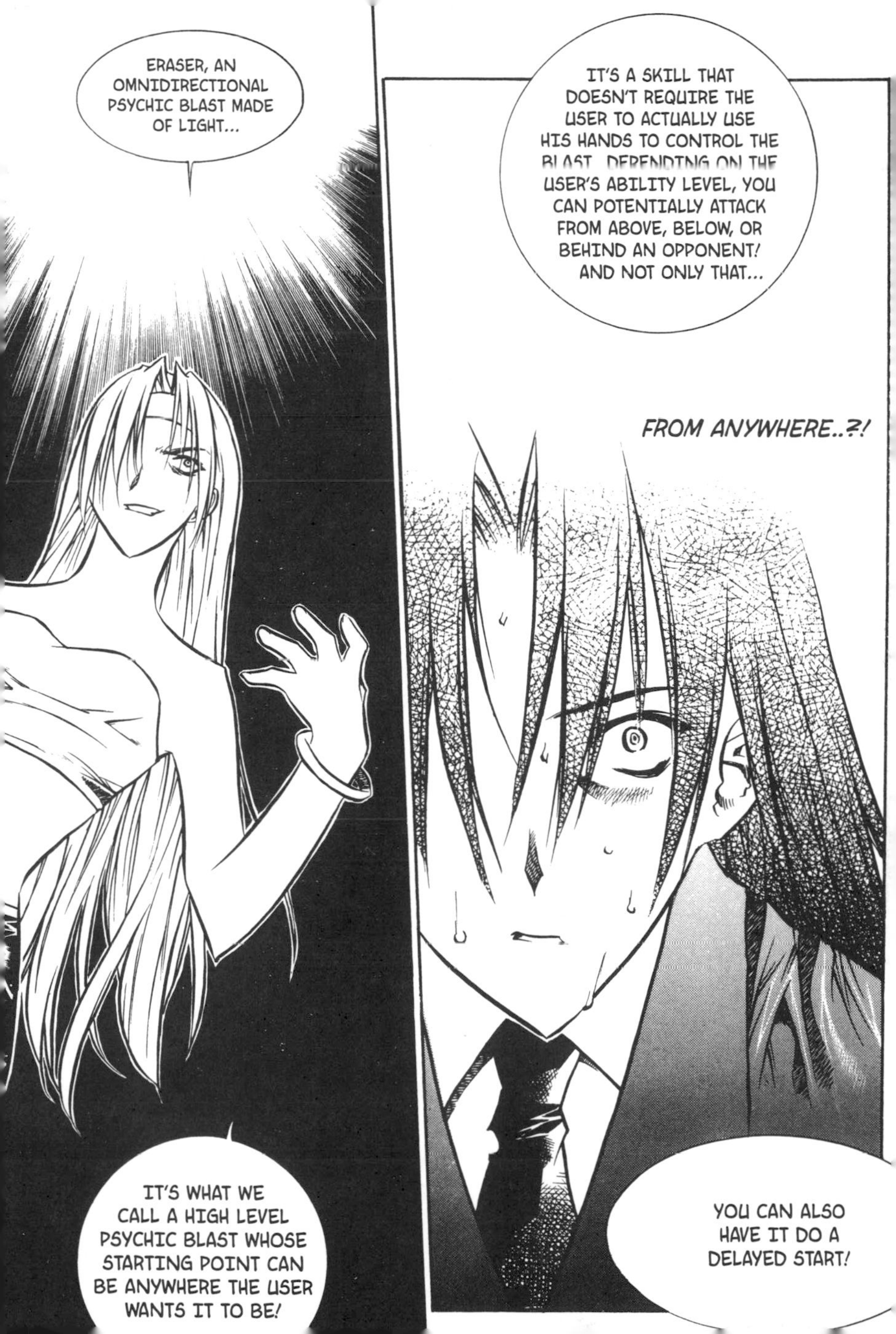
ERASER, AN OMNIDIRECTIONAL PSYCHIC BLAST MADE OF LIGHT...
IT'S WHAT WE CALL A HIGH LEVEL PSYCHIC BLAST WHOSE STARTING POINT CAN BE ANYWHERE THE USER WANTS IT TO BE!
IT'S A SKILL THAT DOESN'T REQUIRE THE USER TO ACTUALLY USE HIS HANDS TO CONTROL THE BLAST. DEPENDING ON THE USER'S ABILITY LEVEL, YOU CAN POTENTIALLY ATTACK FROM ABOVE, BELOW, OR BEHIND AN OPPONENT! AND NOT ONLY THAT...
FROM ANYWHERE..?!
YOU CAN ALSO HAVE IT DO A DELAYED START!

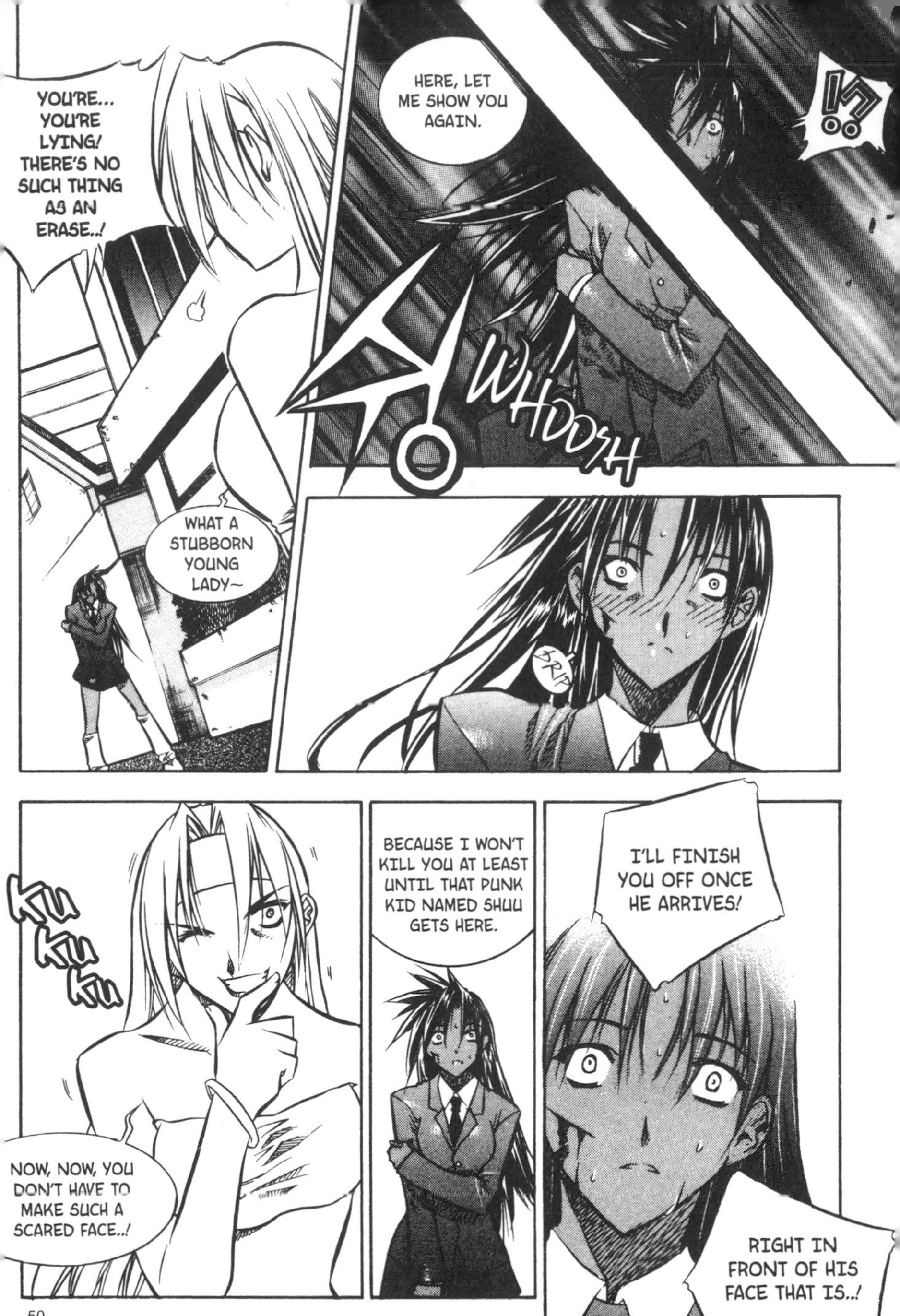

!?
HERE, LET ME SHOW YOU AGAIN.
YOU'RE... YOU'RE LYING! THERE'S NO SUCH THING AS AN ERASE..!
WHOOSH
WHAT A STUBBORN YOUNG LADY~
DRIP
I'LL FINISH YOU OFF ONCE HE ARRIVES!
RIGHT IN FRONT OF HIS FACE THAT IS..!
BECAUSE I WON'T KILL YOU AT LEAST UNTIL THAT PUNK KID NAMED SHUU GETS HERE.
KU KU KU KU
NOW, NOW, YOU DON'T HAVE TO MAKE SUCH A SCARED FACE..!

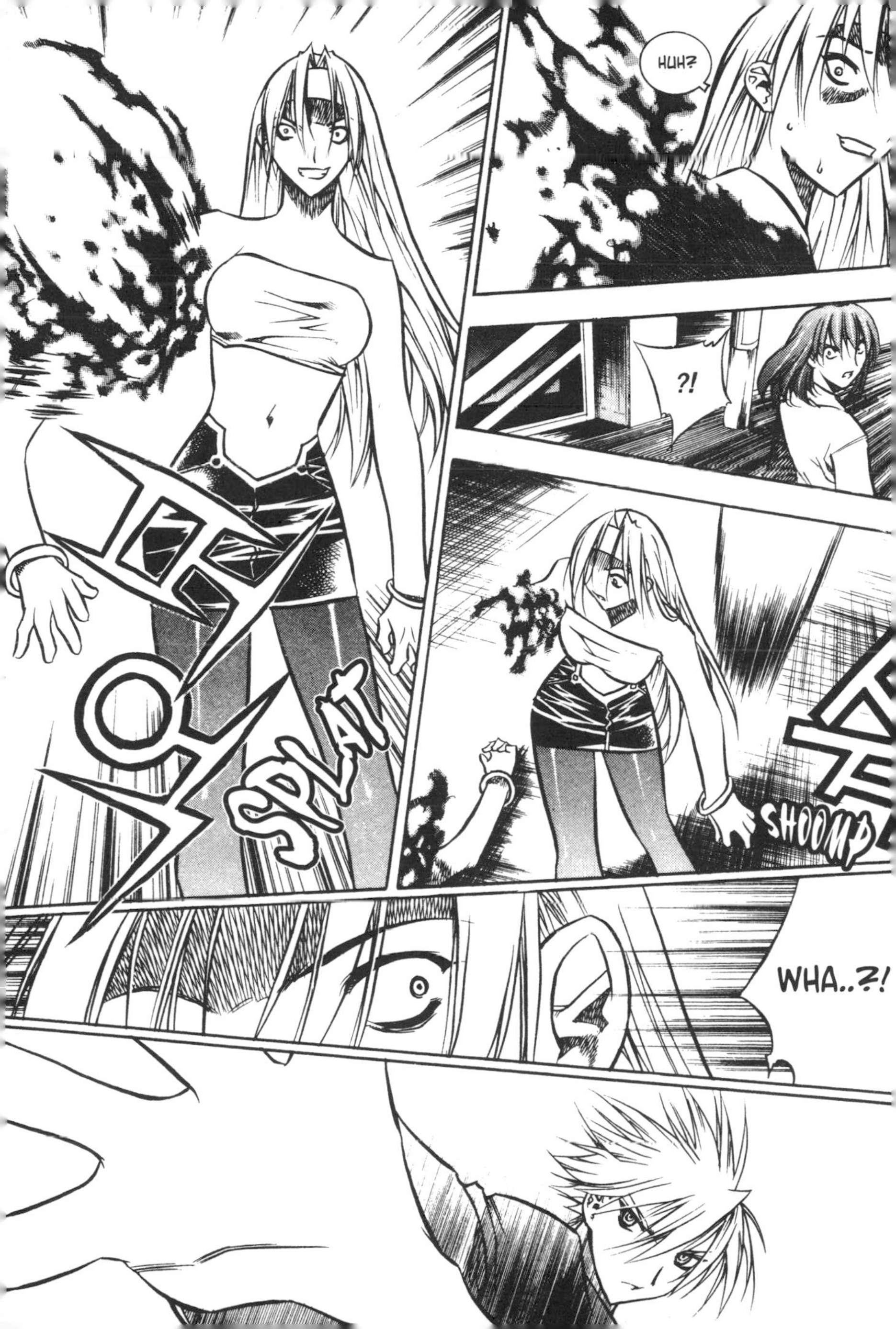

HUH?
?!
SPLAT
SHOOMP
WHA..?!

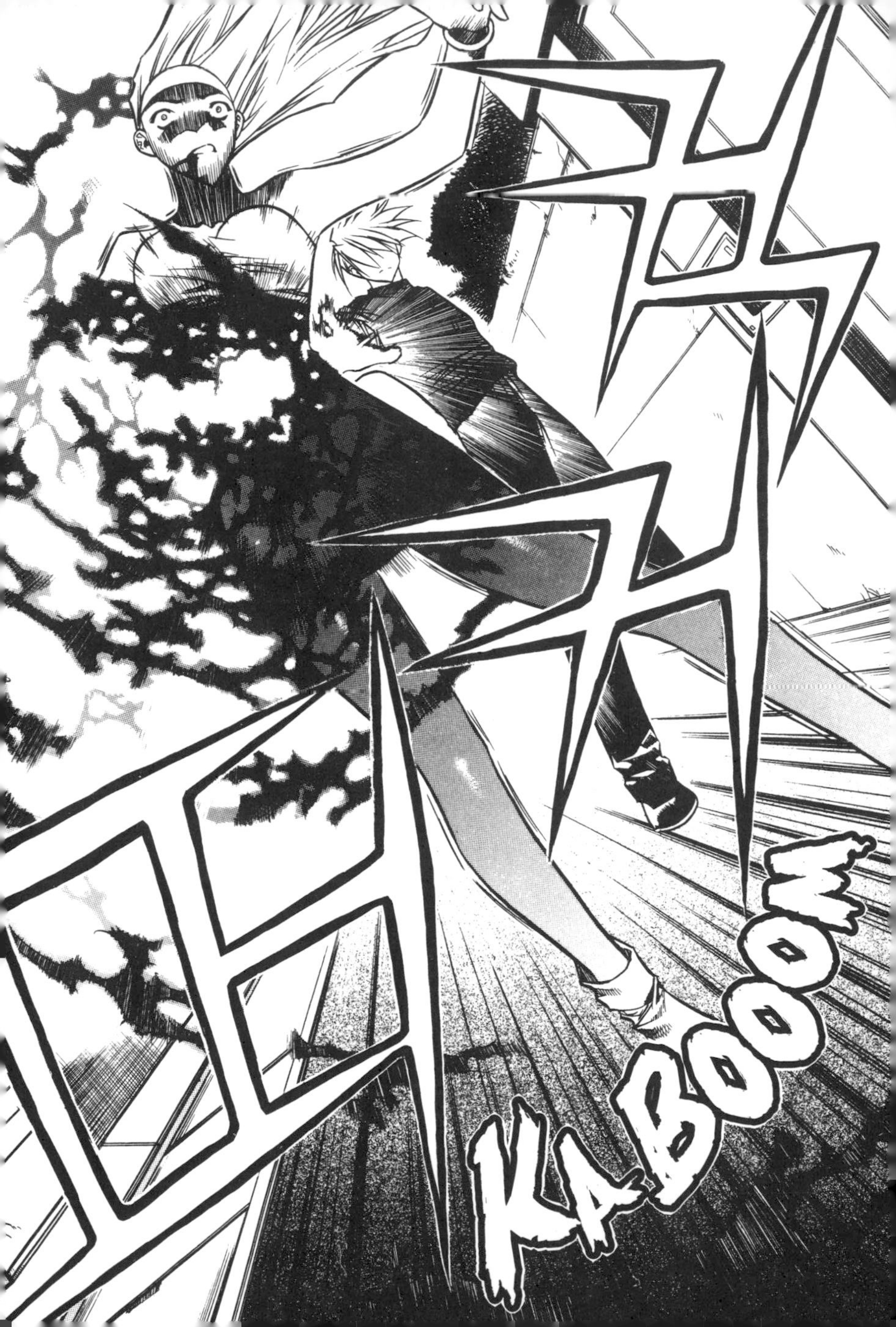
KA-BOOOM

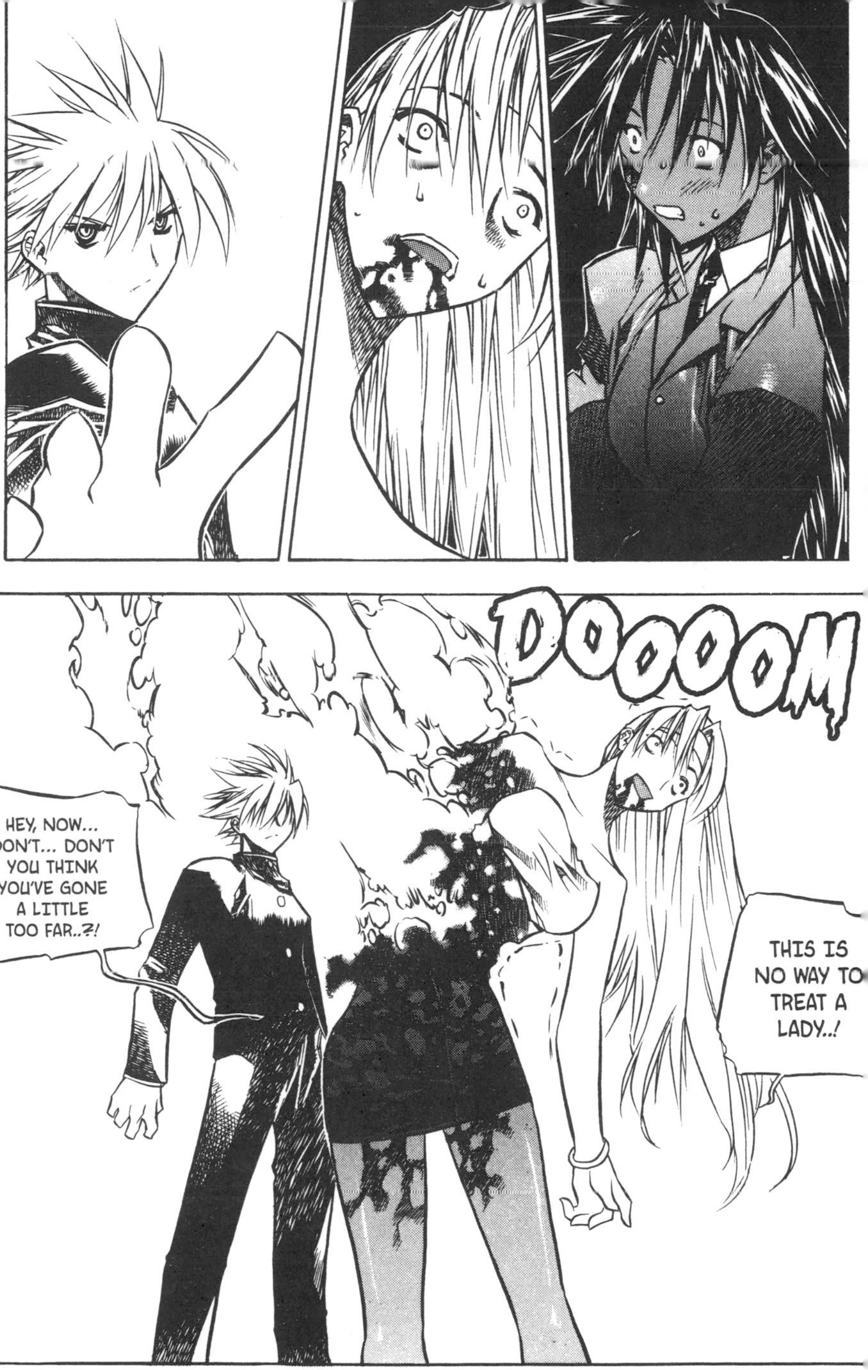
DOOOOM
HEY, NOW... DON'T... DON'T YOU THINK YOU'VE GONE A LITTLE TOO FAR..?!
THIS IS NO WAY TO TREAT A LADY..!

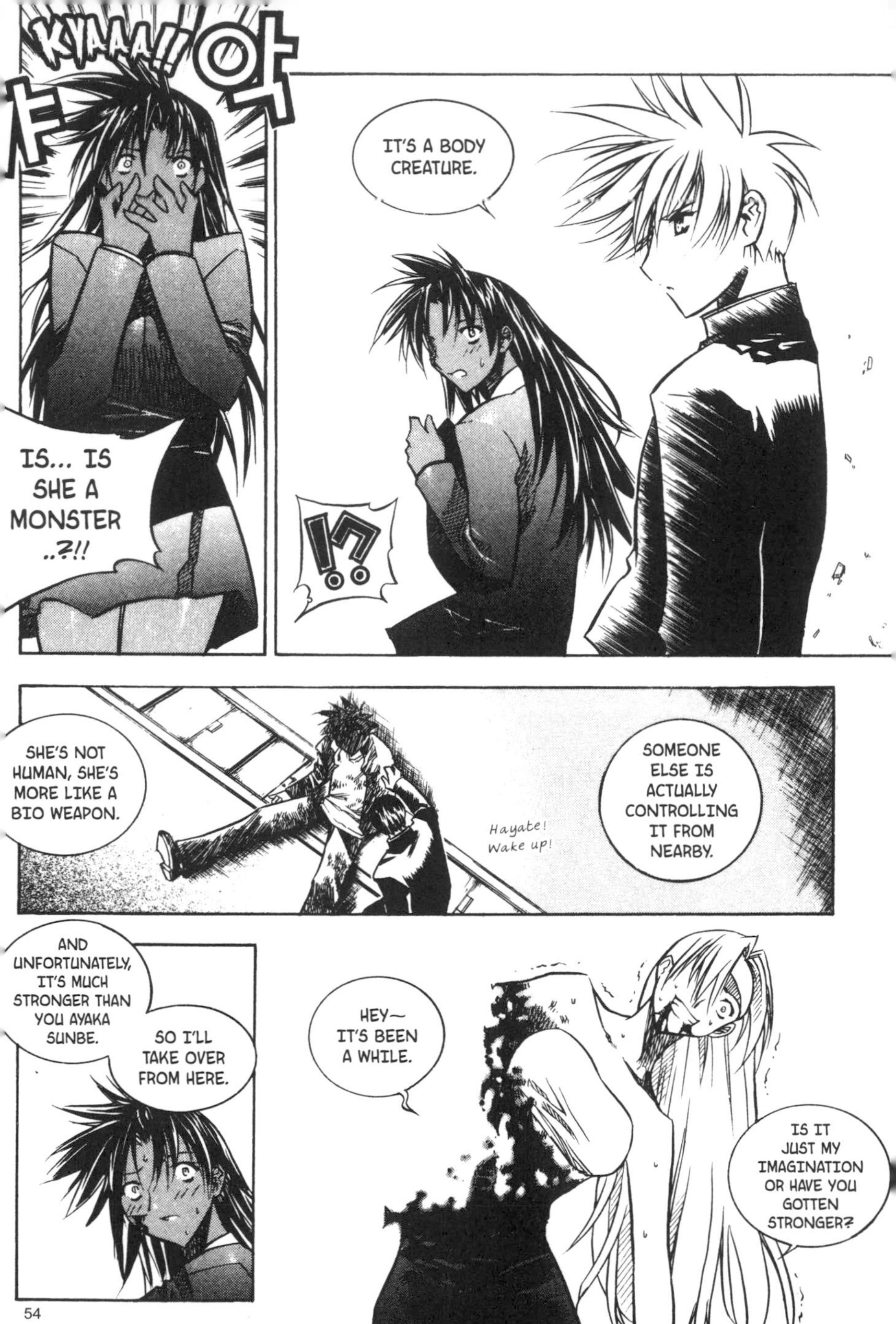
KYAAA!! 야
IS... IS SHE A MONSTER ..?!!
IT'S A BODY CREATURE.
!?
SHE'S NOT HUMAN, SHE'S MORE LIKE A BIO WEAPON.
Hayate! Wake up!
SOMEONE ELSE IS ACTUALLY CONTROLLING IT FROM NEARBY.
AND UNFORTUNATELY, IT'S MUCH STRONGER THAN YOU AYAKA SUNBE.
SO I'LL TAKE OVER FROM HERE.
HEY~ IT'S BEEN A WHILE.
IS IT JUST MY IMAGINATION OR HAVE YOU GOTTEN STRONGER?

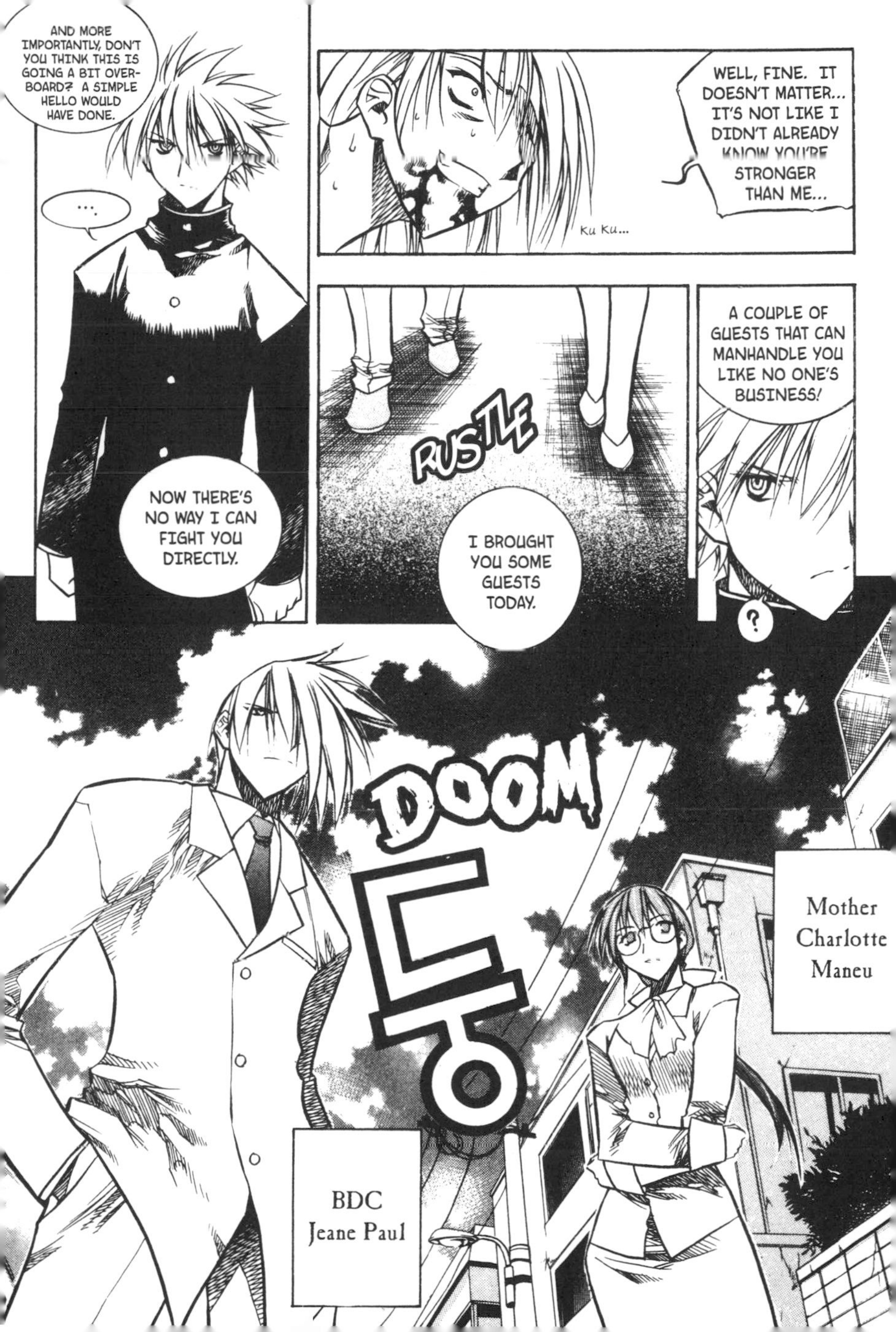

AND MORE IMPORTANTLY, DON'T YOU THINK THIS IS GOING A BIT OVER-BOARD? A SIMPLE HELLO WOULD HAVE DONE.
...
WELL, FINE. IT DOESN'T MATTER... IT'S NOT LIKE I DIDN'T ALREADY KNOW YOU'RE STRONGER THAN ME...
Ku Ku...
NOW THERE'S NO WAY I CAN FIGHT YOU DIRECTLY.
I BROUGHT YOU SOME GUESTS TODAY.
RUSTLE
A COUPLE OF GUESTS THAT CAN MANHANDLE YOU LIKE NO ONE'S BUSINESS!
?
DOOM
둥
Mother Charlotte Maneu
BDC Jeane Paul

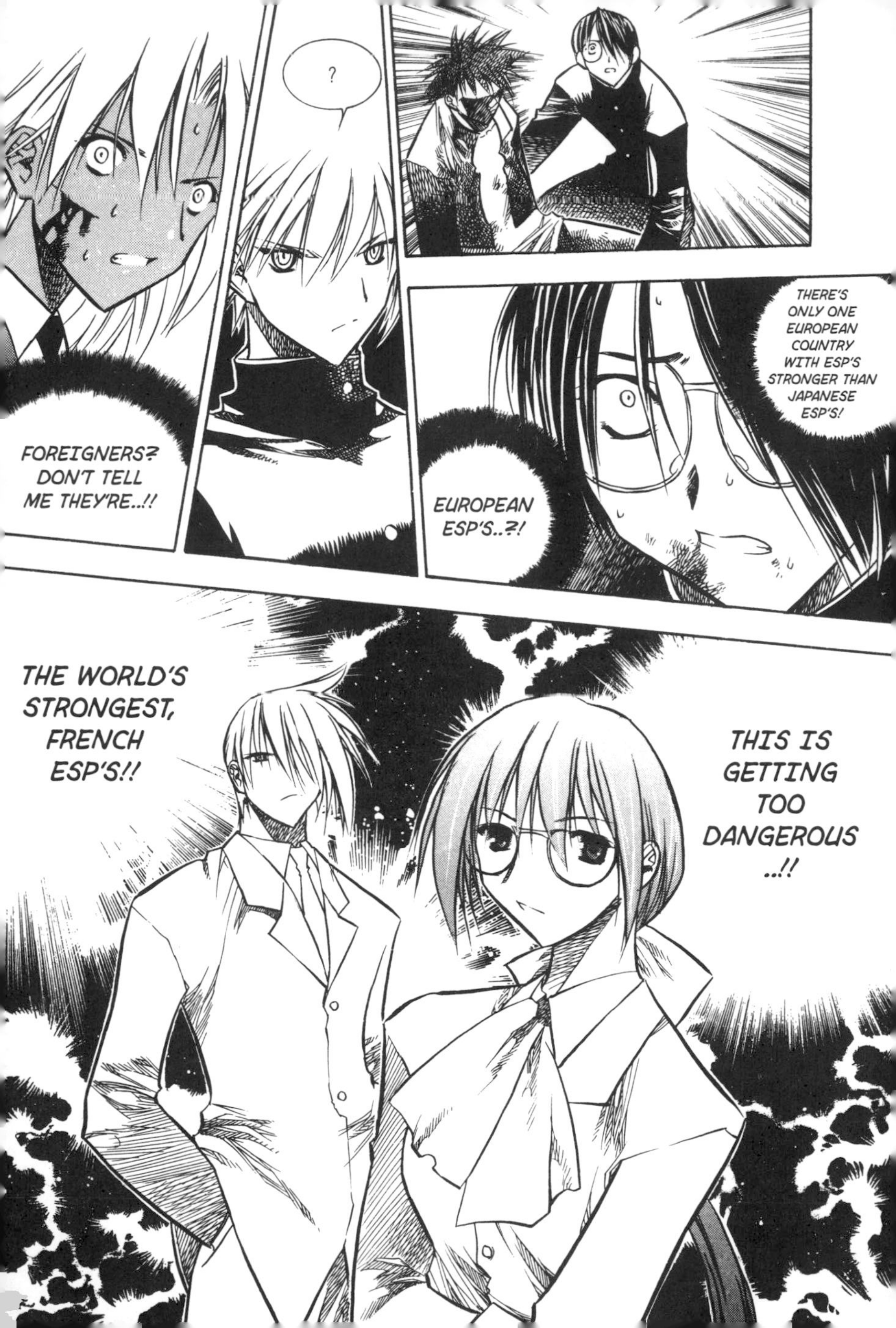
?
THERE'S ONLY ONE EUROPEAN COUNTRY WITH ESP'S STRONGER THAN JAPANESE ESP'S!
EUROPEAN ESP'S..?!
FOREIGNERS? DON'T TELL ME THEY'RE..!!
THIS IS GETTING TOO DANGEROUS ..!!
THE WORLD'S STRONGEST, FRENCH ESP'S!!

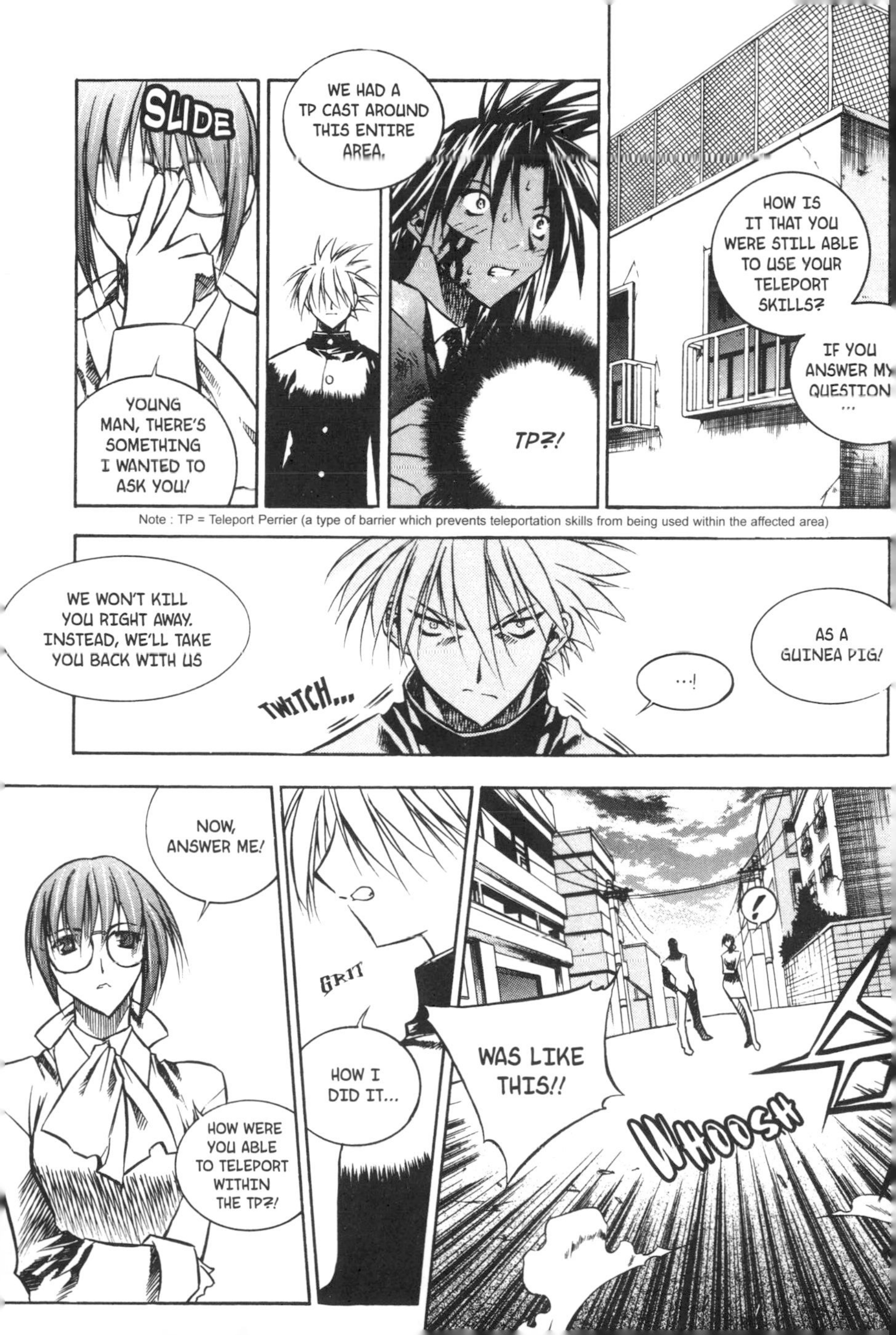
SLIDE
YOUNG MAN, THERE'S SOMETHING I WANTED TO ASK YOU!
WE HAD A TP CAST AROUND THIS ENTIRE AREA.
TP?!
HOW IS IT THAT YOU WERE STILL ABLE TO USE YOUR TELEPORT SKILLS?
IF YOU ANSWER MY QUESTION ...
WE WON'T KILL YOU RIGHT AWAY. INSTEAD, WE'LL TAKE YOU BACK WITH US
TWITCH...
...!
AS A GUINEA PIG!
NOW, ANSWER ME!
HOW WERE YOU ABLE TO TELEPORT WITHIN THE TP?!
GRIT
HOW I DID IT...
WAS LIKE THIS!!
WHOOSH
!

Note : TP = Teleport Perrier (a type of barrier which prevents teleportation skills from being used within the affected area)

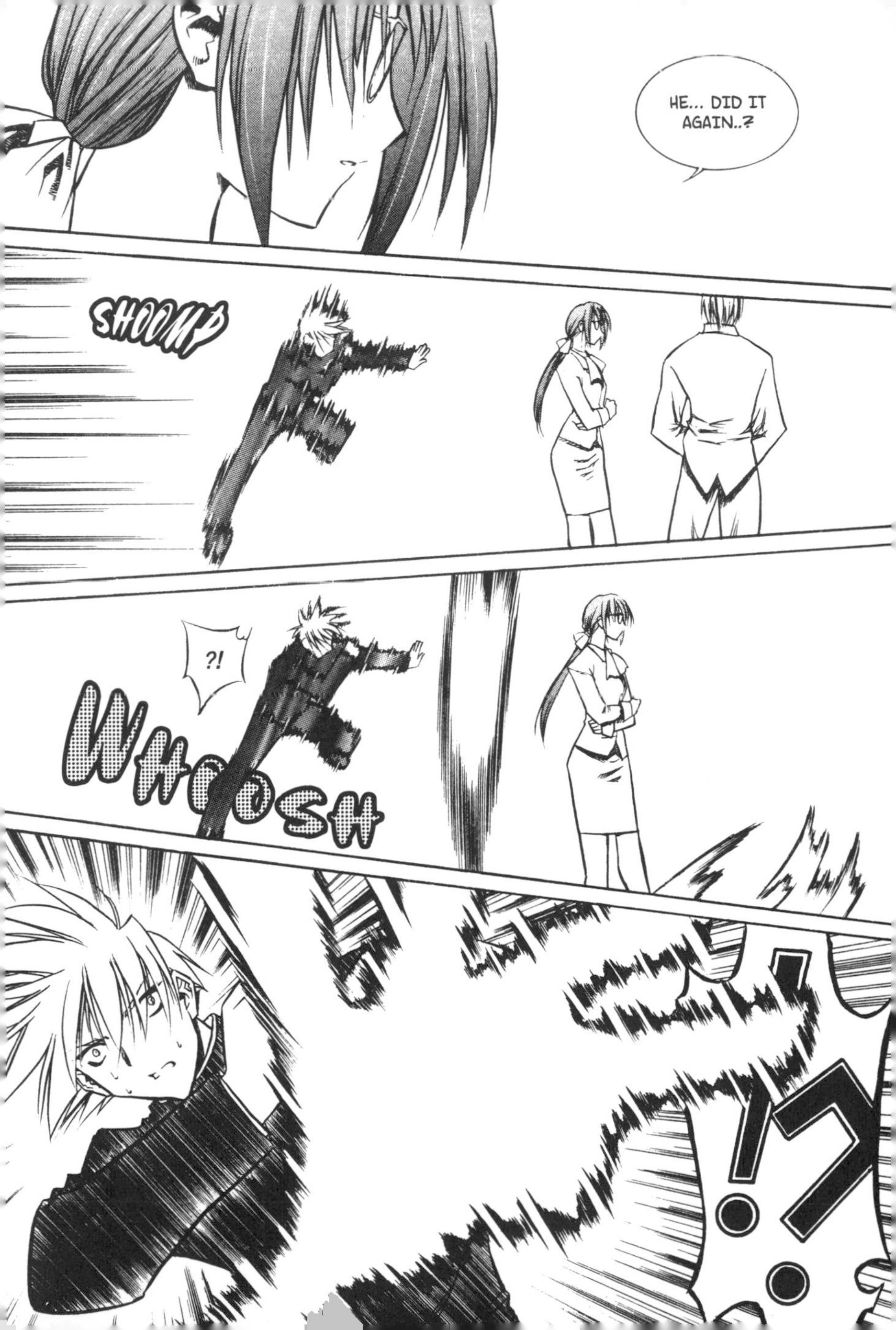
HE... DID IT AGAIN..?
SHOOMP
?!
WHOOSH

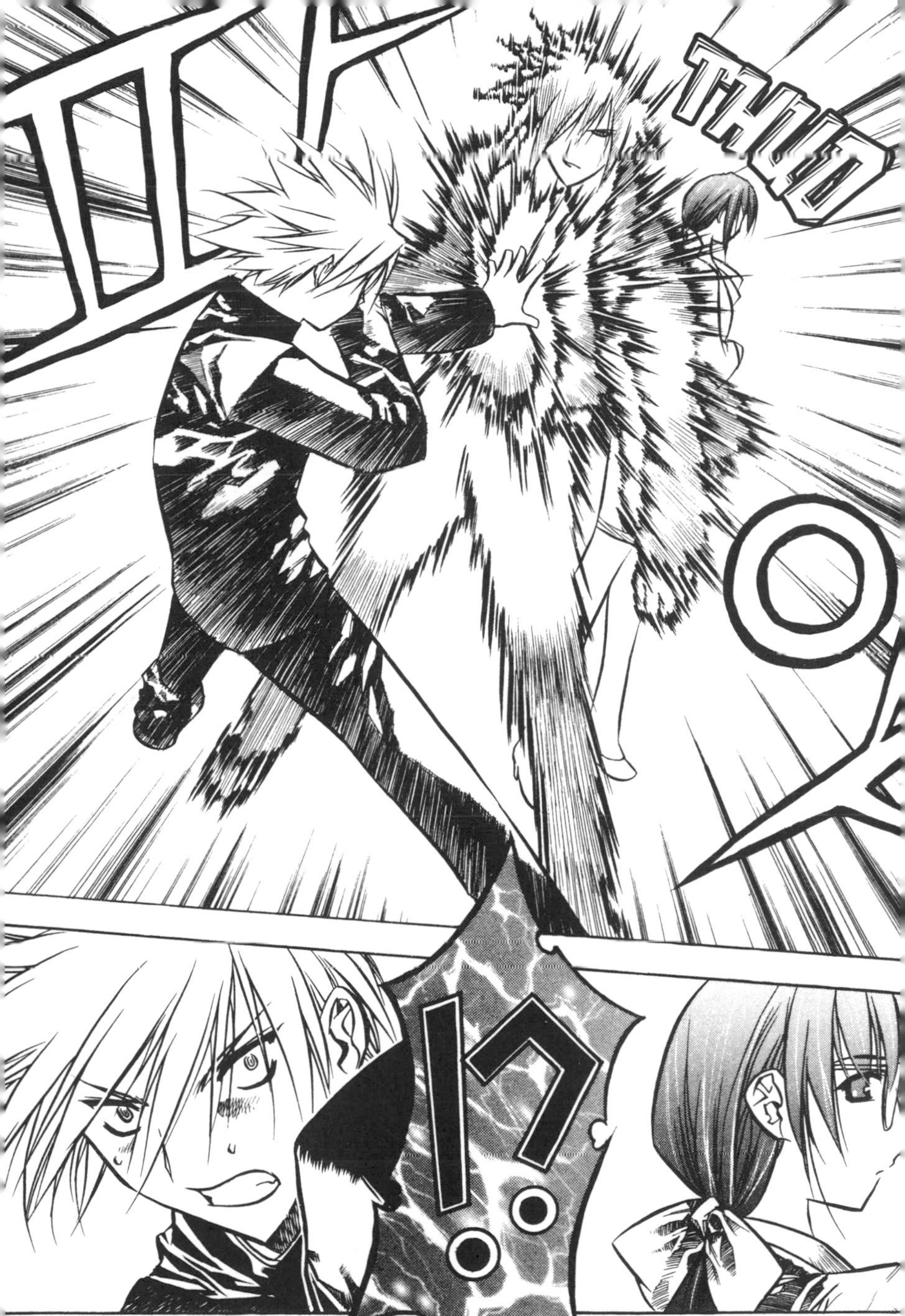
THUD

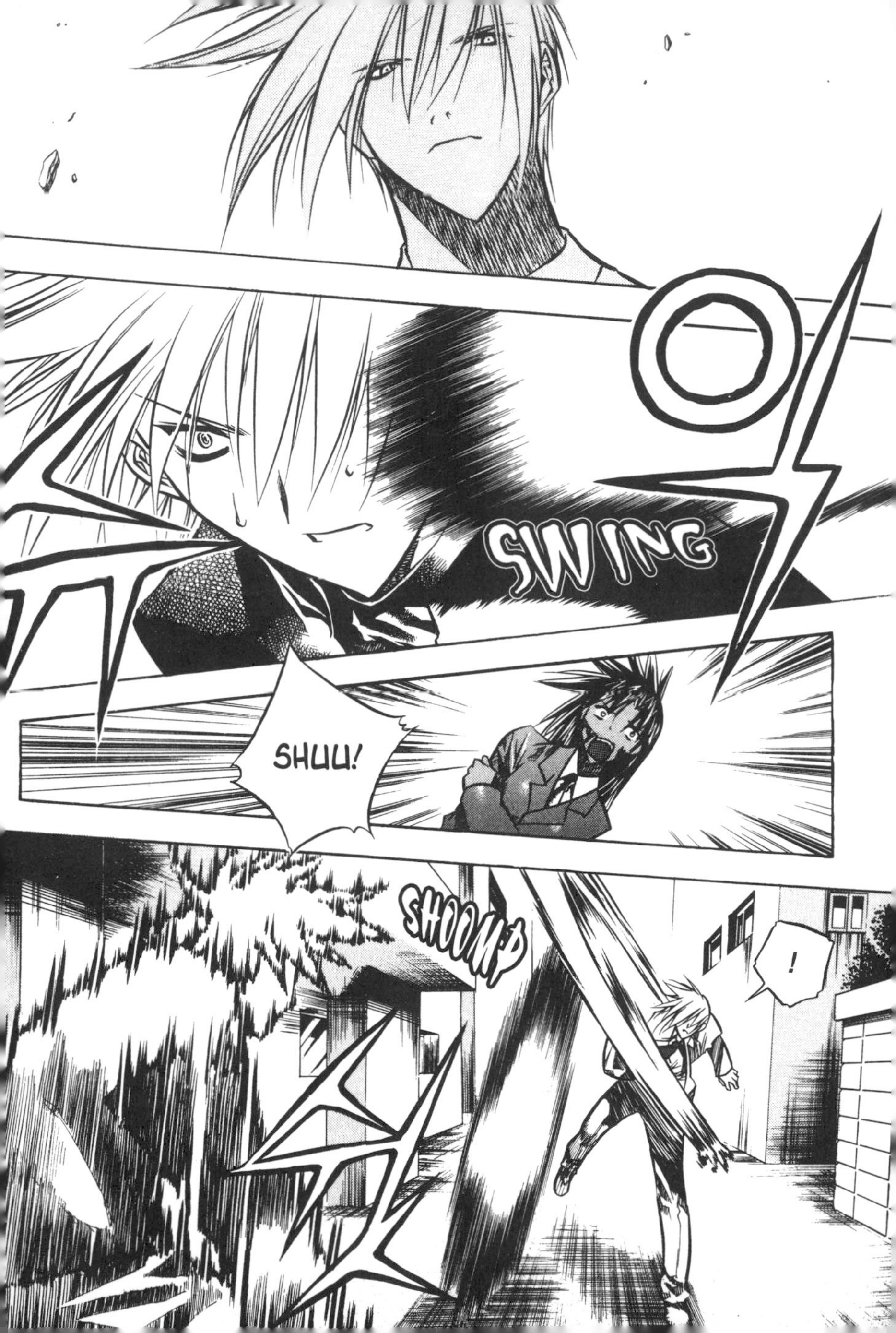
SWING
SHUU!
SHOOM
!

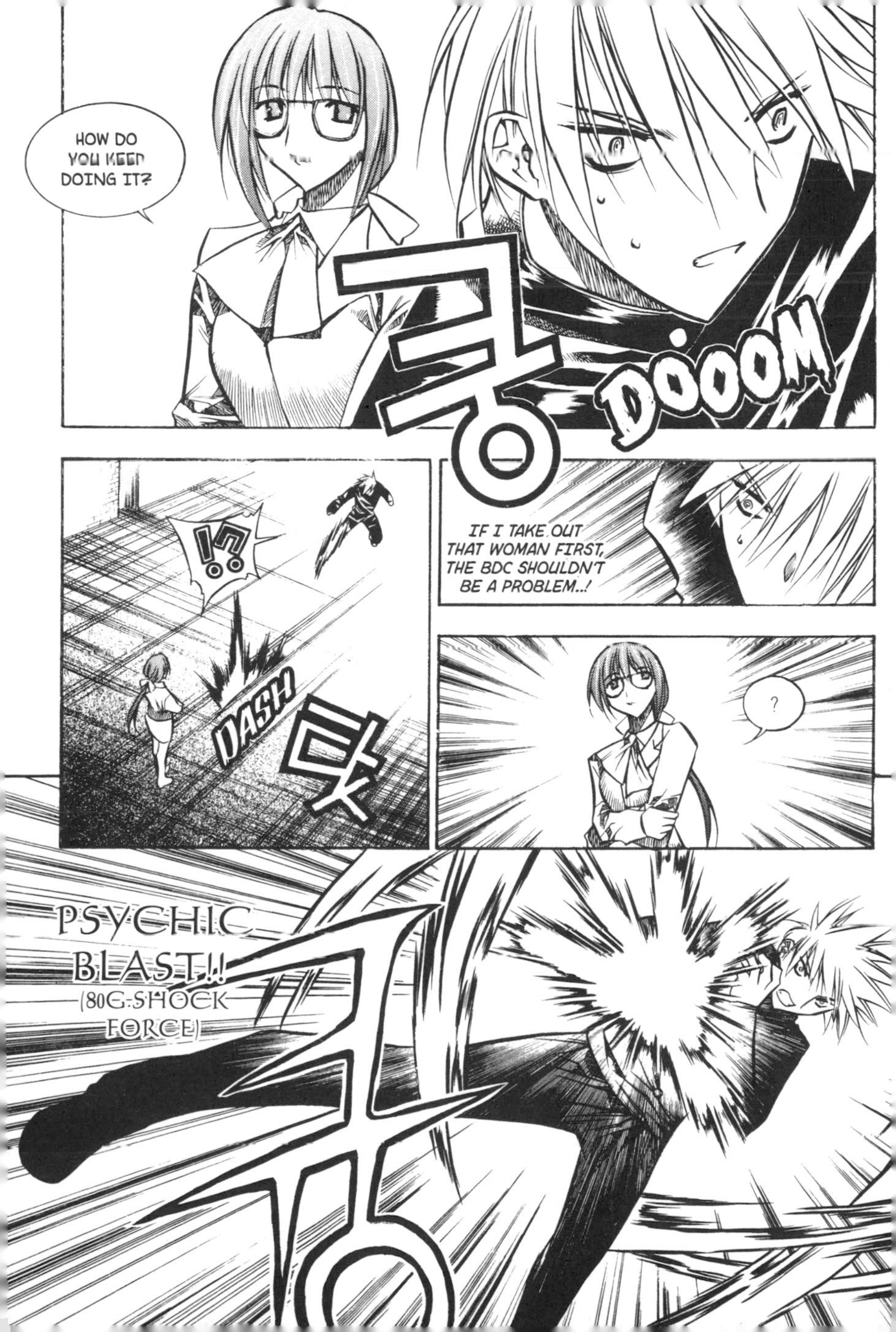
HOW DO YOU KEEP DOING IT?
DOOOM
!?
DASH
IF I TAKE OUT THAT WOMAN FIRST, THE BDC SHOULDN'T BE A PROBLEM...!
?
PSYCHIC BLAST!!
(80G-SHOCK FORCE)

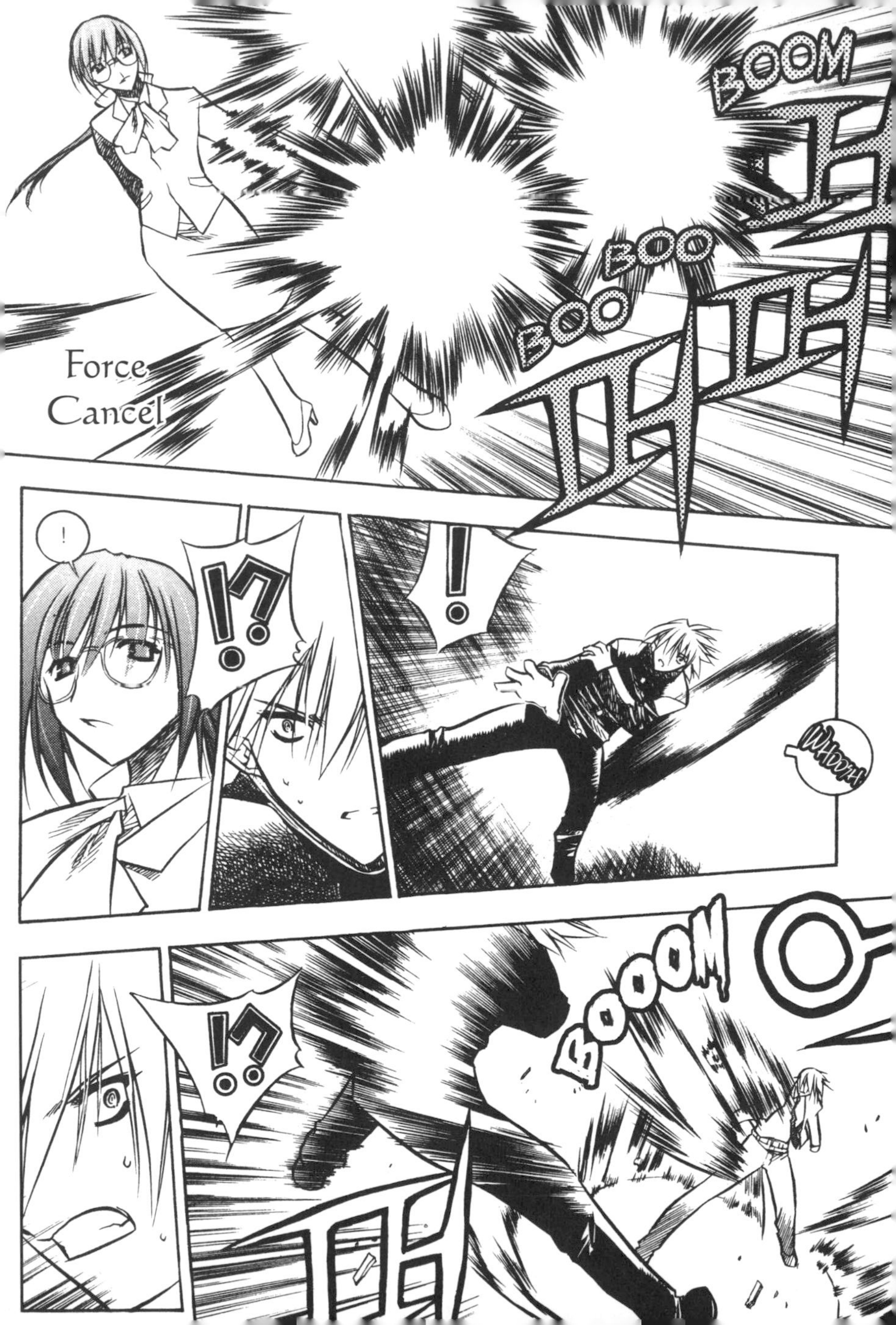
BOOM
BOO BOO BOO
Force Cancel
!
!?
!
WHOOSH
BOOOOM
!?

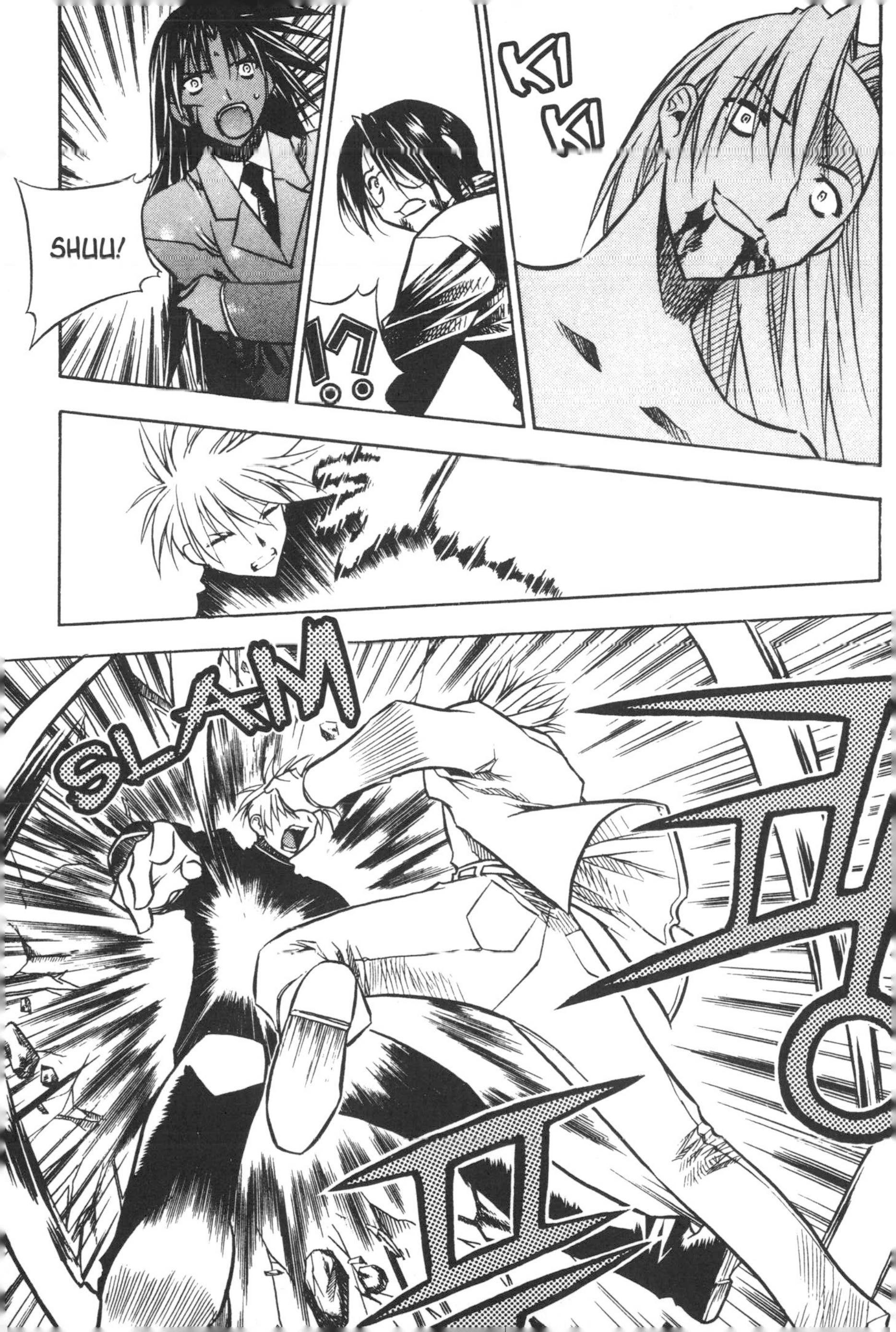
KI KI
!?
SHUU!
SLAM

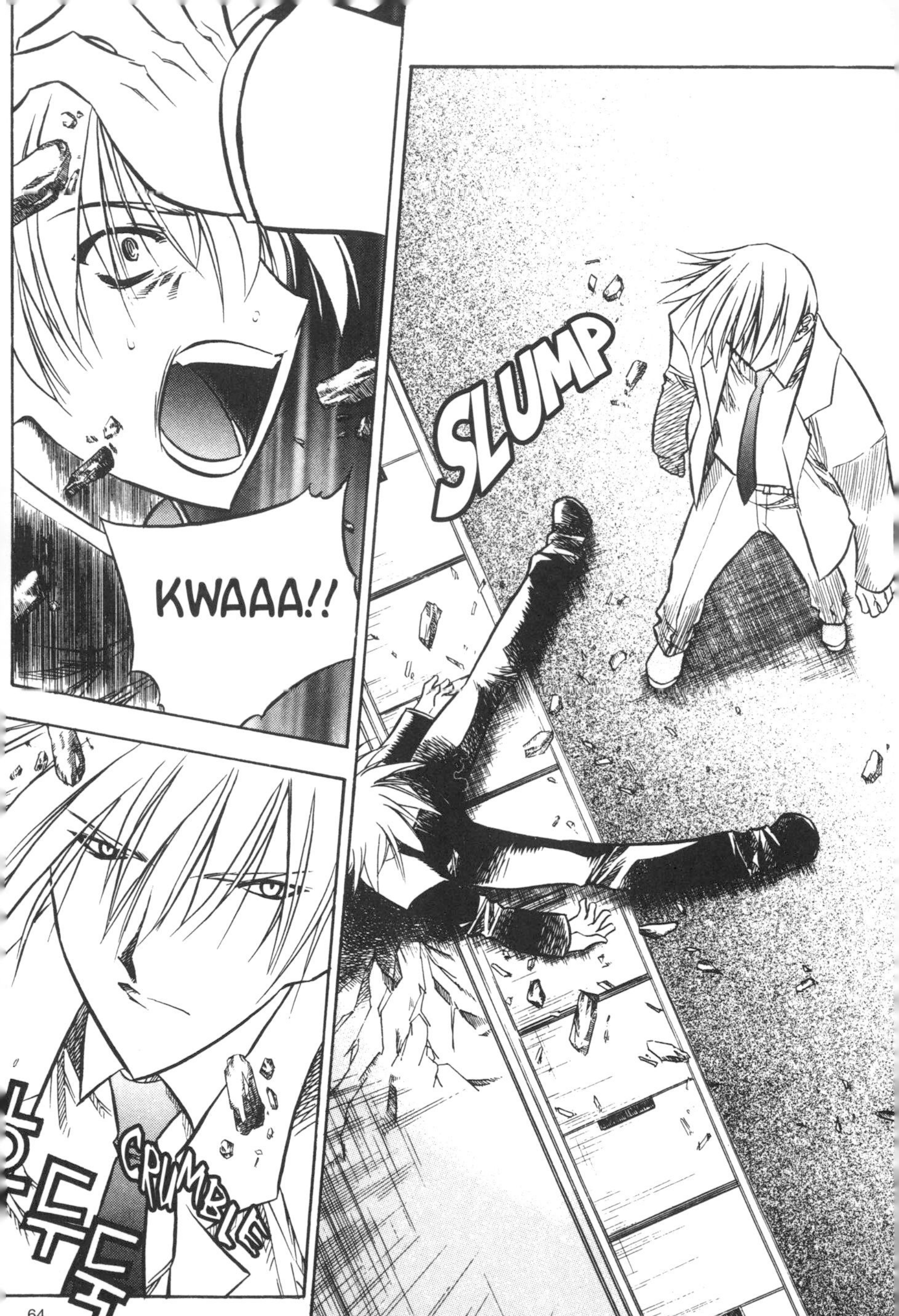
KWAAA!!
CRUMBLE
SLUMP

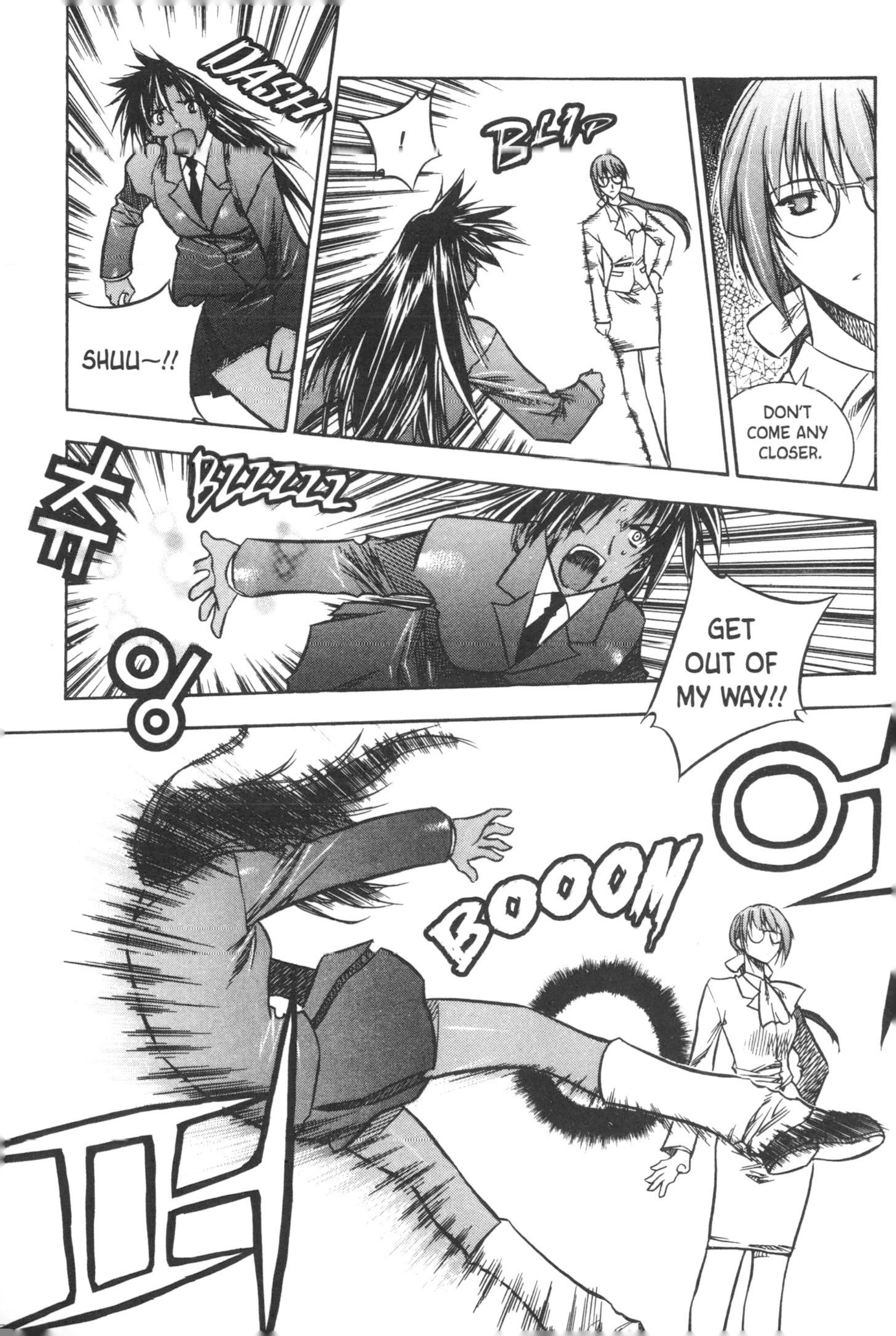
DASH
SHUU~!!
!
BLIP
DON'T COME ANY CLOSER.
GET OUT OF MY WAY!!
BOOOM

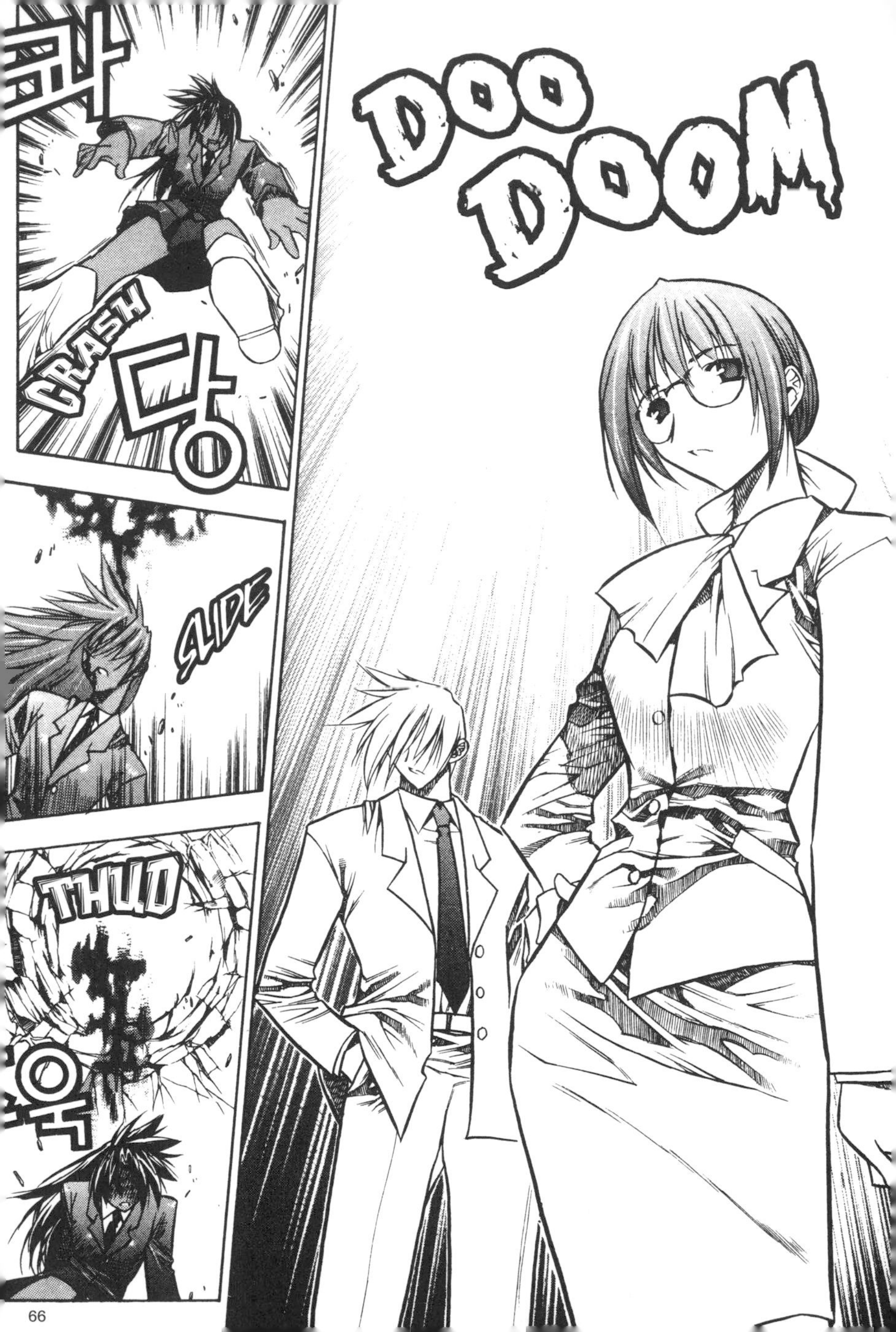
DOO
DOOM
CRASH
당
SLIDE
THUD

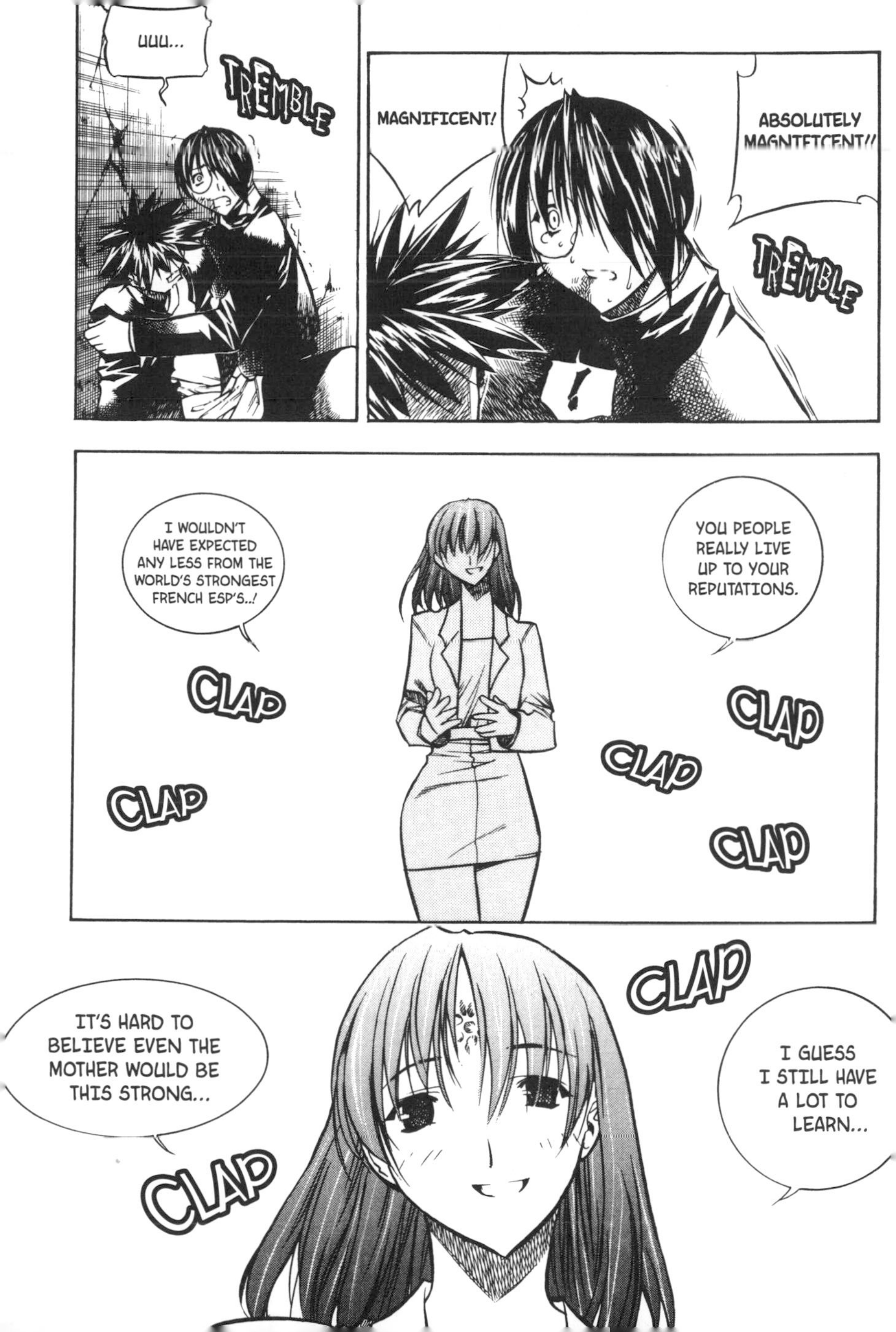

uuu...
TREMBLE
MAGNIFICENT!
ABSOLUTELY MAGNIFICENT!!
TREMBLE
I WOULDN'T HAVE EXPECTED ANY LESS FROM THE WORLD'S STRONGEST FRENCH ESP'S..!
YOU PEOPLE REALLY LIVE UP TO YOUR REPUTATIONS.
CLAP
CLAP
CLAP
CLAP
CLAP
IT'S HARD TO BELIEVE EVEN THE MOTHER WOULD BE THIS STRONG...
CLAP
I GUESS I STILL HAVE A LOT TO LEARN...
CLAP

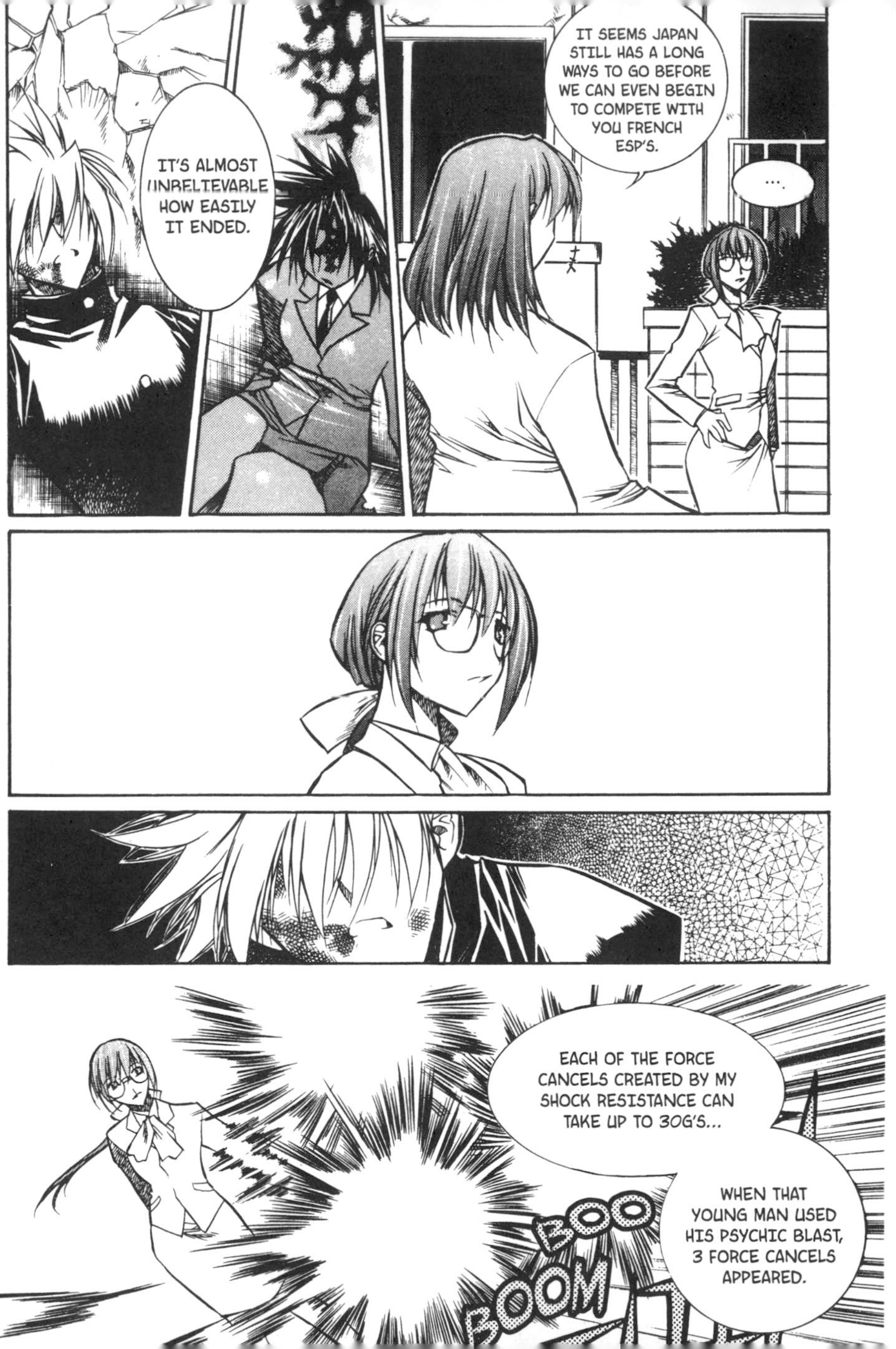
IT'S ALMOST UNBELIEVABLE HOW EASILY IT ENDED.
IT SEEMS JAPAN STILL HAS A LONG WAYS TO GO BEFORE WE CAN EVEN BEGIN TO COMPETE WITH YOU FRENCH ESP'S.
...
EACH OF THE FORCE CANCELS CREATED BY MY SHOCK RESISTANCE CAN TAKE UP TO 30G'S...
BOO
BOOM
WHEN THAT YOUNG MAN USED HIS PSYCHIC BLAST, 3 FORCE CANCELS APPEARED.

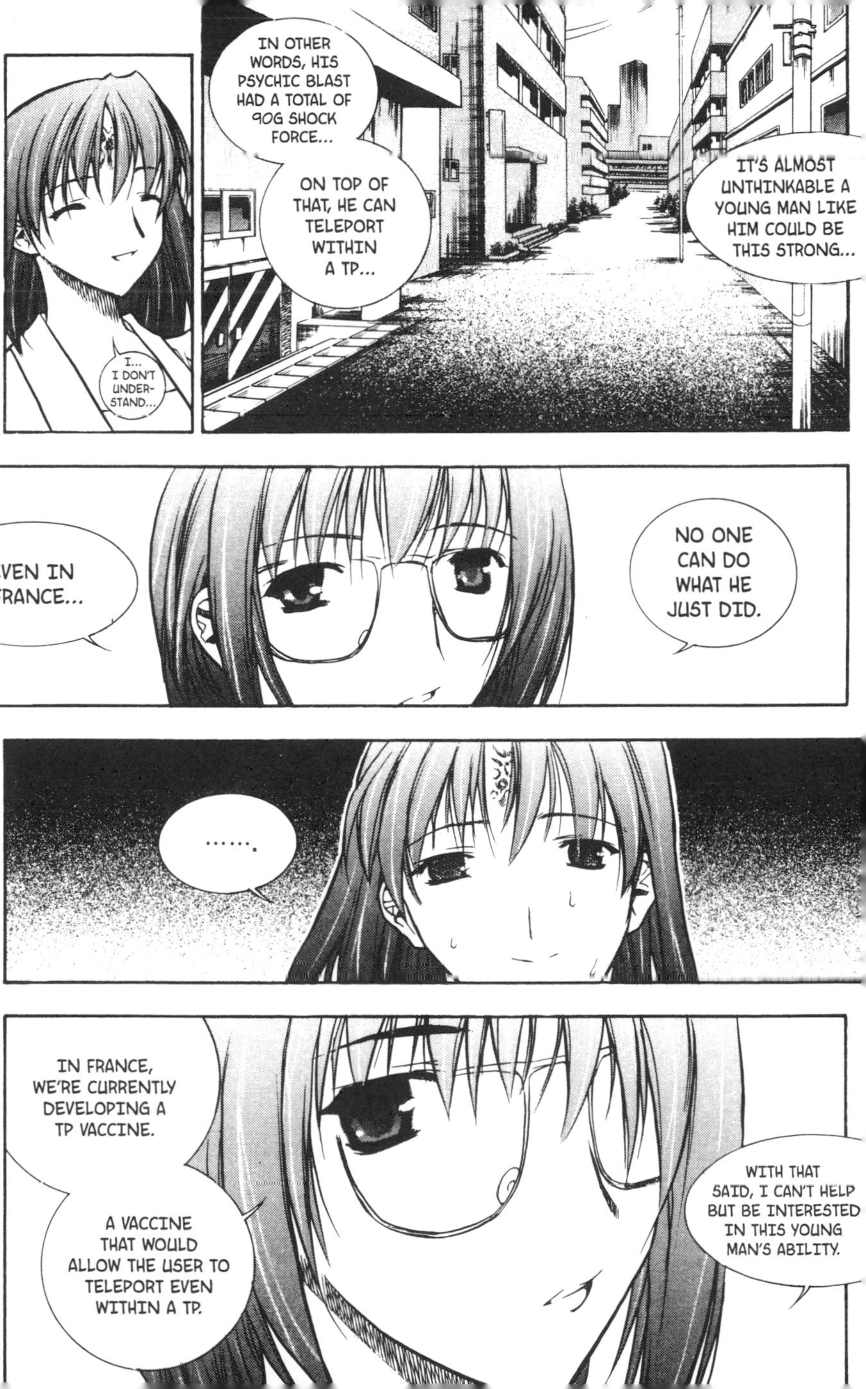

IN OTHER WORDS, HIS PSYCHIC BLAST HAD A TOTAL OF 90G SHOCK FORCE...
ON TOP OF THAT, HE CAN TELEPORT WITHIN A TP...
IT'S ALMOST UNTHINKABLE A YOUNG MAN LIKE HIM COULD BE THIS STRONG...
I... I DON'T UNDER-STAND...
EVEN IN FRANCE...
NO ONE CAN DO WHAT HE JUST DID.
....
IN FRANCE, WE'RE CURRENTLY DEVELOPING A TP VACCINE.
A VACCINE THAT WOULD ALLOW THE USER TO TELEPORT EVEN WITHIN A TP.
WITH THAT SAID, I CAN'T HELP BUT BE INTERESTED IN THIS YOUNG MAN'S ABILITY.

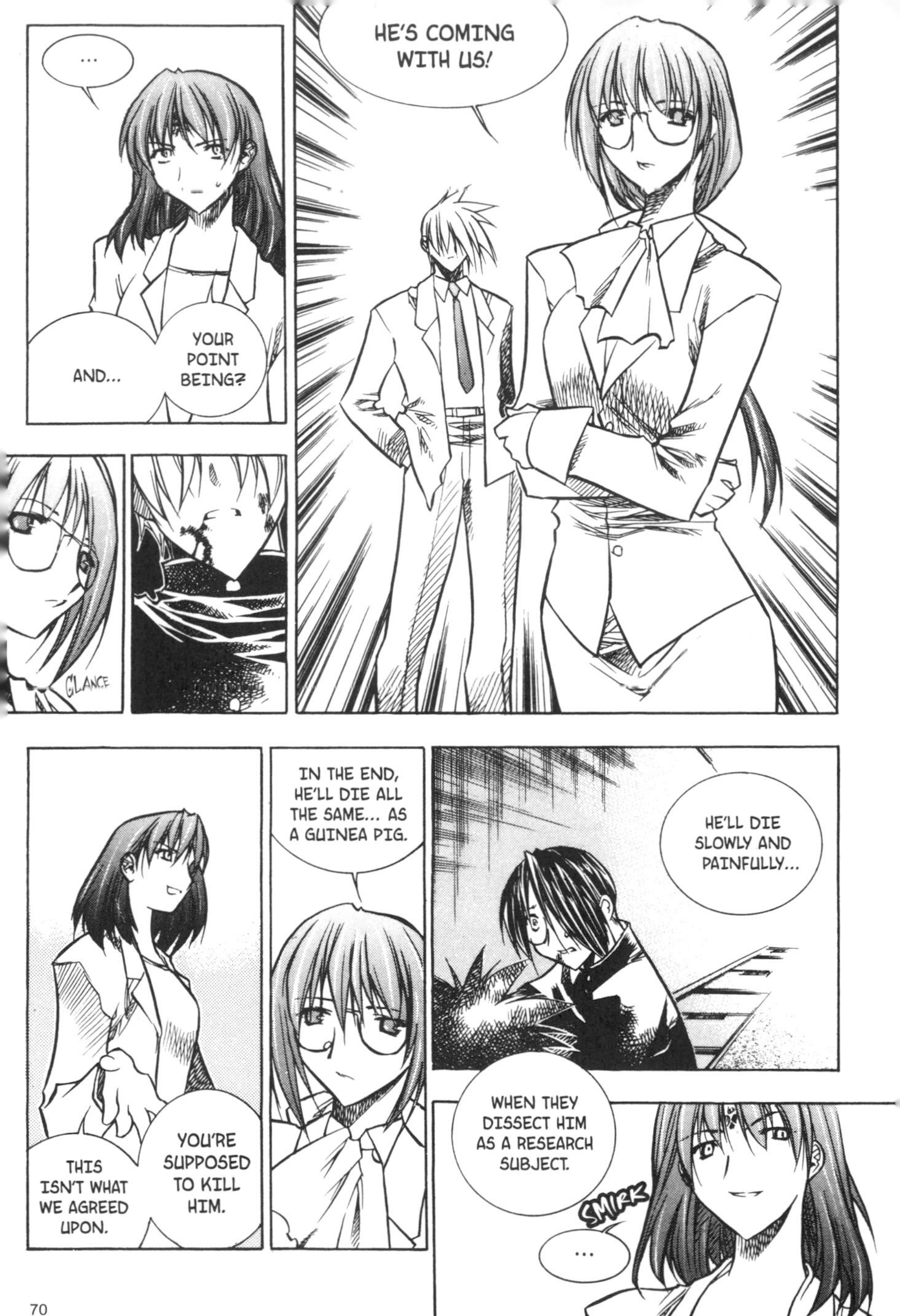
...
AND...
YOUR POINT BEING?
HE'S COMING WITH US!
GLANCE
THIS ISN'T WHAT WE AGREED UPON.
YOU'RE SUPPOSED TO KILL HIM.
IN THE END, HE'LL DIE ALL THE SAME... AS A GUINEA PIG.
HE'LL DIE SLOWLY AND PAINFULLY...
WHEN THEY DISSECT HIM AS A RESEARCH SUBJECT.
SMIRK
...

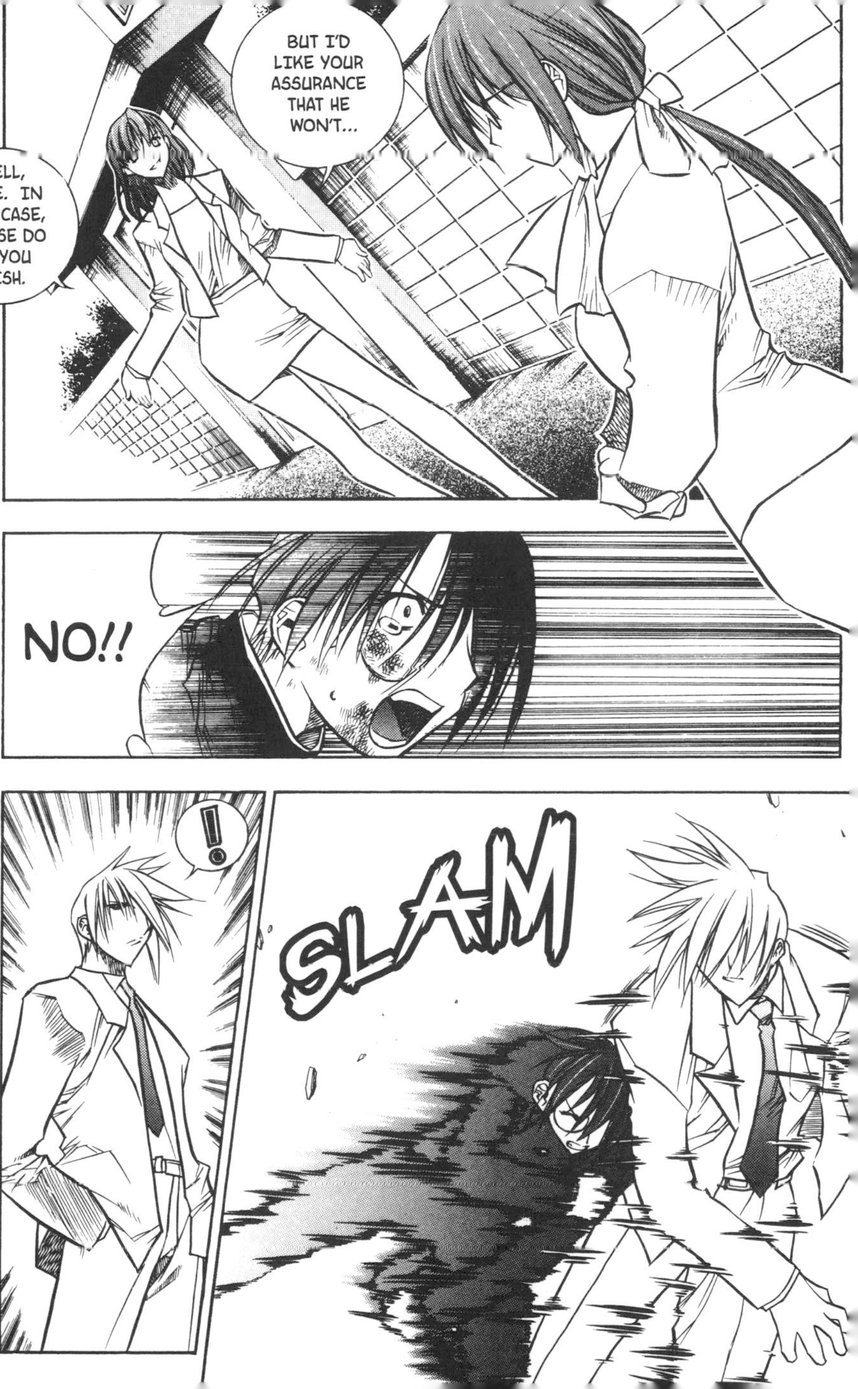
BUT I'D LIKE YOUR ASSURANCE THAT HE WON'T...
WELL, FINE. IN THAT CASE, PLEASE DO AS YOU WISH.
NO!!
!
SLAM

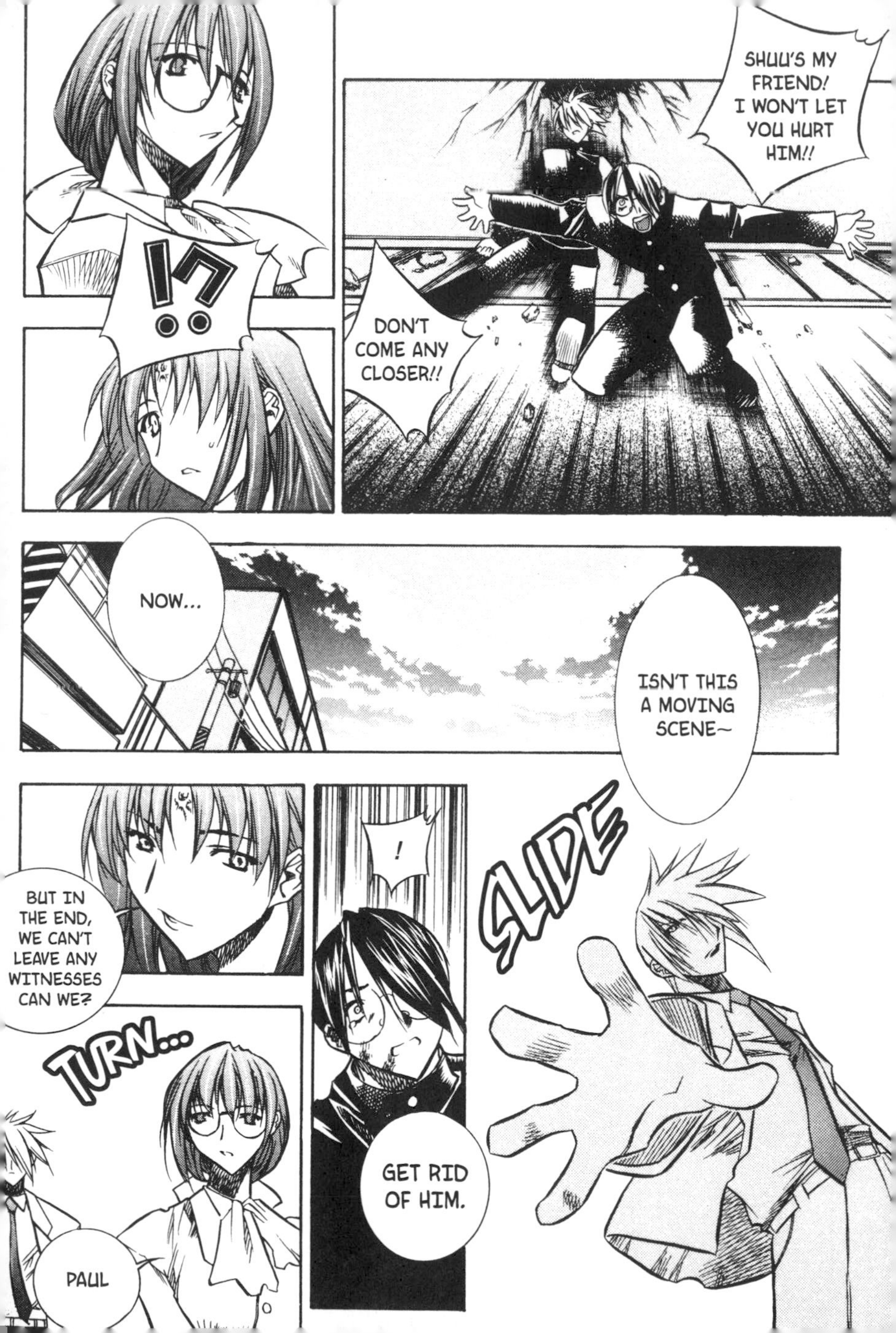
SHUU'S MY FRIEND! I WON'T LET YOU HURT HIM!!
DON'T COME ANY CLOSER!!
!?
NOW...
ISN'T THIS A MOVING SCENE~
SLIDE
!
GET RID OF HIM.
BUT IN THE END, WE CAN'T LEAVE ANY WITNESSES CAN WE?
TURN...
PAUL

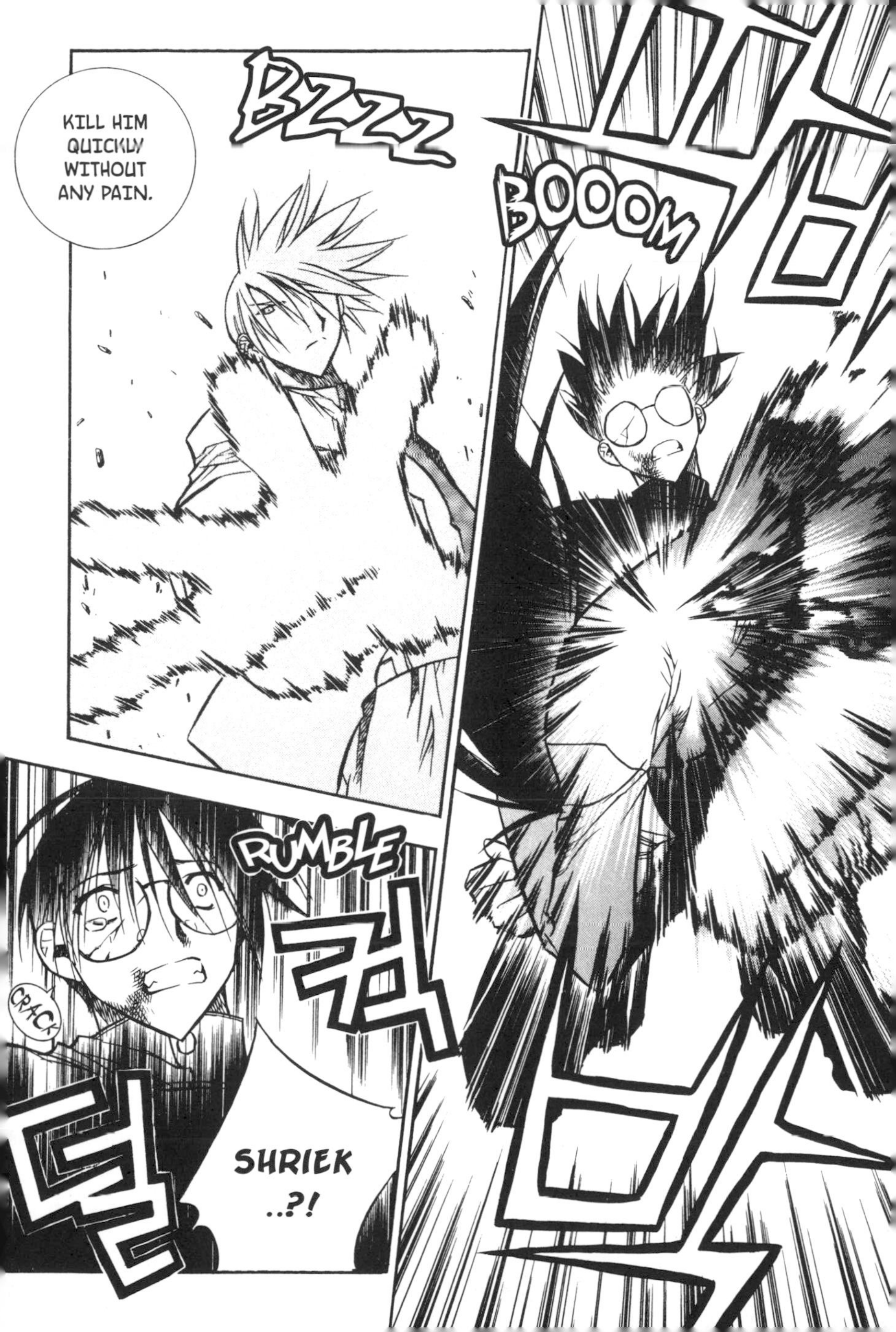
BOOOM
KILL HIM QUICKLY WITHOUT ANY PAIN.
BZZZ
RUMBLE
CRACK
SHRIEK ..?!

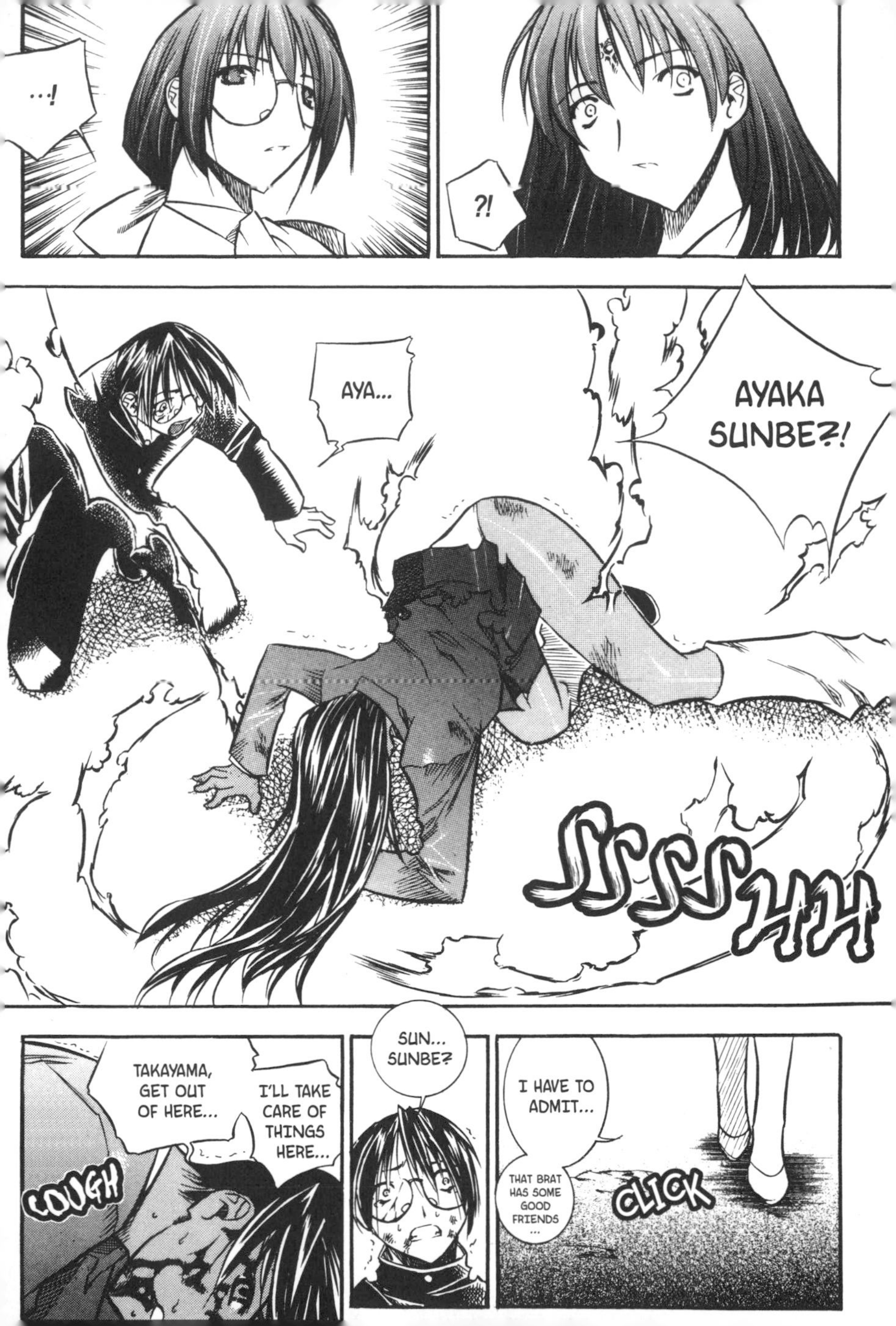
?!
...!
AYAKA SUNBE?!
AYA...
I HAVE TO ADMIT...
THAT BRAT HAS SOME GOOD FRIENDS ...
CLICK
SUN... SUNBE?
TAKAYAMA, GET OUT OF HERE...
I'LL TAKE CARE OF THINGS HERE...
COUGH

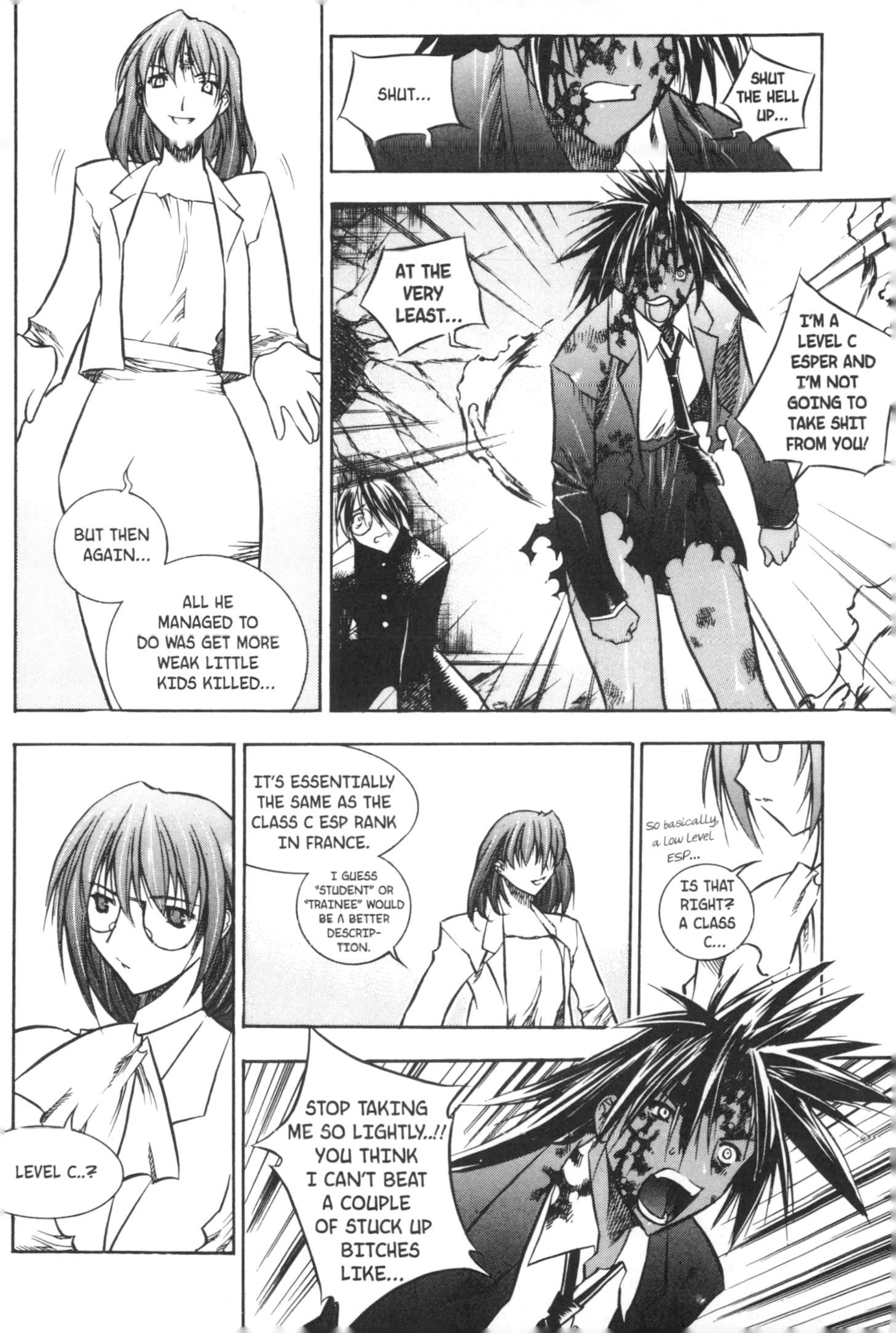
BUT THEN AGAIN...
ALL HE MANAGED TO DO WAS GET MORE WEAK LITTLE KIDS KILLED...
SHUT...
SHUT THE HELL UP...
AT THE VERY LEAST...
I'M A LEVEL C ESPER AND I'M NOT GOING TO TAKE SHIT FROM YOU!
LEVEL C..?
IT'S ESSENTIALLY THE SAME AS THE CLASS C ESP RANK IN FRANCE.
I GUESS "STUDENT" OR "TRAINEE" WOULD BE A BETTER DESCRIP-TION.
IS THAT RIGHT? A CLASS C...
So basically, a Low Level ESP...
STOP TAKING ME SO LIGHTLY..!! YOU THINK I CAN'T BEAT A COUPLE OF STUCK UP BITCHES LIKE...

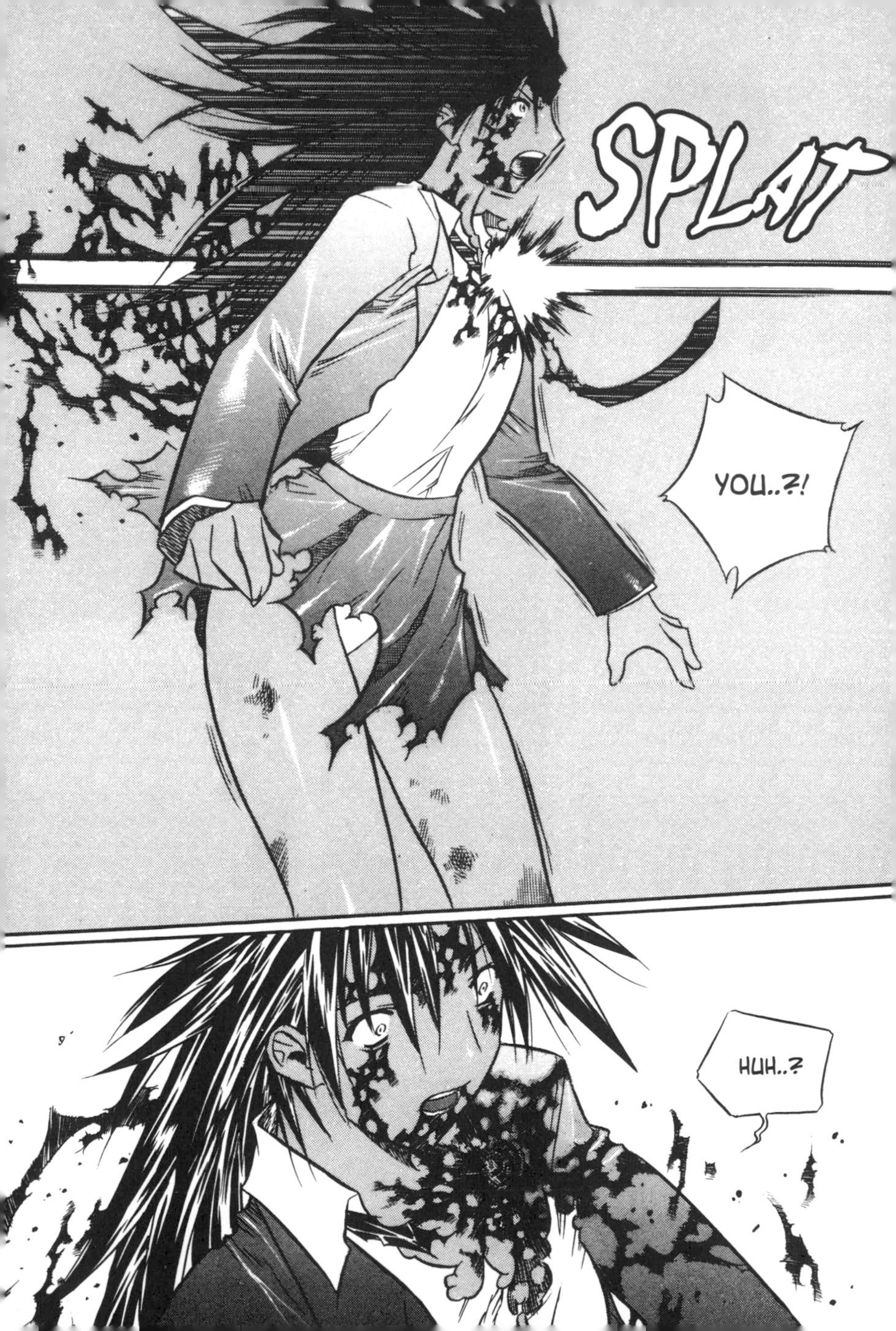
SPLAT
YOU..?!
HUH..?

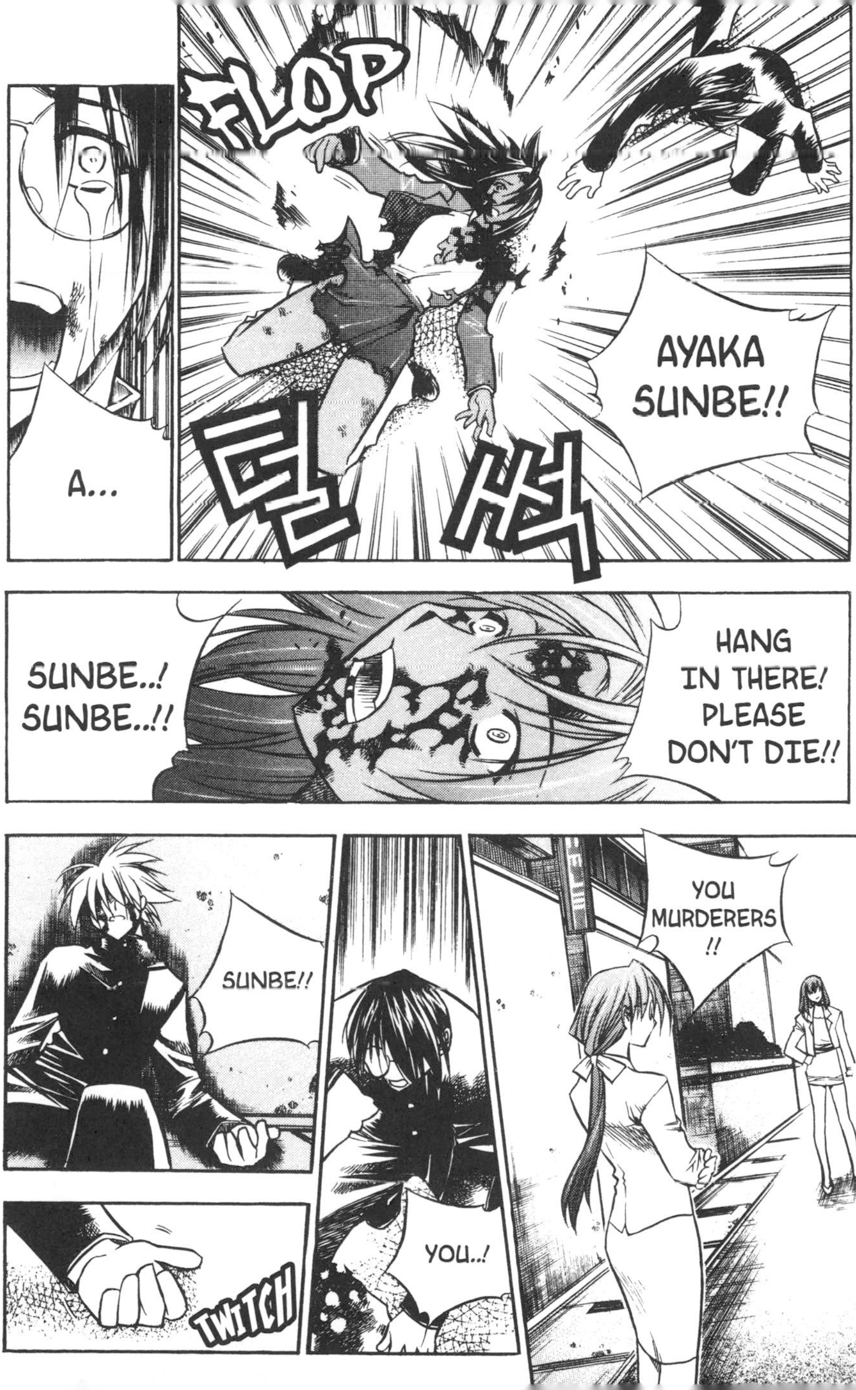
A...
FLOP
AYAKA SUNBE!!
SUNBE..! SUNBE..!!
HANG IN THERE! PLEASE DON'T DIE!!
SUNBE!!
TWITCH
YOU..!
YOU MURDERERS !!

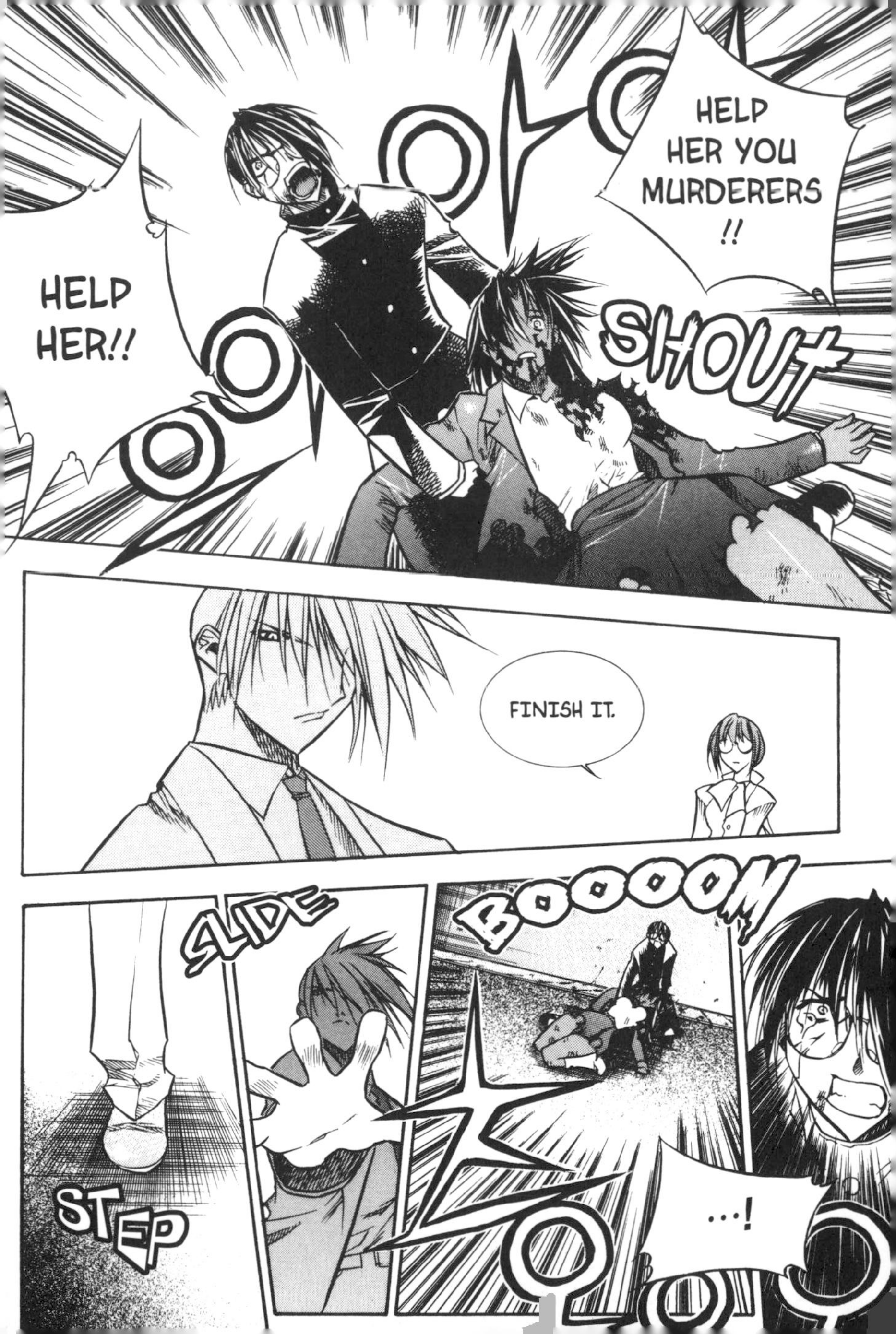
HELP HER YOU MURDERERS !!
SHOUT
HELP HER!!
FINISH IT.
BOOOOOM
...!
SLIDE
STEP

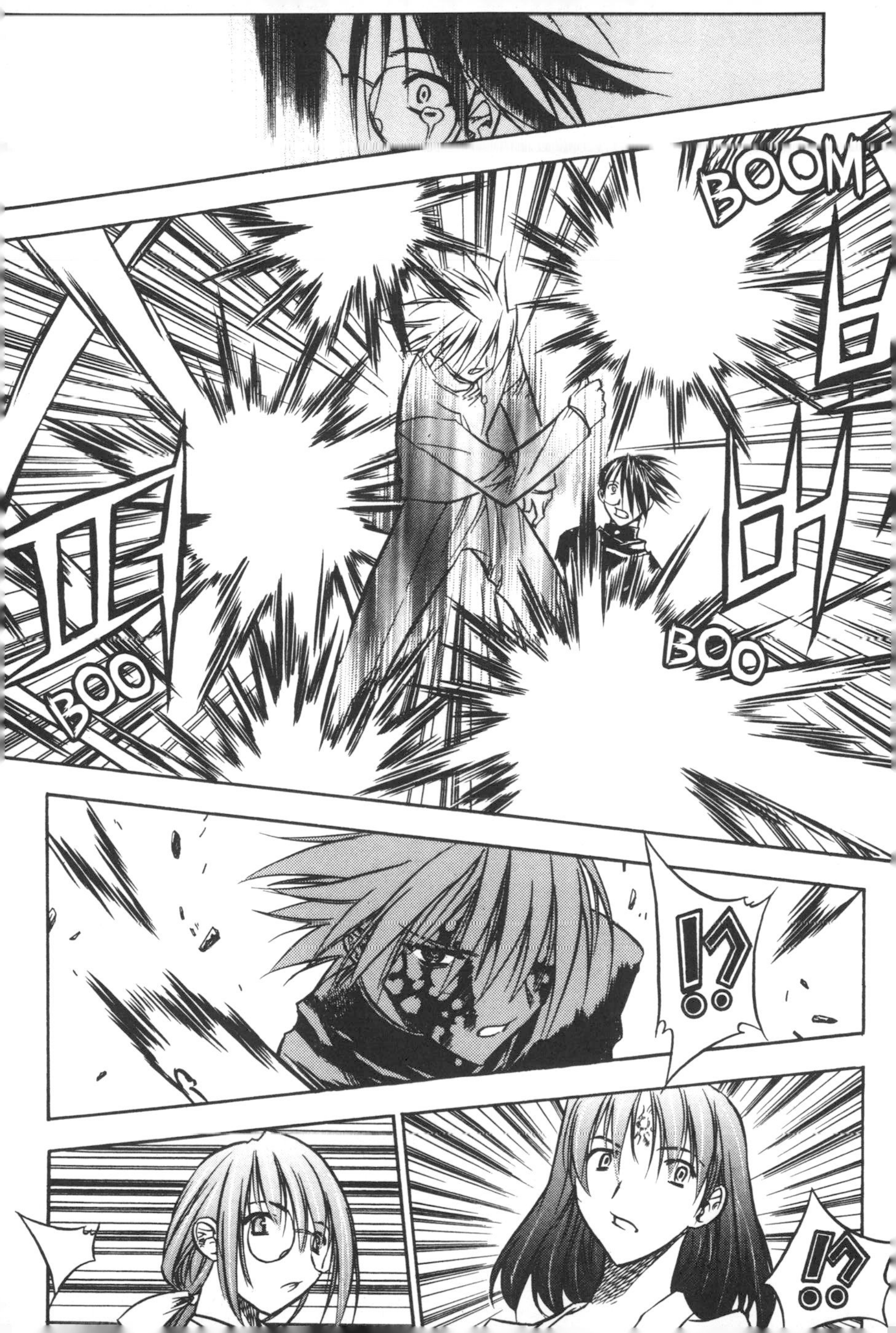
BOOM
BOO
BOO
!?
!?

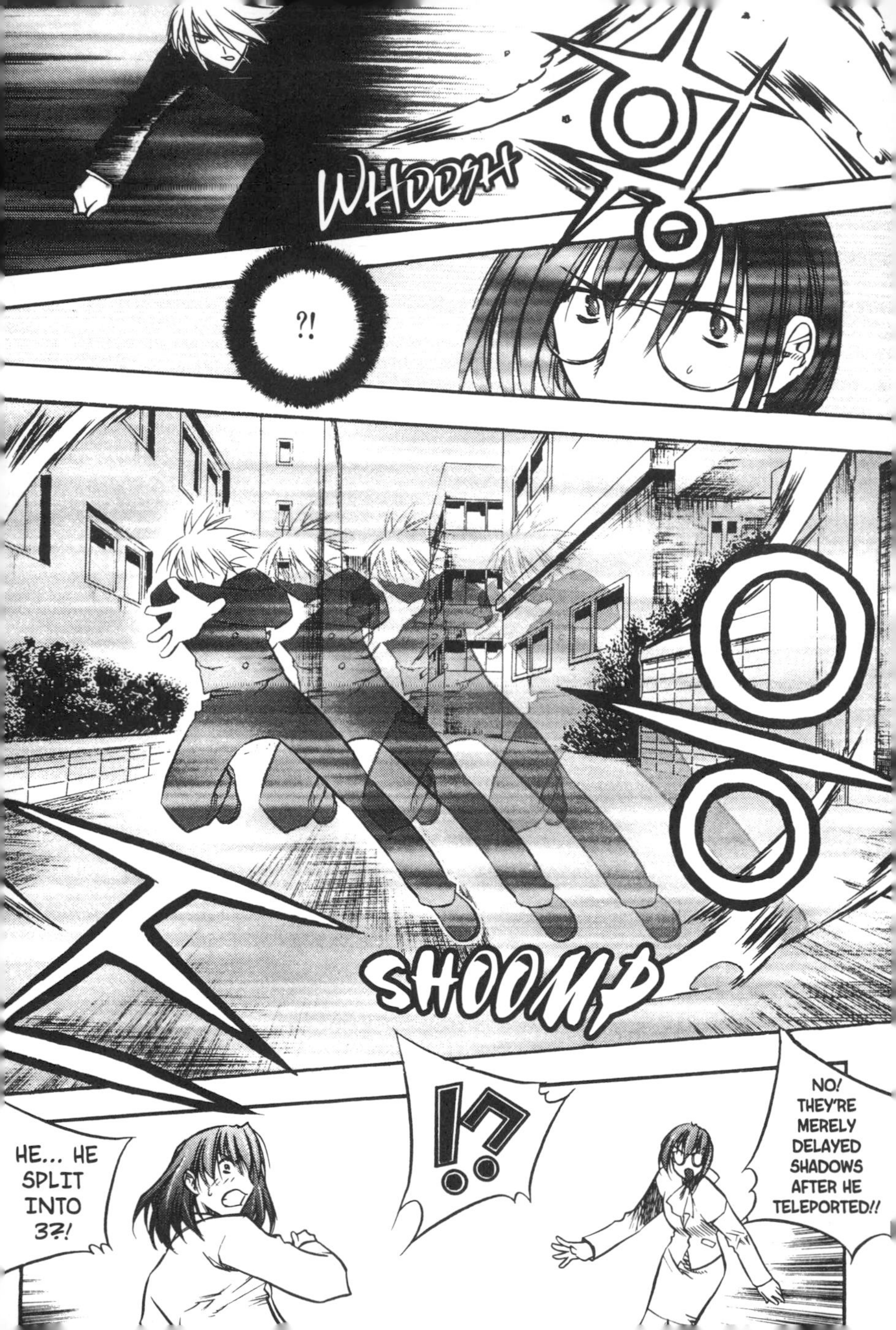
WHOOSH
?!
SHOOMP
NO! THEY'RE MERELY DELAYED SHADOWS AFTER HE TELEPORTED!!
!?
HE... HE SPLIT INTO 3?!

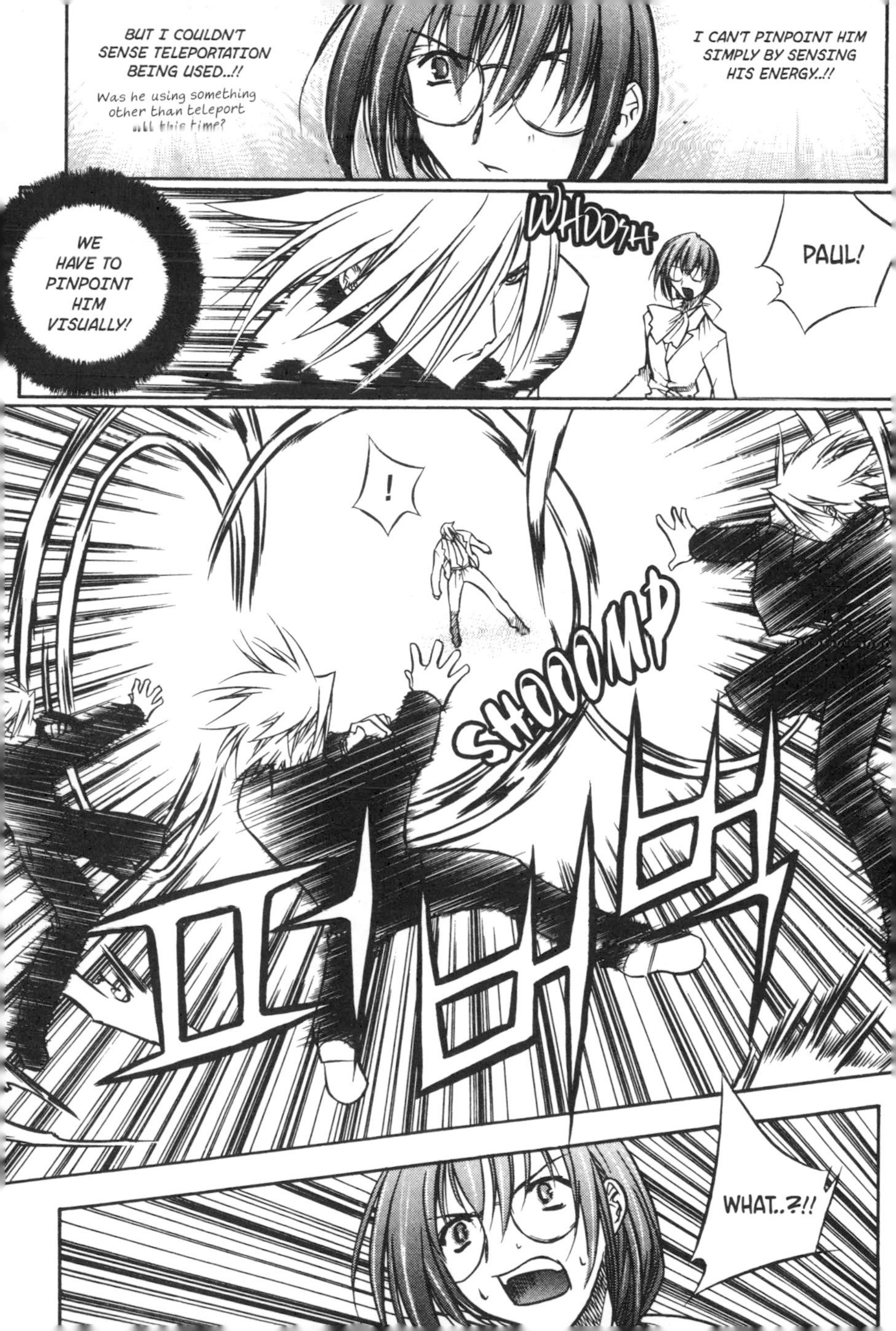
I CAN'T PINPOINT HIM SIMPLY BY SENSING HIS ENERGY..!!
BUT I COULDN'T SENSE TELEPORTATION BEING USED..!!
Was he using something other than teleport all this time?
PAUL!
WHOOSH
WE HAVE TO PINPOINT HIM VISUALLY!
!
SHOOOOMP
WHAT..?!!

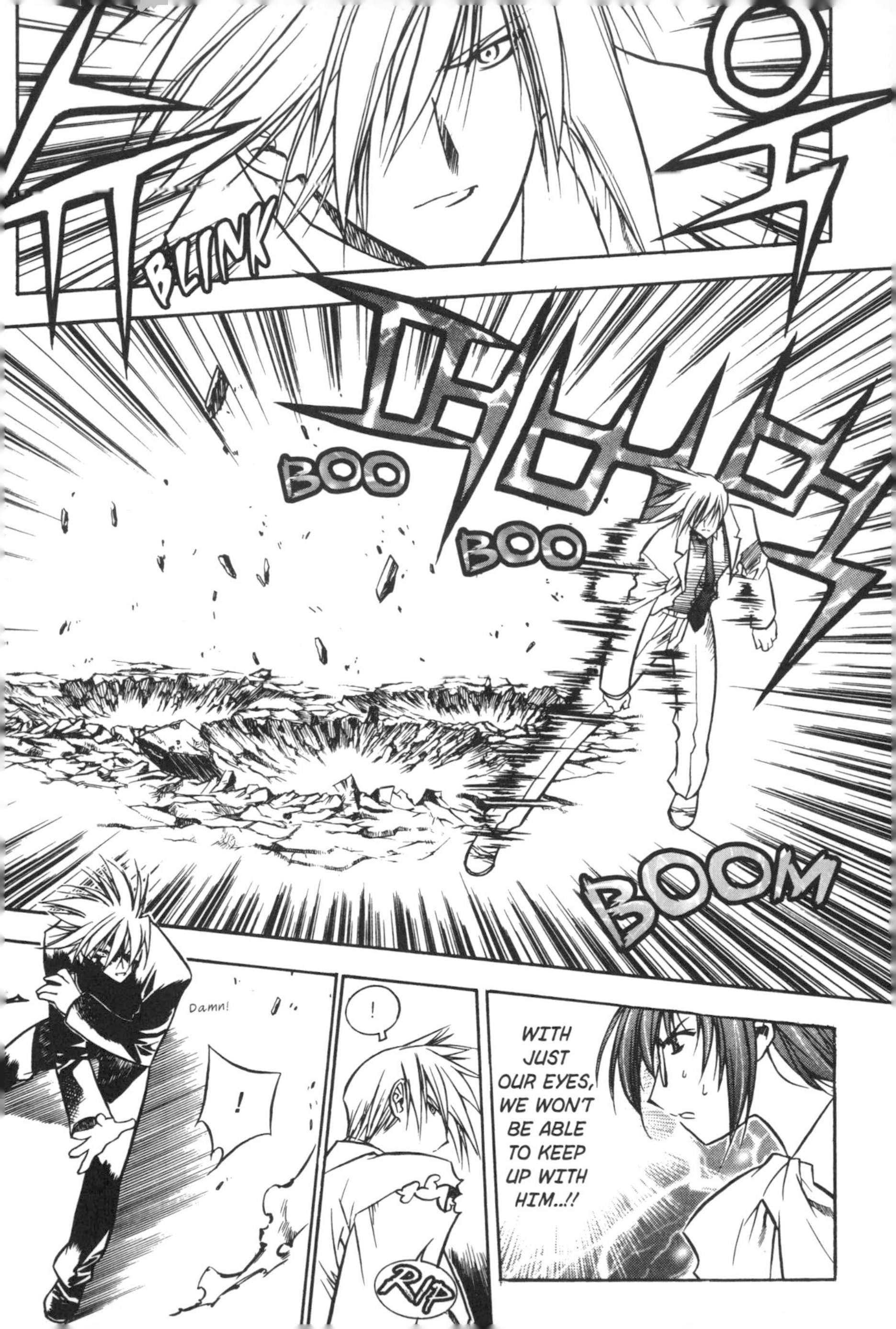
BLINK
BOO
BOO
BOOM
!
Damn!
!
RIP
WITH JUST OUR EYES, WE WON'T BE ABLE TO KEEP UP WITH HIM..!!

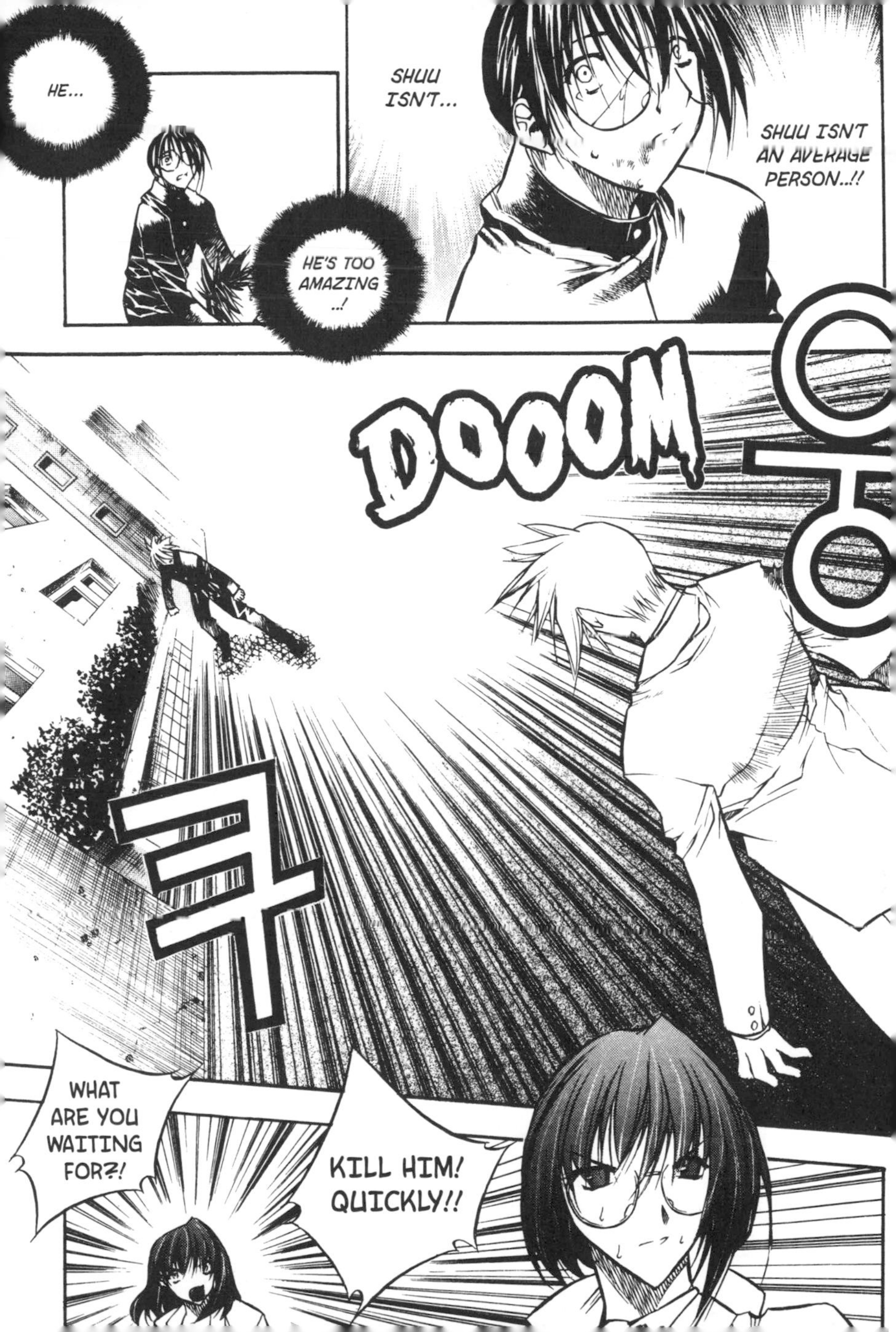
HE...
HE'S TOO AMAZING ..!
SHUU ISN'T...
SHUU ISN'T AN AVERAGE PERSON..!!
DOOOM
WHAT ARE YOU WAITING FOR?!
KILL HIM! QUICKLY!!

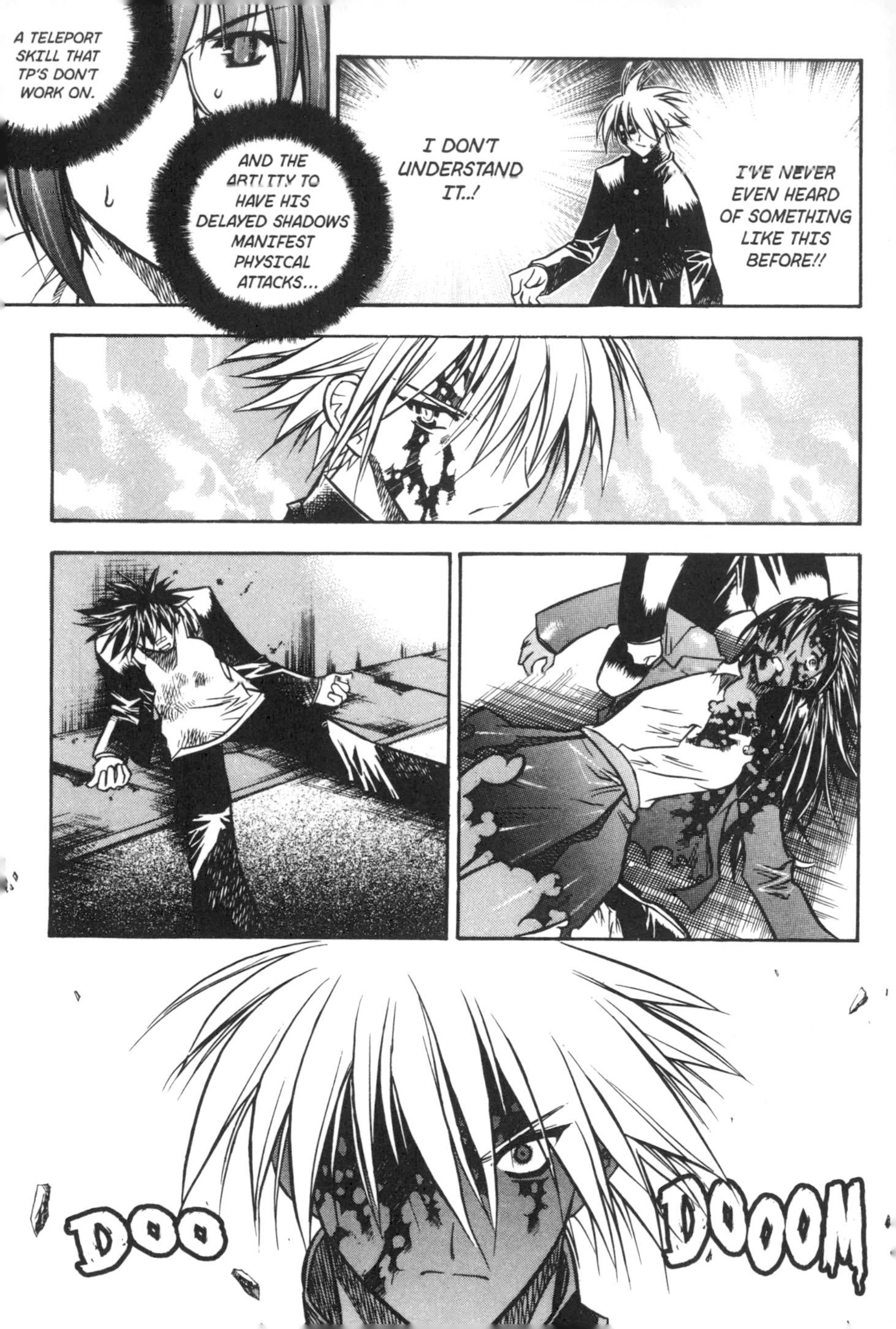
A TELEPORT SKILL THAT TP'S DON'T WORK ON.
AND THE ABILITY TO HAVE HIS DELAYED SHADOWS MANIFEST PHYSICAL ATTACKS...
I DON'T UNDERSTAND IT..!
I'VE NEVER EVEN HEARD OF SOMETHING LIKE THIS BEFORE!!
DOO
DOOOM

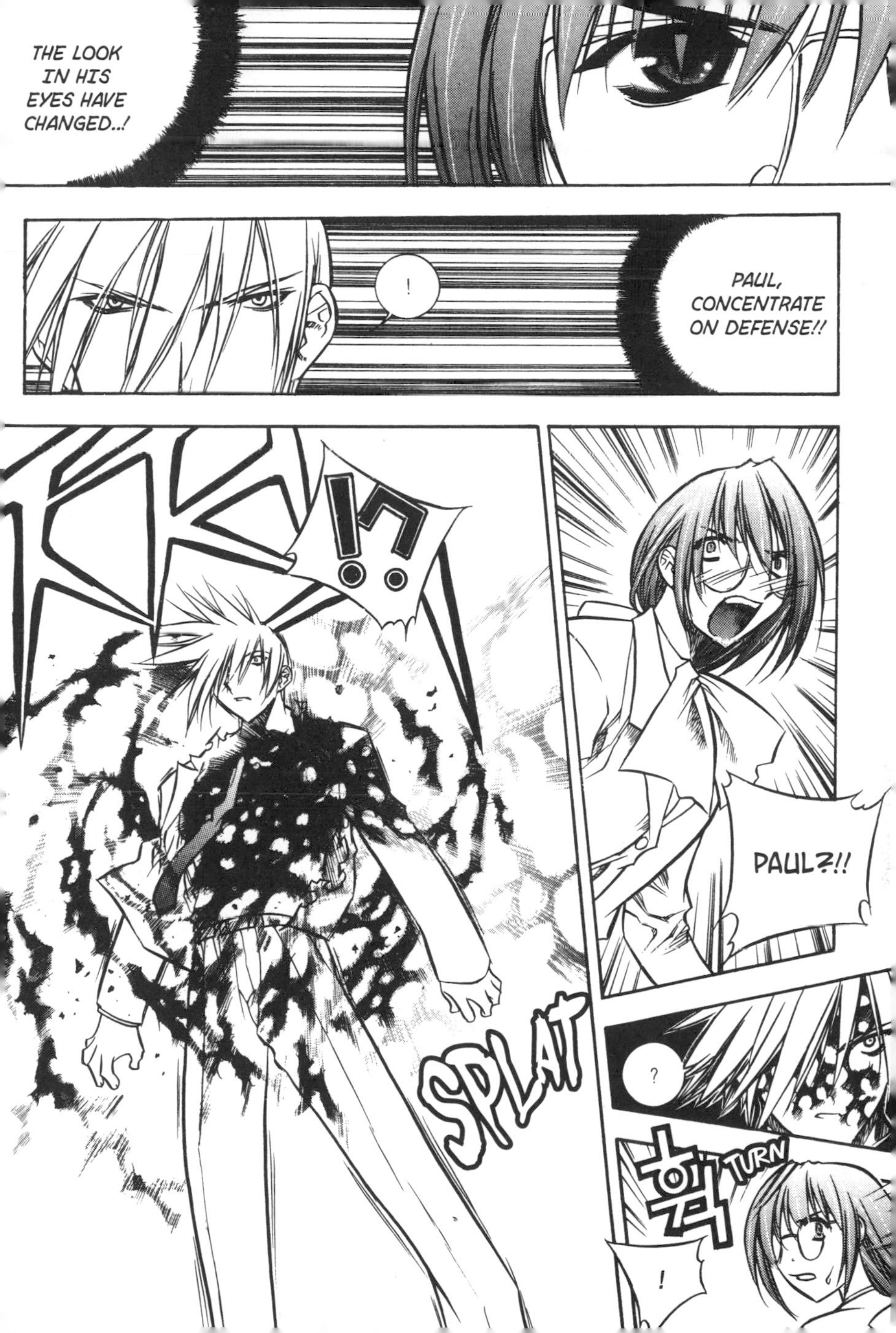
THE LOOK IN HIS EYES HAVE CHANGED..!
PAUL, CONCENTRATE ON DEFENSE!!
!
!?
PAUL?!!
SPLAT
?
TURN
!

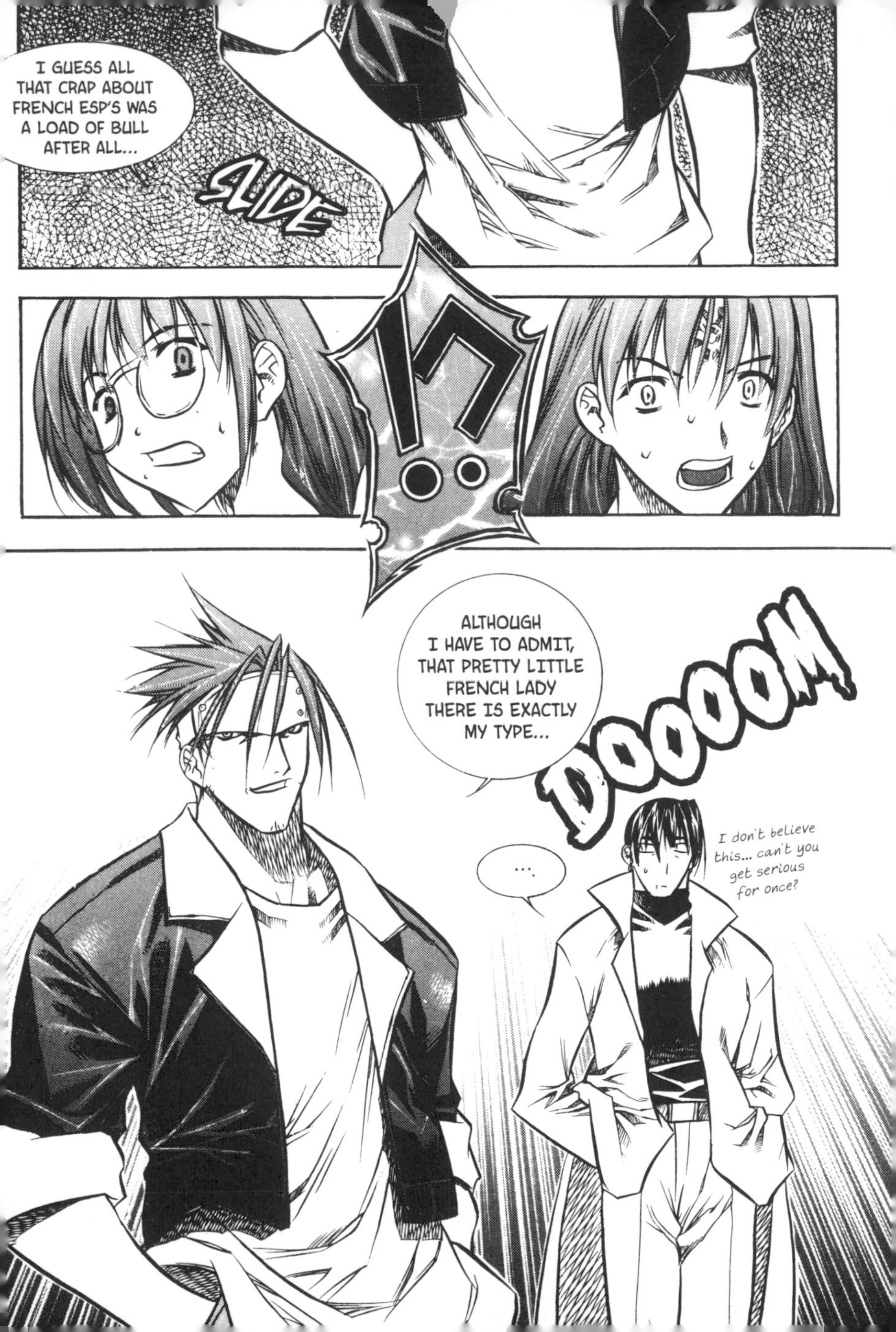
I GUESS ALL THAT CRAP ABOUT FRENCH ESP'S WAS A LOAD OF BULL AFTER ALL...
SLIDE
!?
ALTHOUGH I HAVE TO ADMIT, THAT PRETTY LITTLE FRENCH LADY THERE IS EXACTLY MY TYPE...
DOOOOM
...
I don't believe this... can't you get serious for once?

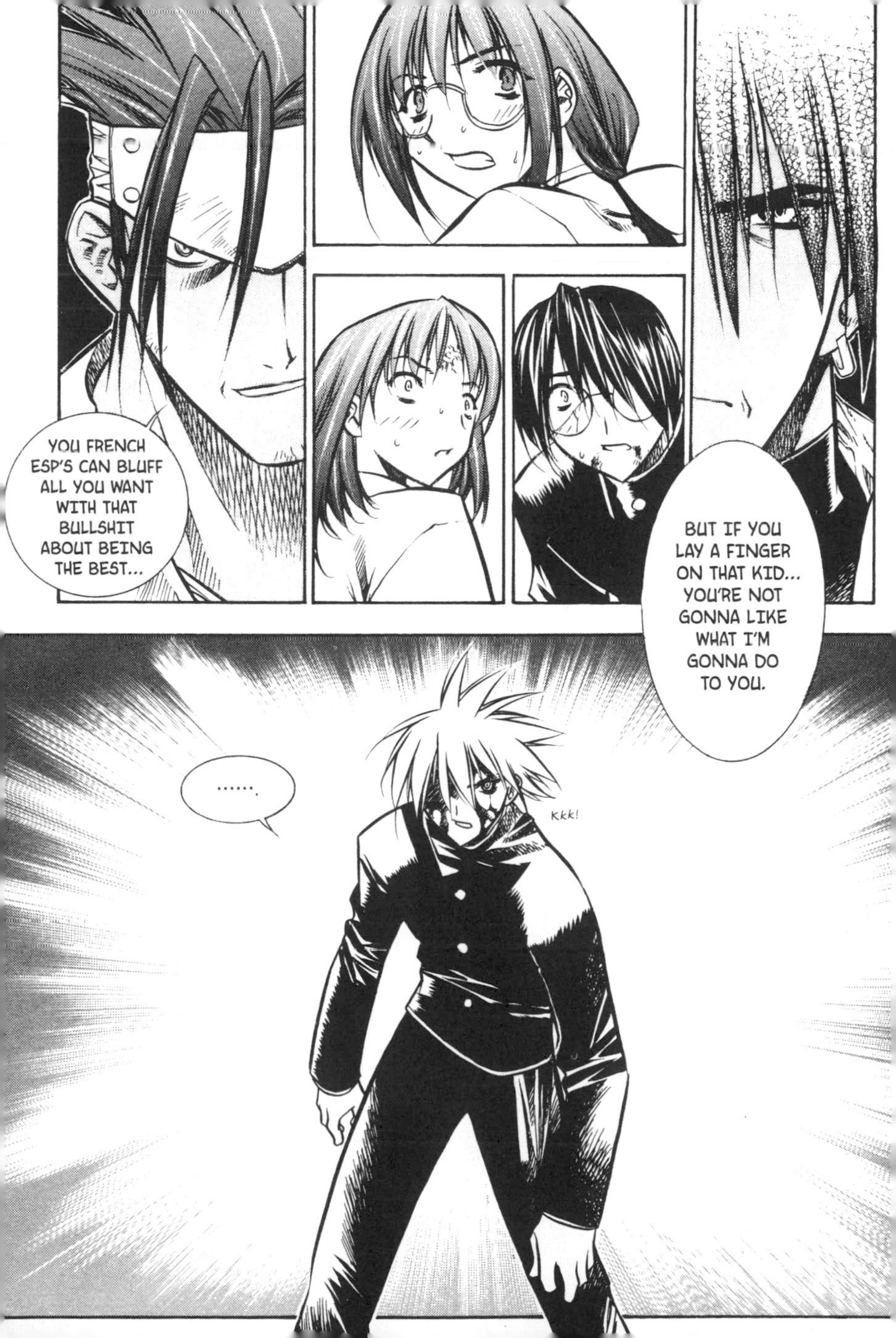
YOU FRENCH ESP'S CAN BLUFF ALL YOU WANT WITH THAT BULLSHIT ABOUT BEING THE BEST...
BUT IF YOU LAY A FINGER ON THAT KID... YOU'RE NOT GONNA LIKE WHAT I'M GONNA DO TO YOU.
......
Kkk!

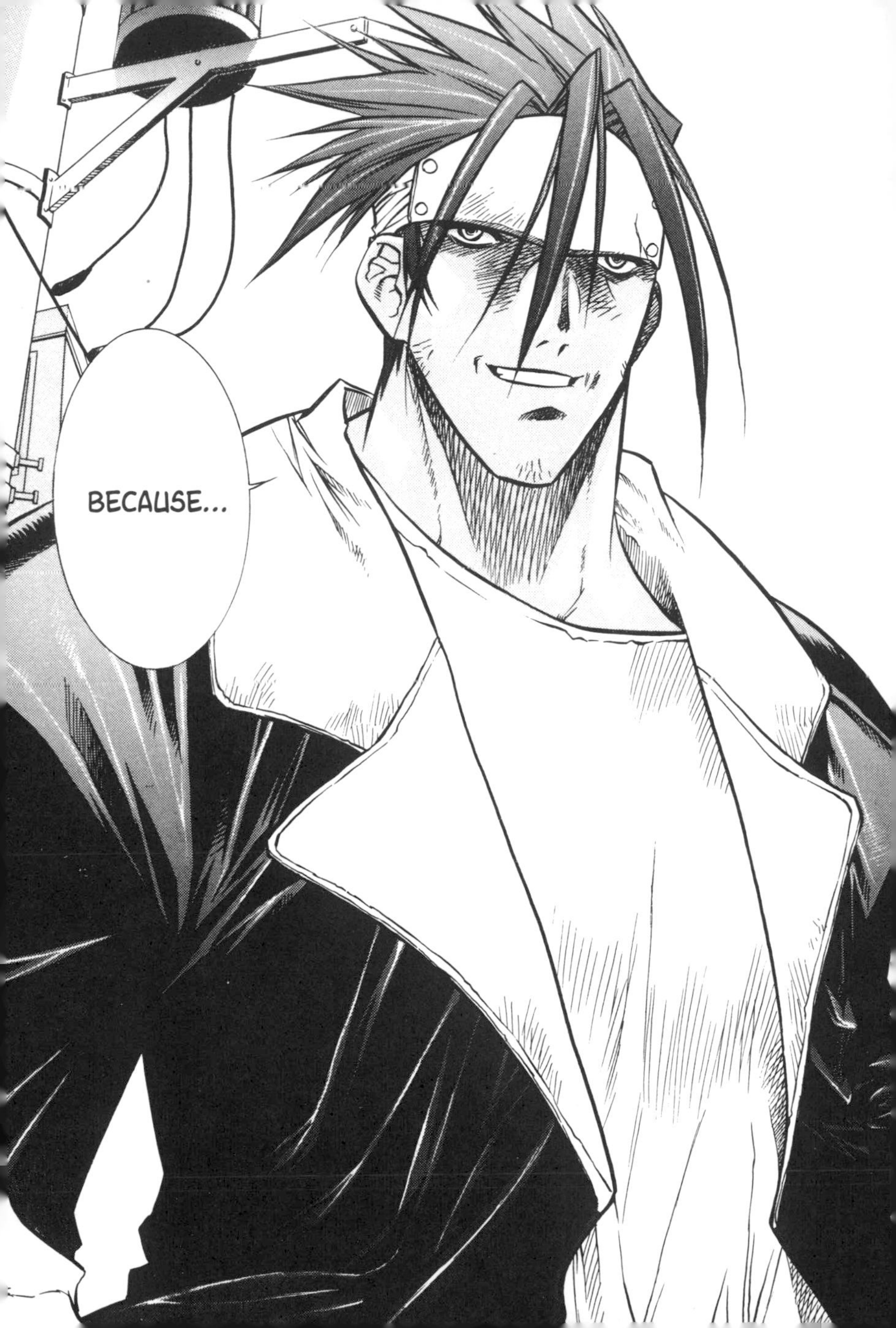
BECAUSE...

CIRCLE 11
Double Impact

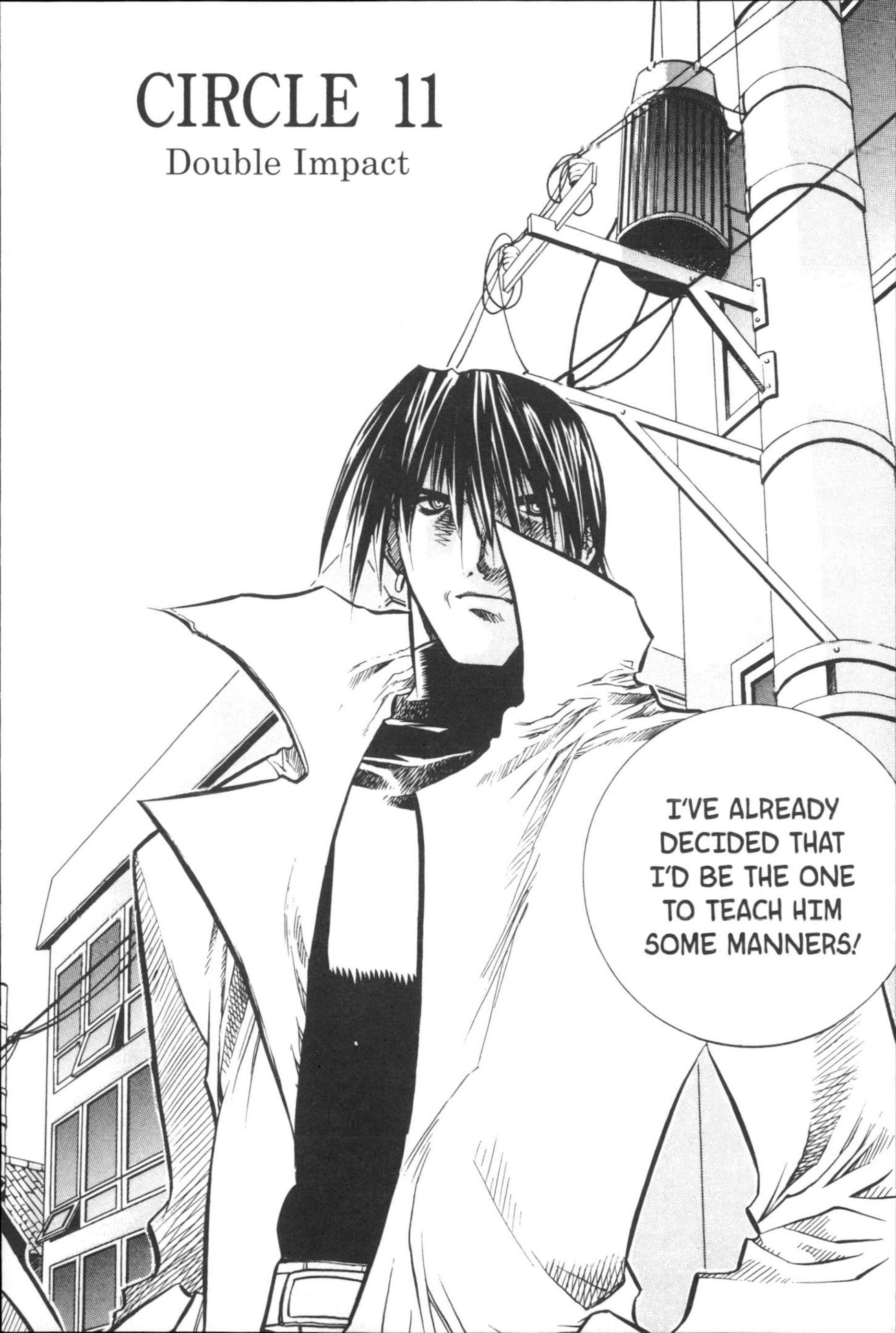
I'VE ALREADY DECIDED THAT I'D BE THE ONE TO TEACH HIM SOME MANNERS!

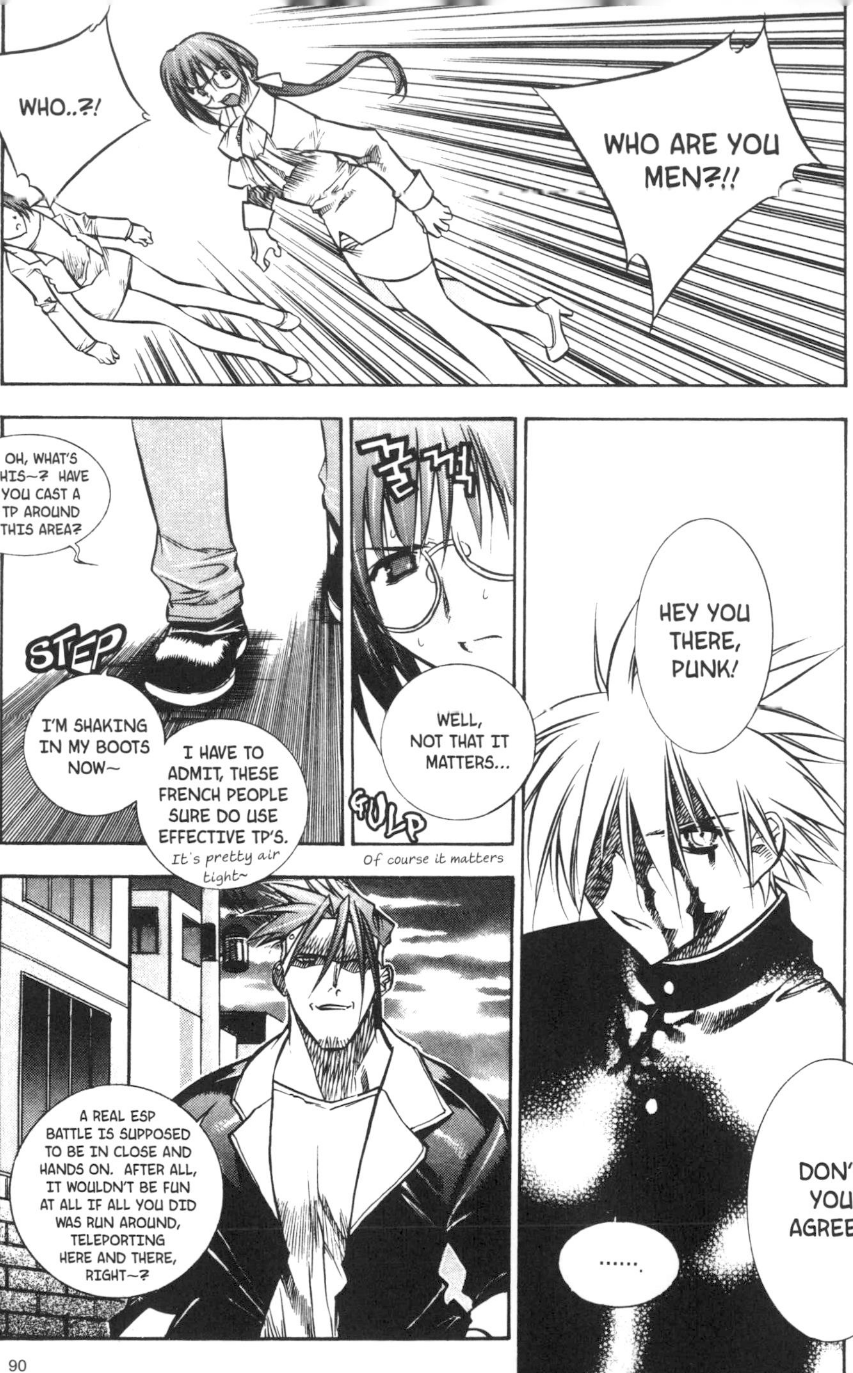

WHO..?!
WHO ARE YOU MEN?!!
OH, WHAT'S THIS~? HAVE YOU CAST A TP AROUND THIS AREA?
STEP
I'M SHAKING IN MY BOOTS NOW~
I HAVE TO ADMIT, THESE FRENCH PEOPLE SURE DO USE EFFECTIVE TP'S.
It's pretty air tight~
꿀꺽
WELL, NOT THAT IT MATTERS...
GULP
Of course it matters
HEY YOU THERE, PUNK!
A REAL ESP BATTLE IS SUPPOSED TO BE IN CLOSE AND HANDS ON. AFTER ALL, IT WOULDN'T BE FUN AT ALL IF ALL YOU DID WAS RUN AROUND, TELEPORTING HERE AND THERE, RIGHT~?
DON'T YOU AGREE?
....

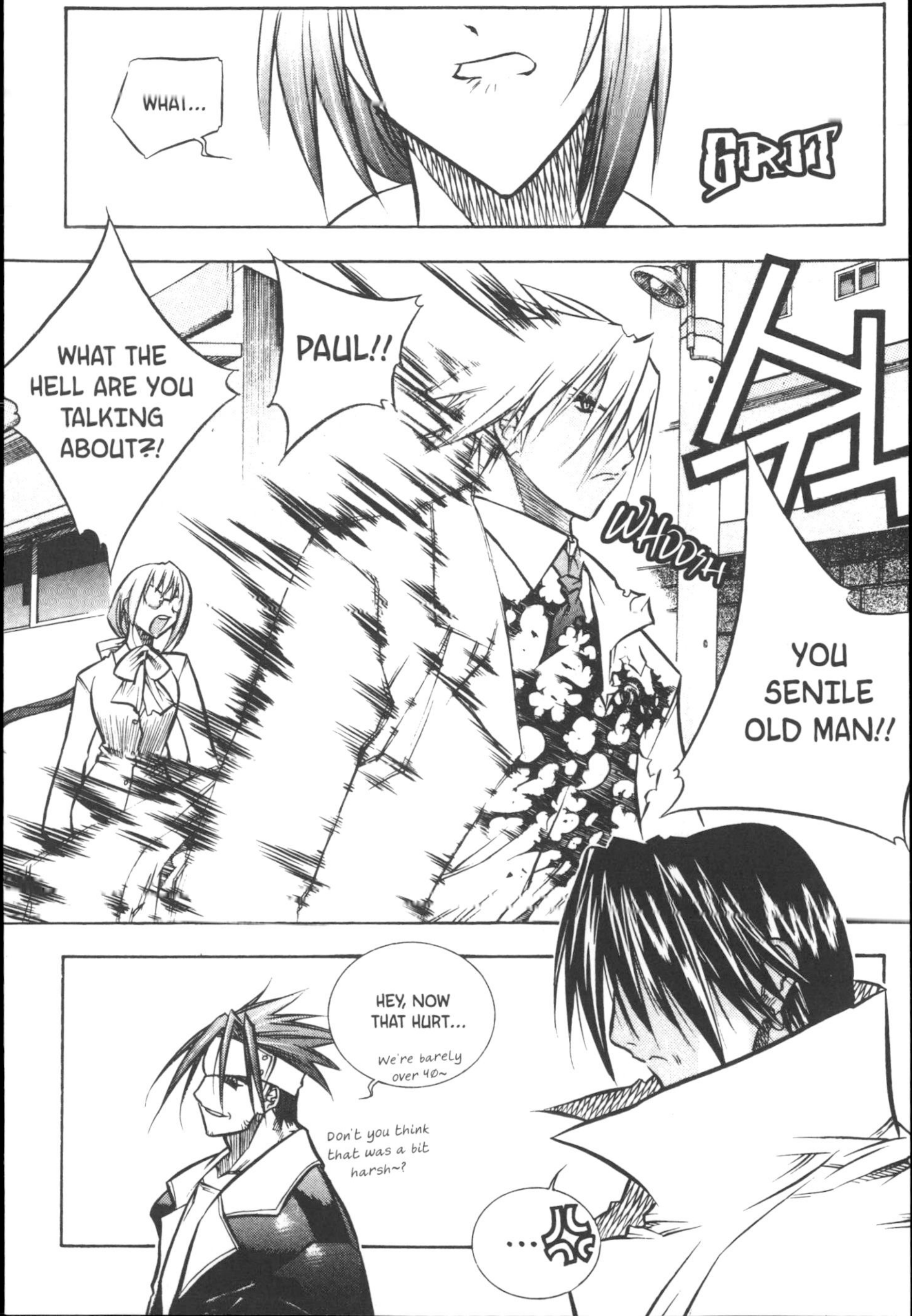
WHAT...
GRIT
PAUL!!
WHAT THE HELL ARE YOU TALKING ABOUT?!
YOU SENILE OLD MAN!!
HEY, NOW THAT HURT...
We're barely over 40~
Don't you think that was a bit harsh~?
...

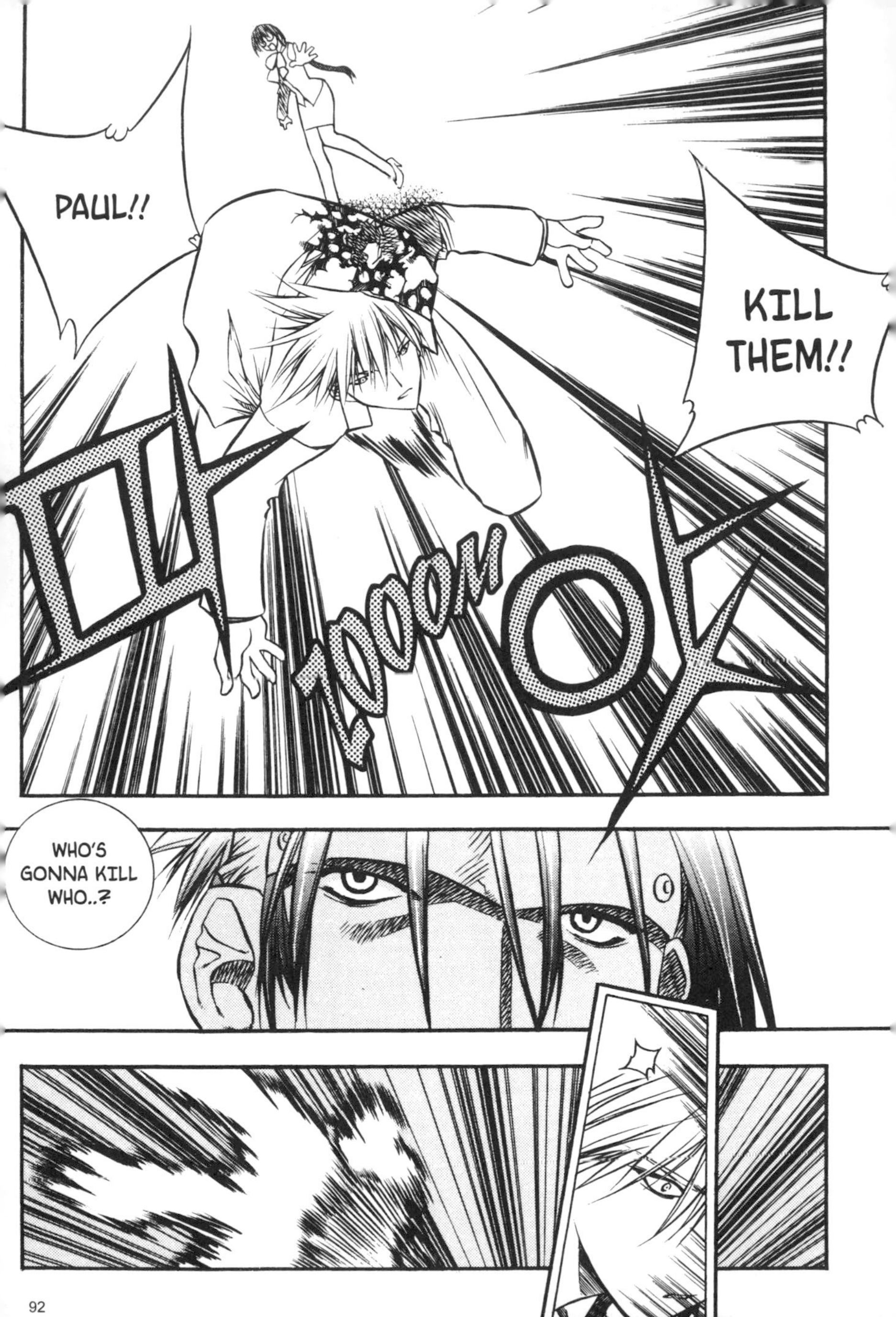
KILL THEM!!
PAUL!!
DOOOOOM
WHO'S GONNA KILL WHO..?

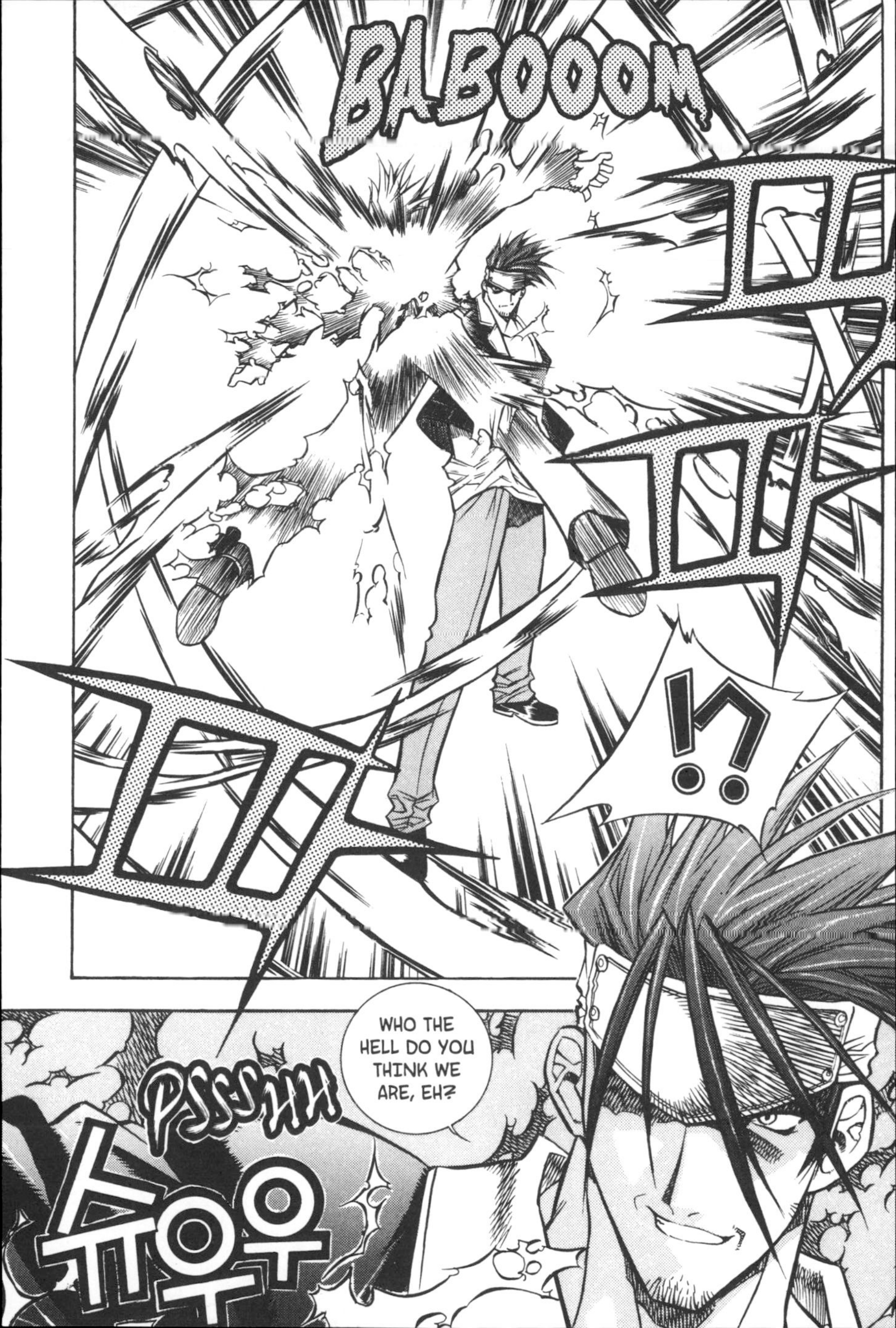
BABOOOM
!?
WHO THE HELL DO YOU THINK WE ARE, EH?
PSSSHH

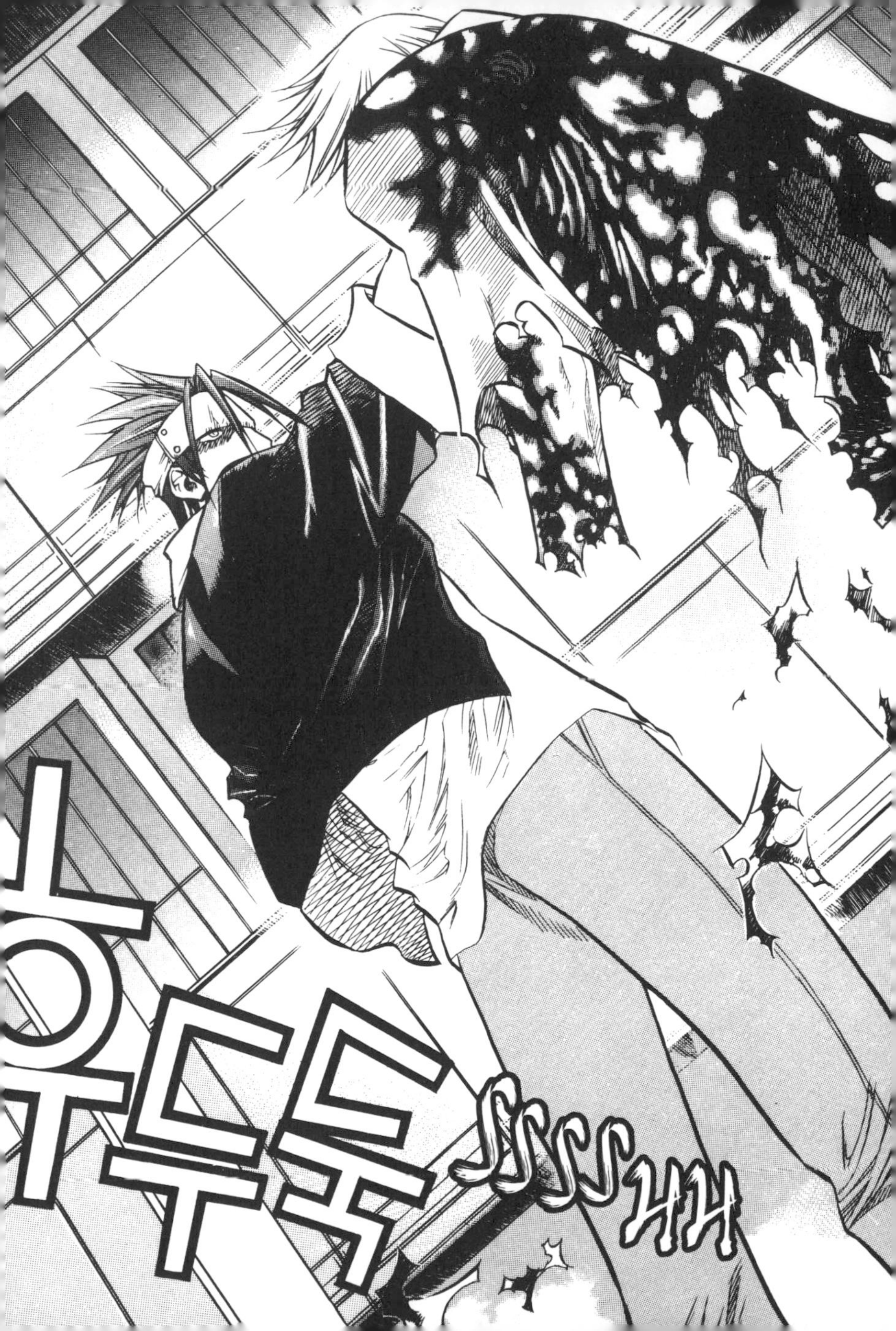
SSSSHH

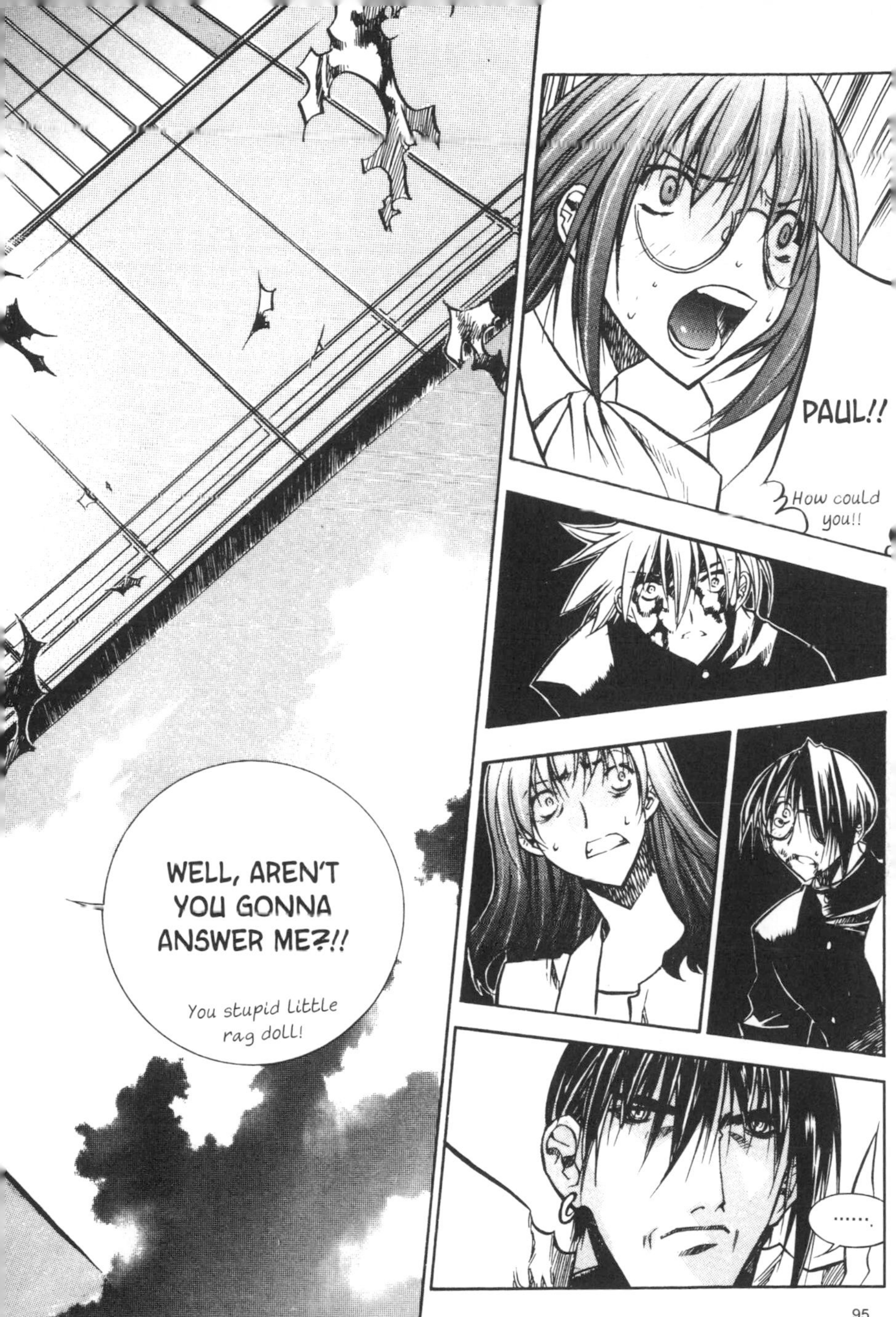
PAUL!!
How could you!!
WELL, AREN'T YOU GONNA ANSWER ME?!!
You stupid little rag doll!
....

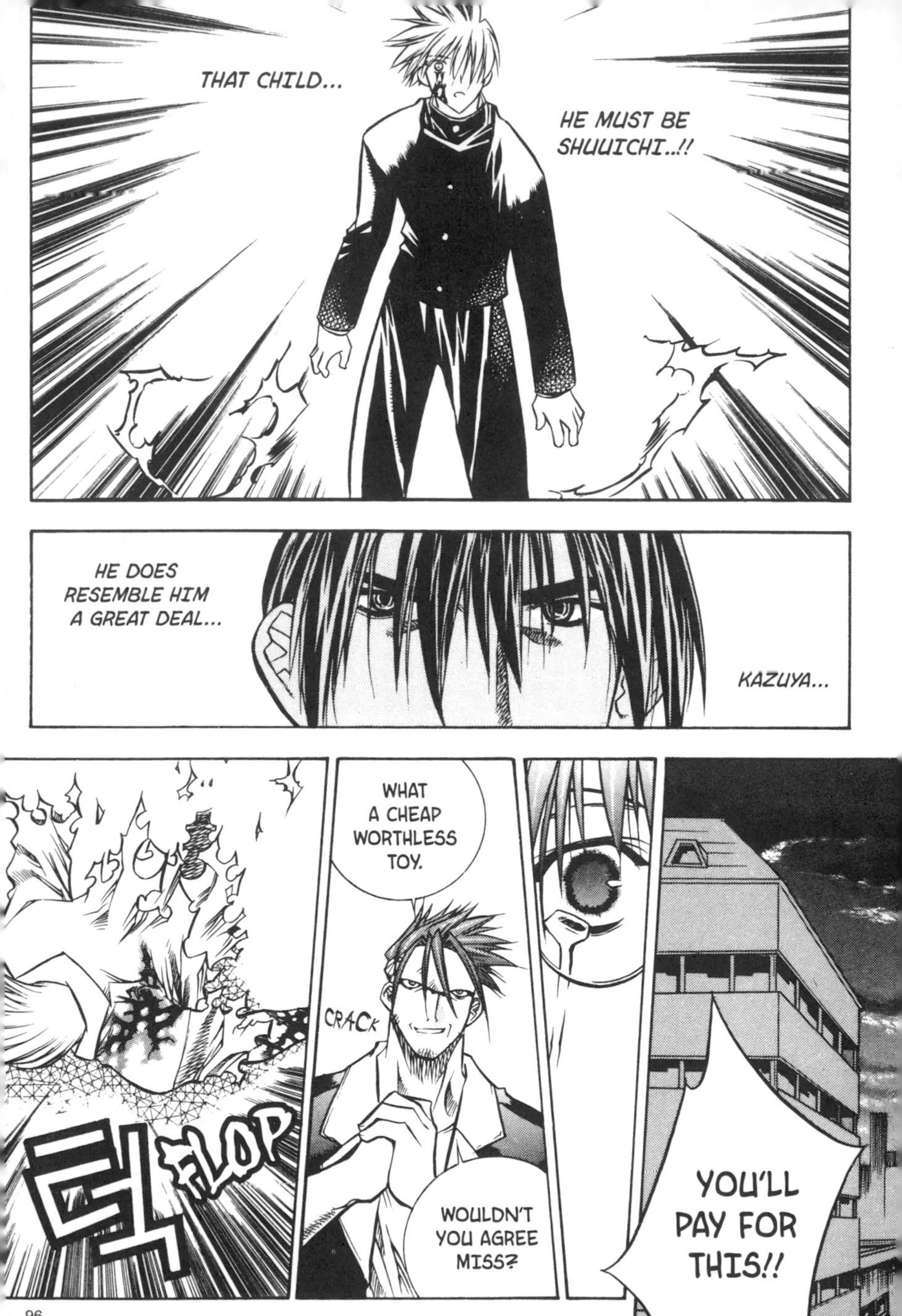

THAT CHILD...
HE MUST BE SHUUICHI..!!
HE DOES RESEMBLE HIM A GREAT DEAL...
KAZUYA...
FLOP
WHAT A CHEAP WORTHLESS TOY.
CRACK
WOULDN'T YOU AGREE MISS?
YOU'LL PAY FOR THIS!!

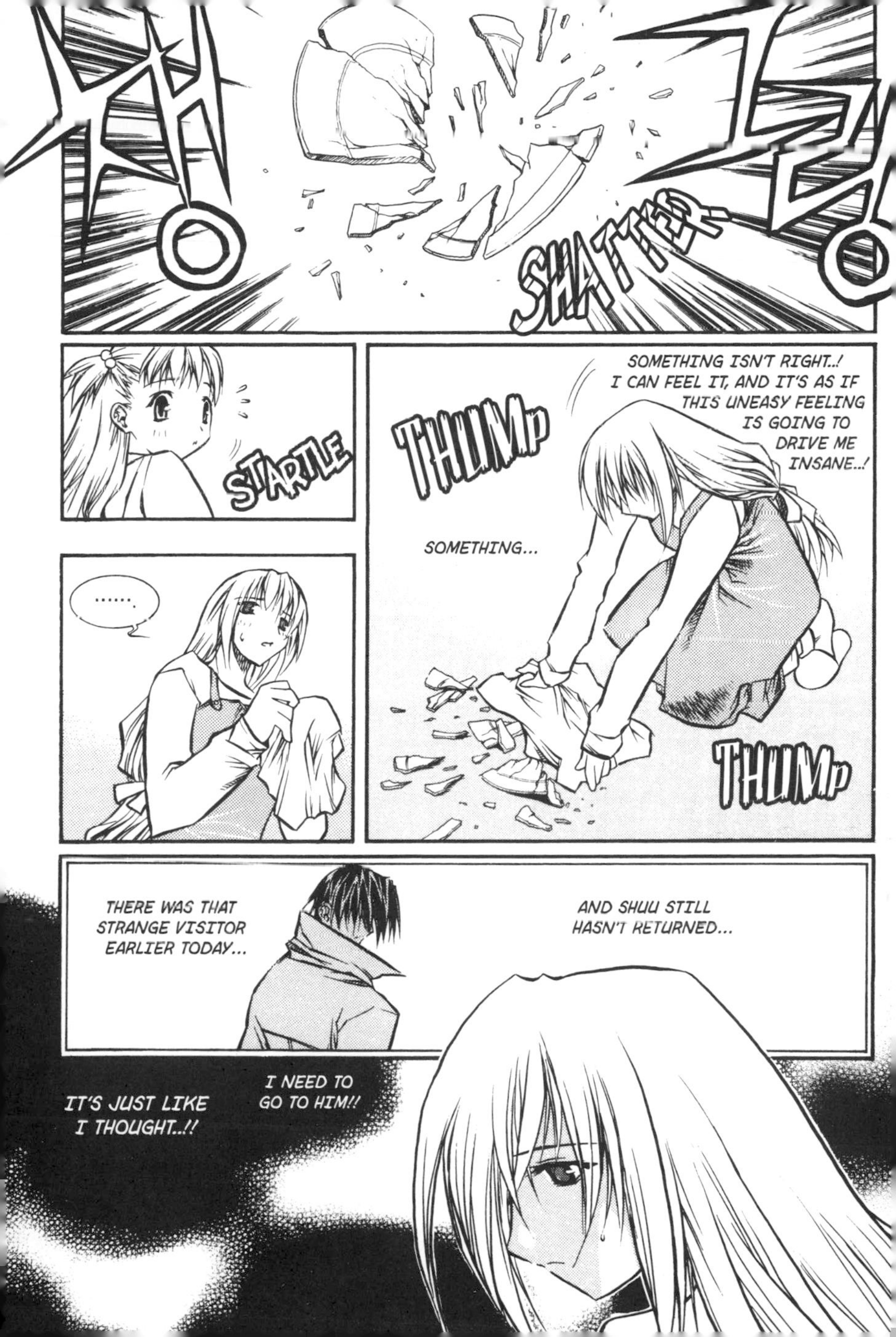
SHATTER
SOMETHING ISN'T RIGHT..! I CAN FEEL IT, AND IT'S AS IF THIS UNEASY FEELING IS GOING TO DRIVE ME INSANE..!
THUMP
SOMETHING...
THUMP
STARTLE
....
AND SHUU STILL HASN'T RETURNED...
THERE WAS THAT STRANGE VISITOR EARLIER TODAY...
I NEED TO GO TO HIM!!
IT'S JUST LIKE I THOUGHT..!!

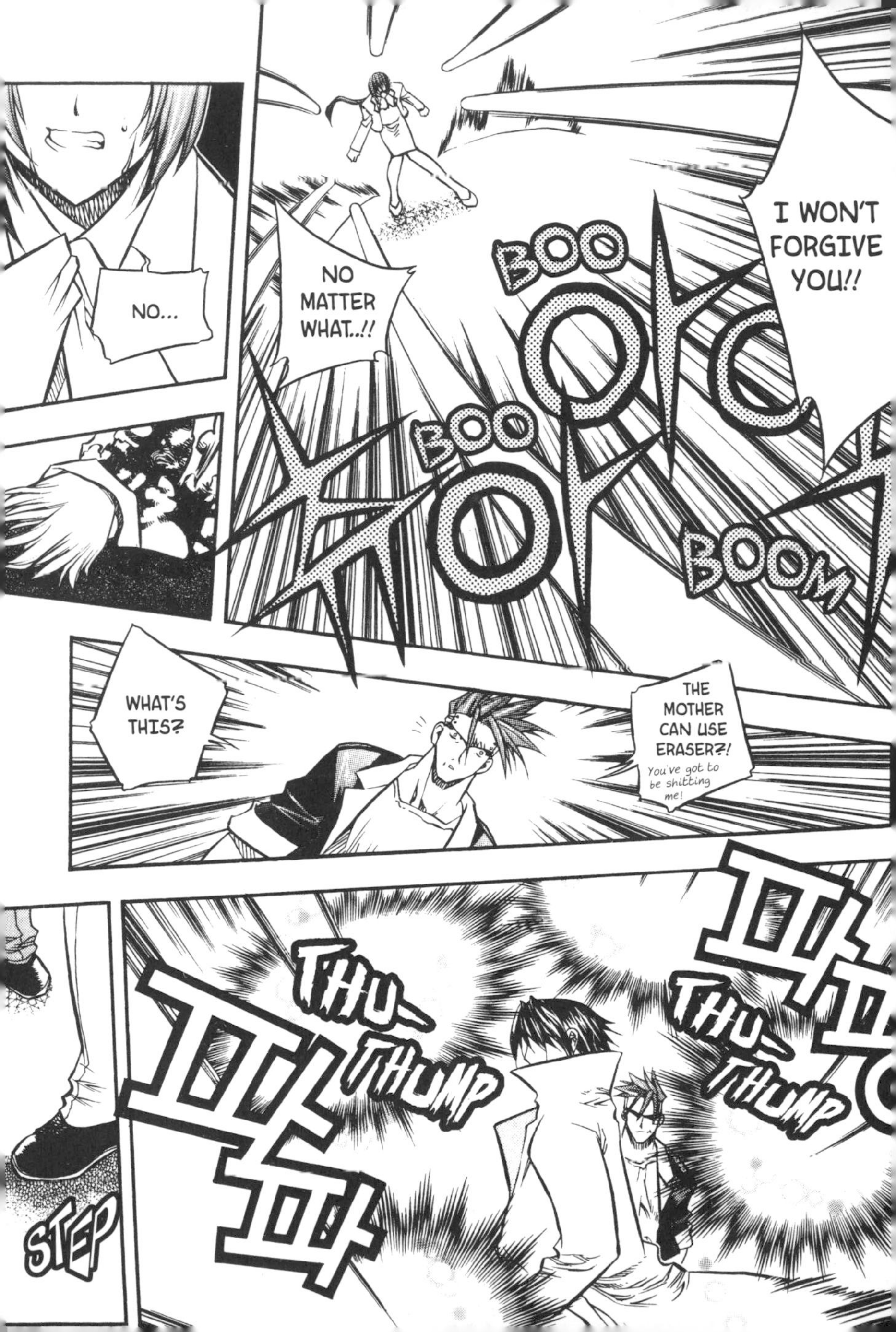

I WON'T FORGIVE YOU!!
NO MATTER WHAT..!!
NO...
BOOOOM
BOOOOM
BOOM
THE MOTHER CAN USE ERASER?!
You've got to be shitting me!
WHAT'S THIS?
THU-THUMP
THU-THUMP
STEP

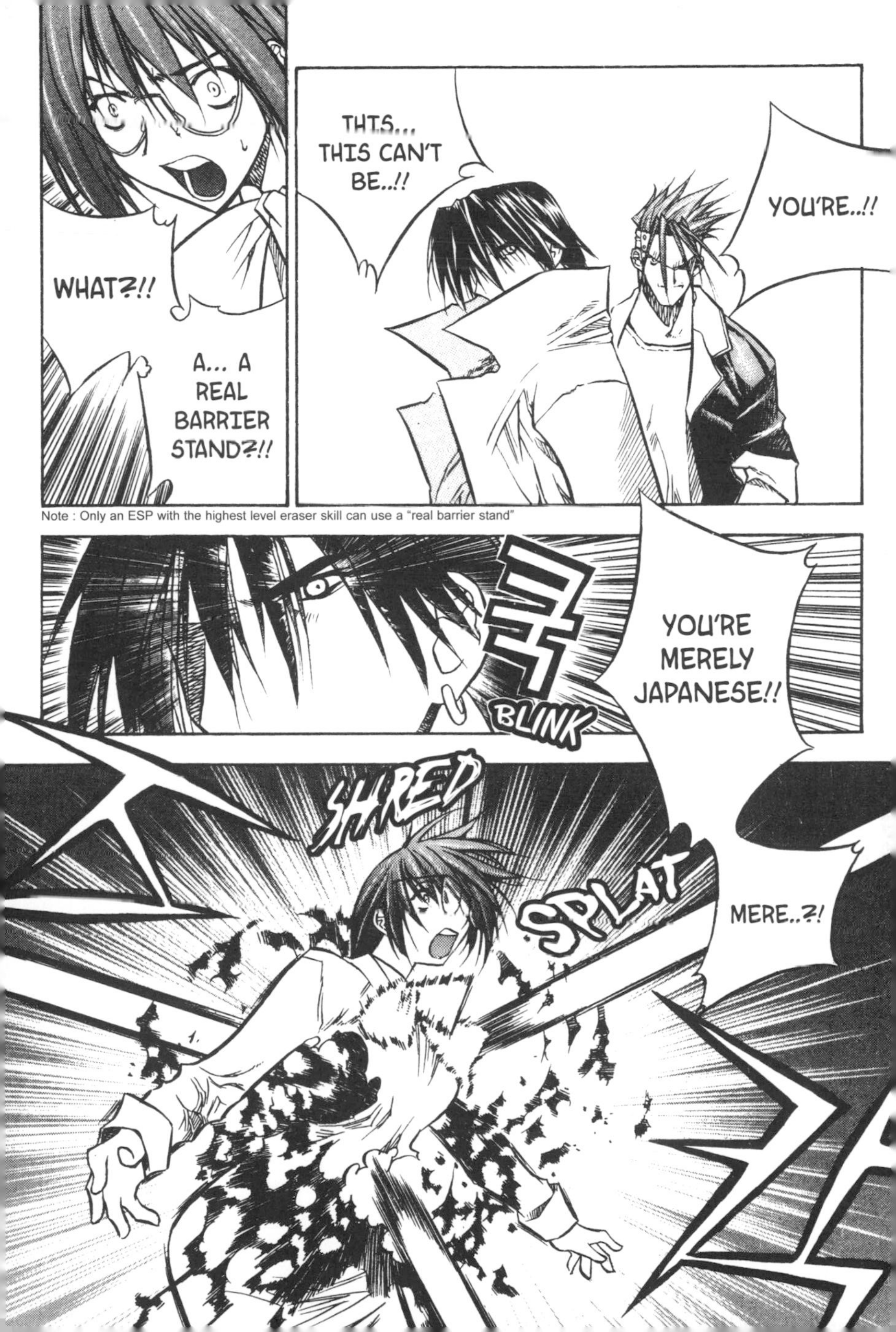
YOU'RE..!!
THTS... THIS CAN'T BE..!!
WHAT?!!
A... A REAL BARRIER STAND?!!
YOU'RE MERELY JAPANESE!!
BLINK
MERE..?!
SPLAT
SHRED
Note : Only an ESP with the highest level eraser skill can use a "real barrier stand"

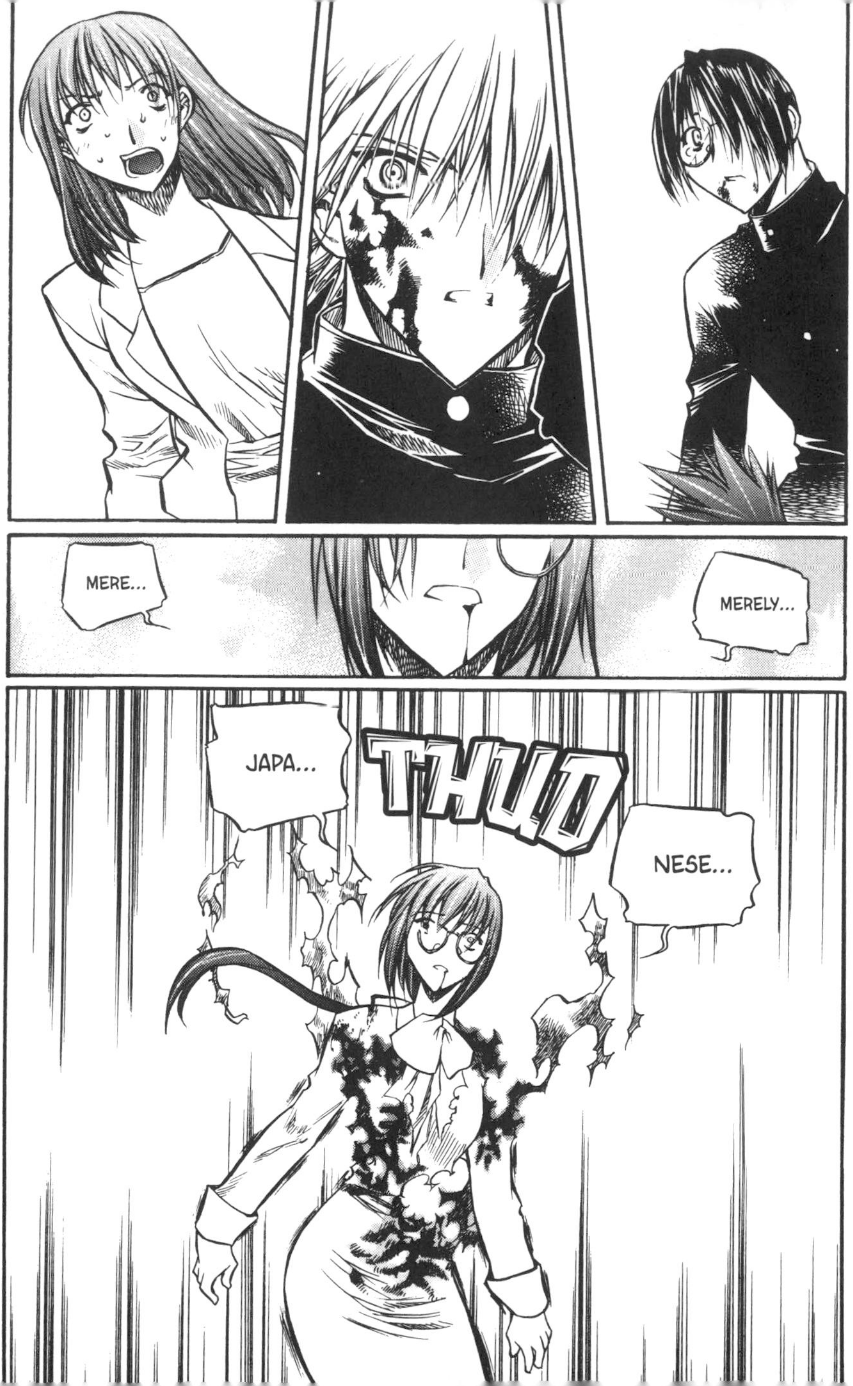
MERELY...
MERE...
THUD
NESE...
JAPA...

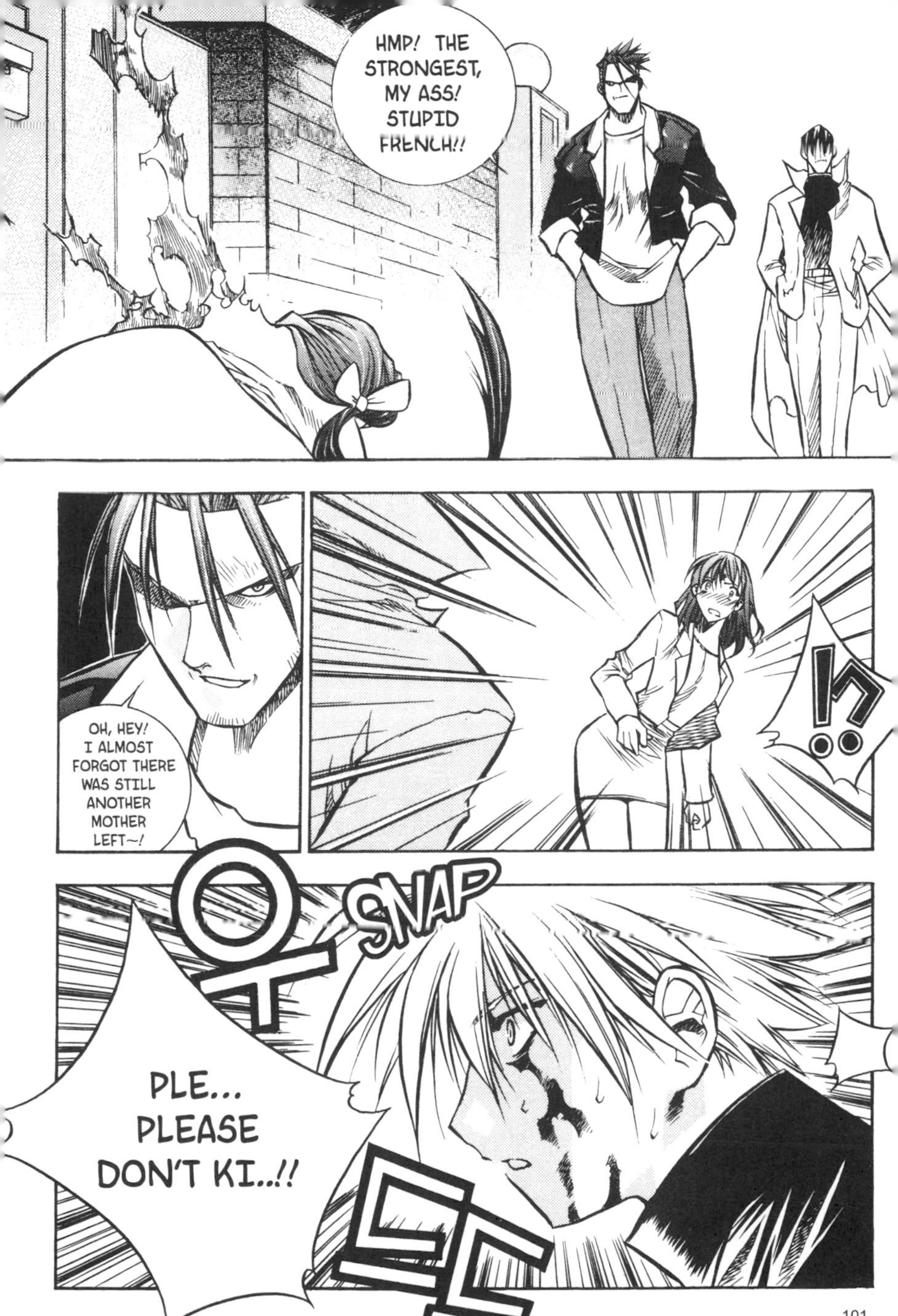
HMP! THE STRONGEST, MY ASS! STUPID FRENCH!!
OH, HEY! I ALMOST FORGOT THERE WAS STILL ANOTHER MOTHER LEFT~!
SNAP
PLE... PLEASE DON'T KI..!!

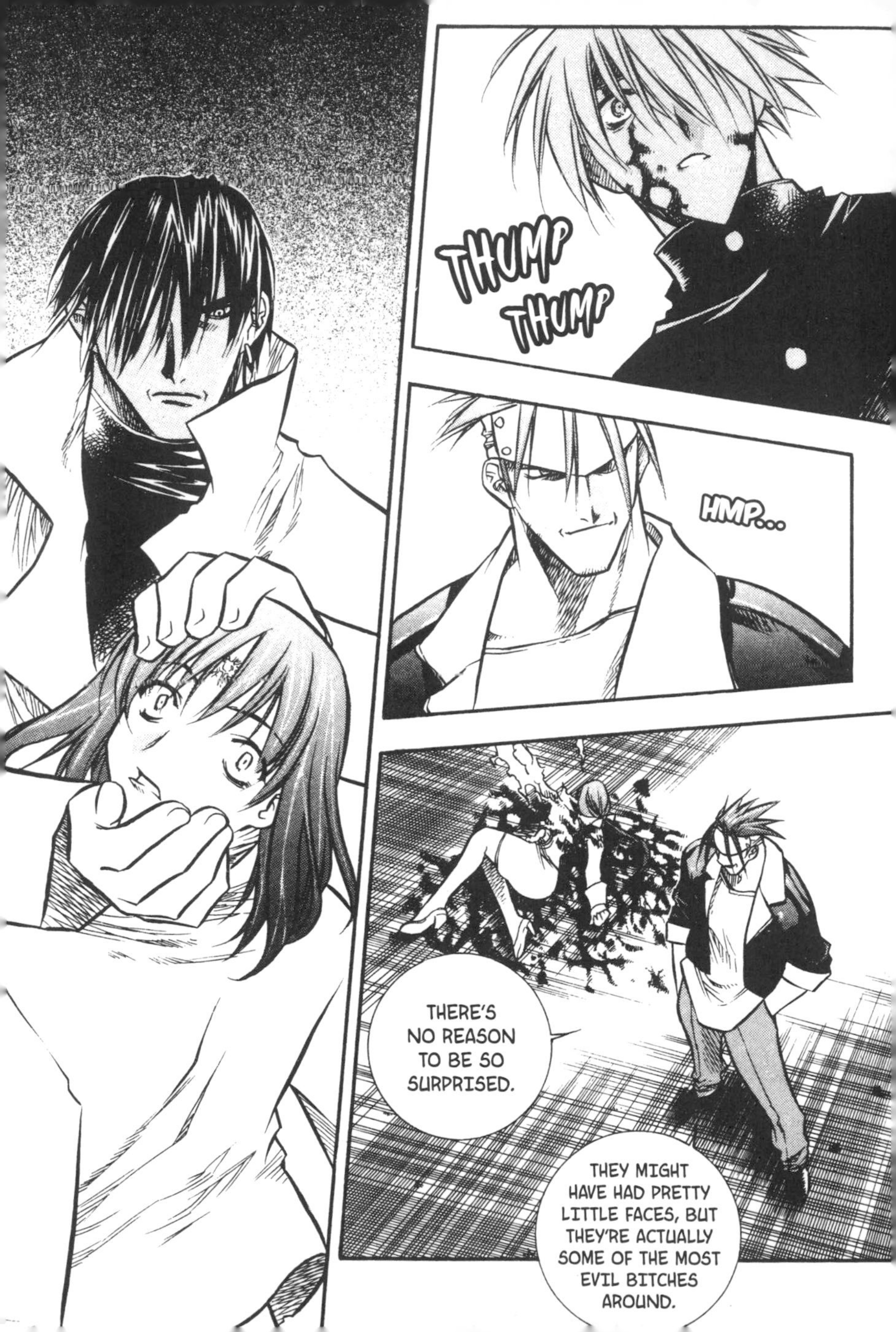
THUMP
THUMP
HMP...
THERE'S NO REASON TO BE SO SURPRISED.
THEY MIGHT HAVE HAD PRETTY LITTLE FACES, BUT THEY'RE ACTUALLY SOME OF THE MOST EVIL BITCHES AROUND.

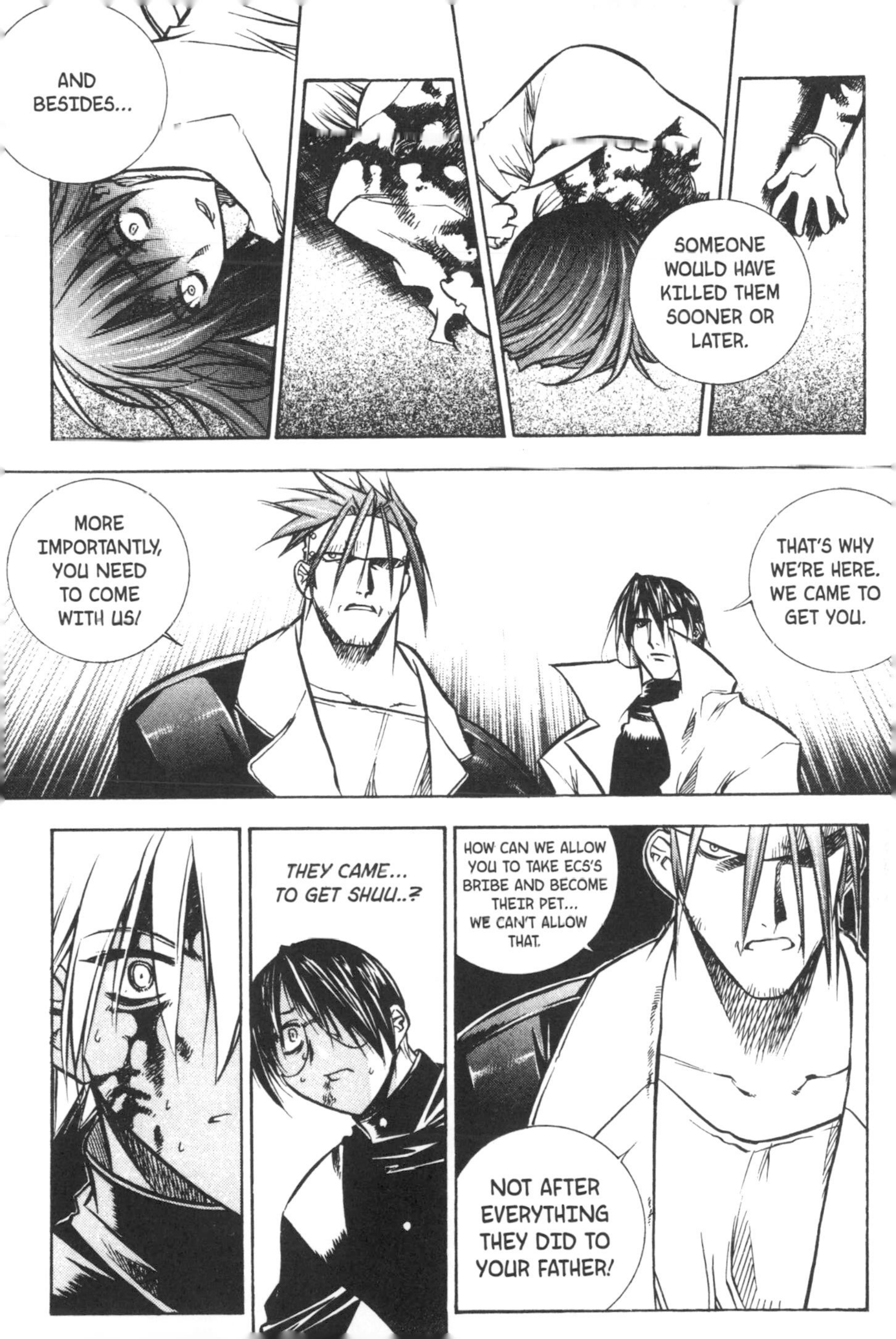
AND BESIDES...
SOMEONE WOULD HAVE KILLED THEM SOONER OR LATER.
MORE IMPORTANTLY, YOU NEED TO COME WITH US!
THAT'S WHY WE'RE HERE. WE CAME TO GET YOU.
THEY CAME... TO GET SHUU..?
HOW CAN WE ALLOW YOU TO TAKE ECS'S BRIBE AND BECOME THEIR PET... WE CAN'T ALLOW THAT.
NOT AFTER EVERYTHING THEY DID TO YOUR FATHER!

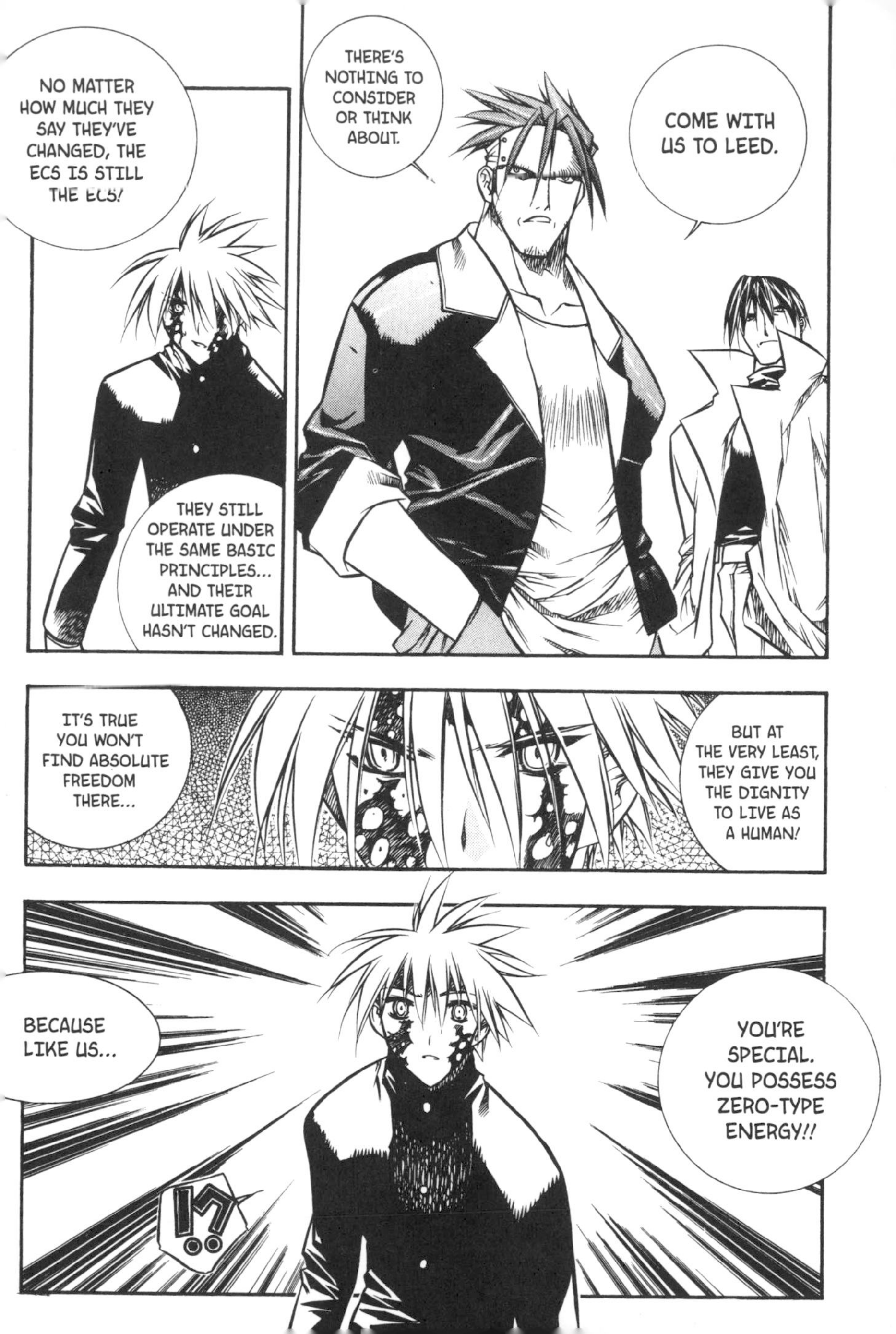

COME WITH US TO LEED.
THERE'S NOTHING TO CONSIDER OR THINK ABOUT.
NO MATTER HOW MUCH THEY SAY THEY'VE CHANGED, THE ECS IS STILL THE ECS!
THEY STILL OPERATE UNDER THE SAME BASIC PRINCIPLES... AND THEIR ULTIMATE GOAL HASN'T CHANGED.
BUT AT THE VERY LEAST, THEY GIVE YOU THE DIGNITY TO LIVE AS A HUMAN!
IT'S TRUE YOU WON'T FIND ABSOLUTE FREEDOM THERE...
YOU'RE SPECIAL. YOU POSSESS ZERO-TYPE ENERGY!!
BECAUSE LIKE US...
!?

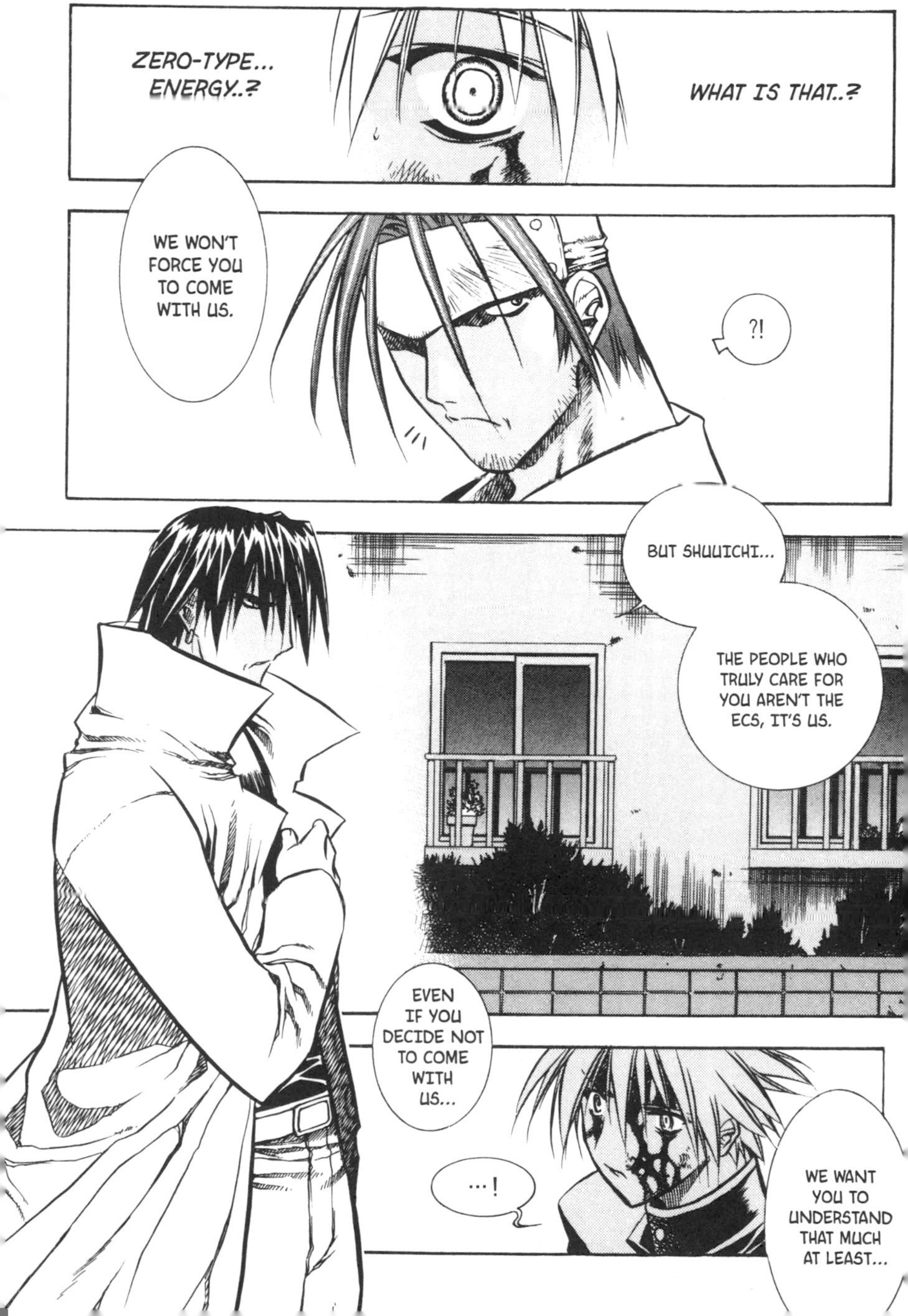
ZERO-TYPE... ENERGY..?
WHAT IS THAT..?
WE WON'T FORCE YOU TO COME WITH US.
?!
BUT SHUUICHI...
THE PEOPLE WHO TRULY CARE FOR YOU AREN'T THE ECS, IT'S US.
EVEN IF YOU DECIDE NOT TO COME WITH US...
WE WANT YOU TO UNDERSTAND THAT MUCH AT LEAST...
...!

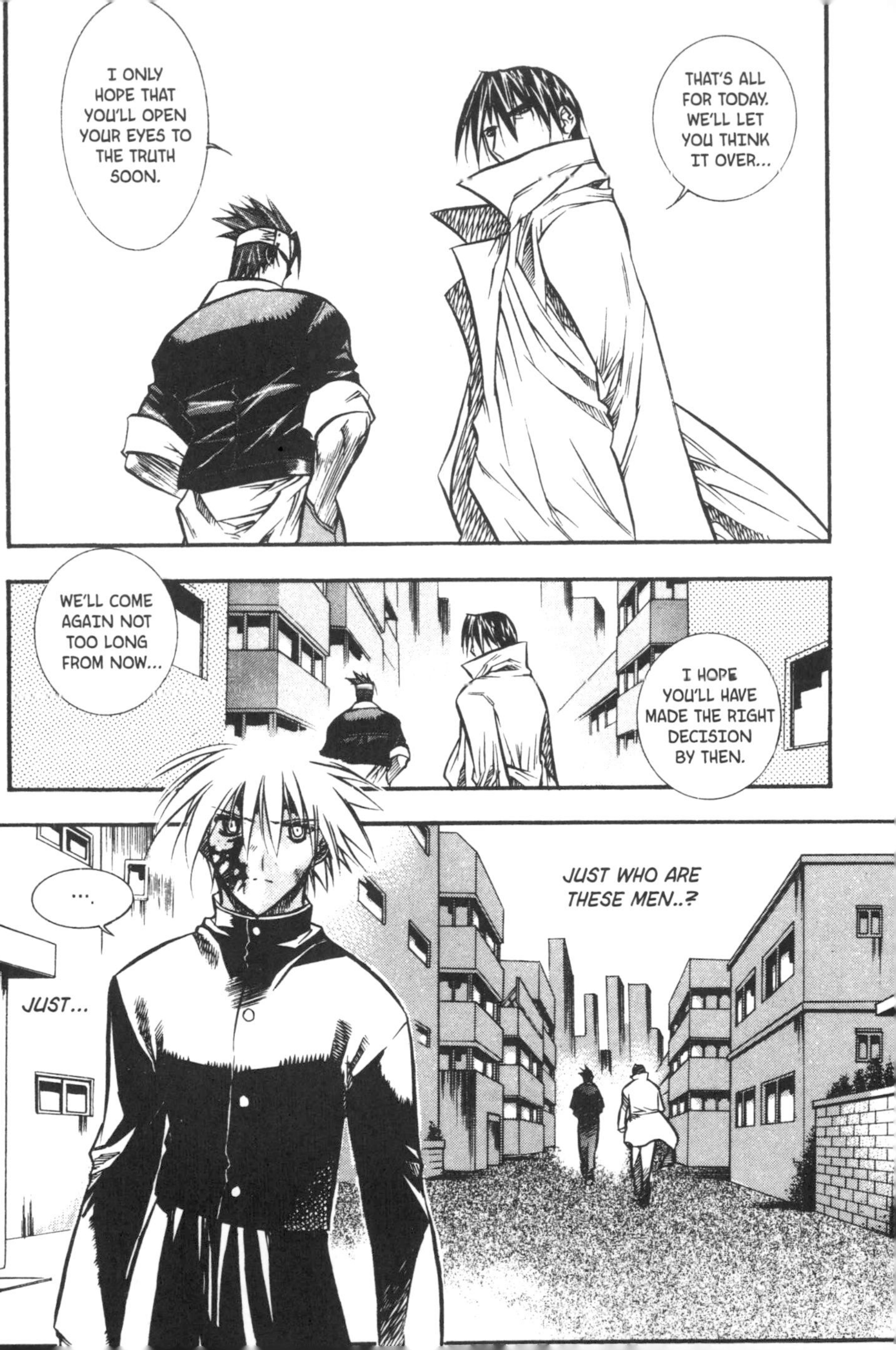
THAT'S ALL FOR TODAY. WE'LL LET YOU THINK IT OVER...
I ONLY HOPE THAT YOU'LL OPEN YOUR EYES TO THE TRUTH SOON.
WE'LL COME AGAIN NOT TOO LONG FROM NOW...
I HOPE YOU'LL HAVE MADE THE RIGHT DECISION BY THEN.
....
JUST...
JUST WHO ARE THESE MEN..?

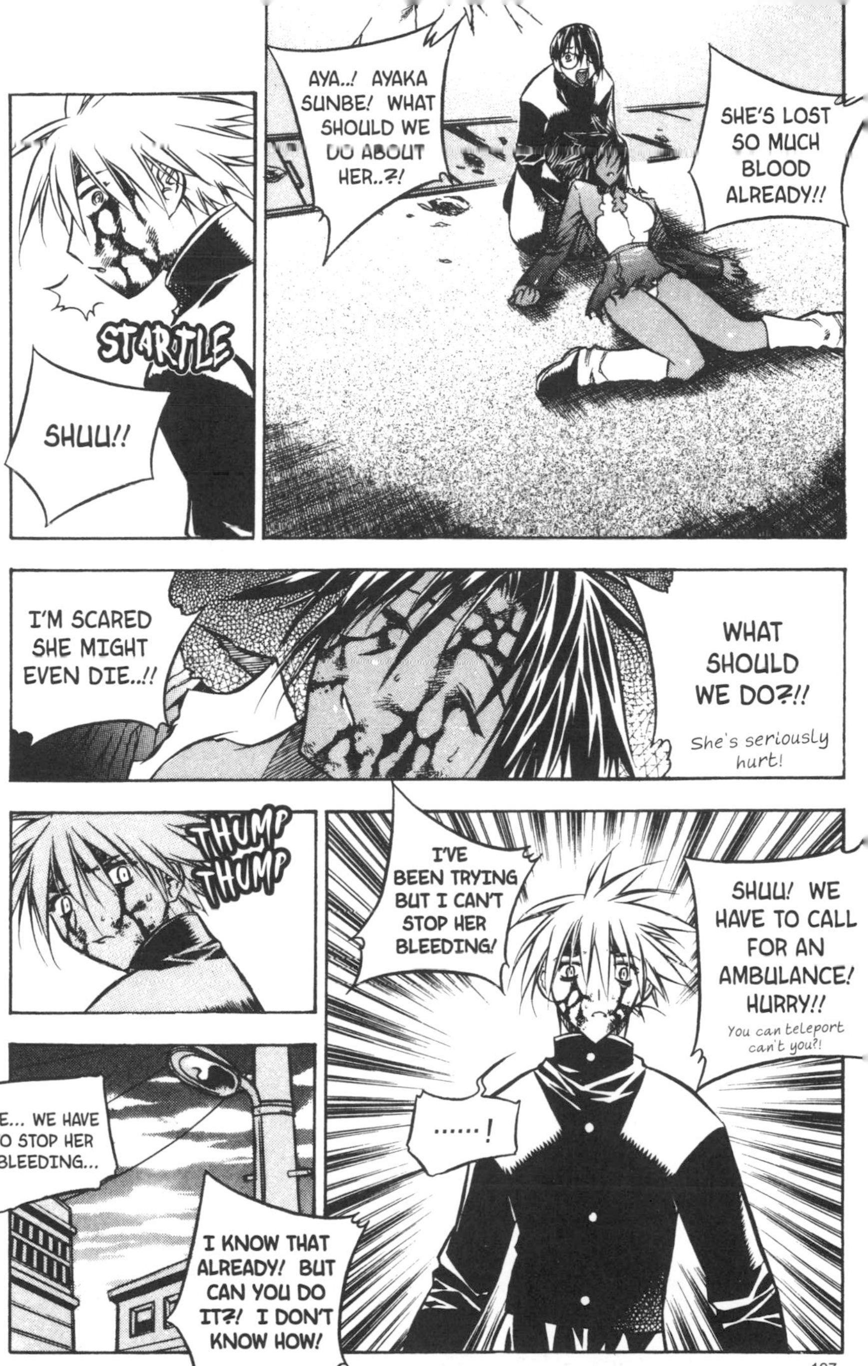
SHUU!!
STARTLE
AYA..! AYAKA SUNBE! WHAT SHOULD WE DO ABOUT HER..?!
SHE'S LOST SO MUCH BLOOD ALREADY!!
I'M SCARED SHE MIGHT EVEN DIE..!!
WHAT SHOULD WE DO?!!
She's seriously hurt!
THUMP THUMP
I'VE BEEN TRYING BUT I CAN'T STOP HER BLEEDING!
SHUU! WE HAVE TO CALL FOR AN AMBULANCE! HURRY!!
You can teleport can't you?!
......!
WE... WE HAVE TO STOP HER BLEEDING...
I KNOW THAT ALREADY! BUT CAN YOU DO IT?! I DON'T KNOW HOW!

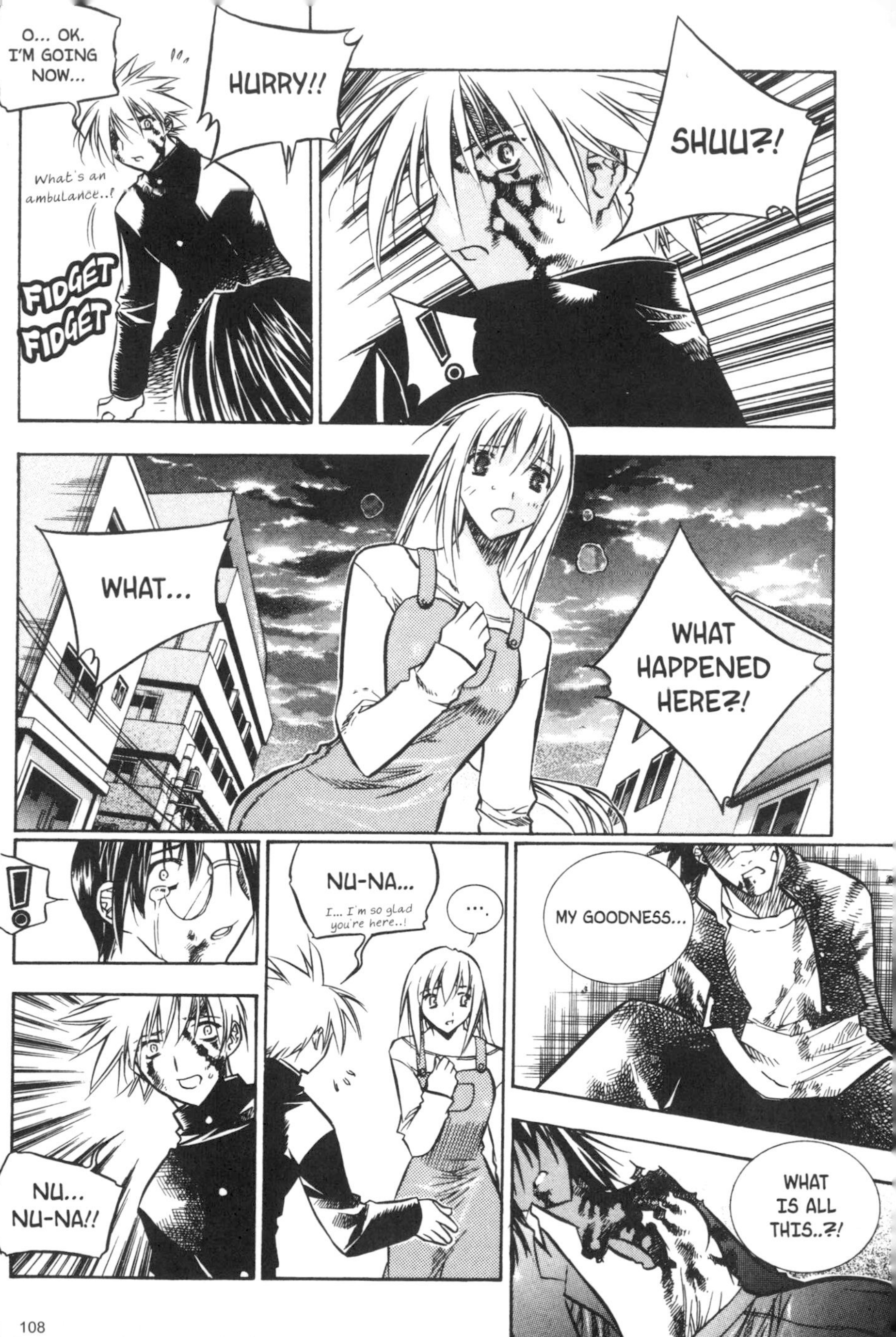

O... OK. I'M GOING NOW...
HURRY!!
What's an ambulance..!
FIDGET FIDGET
SHUU?!
!
WHAT...
WHAT HAPPENED HERE?!
!
NU... NU-NA!!
NU-NA...
I... I'm so glad you're here..!
....
MY GOODNESS...
WHAT IS ALL THIS..?!

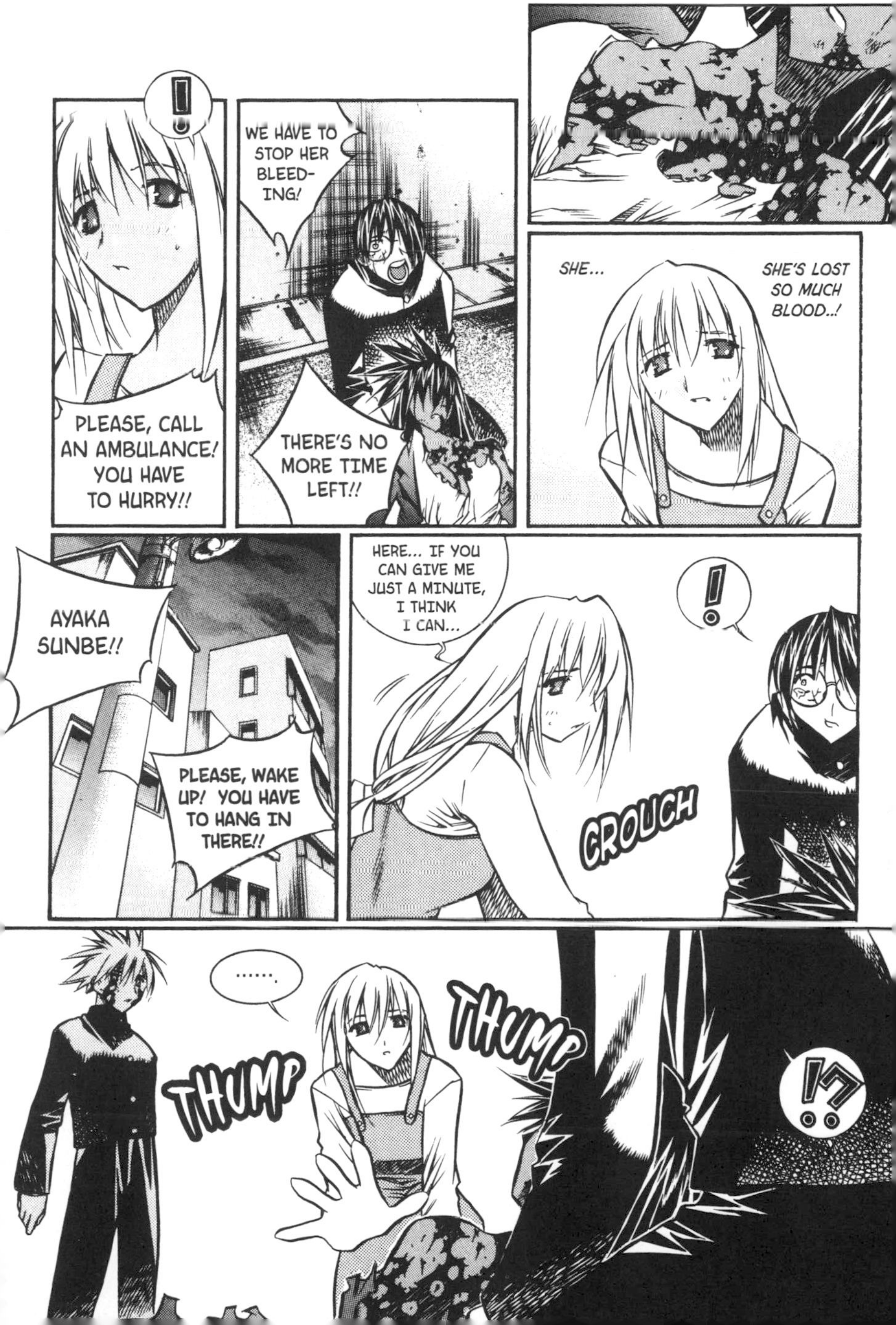

!
PLEASE, CALL AN AMBULANCE! YOU HAVE TO HURRY!!
WE HAVE TO STOP HER BLEED-ING!
THERE'S NO MORE TIME LEFT!!
SHE...
SHE'S LOST SO MUCH BLOOD..!
AYAKA SUNBE!!
PLEASE, WAKE UP! YOU HAVE TO HANG IN THERE!!
HERE... IF YOU CAN GIVE ME JUST A MINUTE, I THINK I CAN...
!
CROUCH
....
THUMP
THUMP
!?

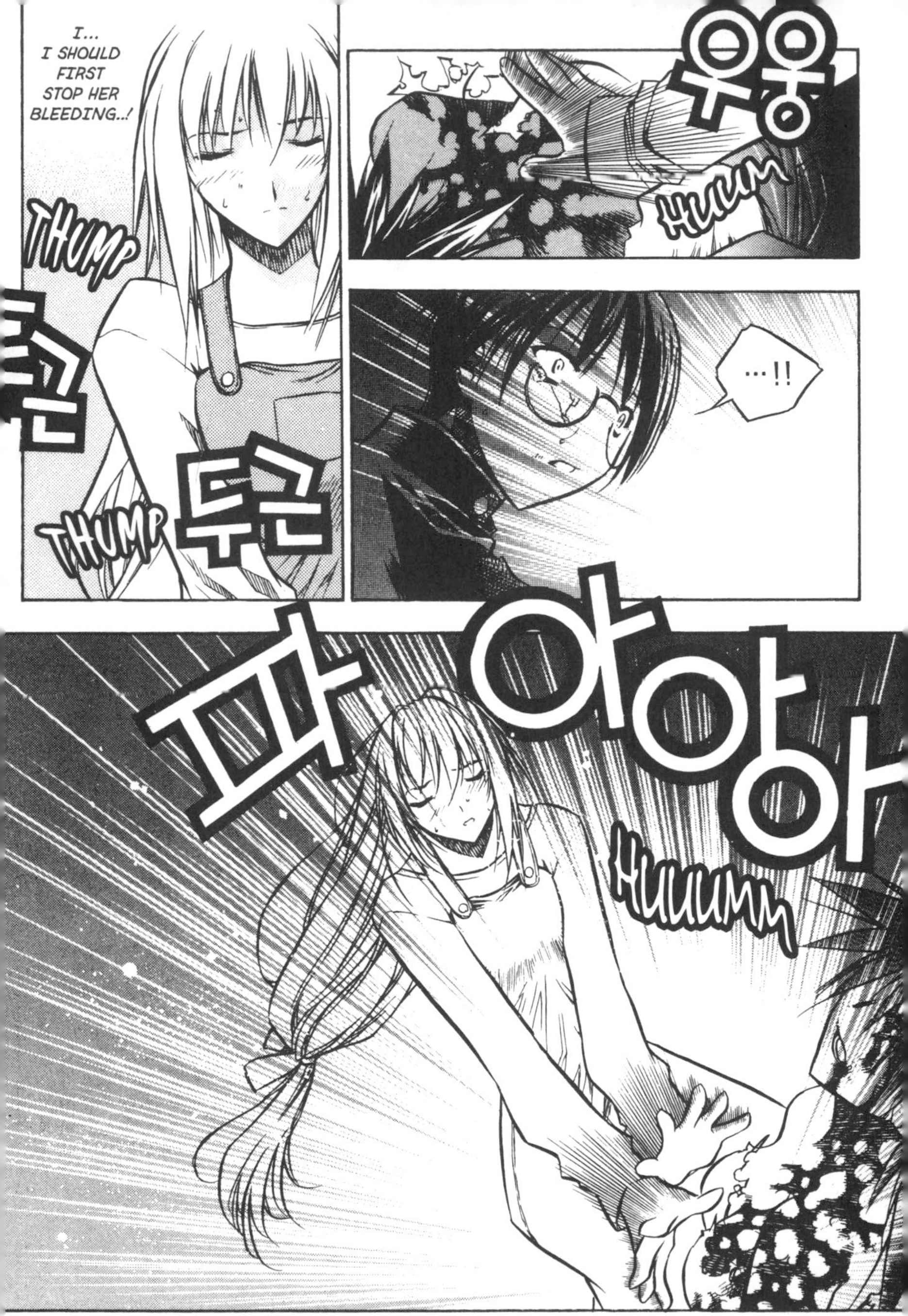
I... I SHOULD FIRST STOP HER BLEEDING..!
THUMP
두근
THUMP
두근
우웅
HUUM
...!!
파아앙아
HUUUMM

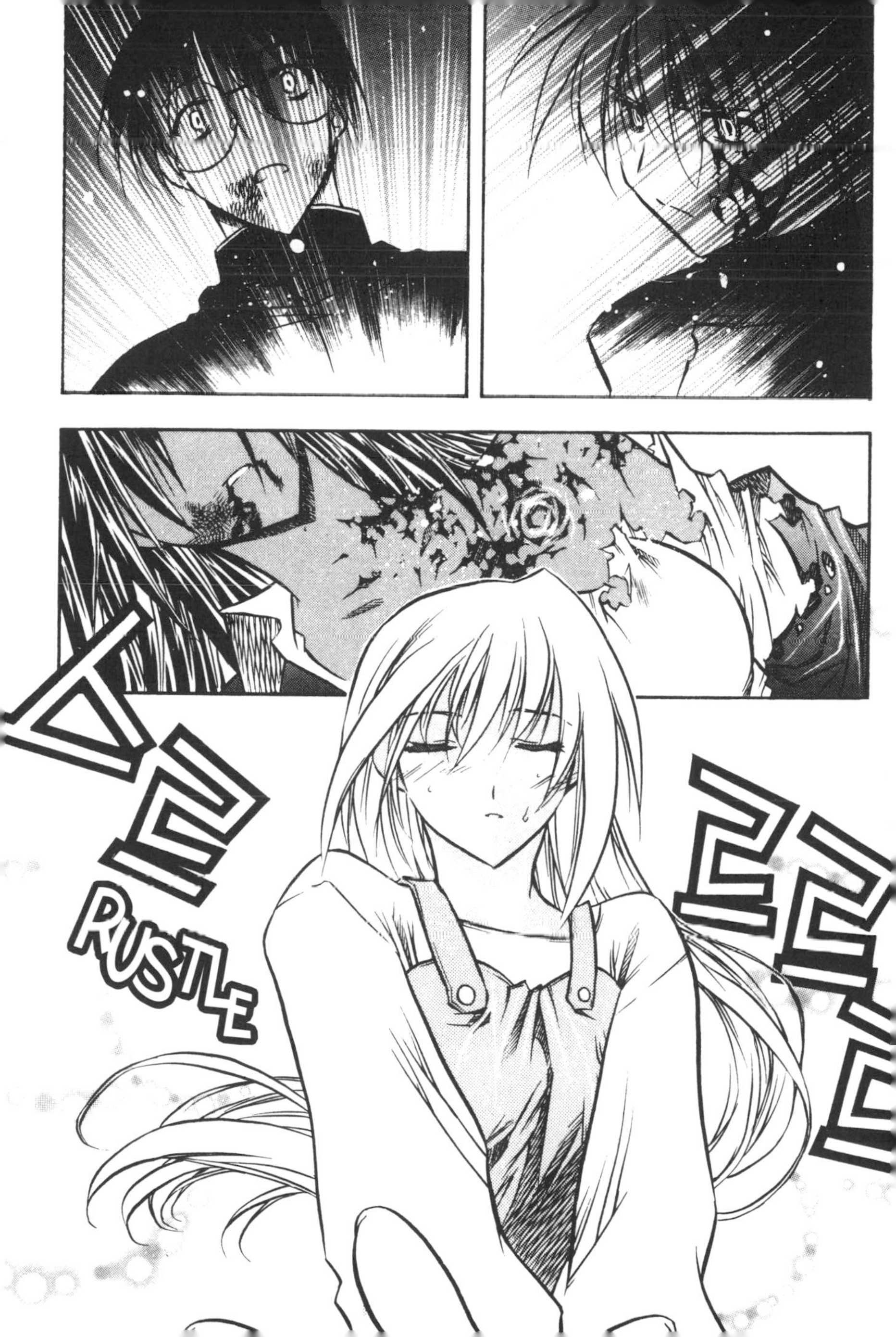
RUSTLE

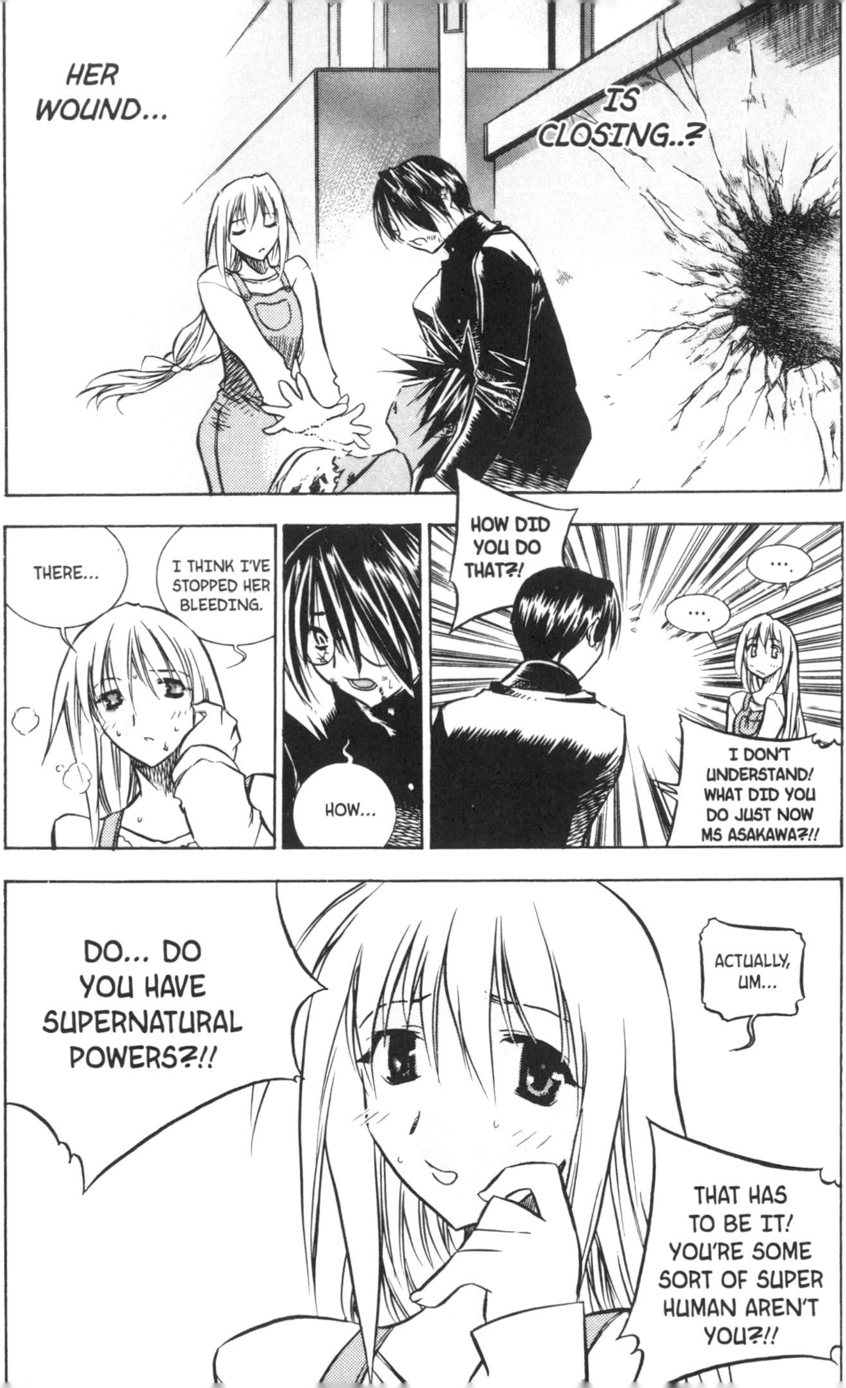

HER WOUND...
IS CLOSING..?
THERE...
I THINK I'VE STOPPED HER BLEEDING.
HOW...
HOW DID YOU DO THAT?!
...
...
I DON'T UNDERSTAND! WHAT DID YOU DO JUST NOW MS ASAKAWA?!!
DO... DO YOU HAVE SUPERNATURAL POWERS?!!
ACTUALLY, UM...
THAT HAS TO BE IT! YOU'RE SOME SORT OF SUPER HUMAN AREN'T YOU?!!

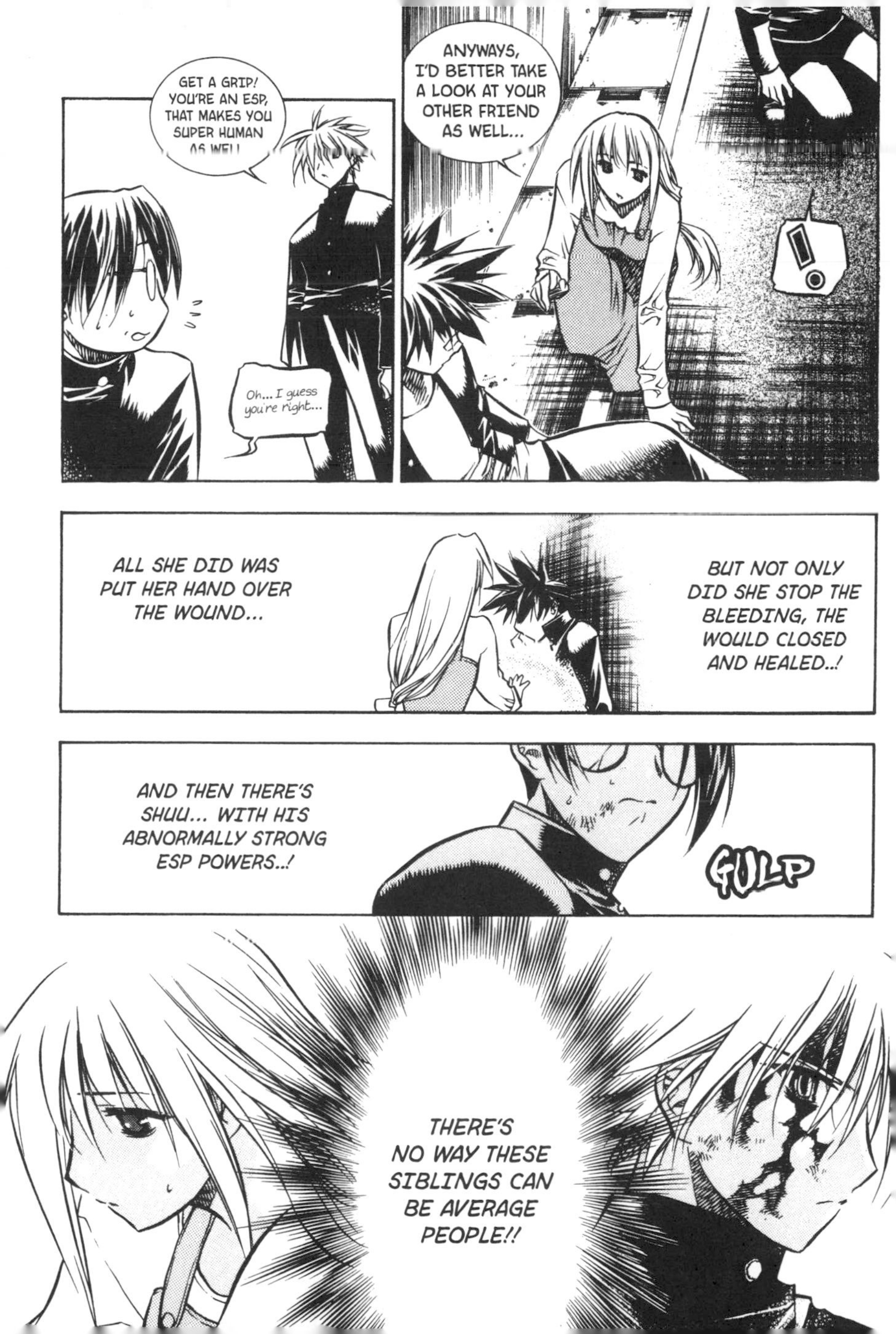
GET A GRIP! YOU'RE AN ESP, THAT MAKES YOU SUPER HUMAN AS WELL
Oh... I guess you're right...
ANYWAYS, I'D BETTER TAKE A LOOK AT YOUR OTHER FRIEND AS WELL...
!
ALL SHE DID WAS PUT HER HAND OVER THE WOUND...
BUT NOT ONLY DID SHE STOP THE BLEEDING, THE WOULD CLOSED AND HEALED..!
AND THEN THERE'S SHUU... WITH HIS ABNORMALLY STRONG ESP POWERS..!
GULP
THERE'S NO WAY THESE SIBLINGS CAN BE AVERAGE PEOPLE!!

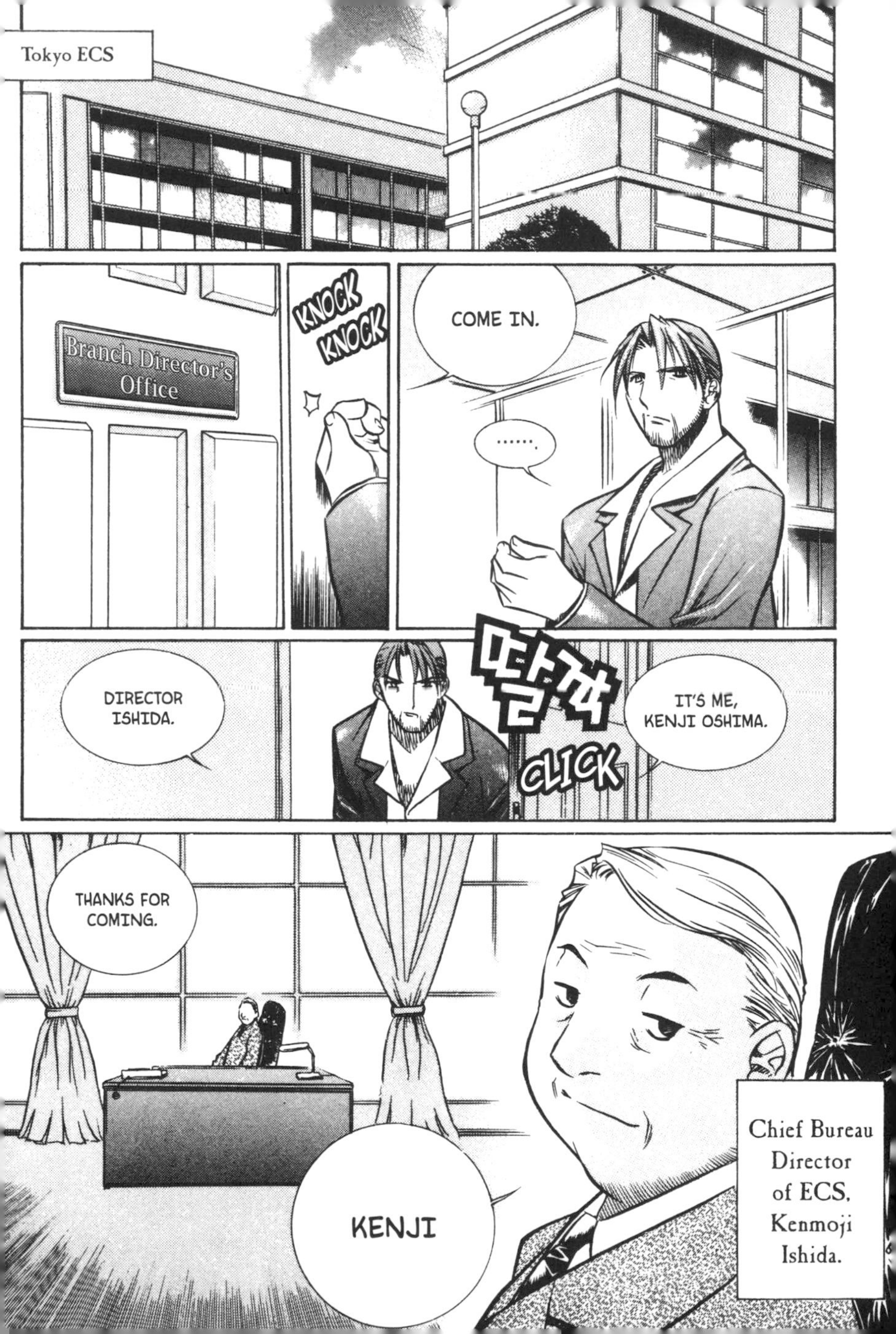
Tokyo ECS
Branch Director's Office
KNOCK KNOCK
COME IN.
....
DIRECTOR ISHIDA.
딸깍
CLICK
IT'S ME, KENJI OSHIMA.
THANKS FOR COMING.
KENJI
Chief Bureau Director of ECS, Kenmoji Ishida.

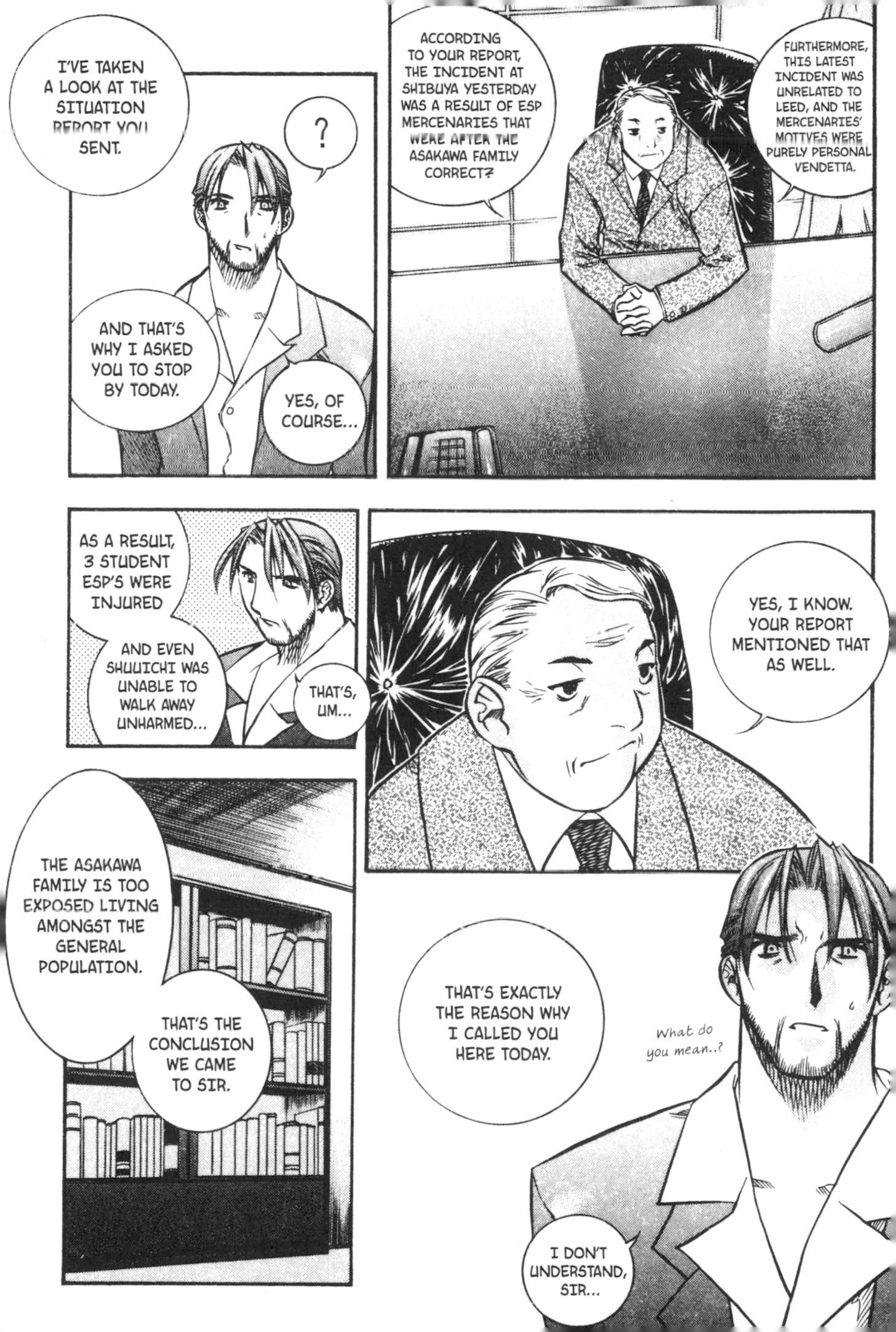
I'VE TAKEN A LOOK AT THE SITUATION REPORT YOU SENT.
?
AND THAT'S WHY I ASKED YOU TO STOP BY TODAY.
YES, OF COURSE...
ACCORDING TO YOUR REPORT, THE INCIDENT AT SHIBUYA YESTERDAY WAS A RESULT OF ESP MERCENARIES THAT WERE AFTER THE ASAKAWA FAMILY CORRECT?
FURTHERMORE, THIS LATEST INCIDENT WAS UNRELATED TO LEED, AND THE MERCENARIES' MOTIVES WERE PURELY PERSONAL VENDETTA.
AS A RESULT, 3 STUDENT ESP'S WERE INJURED
AND EVEN SHUUICHI WAS UNABLE TO WALK AWAY UNHARMED...
THAT'S, UM...
YES, I KNOW. YOUR REPORT MENTIONED THAT AS WELL.
THE ASAKAWA FAMILY IS TOO EXPOSED LIVING AMONGST THE GENERAL POPULATION.
THAT'S THE CONCLUSION WE CAME TO SIR.
THAT'S EXACTLY THE REASON WHY I CALLED YOU HERE TODAY.
What do you mean..?
I DON'T UNDERSTAND, SIR...

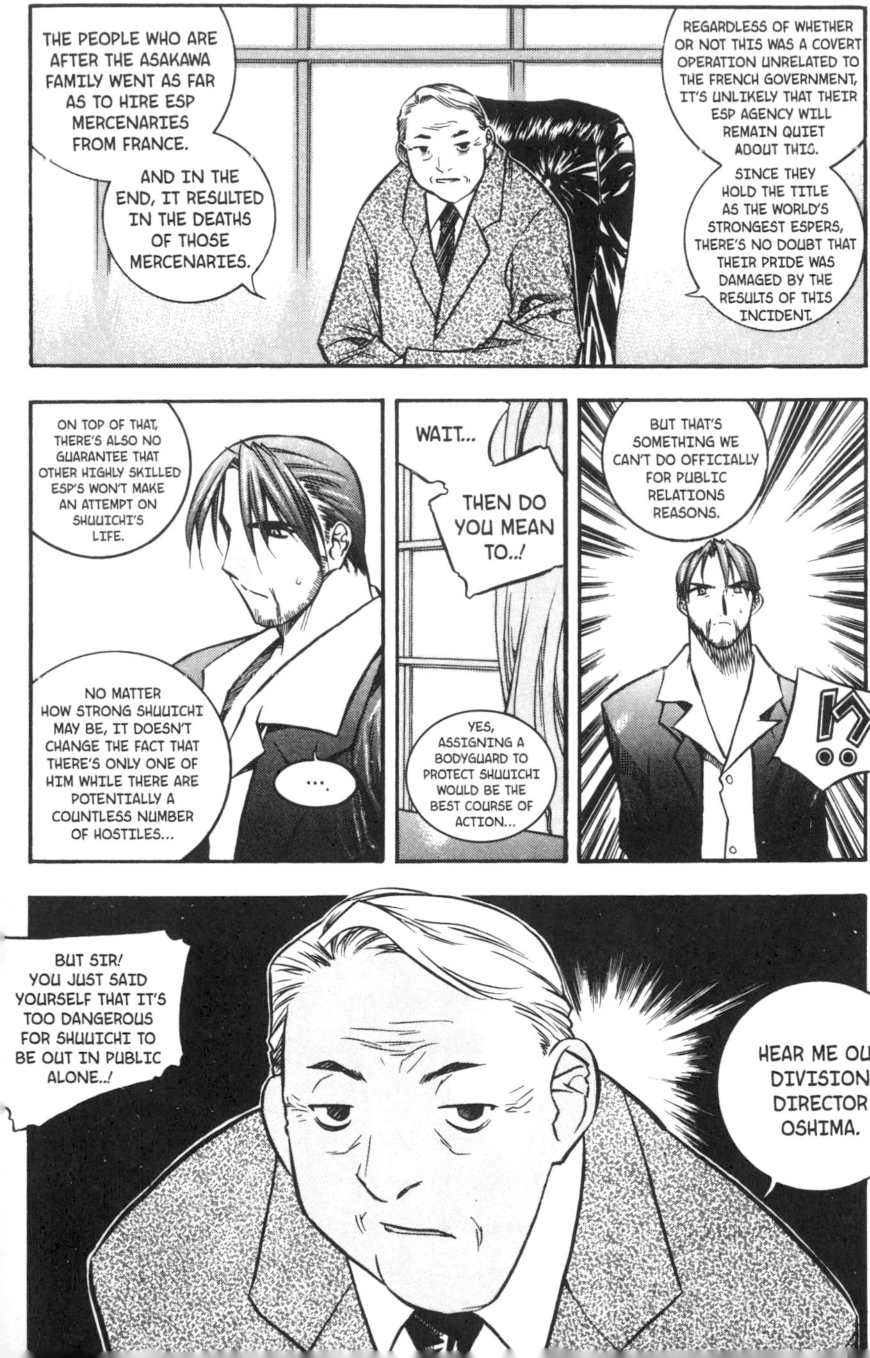
THE PEOPLE WHO ARE AFTER THE ASAKAWA FAMILY WENT AS FAR AS TO HIRE ESP MERCENARIES FROM FRANCE.
AND IN THE END, IT RESULTED IN THE DEATHS OF THOSE MERCENARIES.
REGARDLESS OF WHETHER OR NOT THIS WAS A COVERT OPERATION UNRELATED TO THE FRENCH GOVERNMENT, IT'S UNLIKELY THAT THEIR ESP AGENCY WILL REMAIN QUIET ABOUT THIS.
SINCE THEY HOLD THE TITLE AS THE WORLD'S STRONGEST ESPERS, THERE'S NO DOUBT THAT THEIR PRIDE WAS DAMAGED BY THE RESULTS OF THIS INCIDENT.
ON TOP OF THAT, THERE'S ALSO NO GUARANTEE THAT OTHER HIGHLY SKILLED ESP'S WON'T MAKE AN ATTEMPT ON SHUUICHI'S LIFE.
NO MATTER HOW STRONG SHUUICHI MAY BE, IT DOESN'T CHANGE THE FACT THAT THERE'S ONLY ONE OF HIM WHILE THERE ARE POTENTIALLY A COUNTLESS NUMBER OF HOSTILES...
...
WAIT...
THEN DO YOU MEAN TO..!
YES, ASSIGNING A BODYGUARD TO PROTECT SHUUICHI WOULD BE THE BEST COURSE OF ACTION...
BUT THAT'S SOMETHING WE CAN'T DO OFFICIALLY FOR PUBLIC RELATIONS REASONS.
BUT SIR! YOU JUST SAID YOURSELF THAT IT'S TOO DANGEROUS FOR SHUUICHI TO BE OUT IN PUBLIC ALONE..!
HEAR ME OUT DIVISION DIRECTOR OSHIMA.

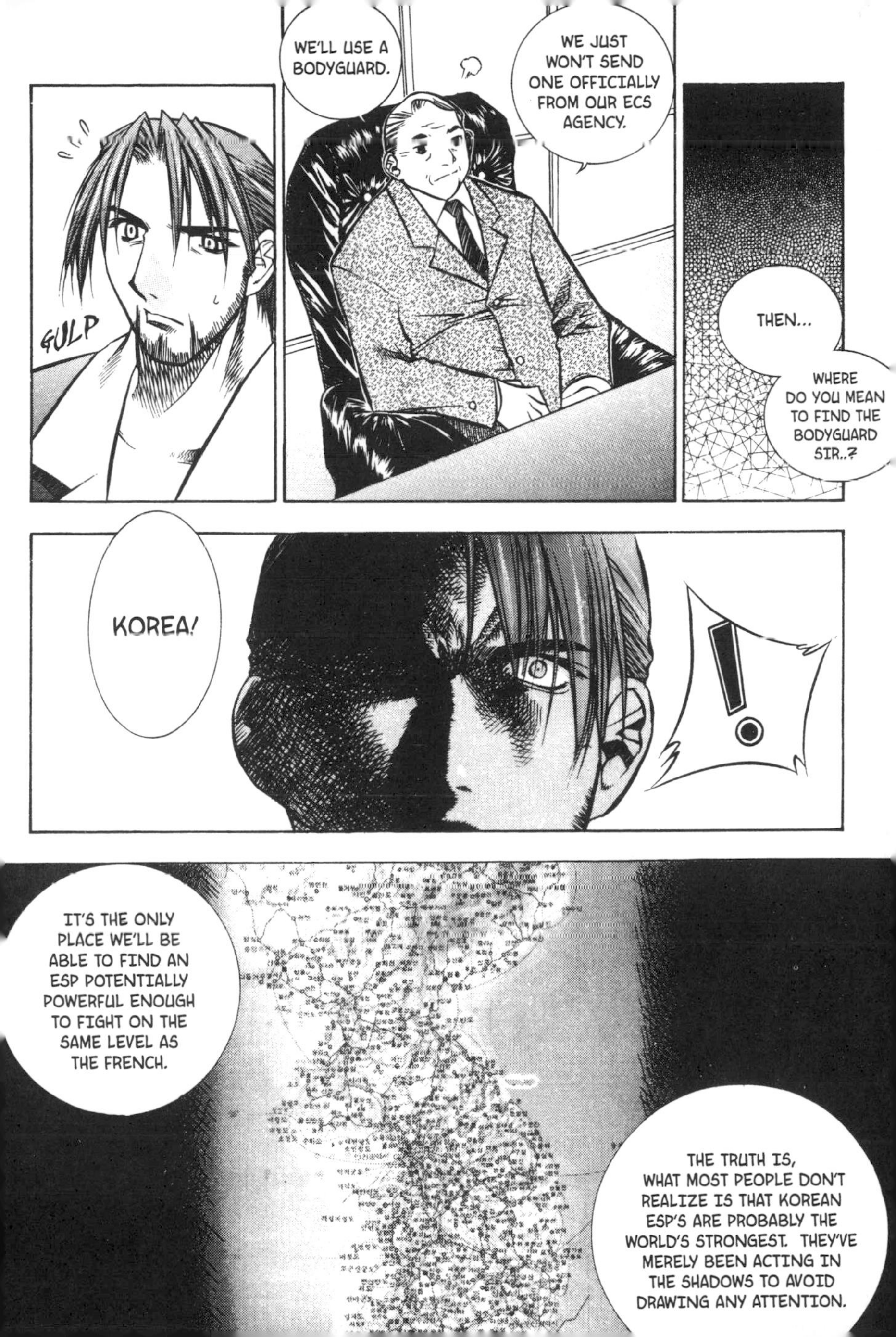
WE'LL USE A BODYGUARD.
WE JUST WON'T SEND ONE OFFICIALLY FROM OUR ECS AGENCY.
GULP
THEN...
WHERE DO YOU MEAN TO FIND THE BODYGUARD SIR..?
KOREA!
!
IT'S THE ONLY PLACE WE'LL BE ABLE TO FIND AN ESP POTENTIALLY POWERFUL ENOUGH TO FIGHT ON THE SAME LEVEL AS THE FRENCH.
THE TRUTH IS, WHAT MOST PEOPLE DON'T REALIZE IS THAT KOREAN ESP'S ARE PROBABLY THE WORLD'S STRONGEST. THEY'VE MERELY BEEN ACTING IN THE SHADOWS TO AVOID DRAWING ANY ATTENTION.

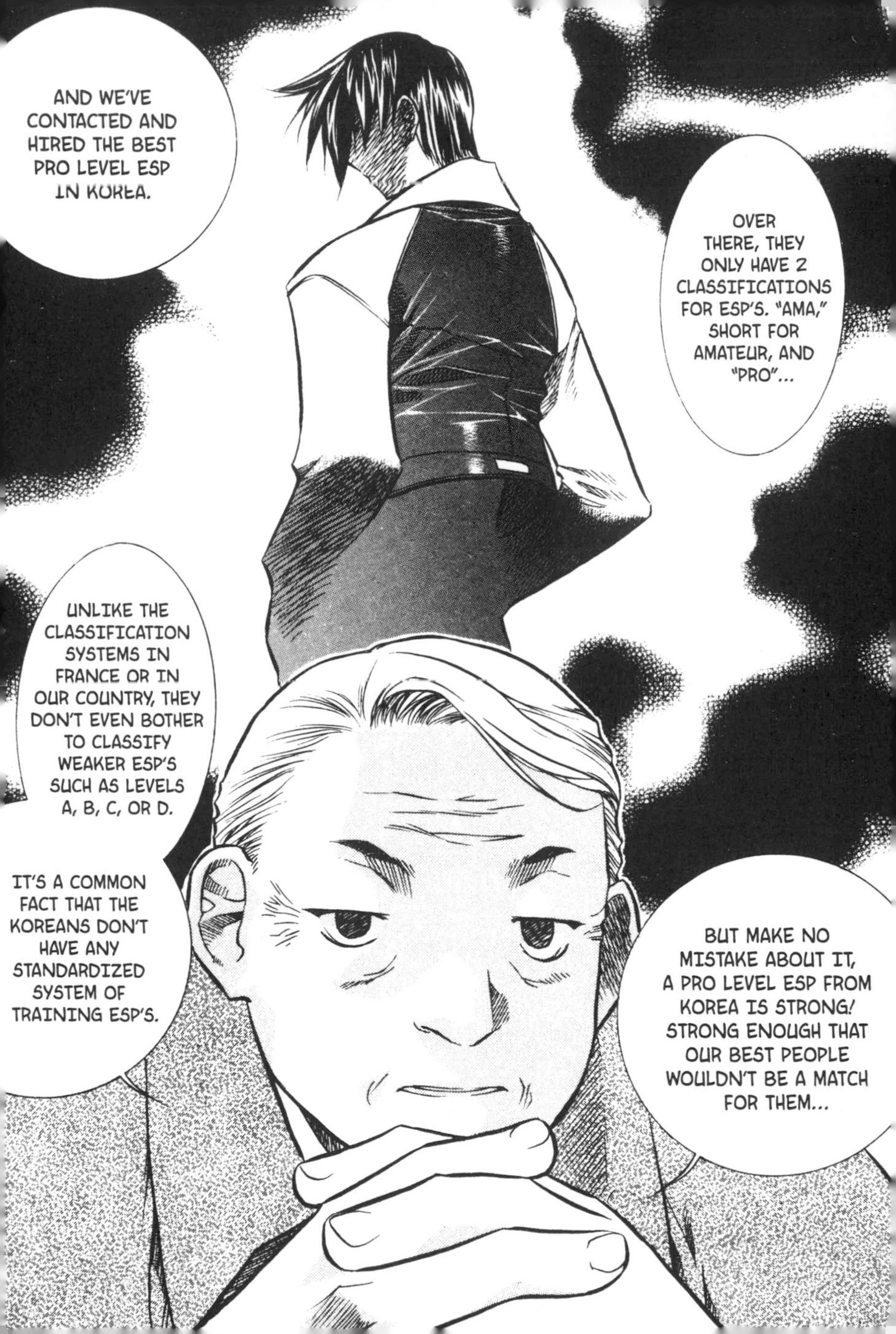
AND WE'VE CONTACTED AND HIRED THE BEST PRO LEVEL ESP IN KOREA.
OVER THERE, THEY ONLY HAVE 2 CLASSIFICATIONS FOR ESP'S. "AMA," SHORT FOR AMATEUR, AND "PRO"...
UNLIKE THE CLASSIFICATION SYSTEMS IN FRANCE OR IN OUR COUNTRY, THEY DON'T EVEN BOTHER TO CLASSIFY WEAKER ESP'S SUCH AS LEVELS A, B, C, OR D.
IT'S A COMMON FACT THAT THE KOREANS DON'T HAVE ANY STANDARDIZED SYSTEM OF TRAINING ESP'S.
BUT MAKE NO MISTAKE ABOUT IT, A PRO LEVEL ESP FROM KOREA IS STRONG! STRONG ENOUGH THAT OUR BEST PEOPLE WOULDN'T BE A MATCH FOR THEM...

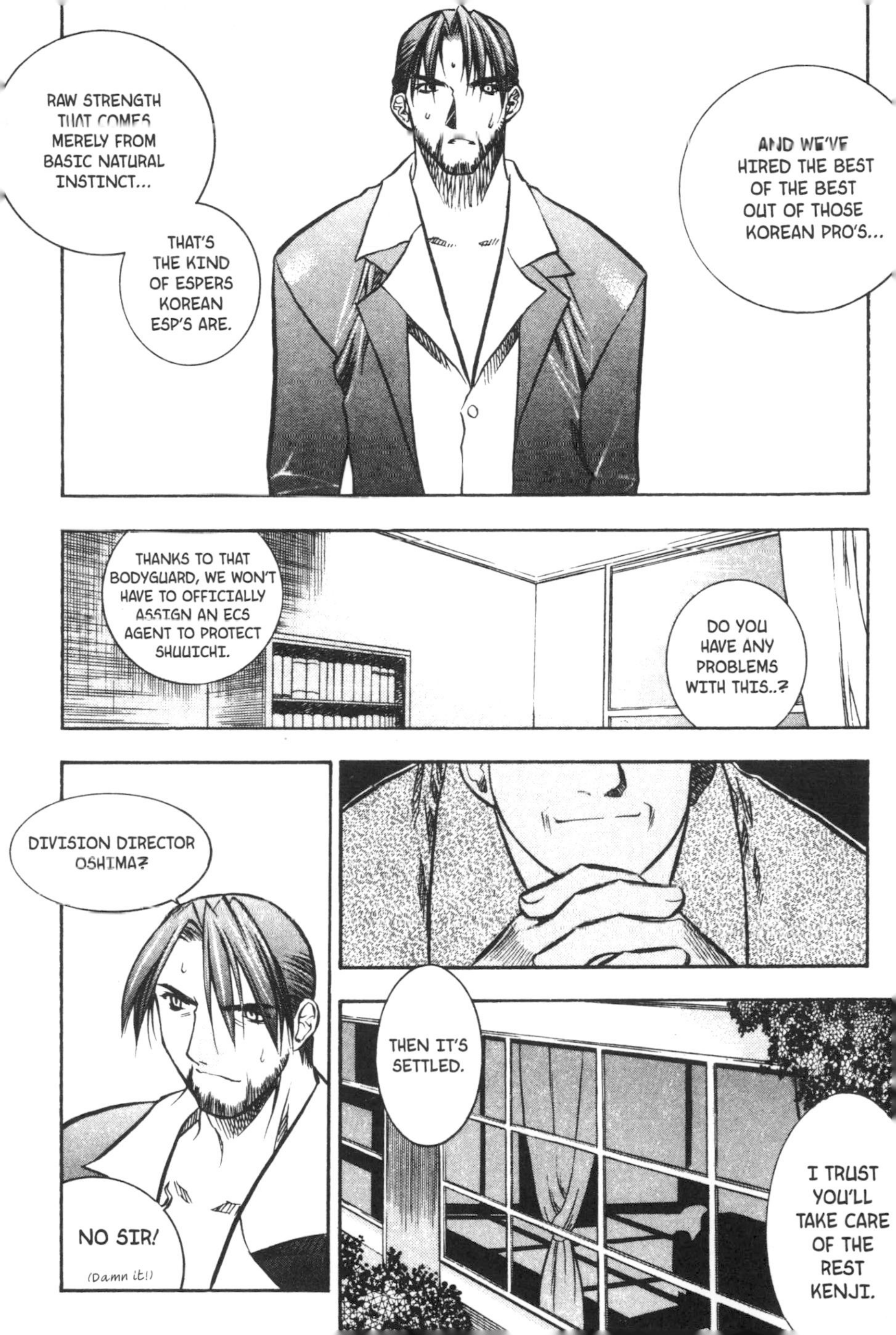
AND WE'VE HIRED THE BEST OF THE BEST OUT OF THOSE KOREAN PRO'S...
RAW STRENGTH THAT COMES MERELY FROM BASIC NATURAL INSTINCT...
THAT'S THE KIND OF ESPERS KOREAN ESP'S ARE.
DO YOU HAVE ANY PROBLEMS WITH THIS..?
THANKS TO THAT BODYGUARD, WE WON'T HAVE TO OFFICIALLY ASSIGN AN ECS AGENT TO PROTECT SHUUICHI.
DIVISION DIRECTOR OSHIMA?
NO SIR!
(Damn it!)
THEN IT'S SETTLED.
I TRUST YOU'LL TAKE CARE OF THE REST KENJI.

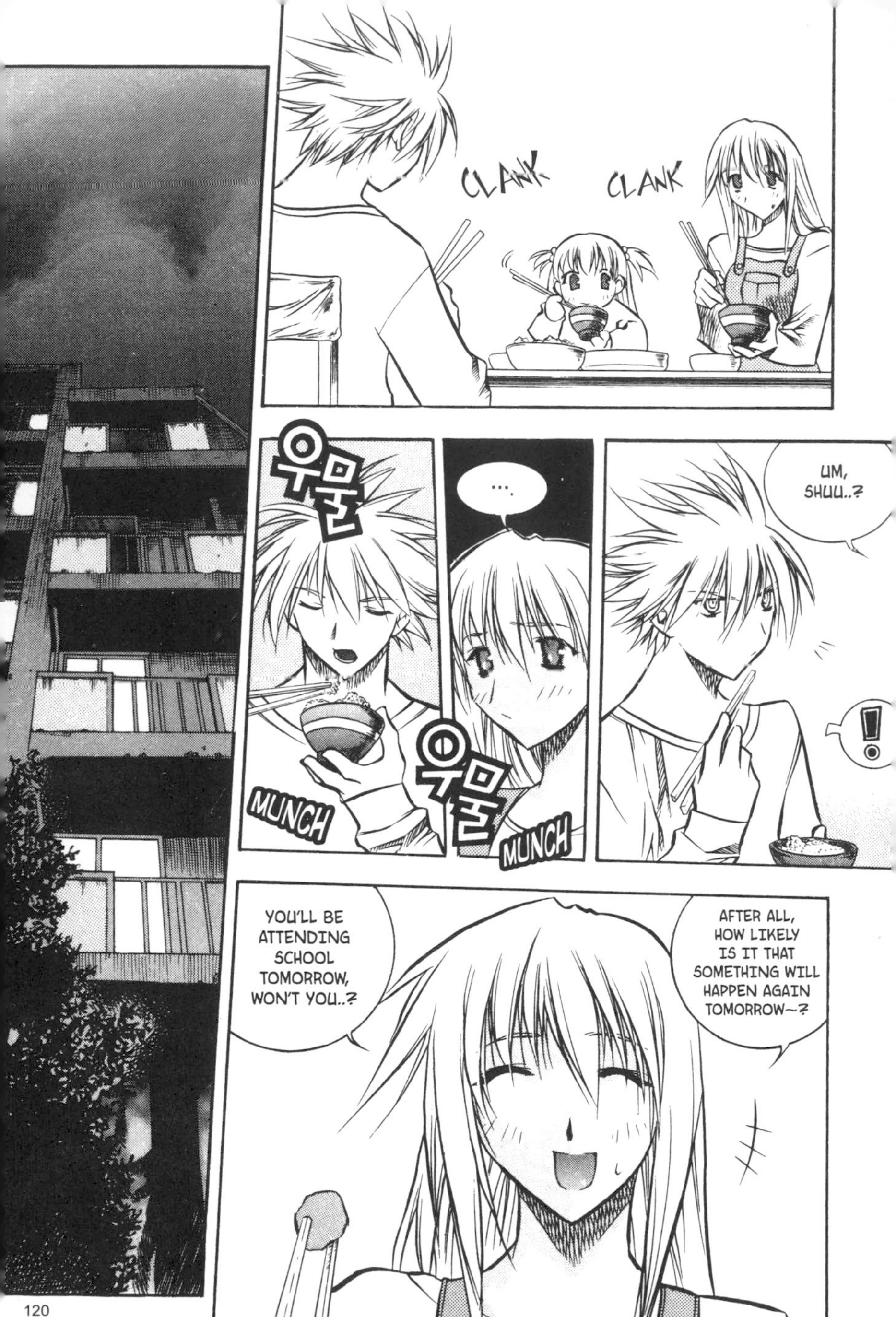

CLANK
CLANK
우물
MUNCH
우물
MUNCH
...
UM, SHUU..?
!
YOU'LL BE ATTENDING SCHOOL TOMORROW, WON'T YOU..?
AFTER ALL, HOW LIKELY IS IT THAT SOMETHING WILL HAPPEN AGAIN TOMORROW~?

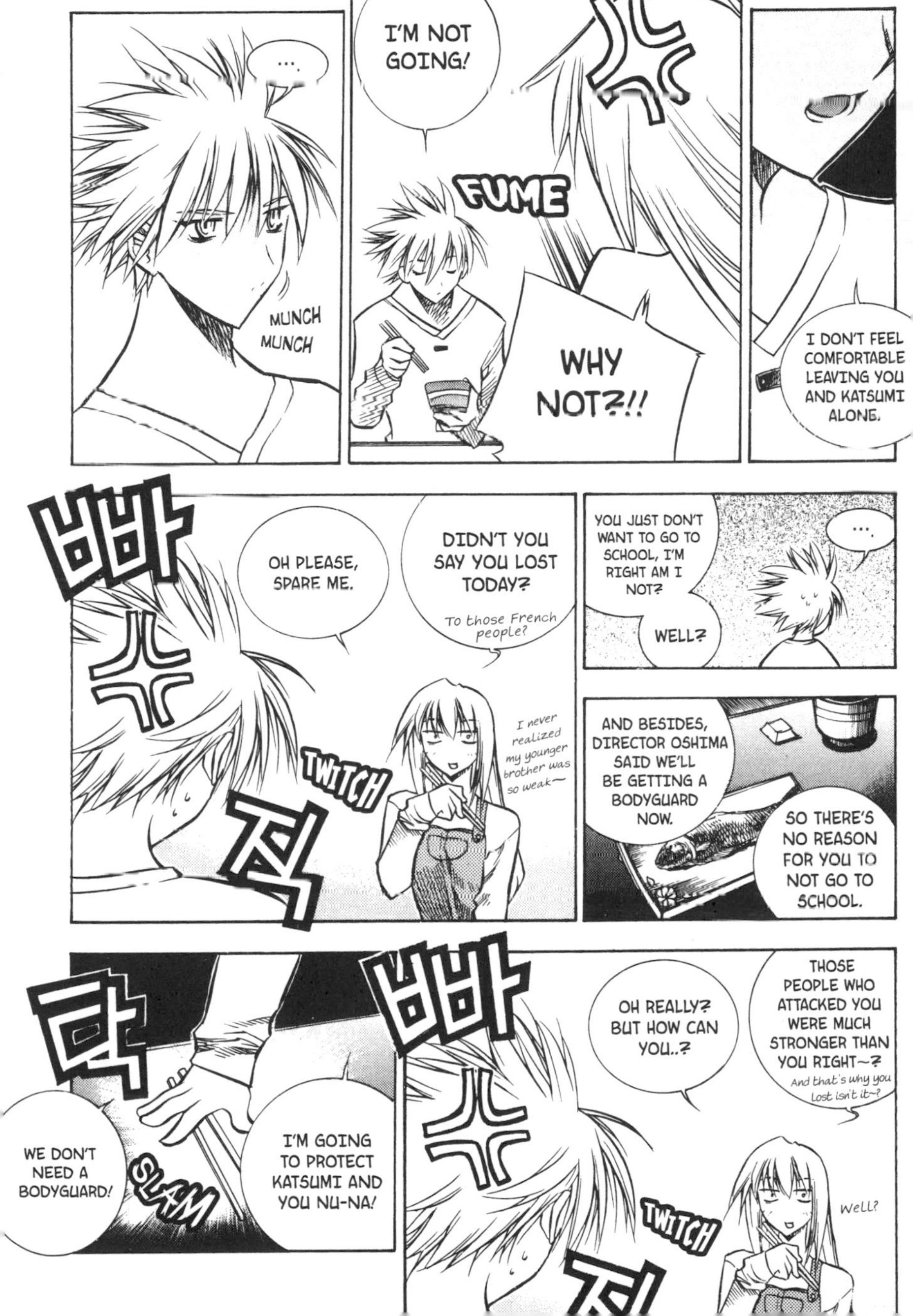

....
MUNCH MUNCH
I'M NOT GOING!
FUME
WHY NOT?!!
I DON'T FEEL COMFORTABLE LEAVING YOU AND KATSUMI ALONE.
빠
OH PLEASE, SPARE ME.
DIDN'T YOU SAY YOU LOST TODAY?
To those French people?
I never realized my younger brother was so weak~
TWITCH
직
YOU JUST DON'T WANT TO GO TO SCHOOL, I'M RIGHT AM I NOT?
WELL?
....
AND BESIDES, DIRECTOR OSHIMA SAID WE'LL BE GETTING A BODYGUARD NOW.
SO THERE'S NO REASON FOR YOU TO NOT GO TO SCHOOL.
탁
WE DON'T NEED A BODYGUARD!
SLAM
I'M GOING TO PROTECT KATSUMI AND YOU NU-NA!
빠
OH REALLY? BUT HOW CAN YOU..?
THOSE PEOPLE WHO ATTACKED YOU WERE MUCH STRONGER THAN YOU RIGHT~?
And that's why you lost isn't it~?
TWITCH
Well?

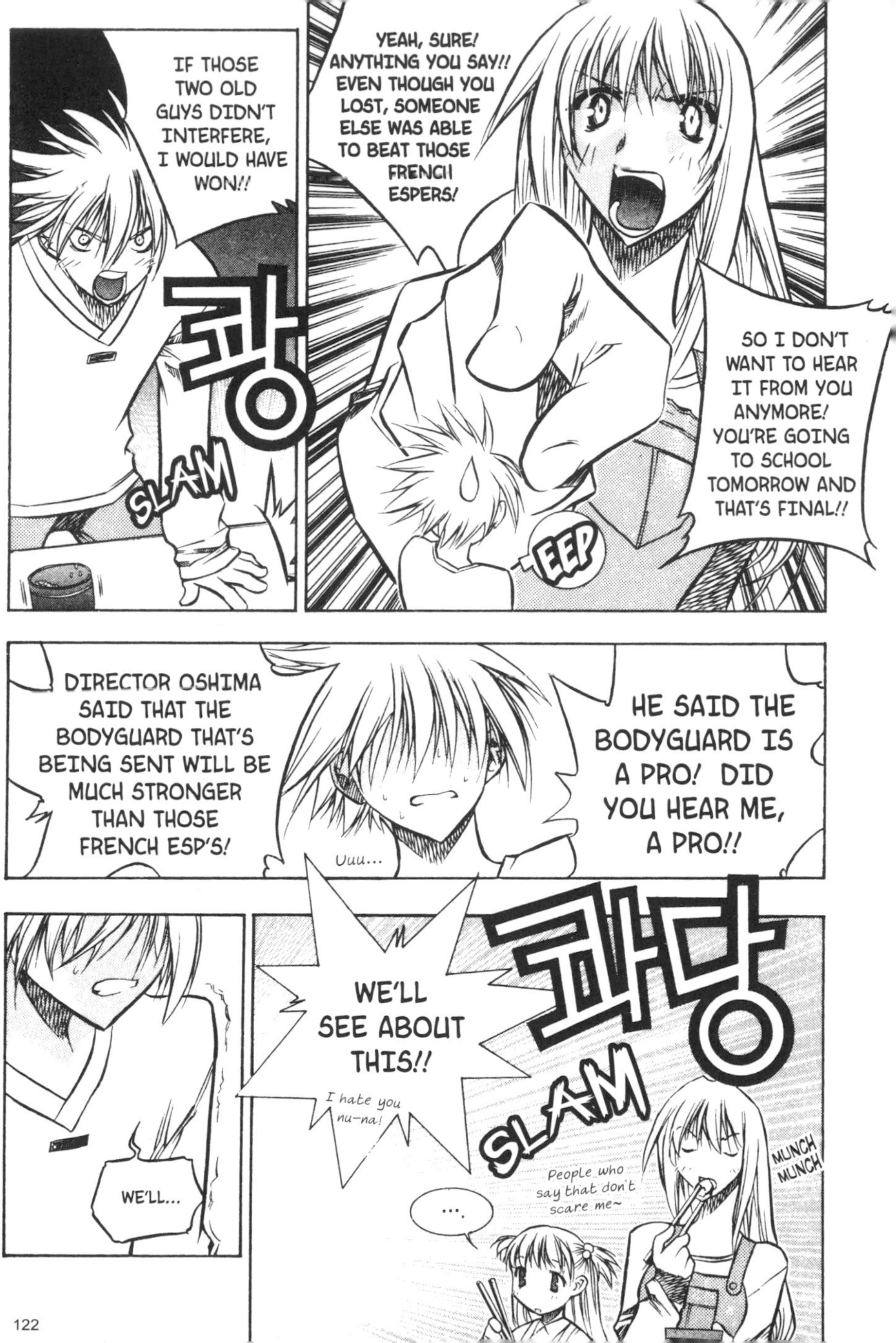
IF THOSE TWO OLD GUYS DIDN'T INTERFERE, I WOULD HAVE WON!!
쾅
SLAM
YEAH, SURE! ANYTHING YOU SAY!! EVEN THOUGH YOU LOST, SOMEONE ELSE WAS ABLE TO BEAT THOSE FRENCH ESPERS!
SO I DON'T WANT TO HEAR IT FROM YOU ANYMORE! YOU'RE GOING TO SCHOOL TOMORROW AND THAT'S FINAL!!
EEP
DIRECTOR OSHIMA SAID THAT THE BODYGUARD THAT'S BEING SENT WILL BE MUCH STRONGER THAN THOSE FRENCH ESP'S!
Uuu...
HE SAID THE BODYGUARD IS A PRO! DID YOU HEAR ME, A PRO!!
WE'LL...
WE'LL SEE ABOUT THIS!!
I hate you nu-na!
콰당
SLAM
...
People who say that don't scare me~
MUNCH MUNCH

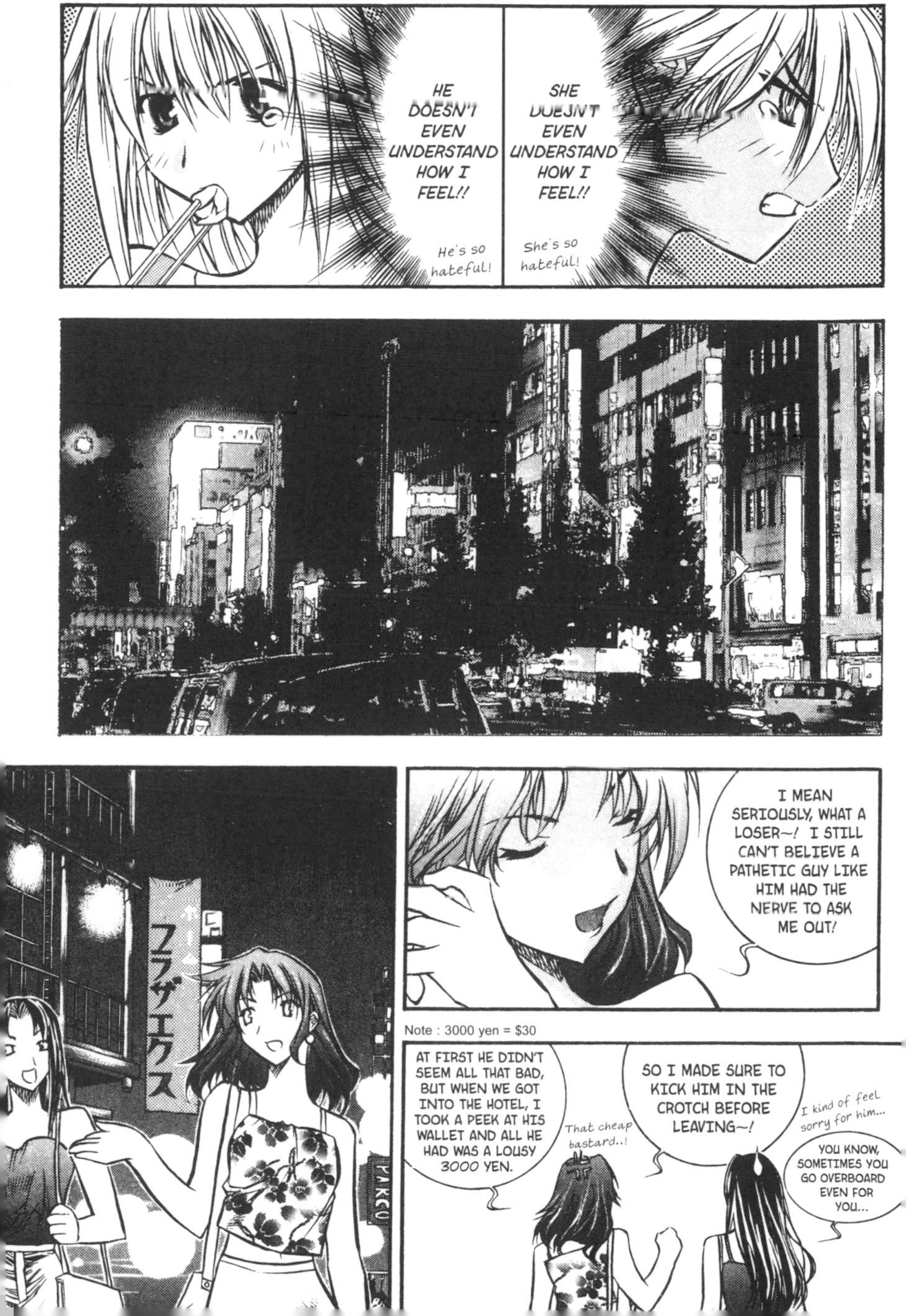
SHE DOESN'T EVEN UNDERSTAND HOW I FEEL!!
She's so hateful!
HE DOESN'T EVEN UNDERSTAND HOW I FEEL!!
He's so hateful!
I MEAN SERIOUSLY, WHAT A LOSER~! I STILL CAN'T BELIEVE A PATHETIC GUY LIKE HIM HAD THE NERVE TO ASK ME OUT!
Note : 3000 yen = $30
AT FIRST HE DIDN'T SEEM ALL THAT BAD, BUT WHEN WE GOT INTO THE HOTEL, I TOOK A PEEK AT HIS WALLET AND ALL HE HAD WAS A LOUSY 3000 YEN.
SO I MADE SURE TO KICK HIM IN THE CROTCH BEFORE LEAVING~!
That cheap bastard..!
I kind of feel sorry for him...
YOU KNOW, SOMETIMES YOU GO OVERBOARD EVEN FOR YOU...
フラザエクス
PARCO

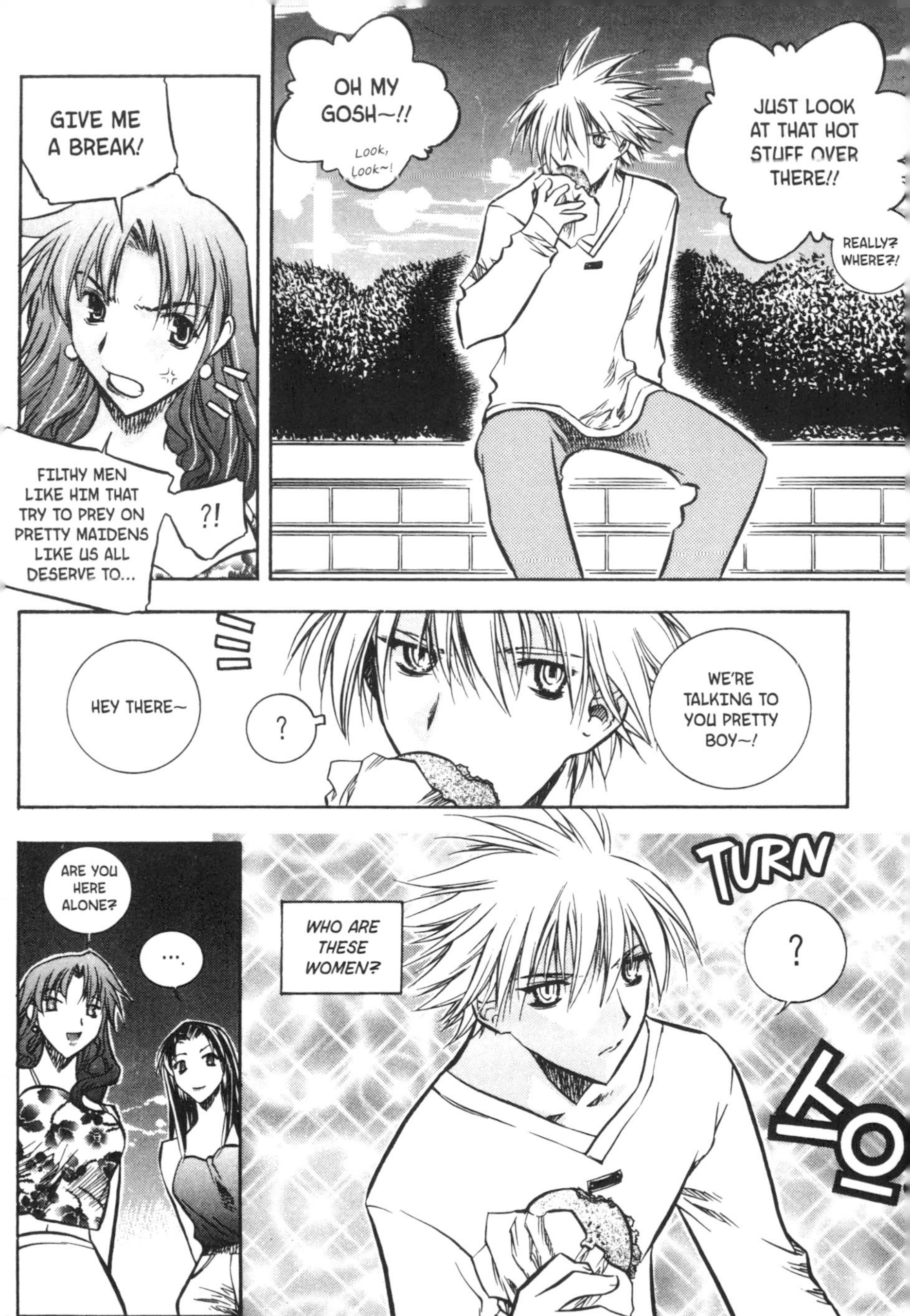
GIVE ME A BREAK!
FILTHY MEN LIKE HIM THAT TRY TO PREY ON PRETTY MAIDENS LIKE US ALL DESERVE TO...
?!
OH MY GOSH~!!
Look, look~!
JUST LOOK AT THAT HOT STUFF OVER THERE!!
REALLY? WHERE?!
HEY THERE~
?
WE'RE TALKING TO YOU PRETTY BOY~!
ARE YOU HERE ALONE?
....
WHO ARE THESE WOMEN?
TURN
?

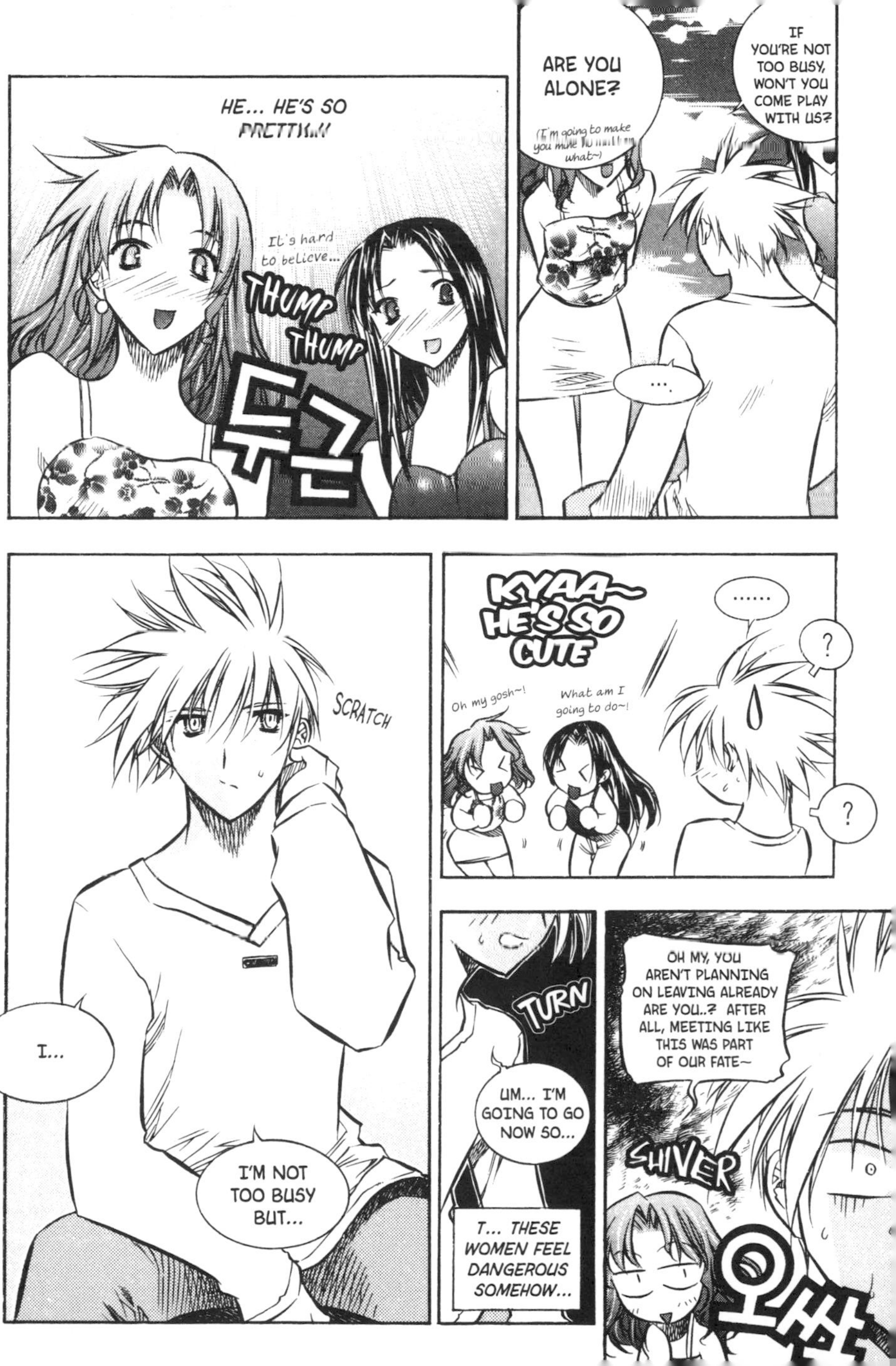

HE... HE'S SO
It's hard to believe...
THUMP THUMP
두근
ARE YOU ALONE?
(I'm going to make you
what~)
IF YOU'RE NOT TOO BUSY, WON'T YOU COME PLAY WITH US?
....
SCRATCH
I...
I'M NOT TOO BUSY BUT...
KYAA~ HE'S SO CUTE
Oh my gosh~!
What am I going to do~!
......
?
?
TURN
UM... I'M GOING TO GO NOW SO...
T... THESE WOMEN FEEL DANGEROUS SOMEHOW...
OH MY, YOU AREN'T PLANNING ON LEAVING ALREADY ARE YOU..? AFTER ALL, MEETING LIKE THIS WAS PART OF OUR FATE~
SHIVER
오싹

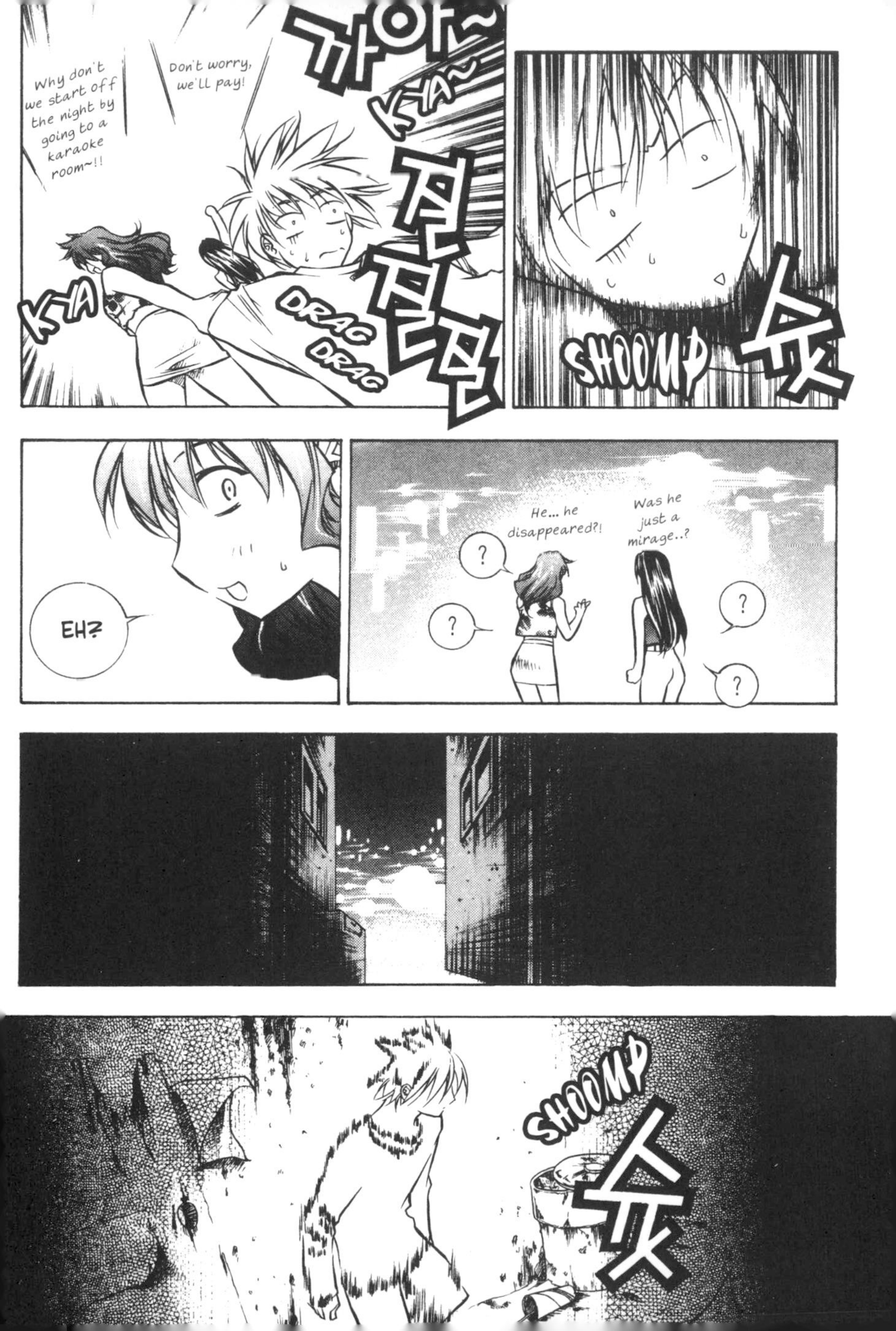

Why don't we start off the night by going to a karaoke room~!!
Don't worry, we'll pay!
KYA~
KYA
DRAG DRAG
SHOOMP
EH?
He... he disappeared?!
Was he just a mirage..?
?
?
?
?
SHOOMP

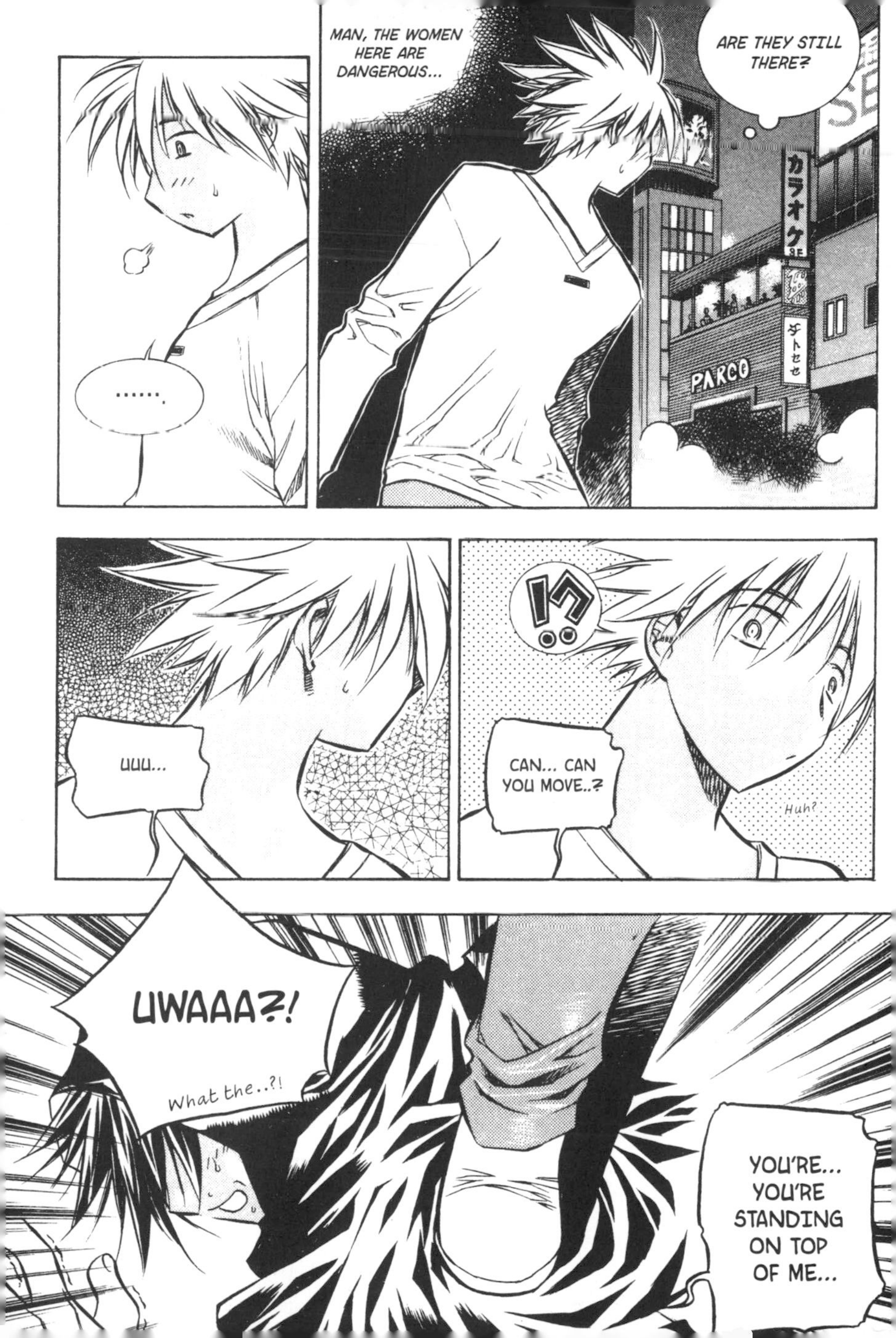
ARE THEY STILL THERE?
MAN, THE WOMEN HERE ARE DANGEROUS...
カラオケ
PARCO
....
CAN... CAN YOU MOVE..?
Huh?
uuu...
YOU'RE... YOU'RE STANDING ON TOP OF ME...
UWAAA?!
What the..?!

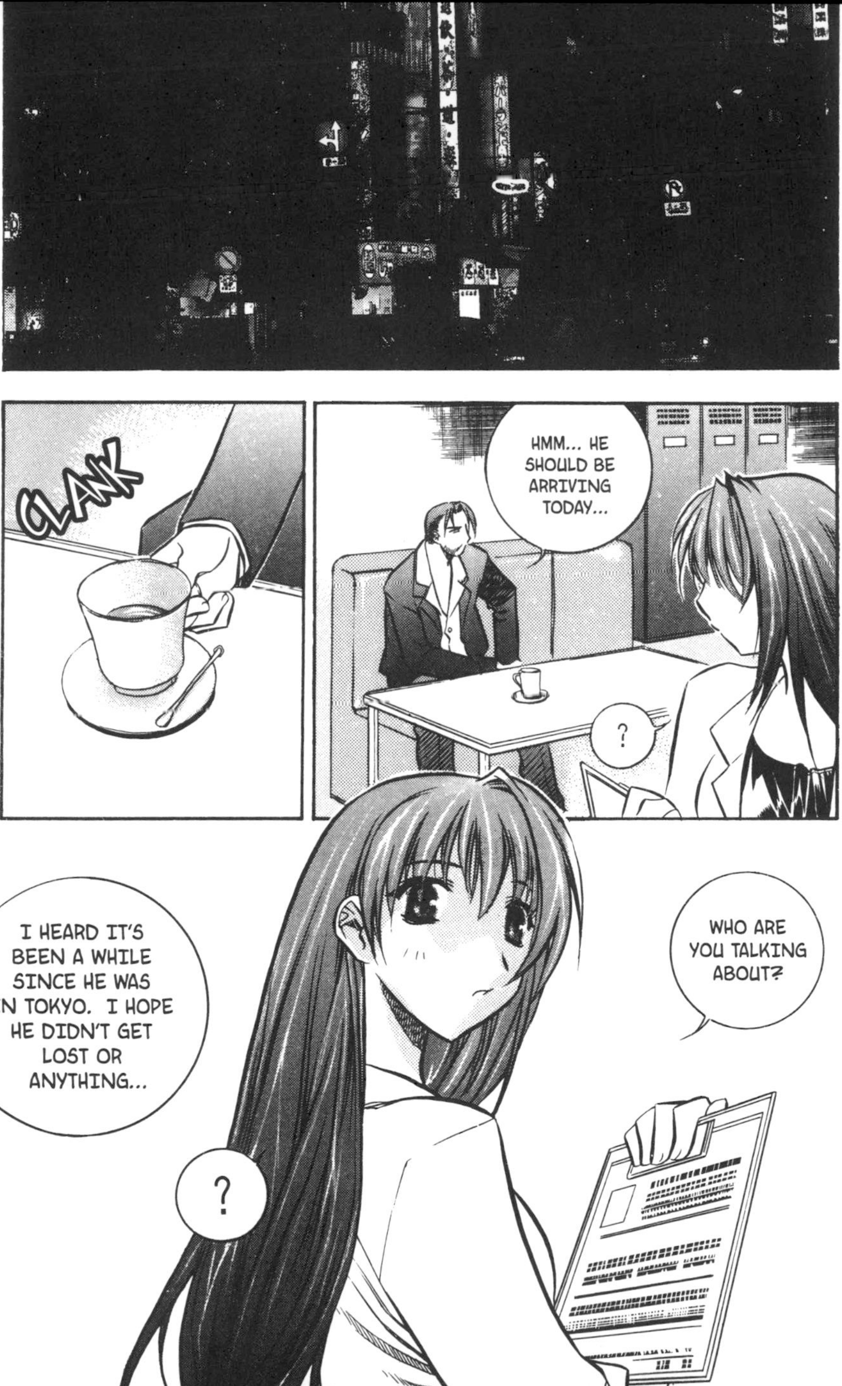

HMM... HE SHOULD BE ARRIVING TODAY...
?
CLANK
WHO ARE YOU TALKING ABOUT?
I HEARD IT'S BEEN A WHILE SINCE HE WAS IN TOKYO. I HOPE HE DIDN'T GET LOST OR ANYTHING...
?

CIRCLE 12

French Espers

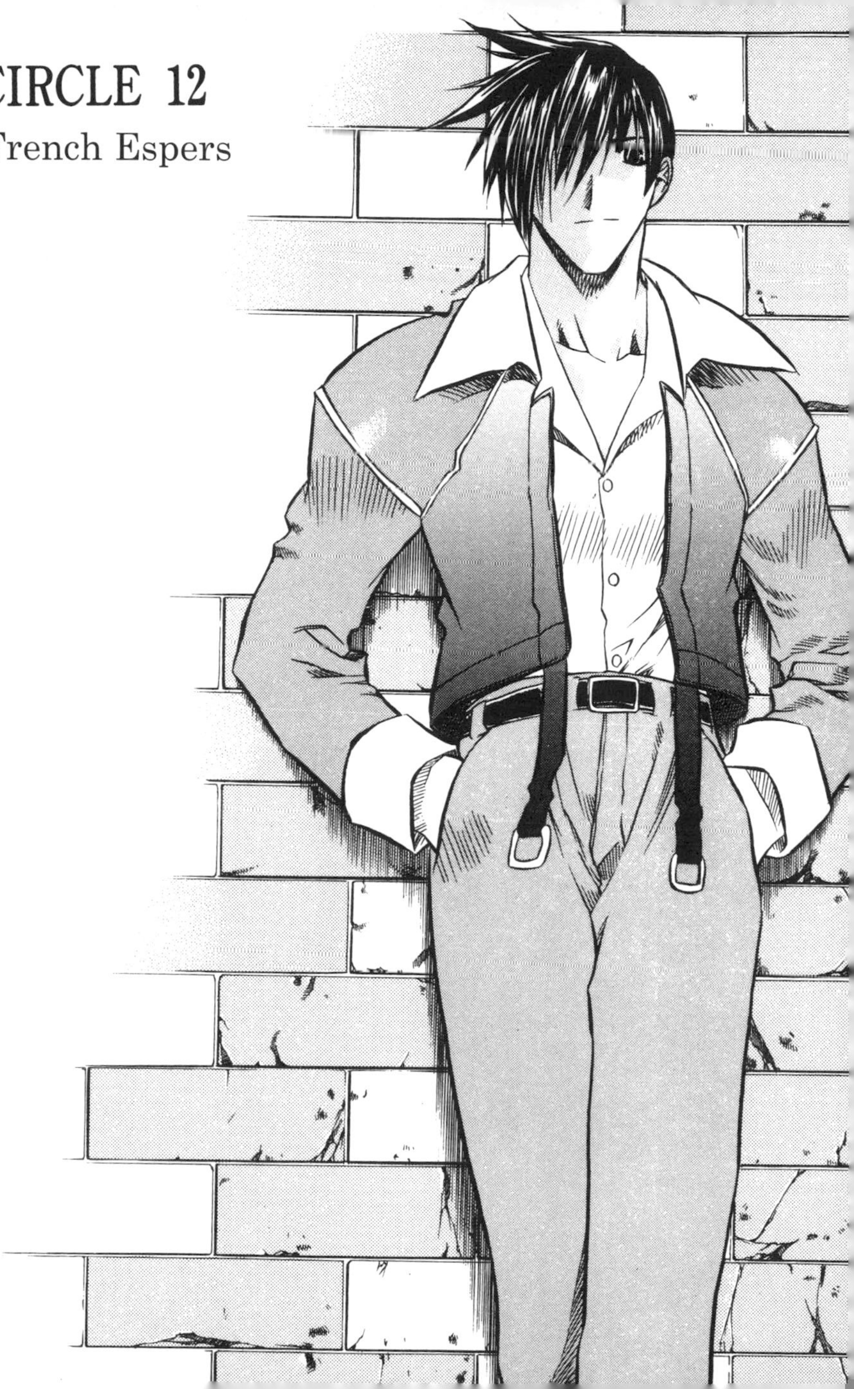

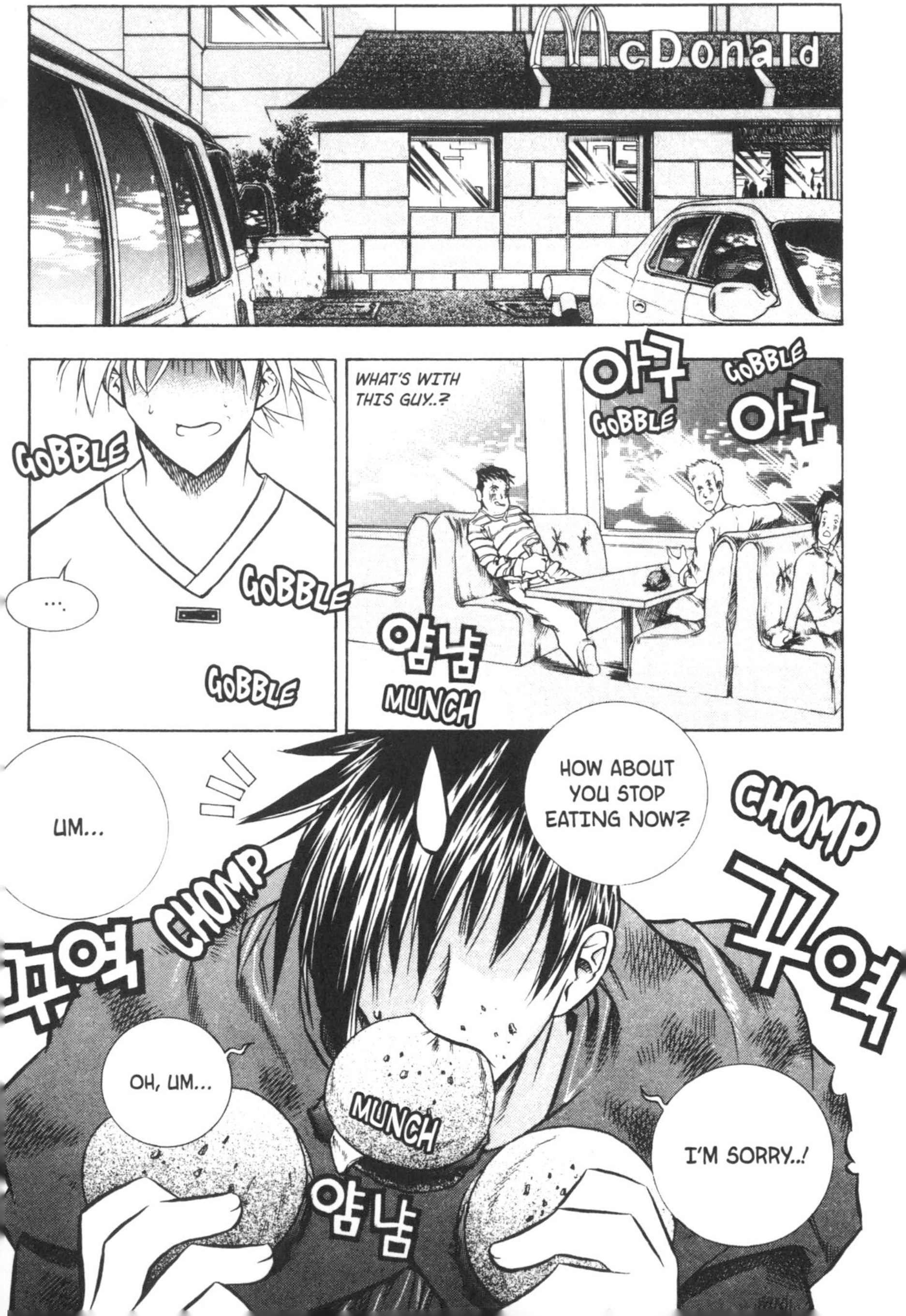
McDonald
GOBBLE
GOBBLE
GOBBLE
...
WHAT'S WITH THIS GUY..?
아구
GOBBLE
GOBBLE
아구
얌냠
MUNCH
HOW ABOUT YOU STOP EATING NOW?
UM...
CHOMP
꾸역
CHOMP
꾸역
OH, UM...
MUNCH
얌냠
I'M SORRY..!

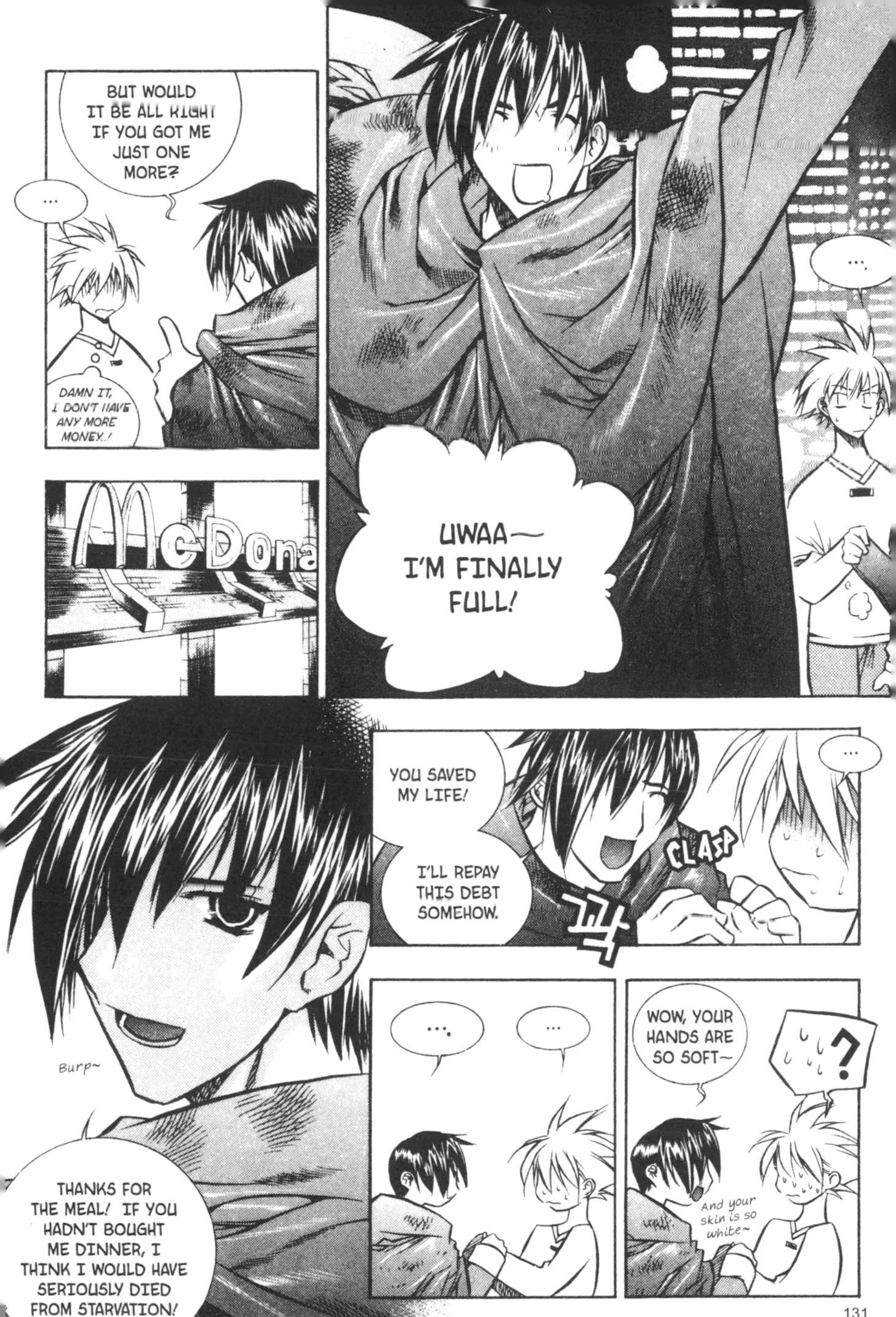
BUT WOULD IT BE ALL RIGHT IF YOU GOT ME JUST ONE MORE?
...
DAMN IT, I DON'T HAVE ANY MORE MONEY..!
McDona
UWAA— I'M FINALLY FULL!
...
Burp~
THANKS FOR THE MEAL! IF YOU HADN'T BOUGHT ME DINNER, I THINK I WOULD HAVE SERIOUSLY DIED FROM STARVATION!
YOU SAVED MY LIFE!
I'LL REPAY THIS DEBT SOMEHOW.
CLASP
...
...
...
WOW, YOUR HANDS ARE SO SOFT~
And your skin is so white~
?

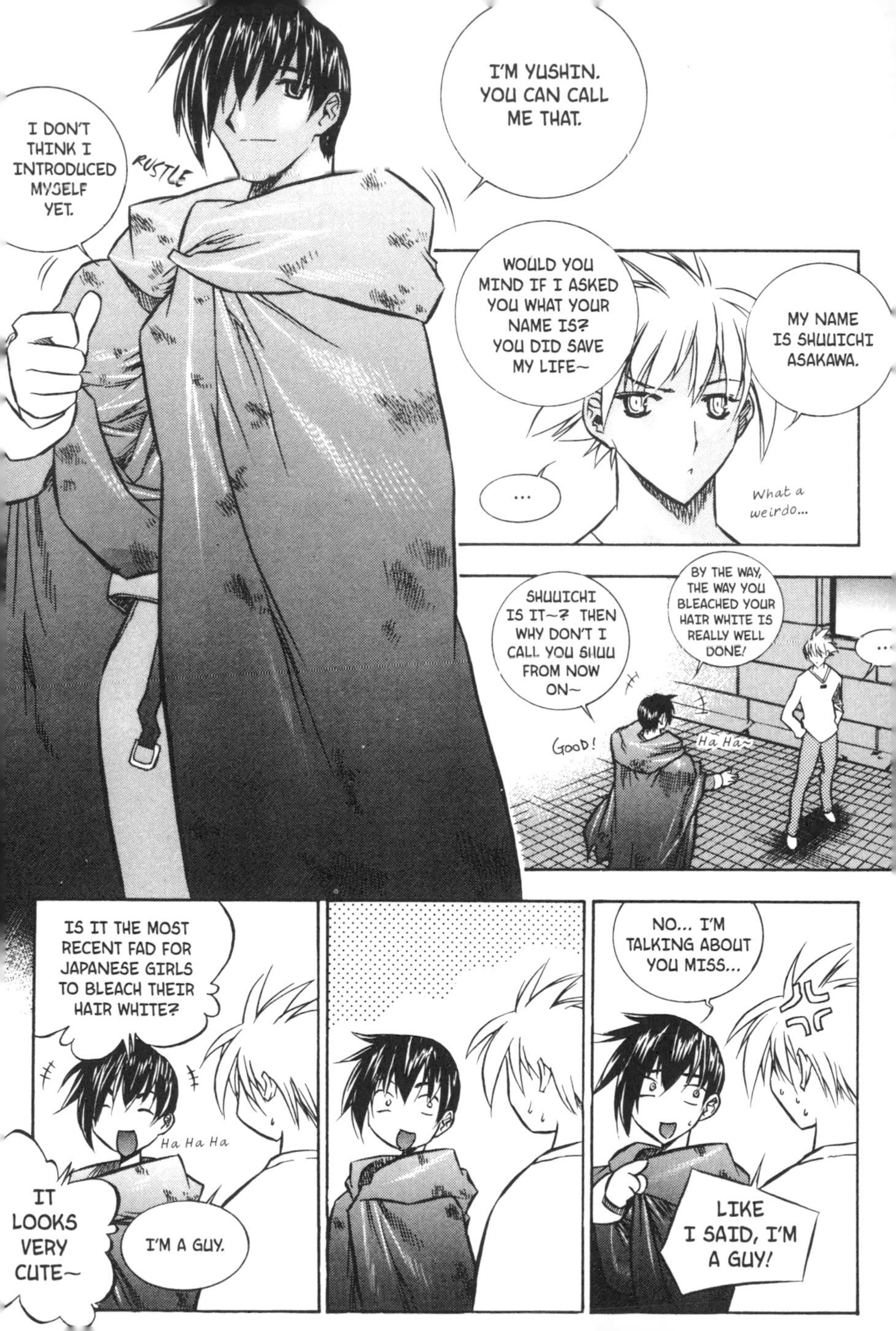

I DON'T THINK I INTRODUCED MYSELF YET.
RUSTLE
I'M YUSHIN. YOU CAN CALL ME THAT.
WOULD YOU MIND IF I ASKED YOU WHAT YOUR NAME IS? YOU DID SAVE MY LIFE~
MY NAME IS SHUUICHI ASAKAWA.
...
What a weirdo...
SHUUICHI IS IT~? THEN WHY DON'T I CALL YOU SHUU FROM NOW ON~
GOOD!
Ha Ha~
BY THE WAY, THE WAY YOU BLEACHED YOUR HAIR WHITE IS REALLY WELL DONE!
...
IS IT THE MOST RECENT FAD FOR JAPANESE GIRLS TO BLEACH THEIR HAIR WHITE?
Ha Ha Ha
IT LOOKS VERY CUTE~
I'M A GUY.
NO... I'M TALKING ABOUT YOU MISS...
LIKE I SAID, I'M A GUY!

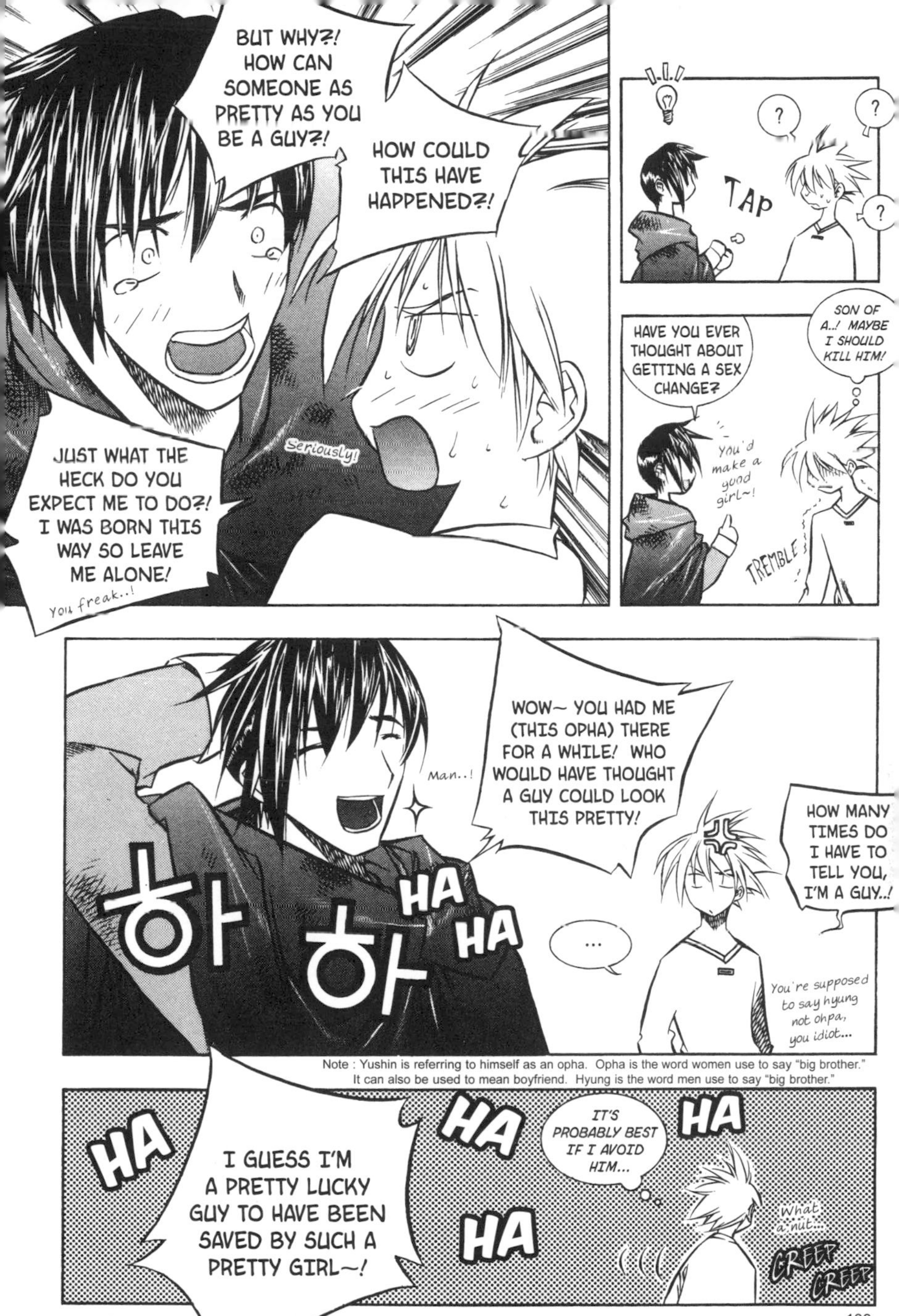

BUT WHY?! HOW CAN SOMEONE AS PRETTY AS YOU BE A GUY?!
HOW COULD THIS HAVE HAPPENED?!
JUST WHAT THE HECK DO YOU EXPECT ME TO DO?! I WAS BORN THIS WAY SO LEAVE ME ALONE!
You freak..!
Seriously!
!.!.!
?
?
?
TAP
HAVE YOU EVER THOUGHT ABOUT GETTING A SEX CHANGE?
SON OF A..! MAYBE I SHOULD KILL HIM!
You'd make a good girl~!
TREMBLE
WOW~ YOU HAD ME (THIS OPHA) THERE FOR A WHILE! WHO WOULD HAVE THOUGHT A GUY COULD LOOK THIS PRETTY!
Man..!
하 하
HA HA
...
HOW MANY TIMES DO I HAVE TO TELL YOU, I'M A GUY..!
You're supposed to say hyung not ohpa, you idiot...
HA
HA
I GUESS I'M A PRETTY LUCKY GUY TO HAVE BEEN SAVED BY SUCH A PRETTY GIRL~!
IT'S PROBABLY BEST IF I AVOID HIM...
HA
HA
What a nut...
CREEP CREEP

Note : Yushin is referring to himself as an opha. Opha is the word women use to say "big brother." It can also be used to mean boyfriend. Hyung is the word men use to say "big brother."

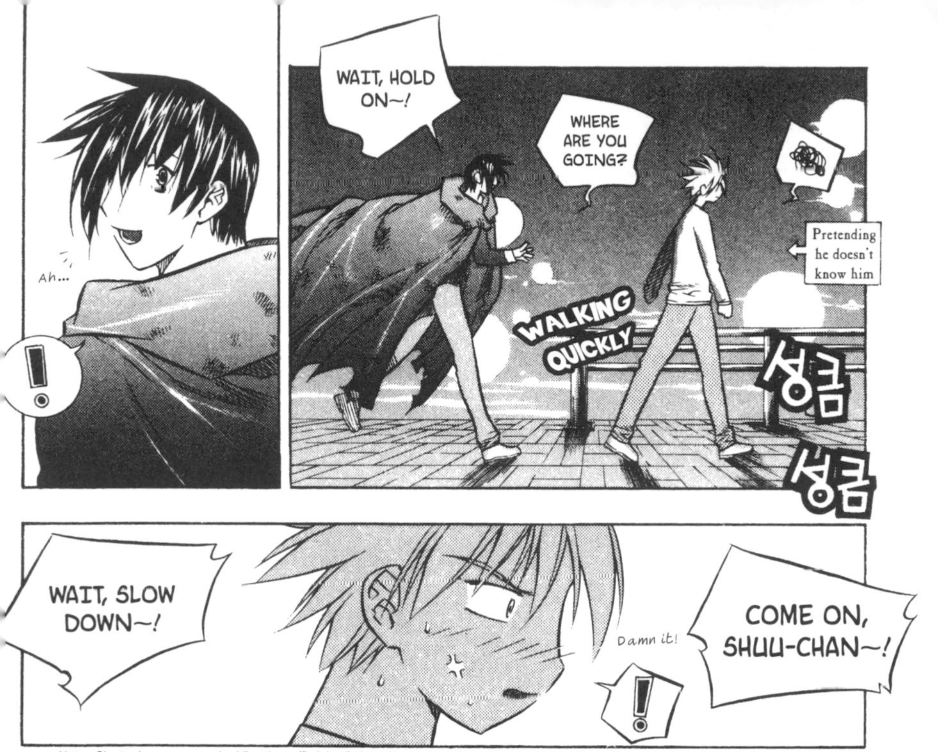
Ah...
WAIT, HOLD ON~!
WHERE ARE YOU GOING?
Pretending he doesn't know him
WALKING QUICKLY
성큼
성큼
WAIT, SLOW DOWN~!
Damn it!
COME ON, SHUU-CHAN~!

Note : Shortening a name and adding the suffix "chan" gives the name a cute and feminine intonation. It implies a certain amount of affection on the part of the speaker.

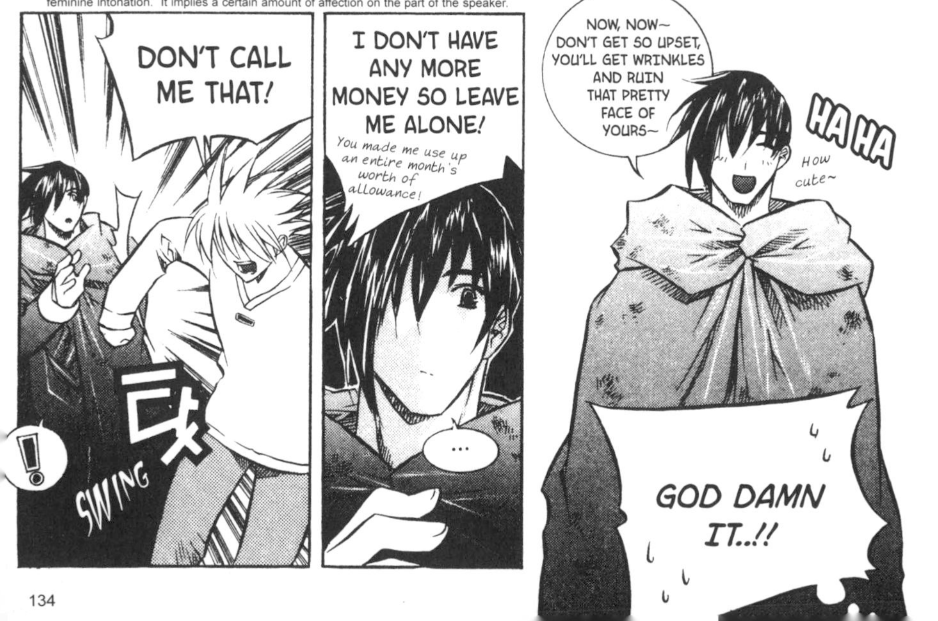
DON'T CALL ME THAT!
SWING
I DON'T HAVE ANY MORE MONEY SO LEAVE ME ALONE!
You made me use up an entire month's worth of allowance!
...
NOW, NOW~ DON'T GET SO UPSET, YOU'LL GET WRINKLES AND RUIN THAT PRETTY FACE OF YOURS~
HA HA
How cute~
GOD DAMN IT..!!

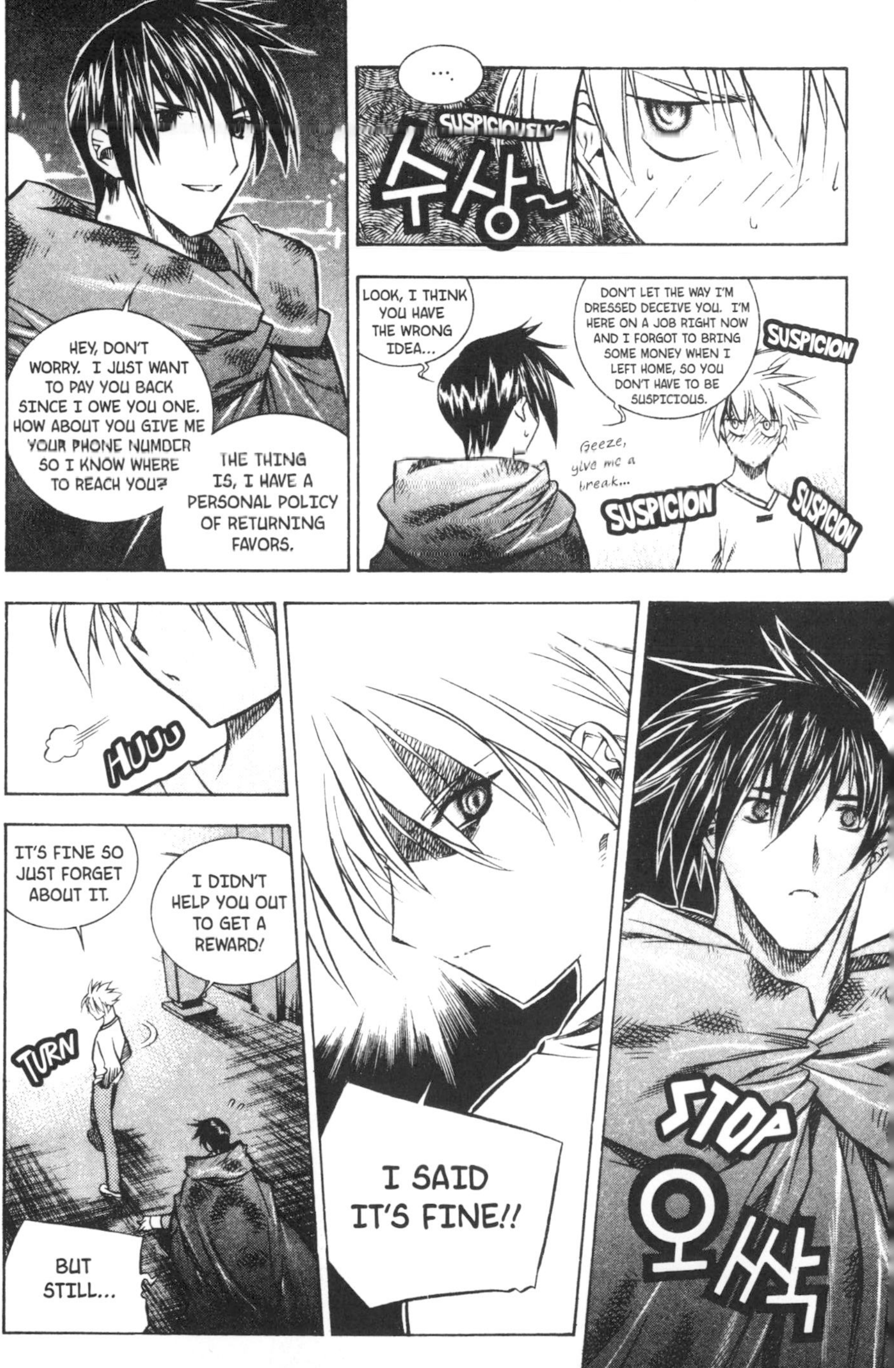
HEY, DON'T WORRY. I JUST WANT TO PAY YOU BACK SINCE I OWE YOU ONE. HOW ABOUT YOU GIVE ME YOUR PHONE NUMBER SO I KNOW WHERE TO REACH YOU?
THE THING IS, I HAVE A PERSONAL POLICY OF RETURNING FAVORS.
...
SUSPICIOUSLY~
수상~
LOOK, I THINK YOU HAVE THE WRONG IDEA...
DON'T LET THE WAY I'M DRESSED DECEIVE YOU. I'M HERE ON A JOB RIGHT NOW AND I FORGOT TO BRING SOME MONEY WHEN I LEFT HOME, SO YOU DON'T HAVE TO BE SUSPICIOUS.
Geeze, give me a break...
SUSPICION
SUSPICION
SUSPICION
HUUU
IT'S FINE SO JUST FORGET ABOUT IT.
I DIDN'T HELP YOU OUT TO GET A REWARD!
TURN
BUT STILL...
I SAID IT'S FINE!!
STOP
오싹

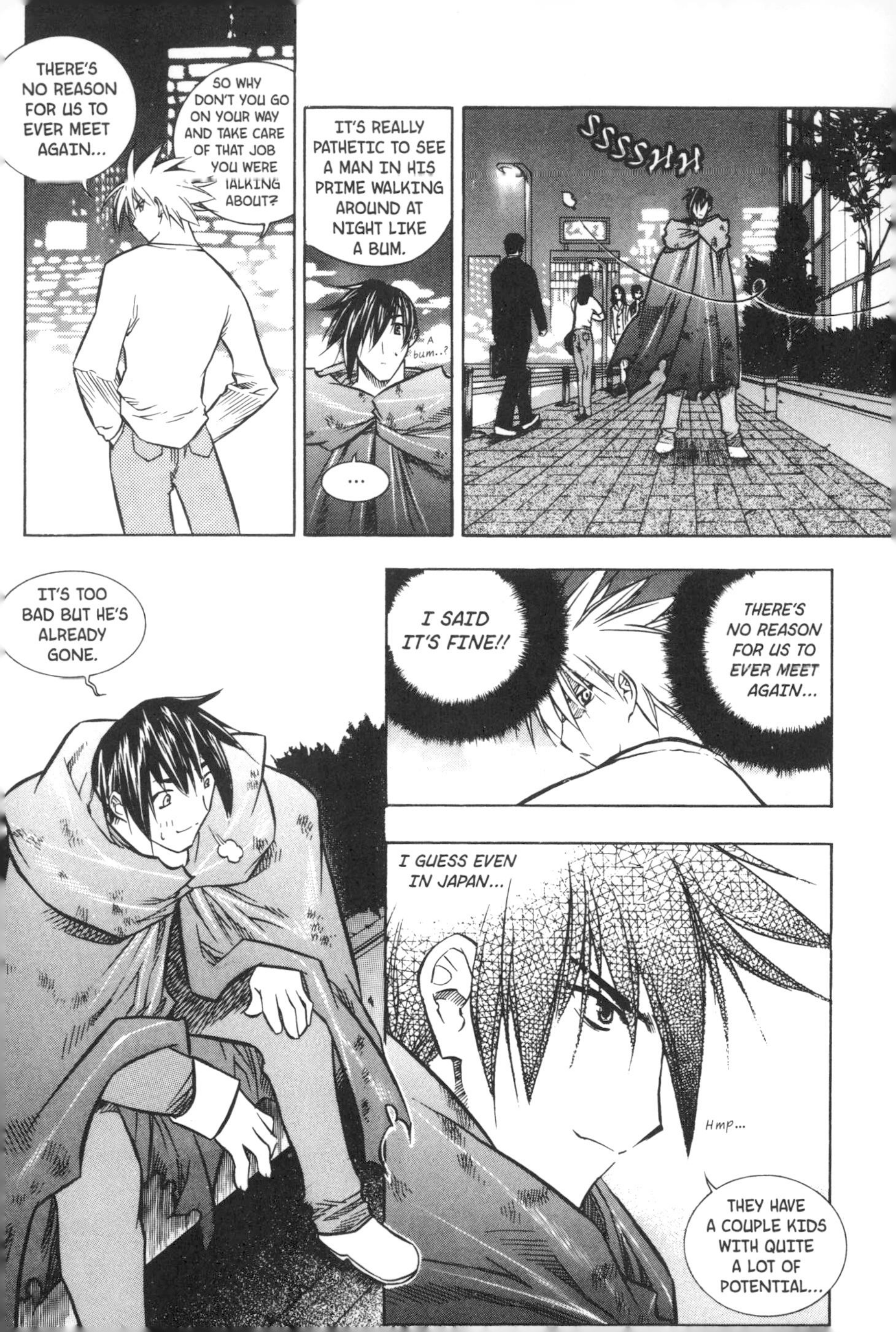
THERE'S NO REASON FOR US TO EVER MEET AGAIN...
SO WHY DON'T YOU GO ON YOUR WAY AND TAKE CARE OF THAT JOB YOU WERE TALKING ABOUT?
IT'S REALLY PATHETIC TO SEE A MAN IN HIS PRIME WALKING AROUND AT NIGHT LIKE A BUM.
A bum..?
...
SSSSHH
IT'S TOO BAD BUT HE'S ALREADY GONE.
I SAID IT'S FINE!!
THERE'S NO REASON FOR US TO EVER MEET AGAIN...
I GUESS EVEN IN JAPAN...
Hmp...
THEY HAVE A COUPLE KIDS WITH QUITE A LOT OF POTENTIAL...

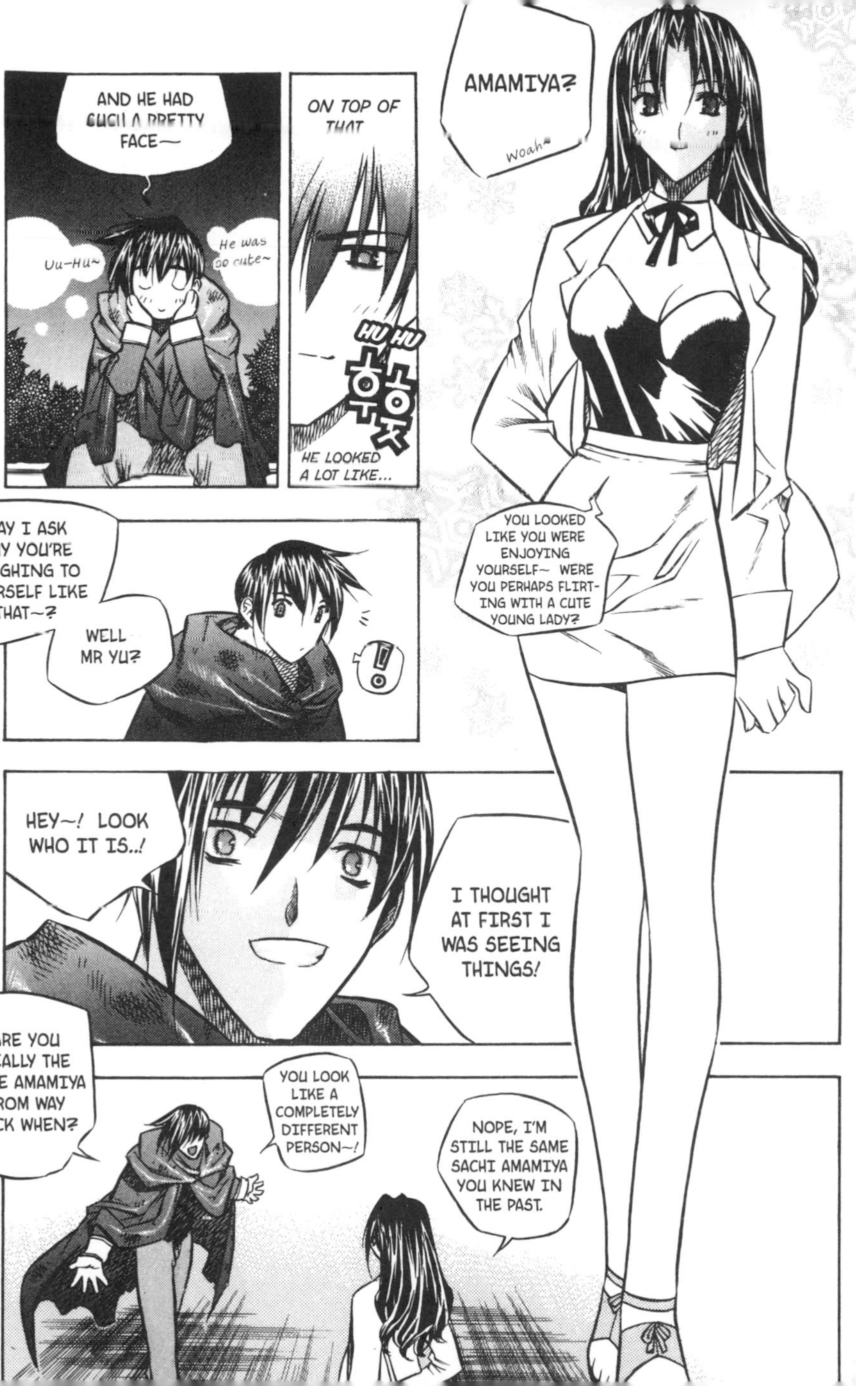
AND HE HAD SUCH A PRETTY FACE~
Uu-Hu~
He was so cute~
ON TOP OF THAT
HU HU
후훗
HE LOOKED A LOT LIKE...
AMAMIYA?
Woah~
MAY I ASK WHY YOU'RE LAUGHING TO YOURSELF LIKE THAT~?
WELL MR YU?
!
YOU LOOKED LIKE YOU WERE ENJOYING YOURSELF~ WERE YOU PERHAPS FLIRTING WITH A CUTE YOUNG LADY?
HEY~! LOOK WHO IT IS..!
I THOUGHT AT FIRST I WAS SEEING THINGS!
ARE YOU REALLY THE SAME AMAMIYA FROM WAY BACK WHEN?
YOU LOOK LIKE A COMPLETELY DIFFERENT PERSON~!
NOPE, I'M STILL THE SAME SACHI AMAMIYA YOU KNEW IN THE PAST.

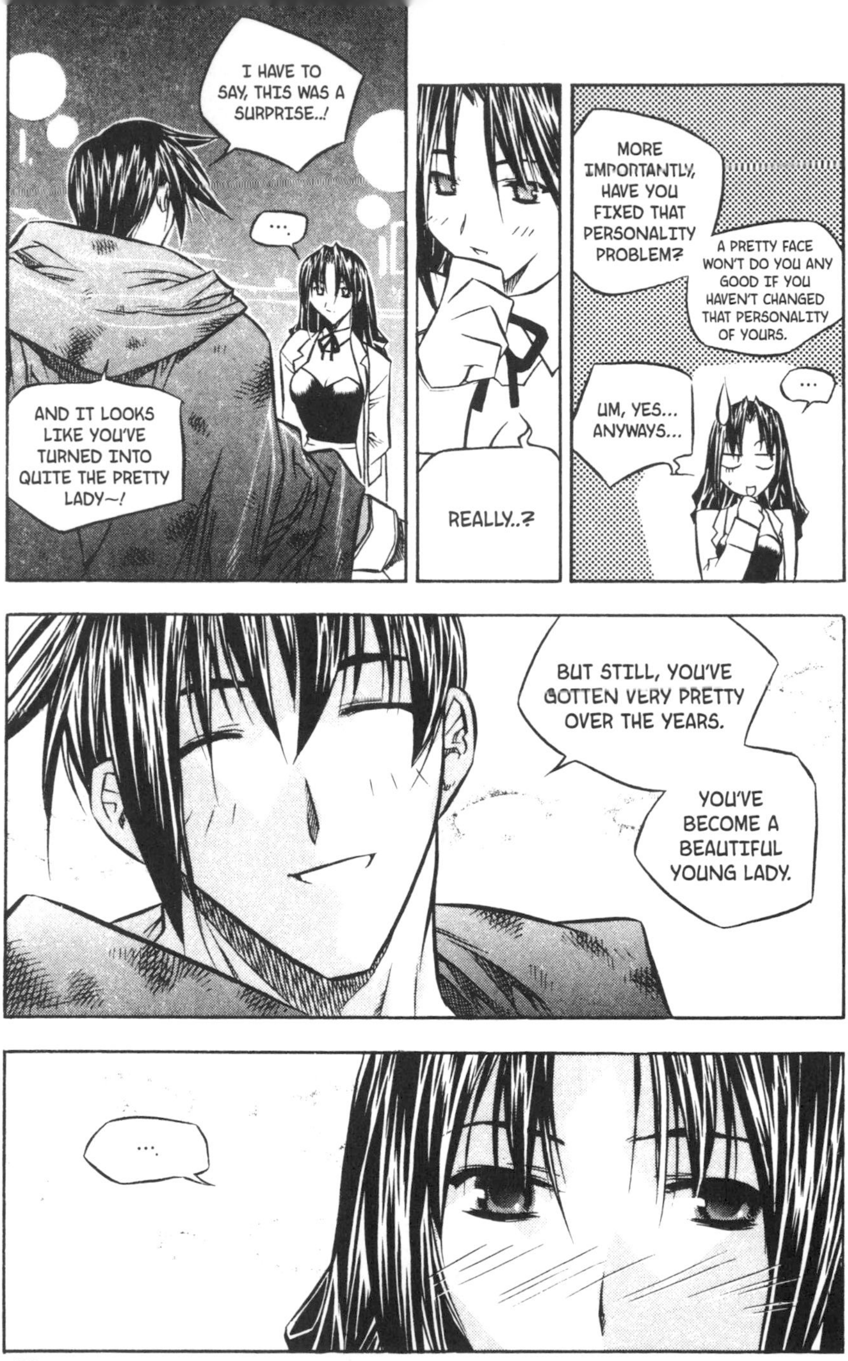
I HAVE TO SAY, THIS WAS A SURPRISE..!
...
AND IT LOOKS LIKE YOU'VE TURNED INTO QUITE THE PRETTY LADY~!
REALLY..?
MORE IMPORTANTLY, HAVE YOU FIXED THAT PERSONALITY PROBLEM?
A PRETTY FACE WON'T DO YOU ANY GOOD IF YOU HAVEN'T CHANGED THAT PERSONALITY OF YOURS.
UM, YES... ANYWAYS...
...
BUT STILL, YOU'VE GOTTEN VERY PRETTY OVER THE YEARS.
YOU'VE BECOME A BEAUTIFUL YOUNG LADY.
...

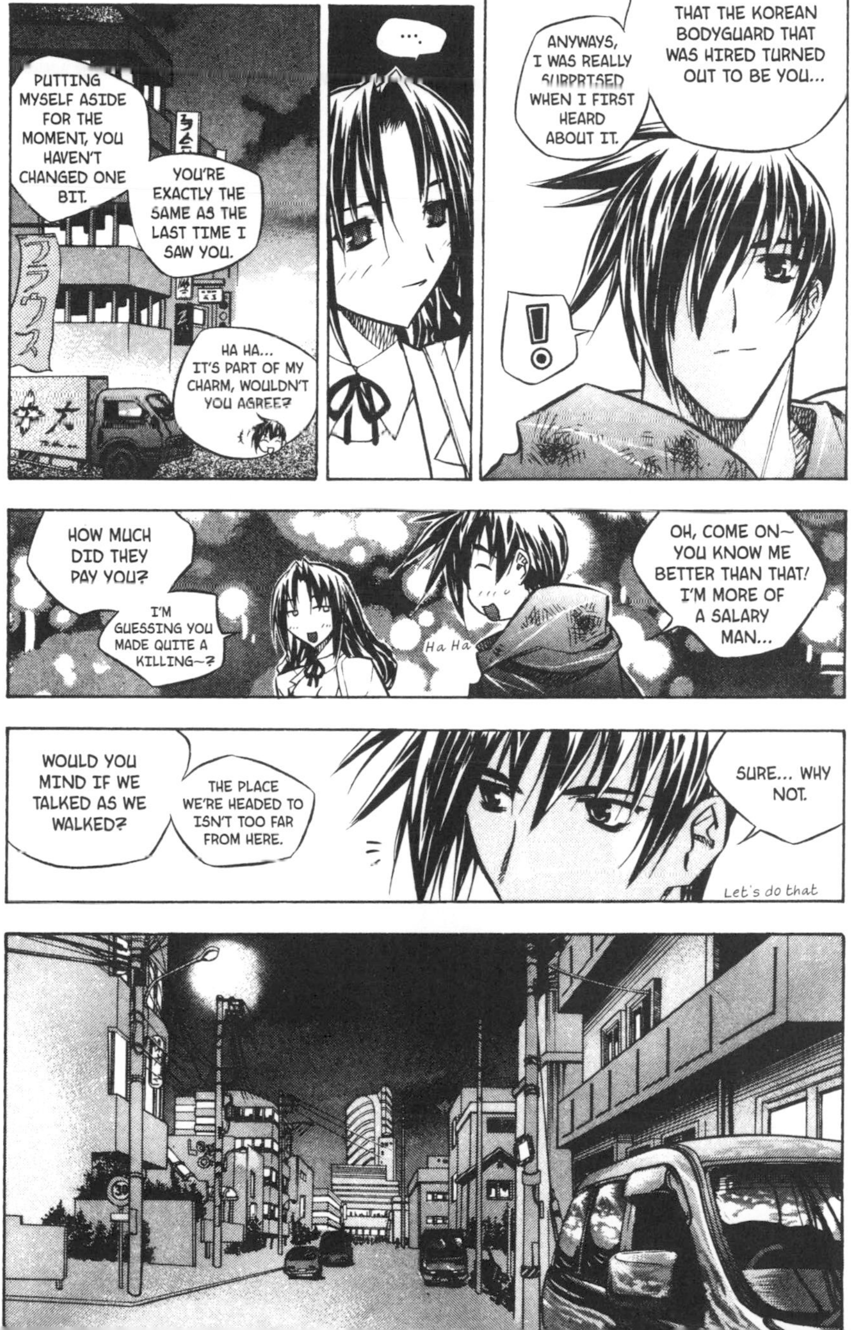
ANYWAYS, I WAS REALLY SURPRISED WHEN I FIRST HEARD ABOUT IT.
THAT THE KOREAN BODYGUARD THAT WAS HIRED TURNED OUT TO BE YOU...
!
...
PUTTING MYSELF ASIDE FOR THE MOMENT, YOU HAVEN'T CHANGED ONE BIT.
YOU'RE EXACTLY THE SAME AS THE LAST TIME I SAW YOU.
HA HA... IT'S PART OF MY CHARM, WOULDN'T YOU AGREE?
OH, COME ON~ YOU KNOW ME BETTER THAN THAT! I'M MORE OF A SALARY MAN...
Ha Ha
HOW MUCH DID THEY PAY YOU?
I'M GUESSING YOU MADE QUITE A KILLING~?
WOULD YOU MIND IF WE TALKED AS WE WALKED?
THE PLACE WE'RE HEADED TO ISN'T TOO FAR FROM HERE.
SURE... WHY NOT.
Let's do that

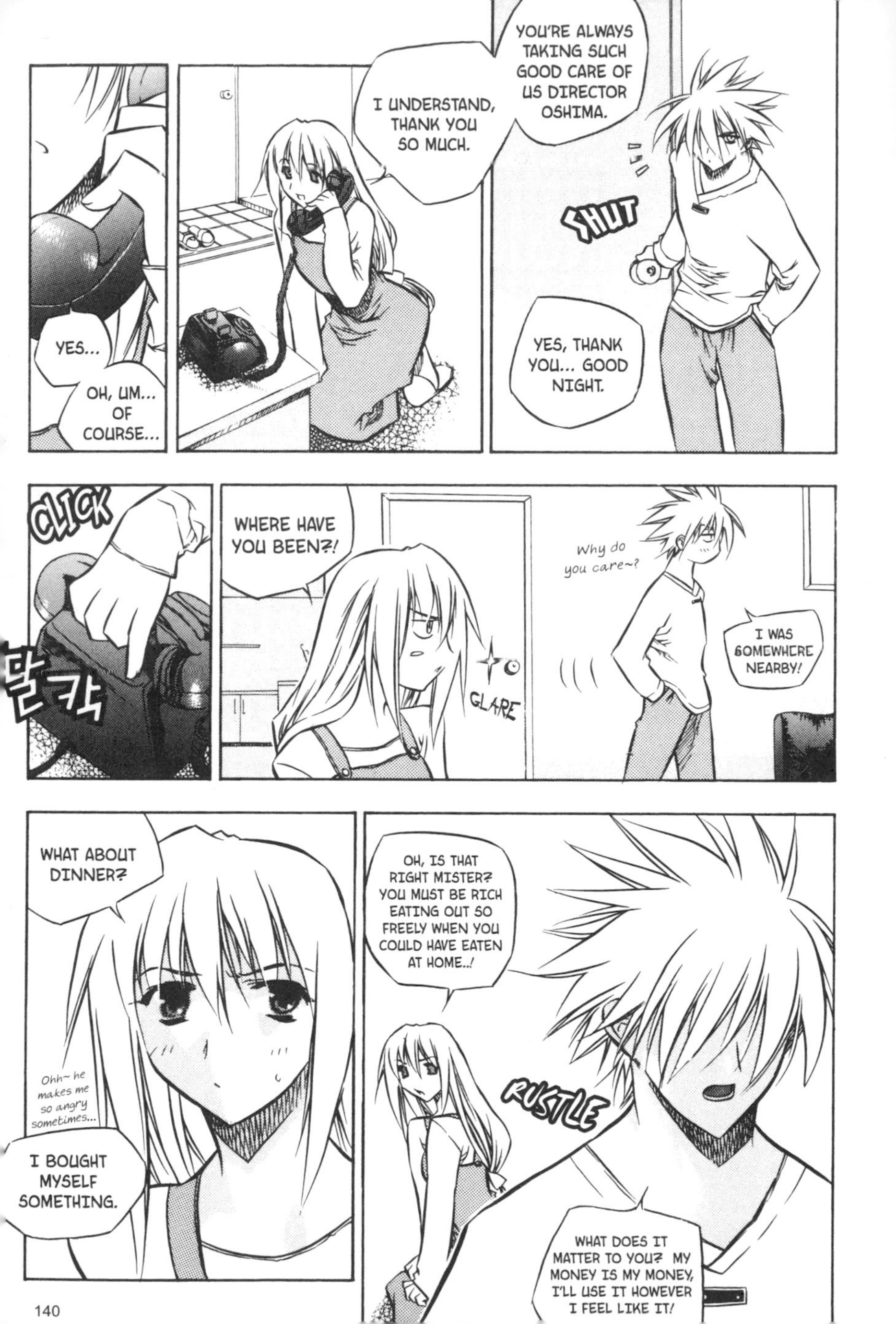
YES...
OH, UM... OF COURSE...
I UNDERSTAND, THANK YOU SO MUCH.
YOU'RE ALWAYS TAKING SUCH GOOD CARE OF US DIRECTOR OSHIMA.
SHUT
YES, THANK YOU... GOOD NIGHT.
CLICK
달칵
WHERE HAVE YOU BEEN?!
GLARE
Why do you care~?
I WAS SOMEWHERE NEARBY!
WHAT ABOUT DINNER?
Ohh~ he makes me so angry sometimes...
I BOUGHT MYSELF SOMETHING.
OH, IS THAT RIGHT MISTER? YOU MUST BE RICH EATING OUT SO FREELY WHEN YOU COULD HAVE EATEN AT HOME..!
RUSTLE
WHAT DOES IT MATTER TO YOU? MY MONEY IS MY MONEY, I'LL USE IT HOWEVER I FEEL LIKE IT!

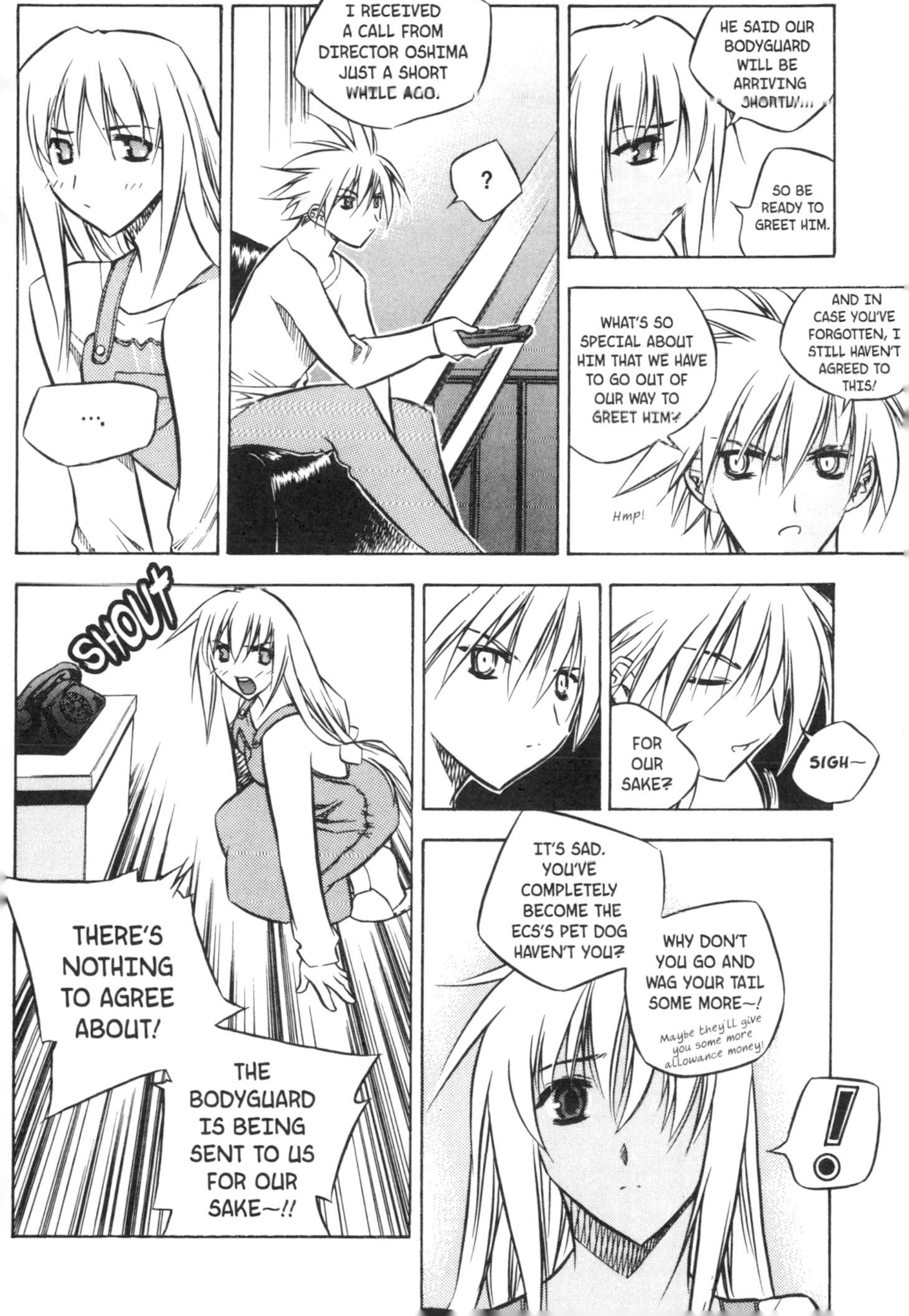

...
I RECEIVED A CALL FROM DIRECTOR OSHIMA JUST A SHORT WHILE AGO.
?
HE SAID OUR BODYGUARD WILL BE ARRIVING SHORTLY...
SO BE READY TO GREET HIM.
WHAT'S SO SPECIAL ABOUT HIM THAT WE HAVE TO GO OUT OF OUR WAY TO GREET HIM?
AND IN CASE YOU'VE FORGOTTEN, I STILL HAVEN'T AGREED TO THIS!
Hmp!
SHOUT
THERE'S NOTHING TO AGREE ABOUT!
THE BODYGUARD IS BEING SENT TO US FOR OUR SAKE~!!
FOR OUR SAKE?
SIGH~
IT'S SAD. YOU'VE COMPLETELY BECOME THE ECS'S PET DOG HAVEN'T YOU?
WHY DON'T YOU GO AND WAG YOUR TAIL SOME MORE~!
Maybe they'll give you some more allowance money!
!

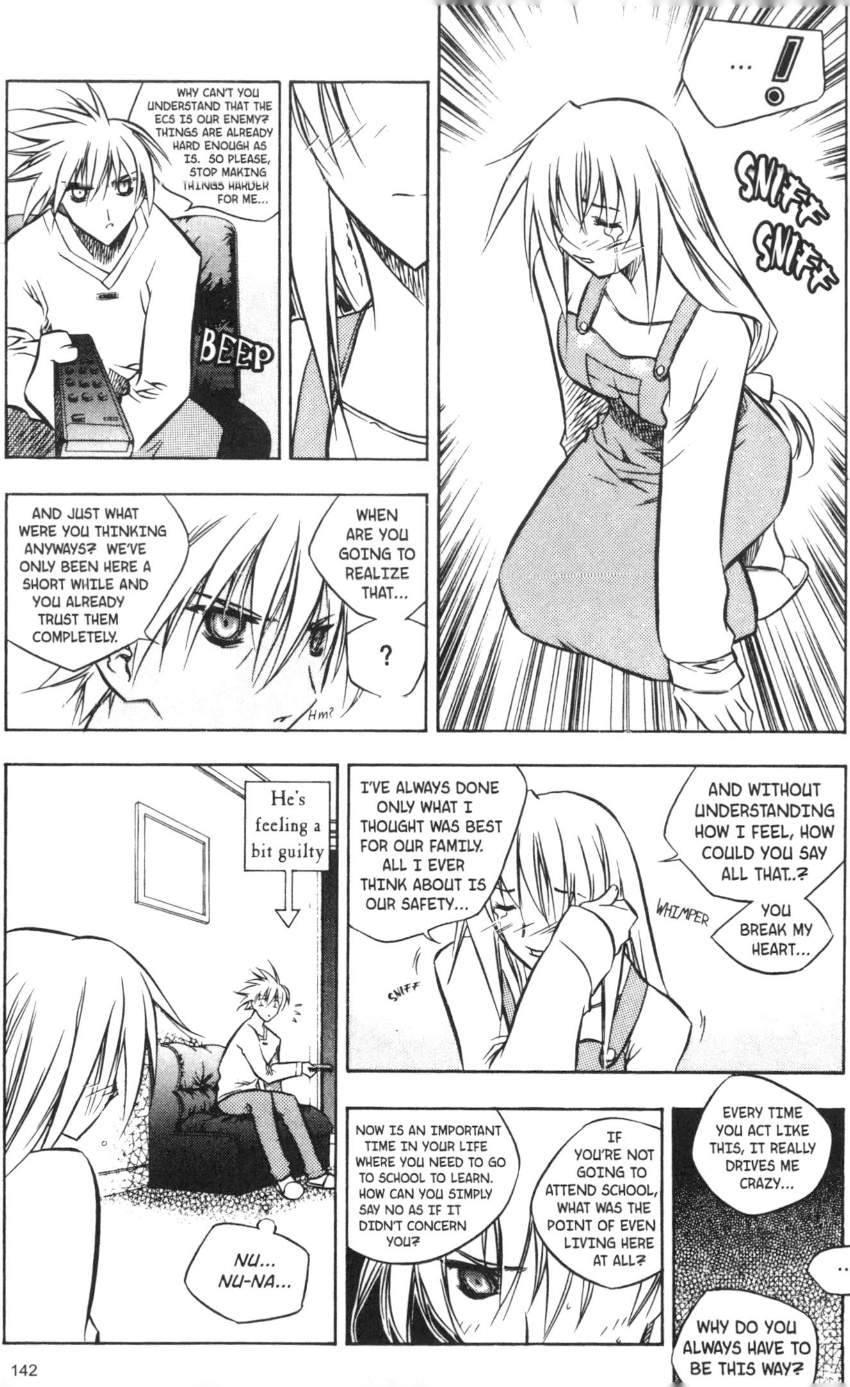
WHY CAN'T YOU UNDERSTAND THAT THE ECS IS OUR ENEMY? THINGS ARE ALREADY HARD ENOUGH AS IS. SO PLEASE, STOP MAKING THINGS HARDER FOR ME...
BEEP
...!
SNIFF SNIFF
AND JUST WHAT WERE YOU THINKING ANYWAYS? WE'VE ONLY BEEN HERE A SHORT WHILE AND YOU ALREADY TRUST THEM COMPLETELY.
WHEN ARE YOU GOING TO REALIZE THAT...
?
Hm?
He's feeling a bit guilty
NU... NU-NA...
I'VE ALWAYS DONE ONLY WHAT I THOUGHT WAS BEST FOR OUR FAMILY. ALL I EVER THINK ABOUT IS OUR SAFETY...
SNIFF
WHIMPER
AND WITHOUT UNDERSTANDING HOW I FEEL, HOW COULD YOU SAY ALL THAT..?
YOU BREAK MY HEART...
NOW IS AN IMPORTANT TIME IN YOUR LIFE WHERE YOU NEED TO GO TO SCHOOL TO LEARN. HOW CAN YOU SIMPLY SAY NO AS IF IT DIDN'T CONCERN YOU?
IF YOU'RE NOT GOING TO ATTEND SCHOOL, WHAT WAS THE POINT OF EVEN LIVING HERE AT ALL?
EVERY TIME YOU ACT LIKE THIS, IT REALLY DRIVES ME CRAZY...
...
WHY DO YOU ALWAYS HAVE TO BE THIS WAY?

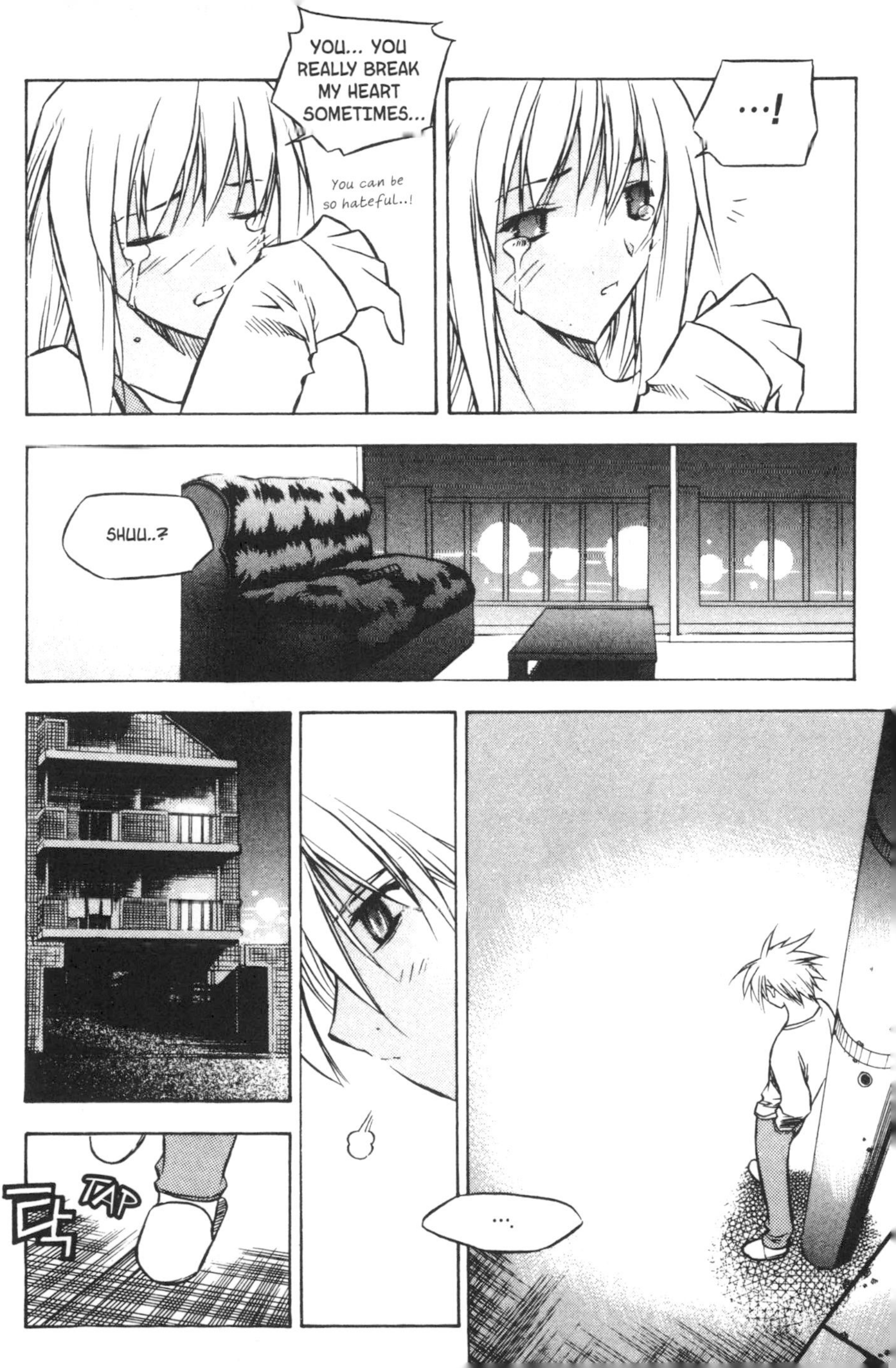
YOU... YOU REALLY BREAK MY HEART SOMETIMES...
You can be so hateful..!
...!
SHUU..?
TAP
...

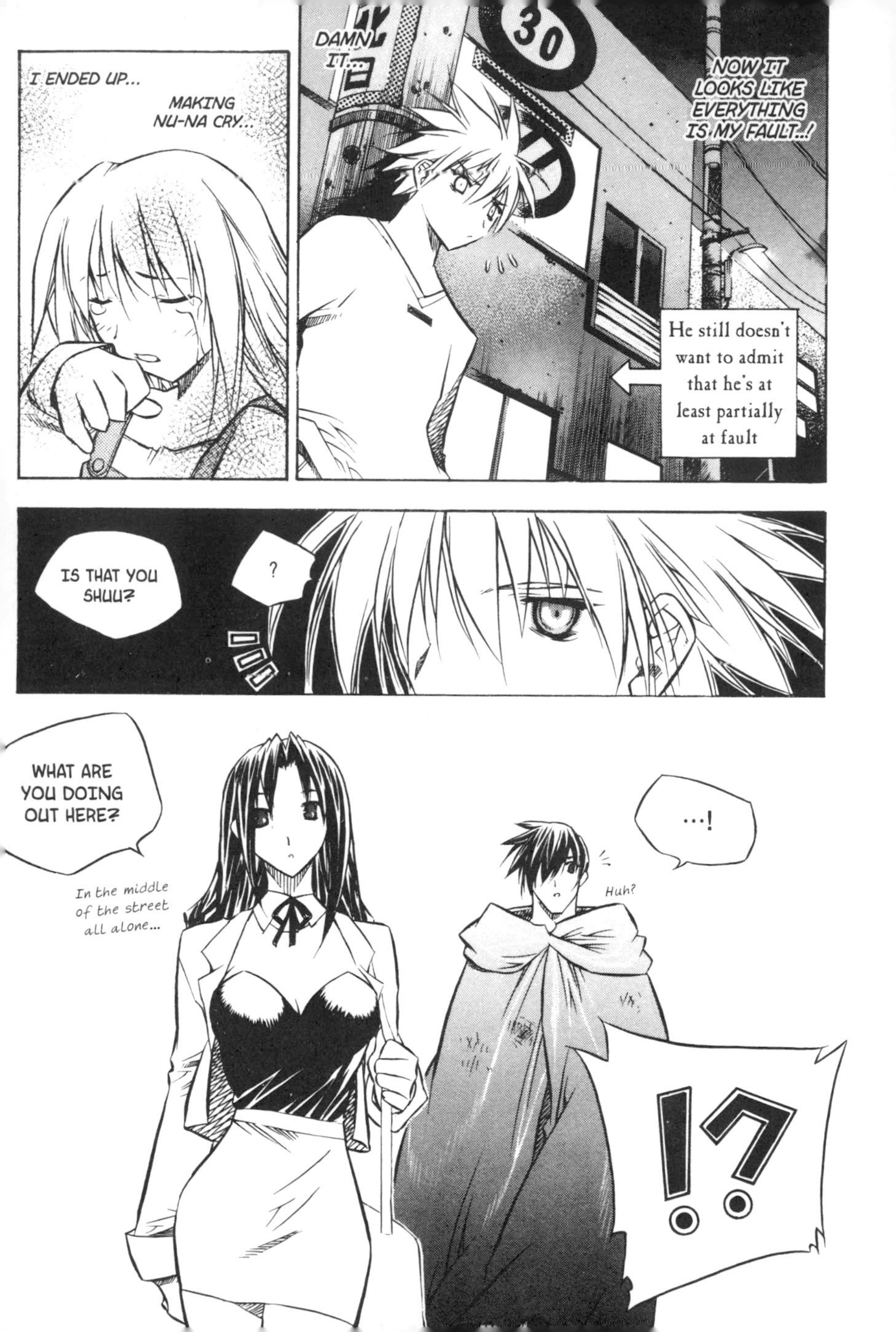
DAMN IT...
NOW IT LOOKS LIKE EVERYTHING IS MY FAULT..!
He still doesn't want to admit that he's at least partially at fault
I ENDED UP...
MAKING NU-NA CRY...
?
IS THAT YOU SHUU?
...!
Huh?
WHAT ARE YOU DOING OUT HERE?
In the middle of the street all alone...
!?

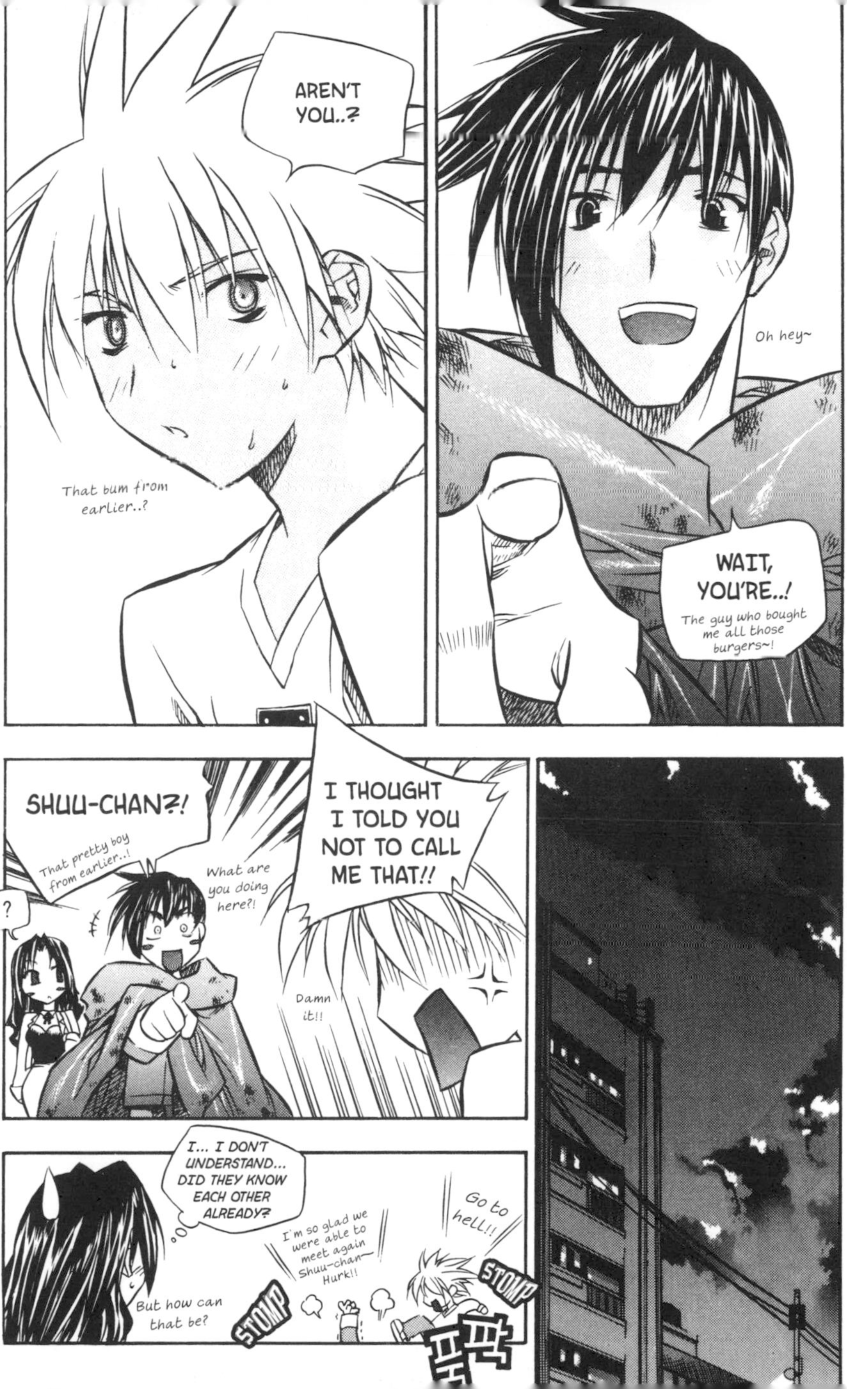

AREN'T YOU..?
That bum from earlier..?
Oh hey~
WAIT, YOU'RE..!
The guy who bought me all those burgers~!
SHUU-CHAN?!
That pretty boy from earlier..!
What are you doing here?!
?
I THOUGHT I TOLD YOU NOT TO CALL ME THAT!!
Damn it!!
I... I DON'T UNDERSTAND... DID THEY KNOW EACH OTHER ALREADY?
But how can that be?
I'm so glad we were able to meet again Shuu-chan~ Hurk!!
Go to hell!!
STOMP
STOMP

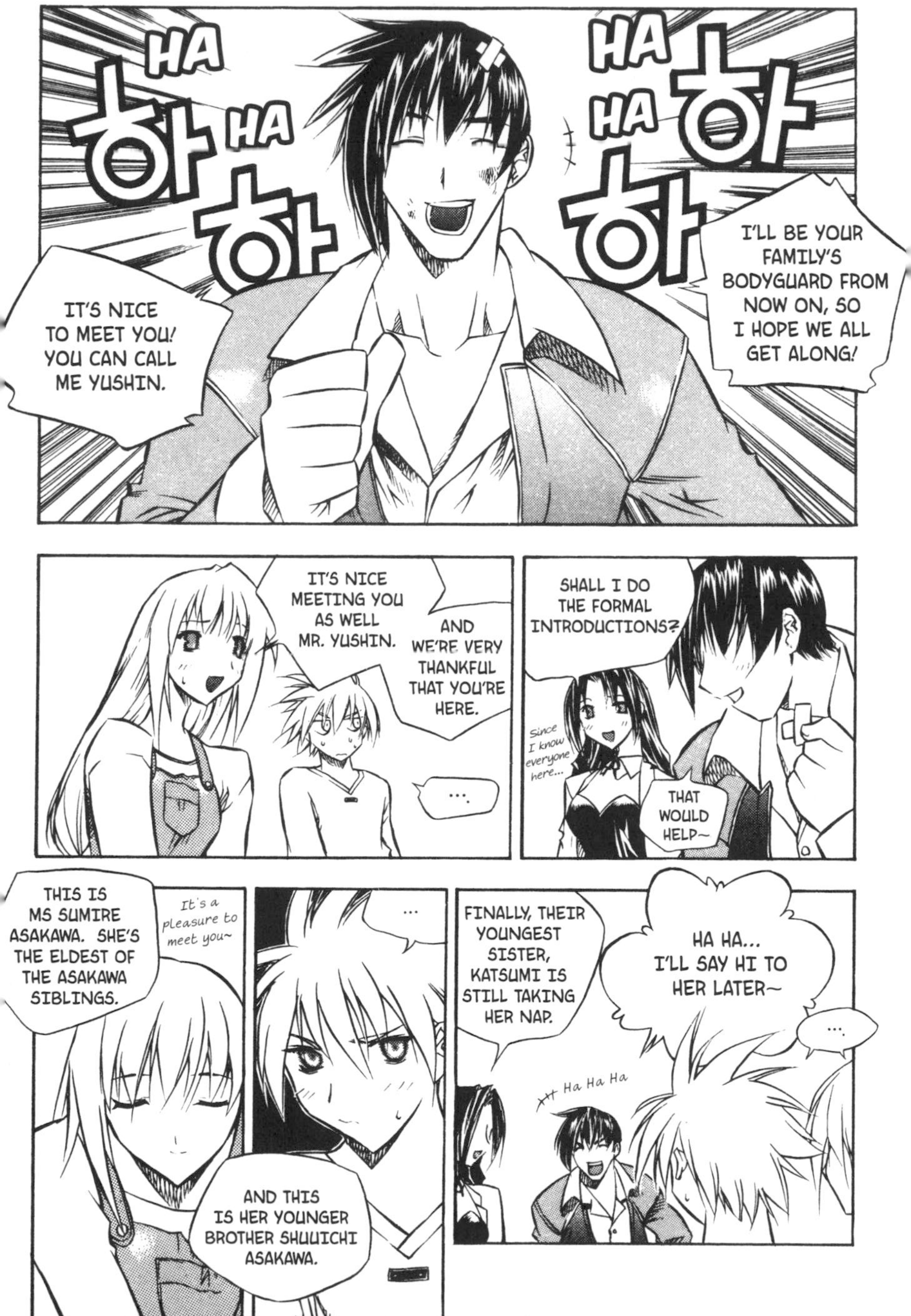

HA
하
HA
하
HA
HA
하
하
IT'S NICE TO MEET YOU! YOU CAN CALL ME YUSHIN.
I'LL BE YOUR FAMILY'S BODYGUARD FROM NOW ON, SO I HOPE WE ALL GET ALONG!
IT'S NICE MEETING YOU AS WELL MR. YUSHIN.
AND WE'RE VERY THANKFUL THAT YOU'RE HERE.
...
SHALL I DO THE FORMAL INTRODUCTIONS?
Since I know everyone here...
THAT WOULD HELP~
THIS IS MS SUMIRE ASAKAWA. SHE'S THE ELDEST OF THE ASAKAWA SIBLINGS.
It's a pleasure to meet you~
...
AND THIS IS HER YOUNGER BROTHER SHUUICHI ASAKAWA.
FINALLY, THEIR YOUNGEST SISTER, KATSUMI IS STILL TAKING HER NAP.
HA HA... I'LL SAY HI TO HER LATER~
Ha Ha Ha
...

Note : Kankoku is the Japanese word for Korea

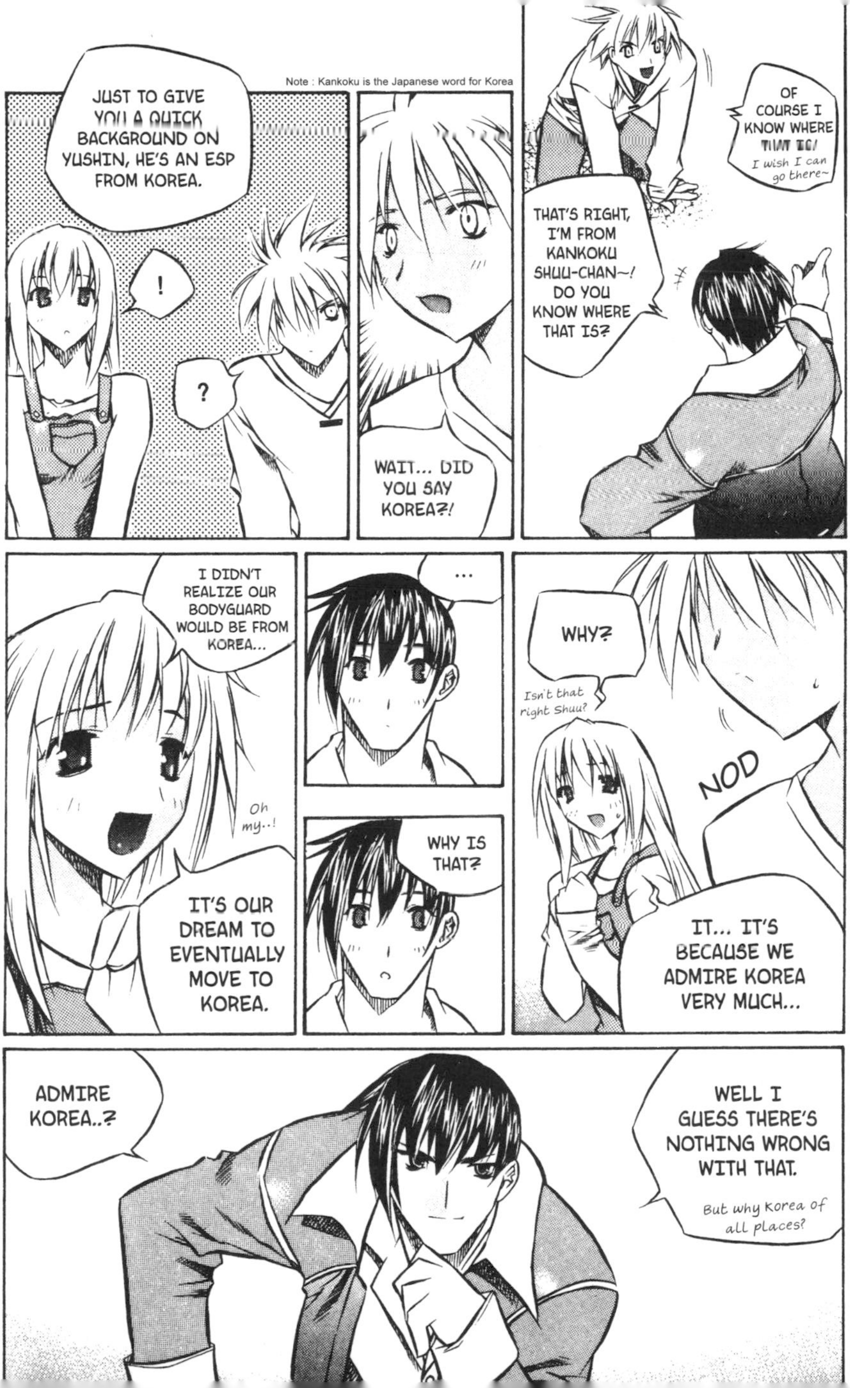

JUST TO GIVE YOU A QUICK BACKGROUND ON YUSHIN, HE'S AN ESP FROM KOREA.
!
?
WAIT... DID YOU SAY KOREA?!
THAT'S RIGHT, I'M FROM KANKOKU SHUU-CHAN~! DO YOU KNOW WHERE THAT IS?
OF COURSE I KNOW WHERE THAT IS!
I wish I can go there~
I DIDN'T REALIZE OUR BODYGUARD WOULD BE FROM KOREA...
Oh my..!
IT'S OUR DREAM TO EVENTUALLY MOVE TO KOREA.
...
WHY IS THAT?
WHY?
Isn't that right Shuu?
NOD
IT... IT'S BECAUSE WE ADMIRE KOREA VERY MUCH...
ADMIRE KOREA..?
WELL I GUESS THERE'S NOTHING WRONG WITH THAT.
But why Korea of all places?

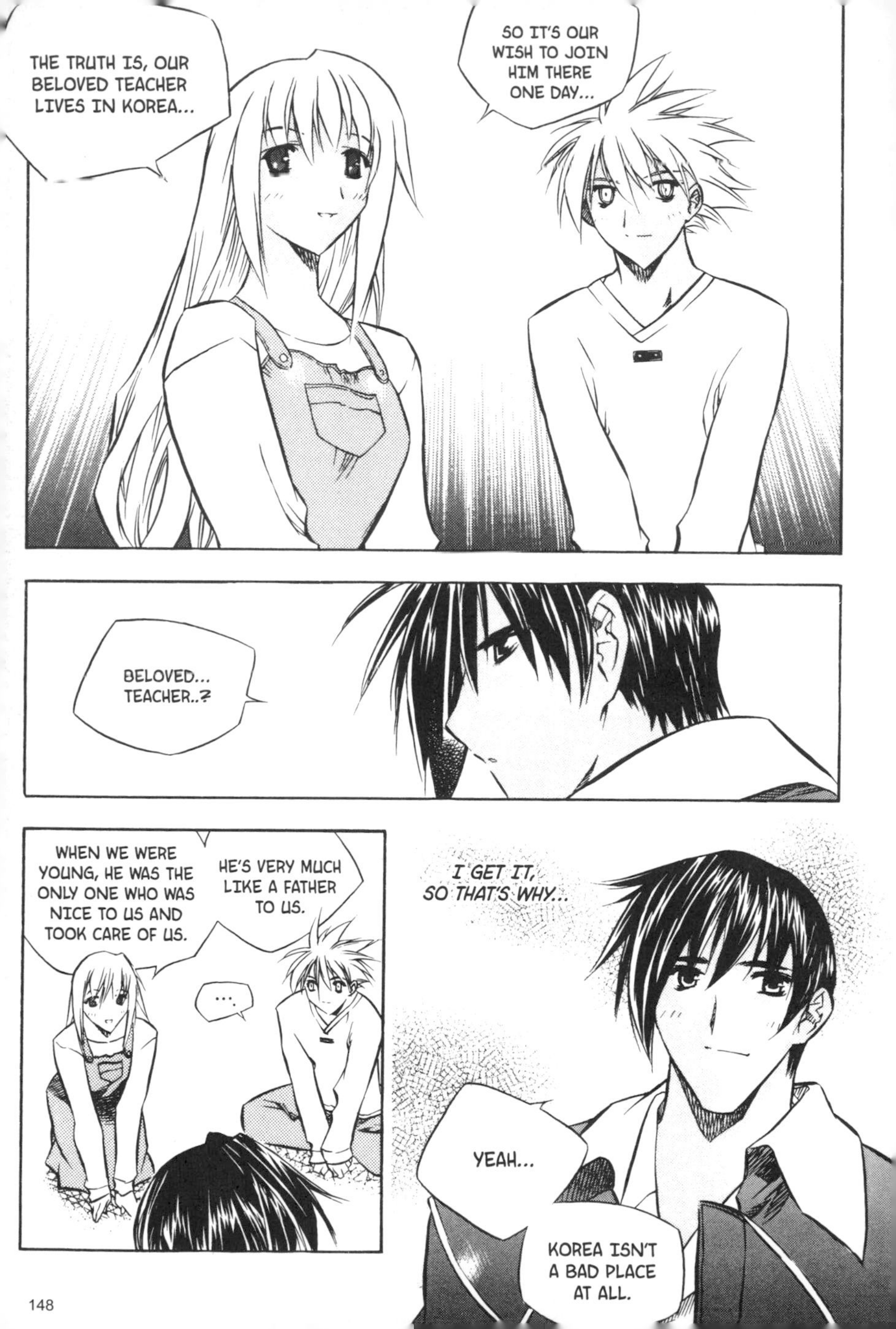
THE TRUTH IS, OUR BELOVED TEACHER LIVES IN KOREA...
SO IT'S OUR WISH TO JOIN HIM THERE ONE DAY...
BELOVED... TEACHER..?
WHEN WE WERE YOUNG, HE WAS THE ONLY ONE WHO WAS NICE TO US AND TOOK CARE OF US.
HE'S VERY MUCH LIKE A FATHER TO US.
...
I GET IT, SO THAT'S WHY...
YEAH...
KOREA ISN'T A BAD PLACE AT ALL.

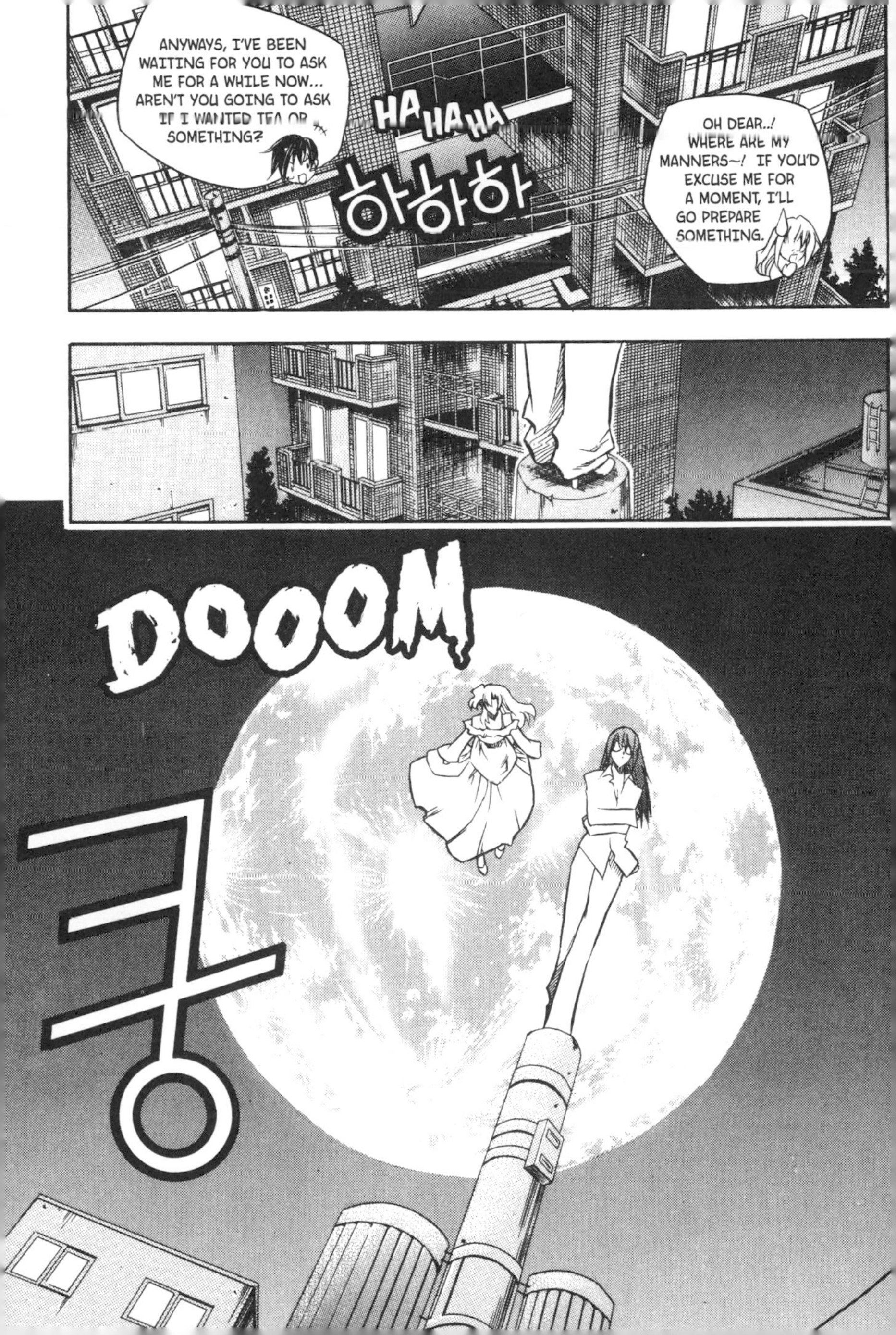
ANYWAYS, I'VE BEEN WAITING FOR YOU TO ASK ME FOR A WHILE NOW... AREN'T YOU GOING TO ASK IF I WANTED TEA OR SOMETHING?
HA HA HA
하하하
OH DEAR..! WHERE ARE MY MANNERS~! IF YOU'D EXCUSE ME FOR A MOMENT, I'LL GO PREPARE SOMETHING.
DOOOM
쿵

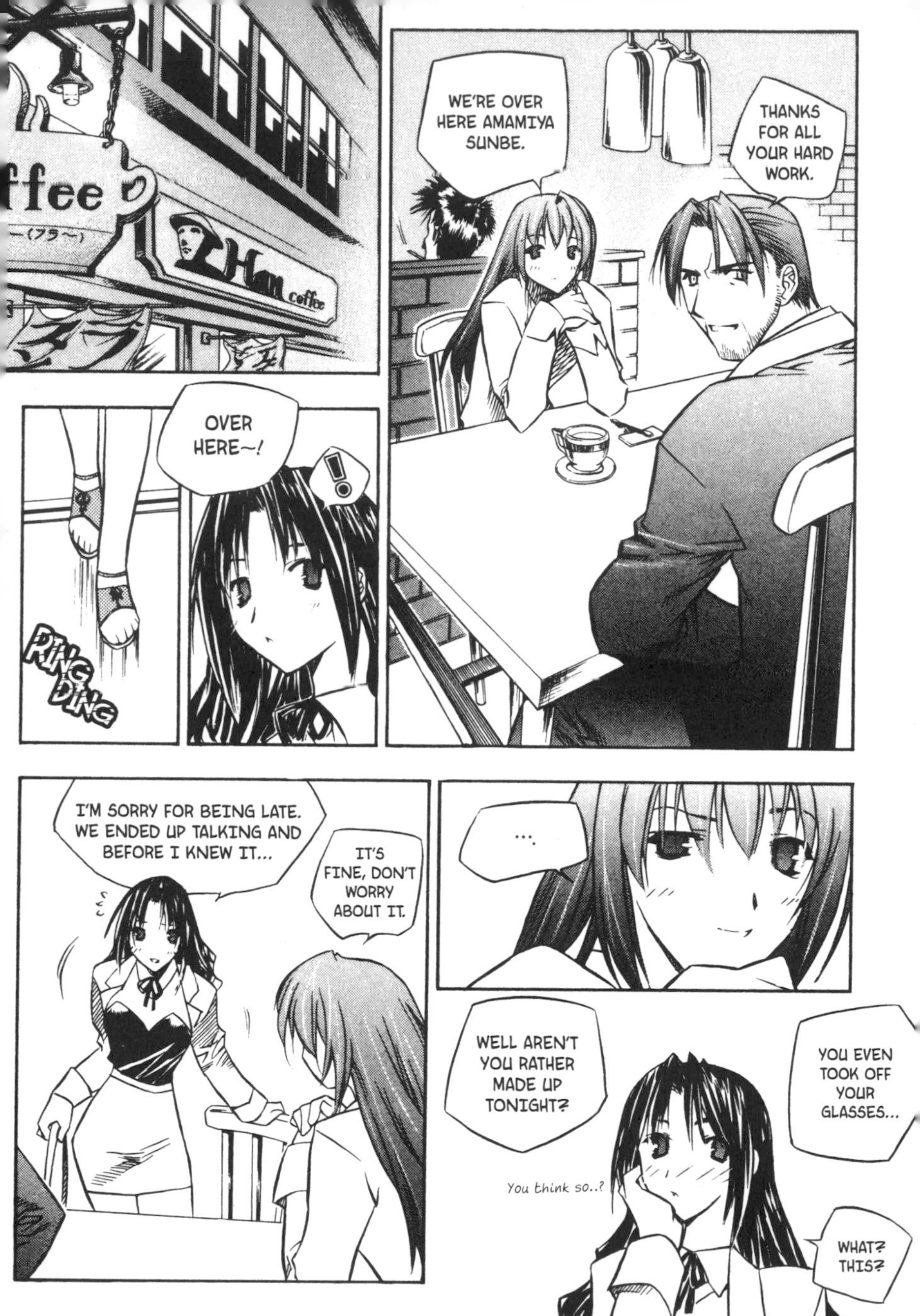
ffee
ー(フラ～)
Han coffee
WE'RE OVER HERE AMAMIYA SUNBE.
THANKS FOR ALL YOUR HARD WORK.
RING DING
OVER HERE~!
I'M SORRY FOR BEING LATE. WE ENDED UP TALKING AND BEFORE I KNEW IT...
IT'S FINE, DON'T WORRY ABOUT IT.
...
WELL AREN'T YOU RATHER MADE UP TONIGHT?
YOU EVEN TOOK OFF YOUR GLASSES...
You think so..?
WHAT? THIS?

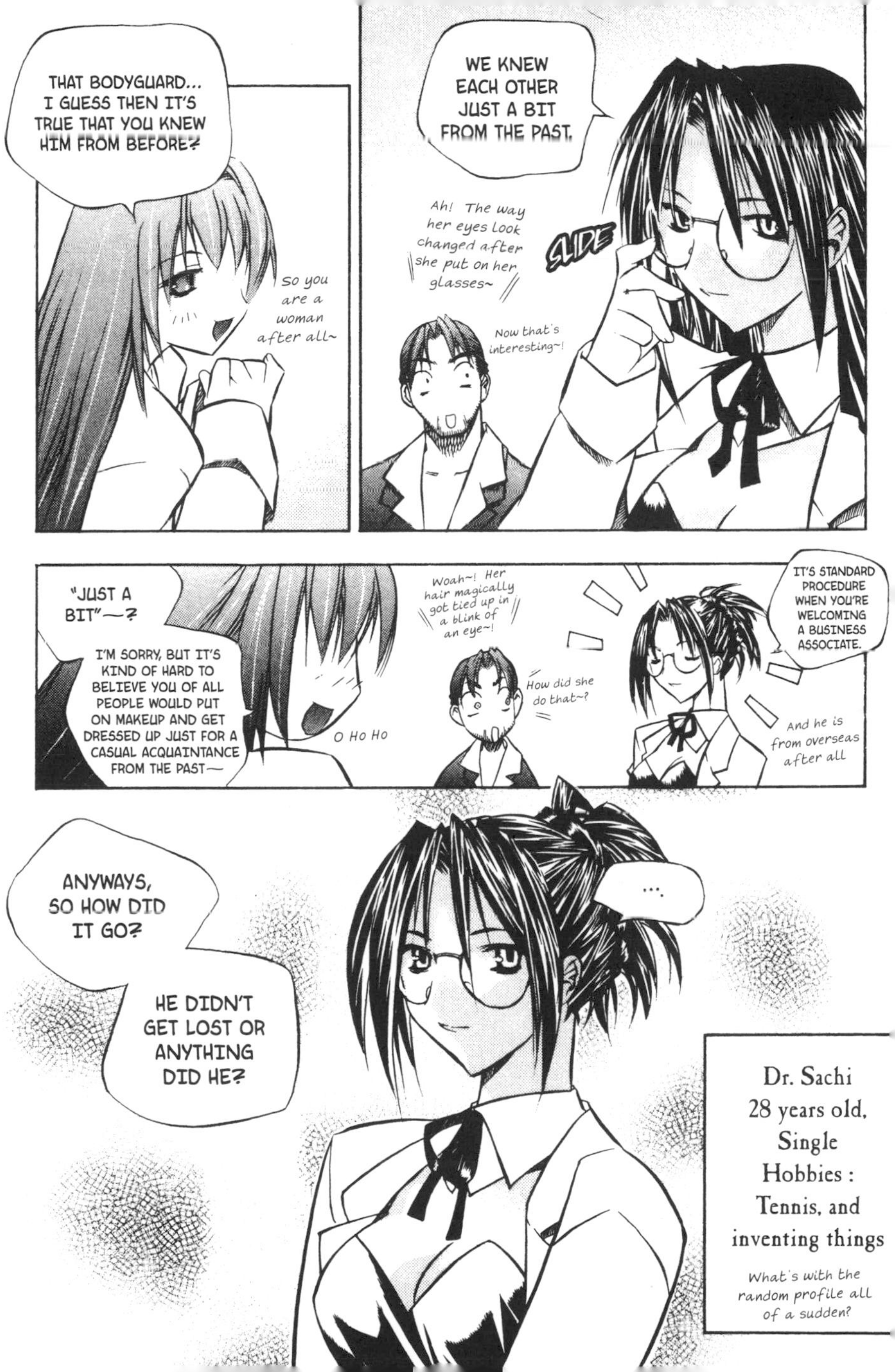
THAT BODYGUARD... I GUESS THEN IT'S TRUE THAT YOU KNEW HIM FROM BEFORE?
So you are a woman after all~
WE KNEW EACH OTHER JUST A BIT FROM THE PAST.
Ah! The way her eyes look changed after she put on her glasses~
SLIDE
Now that's interesting~!
"JUST A BIT"—?
I'M SORRY, BUT IT'S KIND OF HARD TO BELIEVE YOU OF ALL PEOPLE WOULD PUT ON MAKEUP AND GET DRESSED UP JUST FOR A CASUAL ACQUAINTANCE FROM THE PAST—
O Ho Ho
Woah~! Her hair magically got tied up in a blink of an eye~!
How did she do that~?
IT'S STANDARD PROCEDURE WHEN YOU'RE WELCOMING A BUSINESS ASSOCIATE.
And he is from overseas after all
ANYWAYS, SO HOW DID IT GO?
HE DIDN'T GET LOST OR ANYTHING DID HE?
...
Dr. Sachi 28 years old, Single Hobbies : Tennis, and inventing things
What's with the random profile all of a sudden?

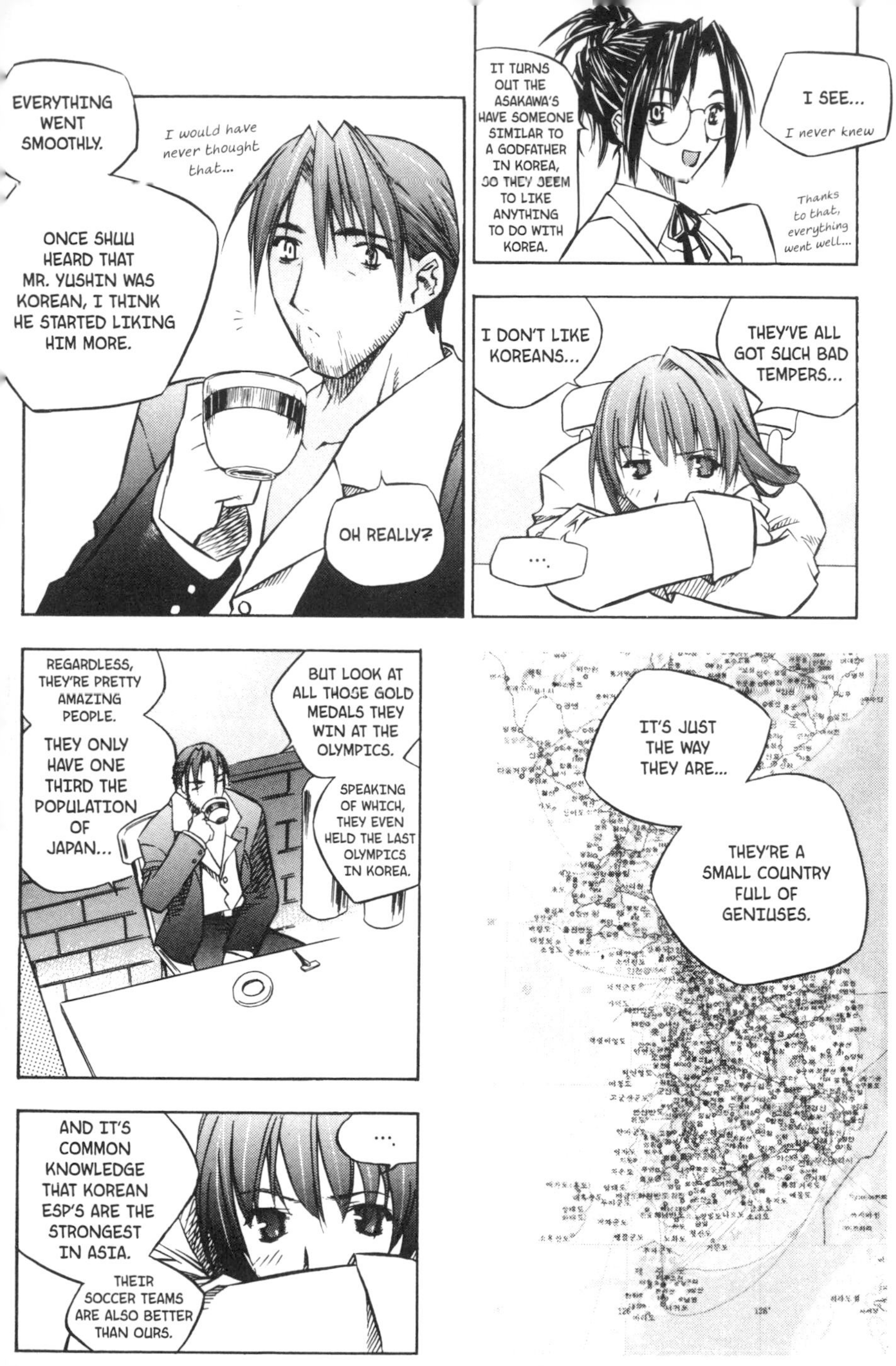
EVERYTHING WENT SMOOTHLY.
I would have never thought that...
ONCE SHUU HEARD THAT MR. YUSHIN WAS KOREAN, I THINK HE STARTED LIKING HIM MORE.
OH REALLY?
IT TURNS OUT THE ASAKAWA'S HAVE SOMEONE SIMILAR TO A GODFATHER IN KOREA, SO THEY SEEM TO LIKE ANYTHING TO DO WITH KOREA.
I SEE...
I never knew
Thanks to that, everything went well...
I DON'T LIKE KOREANS...
THEY'VE ALL GOT SUCH BAD TEMPERS...
....
REGARDLESS, THEY'RE PRETTY AMAZING PEOPLE.
THEY ONLY HAVE ONE THIRD THE POPULATION OF JAPAN...
BUT LOOK AT ALL THOSE GOLD MEDALS THEY WIN AT THE OLYMPICS.
SPEAKING OF WHICH, THEY EVEN HELD THE LAST OLYMPICS IN KOREA.
AND IT'S COMMON KNOWLEDGE THAT KOREAN ESP'S ARE THE STRONGEST IN ASIA.
THEIR SOCCER TEAMS ARE ALSO BETTER THAN OURS.
....
IT'S JUST THE WAY THEY ARE...
THEY'RE A SMALL COUNTRY FULL OF GENIUSES.

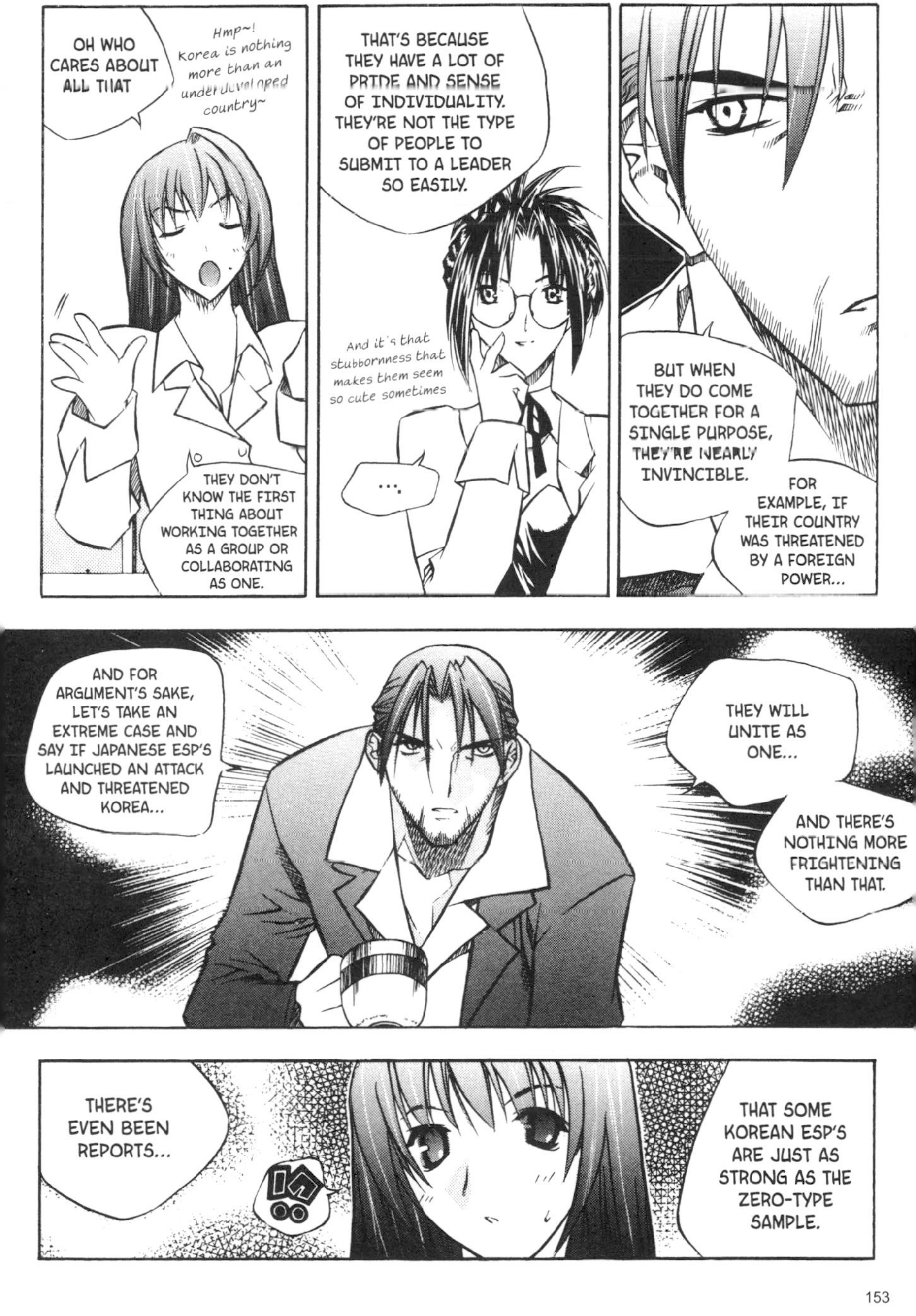

OH WHO CARES ABOUT ALL THAT
Hmp~! Korea is nothing more than an underdeveloped country~
THEY DON'T KNOW THE FIRST THING ABOUT WORKING TOGETHER AS A GROUP OR COLLABORATING AS ONE.
THAT'S BECAUSE THEY HAVE A LOT OF PRIDE AND SENSE OF INDIVIDUALITY. THEY'RE NOT THE TYPE OF PEOPLE TO SUBMIT TO A LEADER SO EASILY.
And it's that stubbornness that makes them seem so cute sometimes
...
BUT WHEN THEY DO COME TOGETHER FOR A SINGLE PURPOSE, THEY'RE NEARLY INVINCIBLE.
FOR EXAMPLE, IF THEIR COUNTRY WAS THREATENED BY A FOREIGN POWER...
AND FOR ARGUMENT'S SAKE, LET'S TAKE AN EXTREME CASE AND SAY IF JAPANESE ESP'S LAUNCHED AN ATTACK AND THREATENED KOREA...
THEY WILL UNITE AS ONE...
AND THERE'S NOTHING MORE FRIGHTENING THAN THAT.
THERE'S EVEN BEEN REPORTS...
THAT SOME KOREAN ESP'S ARE JUST AS STRONG AS THE ZERO-TYPE SAMPLE.

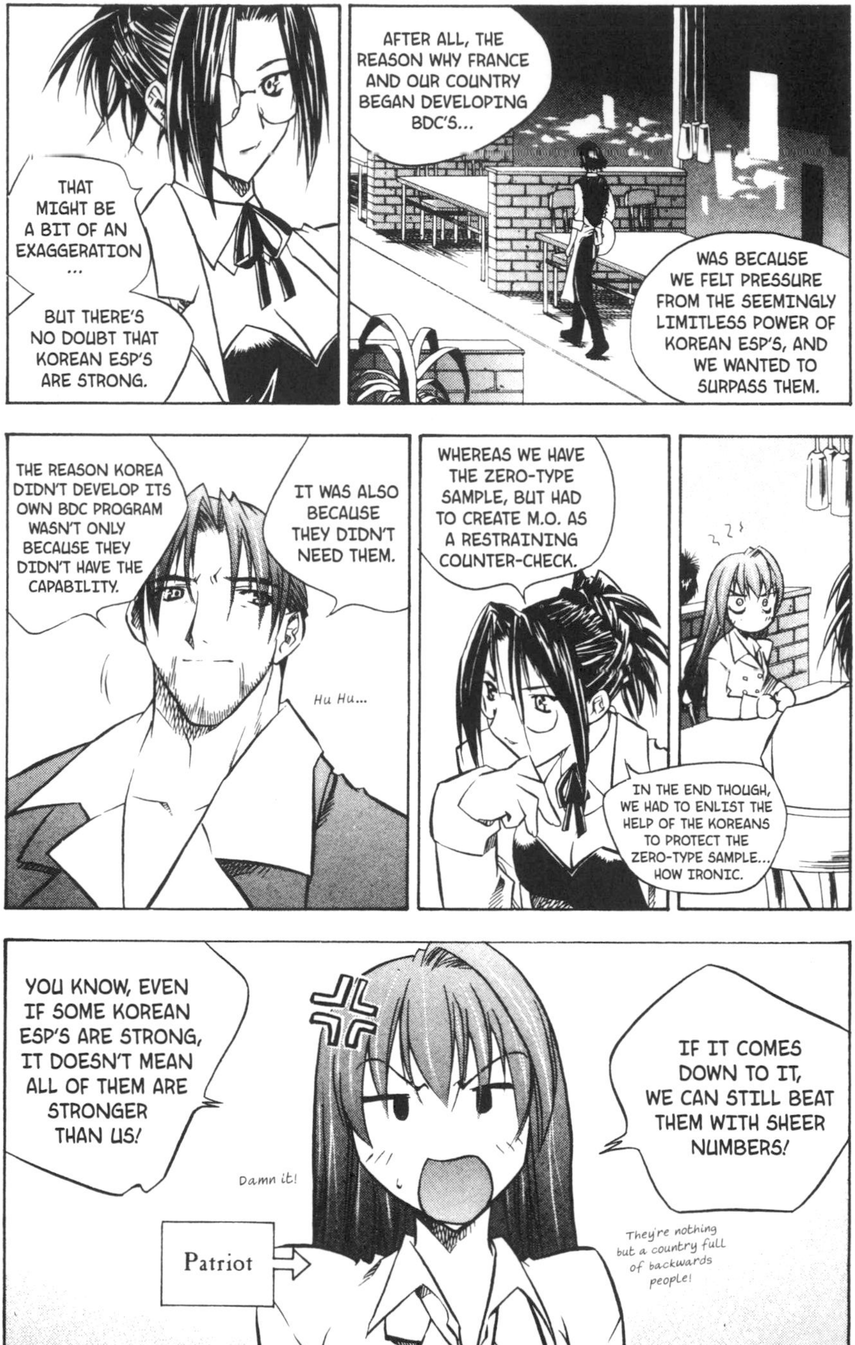
THAT MIGHT BE A BIT OF AN EXAGGERATION ...
BUT THERE'S NO DOUBT THAT KOREAN ESP'S ARE STRONG.
AFTER ALL, THE REASON WHY FRANCE AND OUR COUNTRY BEGAN DEVELOPING BDC'S...
WAS BECAUSE WE FELT PRESSURE FROM THE SEEMINGLY LIMITLESS POWER OF KOREAN ESP'S, AND WE WANTED TO SURPASS THEM.
THE REASON KOREA DIDN'T DEVELOP ITS OWN BDC PROGRAM WASN'T ONLY BECAUSE THEY DIDN'T HAVE THE CAPABILITY.
IT WAS ALSO BECAUSE THEY DIDN'T NEED THEM.
Hu Hu...
WHEREAS WE HAVE THE ZERO-TYPE SAMPLE, BUT HAD TO CREATE M.O. AS A RESTRAINING COUNTER-CHECK.
IN THE END THOUGH, WE HAD TO ENLIST THE HELP OF THE KOREANS TO PROTECT THE ZERO-TYPE SAMPLE... HOW IRONIC.
YOU KNOW, EVEN IF SOME KOREAN ESP'S ARE STRONG, IT DOESN'T MEAN ALL OF THEM ARE STRONGER THAN US!
IF IT COMES DOWN TO IT, WE CAN STILL BEAT THEM WITH SHEER NUMBERS!
Damn it!
Patriot
They're nothing but a country full of backwards people!

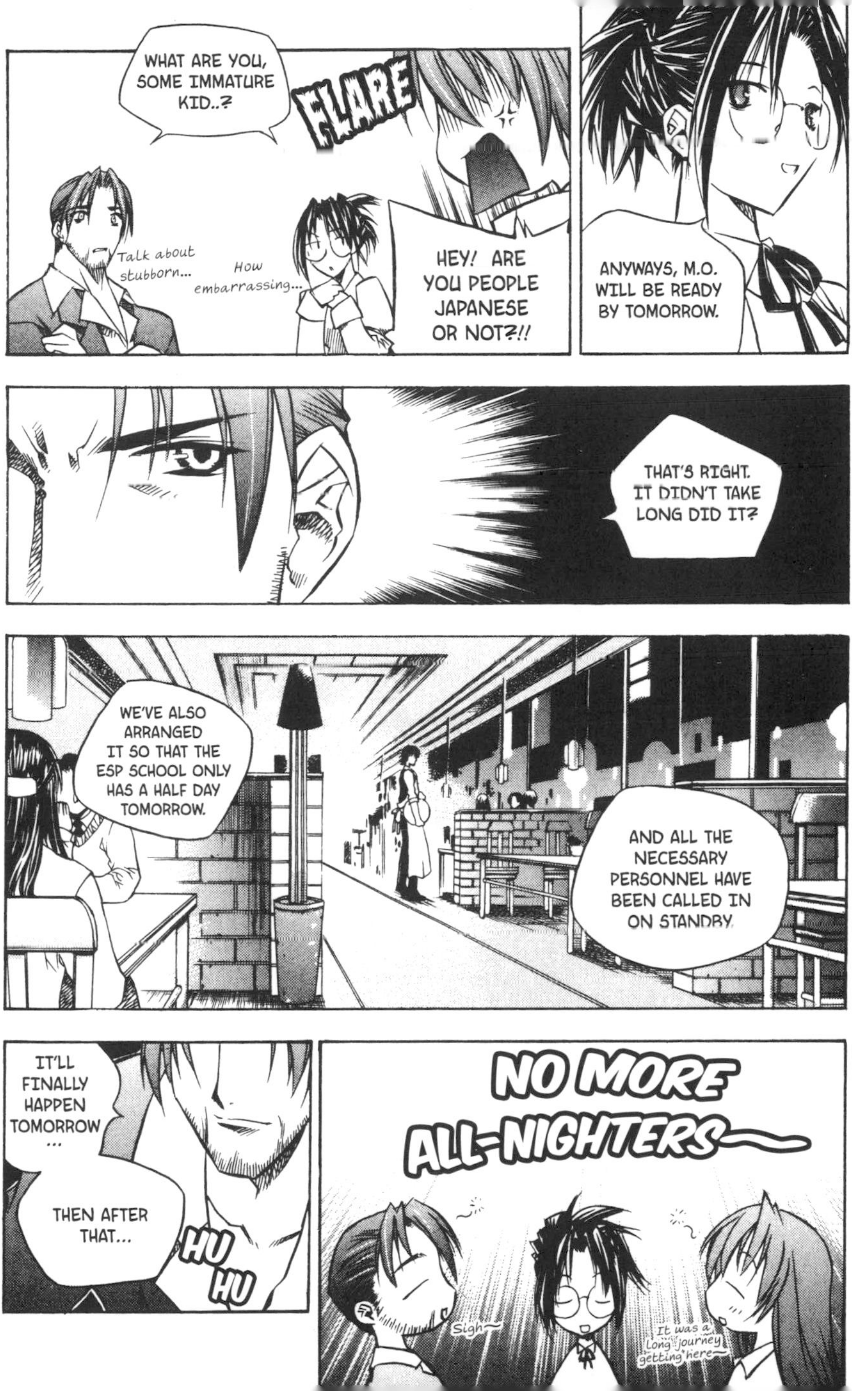
WHAT ARE YOU, SOME IMMATURE KID..?
FLARE
Talk about stubborn...
How embarrassing...
HEY! ARE YOU PEOPLE JAPANESE OR NOT?!!
ANYWAYS, M.O. WILL BE READY BY TOMORROW.
THAT'S RIGHT. IT DIDN'T TAKE LONG DID IT?
WE'VE ALSO ARRANGED IT SO THAT THE ESP SCHOOL ONLY HAS A HALF DAY TOMORROW.
AND ALL THE NECESSARY PERSONNEL HAVE BEEN CALLED IN ON STANDBY.
IT'LL FINALLY HAPPEN TOMORROW...
THEN AFTER THAT...
HU HU
NO MORE ALL-NIGHTERS~
Sigh~
It was a long journey getting here~

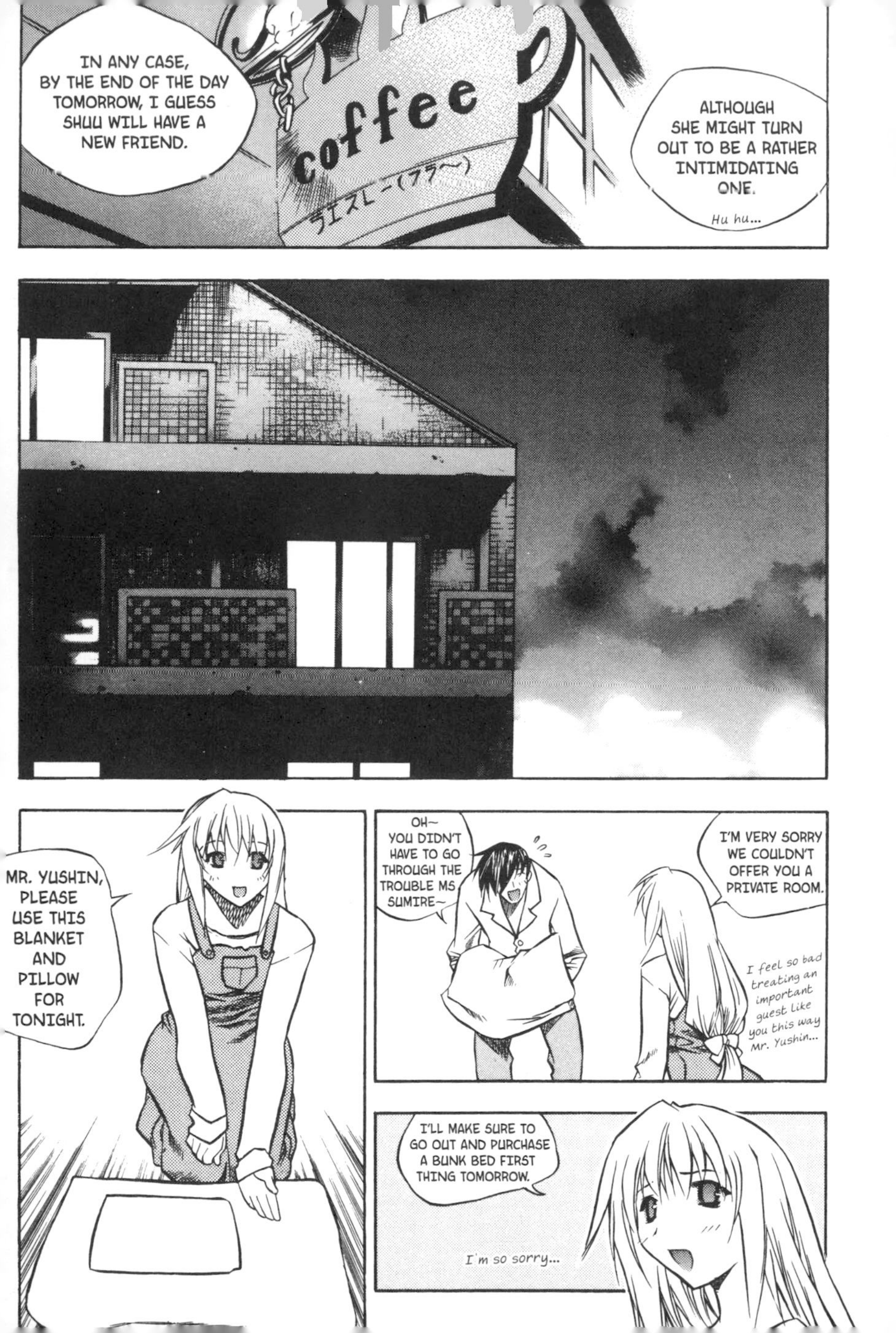

IN ANY CASE, BY THE END OF THE DAY TOMORROW, I GUESS SHUU WILL HAVE A NEW FRIEND.
coffee
ALTHOUGH SHE MIGHT TURN OUT TO BE A RATHER INTIMIDATING ONE.
Hu hu...
MR. YUSHIN, PLEASE USE THIS BLANKET AND PILLOW FOR TONIGHT.
OH~ YOU DIDN'T HAVE TO GO THROUGH THE TROUBLE MS SUMIRE~
I'M VERY SORRY WE COULDN'T OFFER YOU A PRIVATE ROOM.
I feel so bad treating an important guest like you this way Mr. Yushin...
I'LL MAKE SURE TO GO OUT AND PURCHASE A BUNK BED FIRST THING TOMORROW.
I'm so sorry...

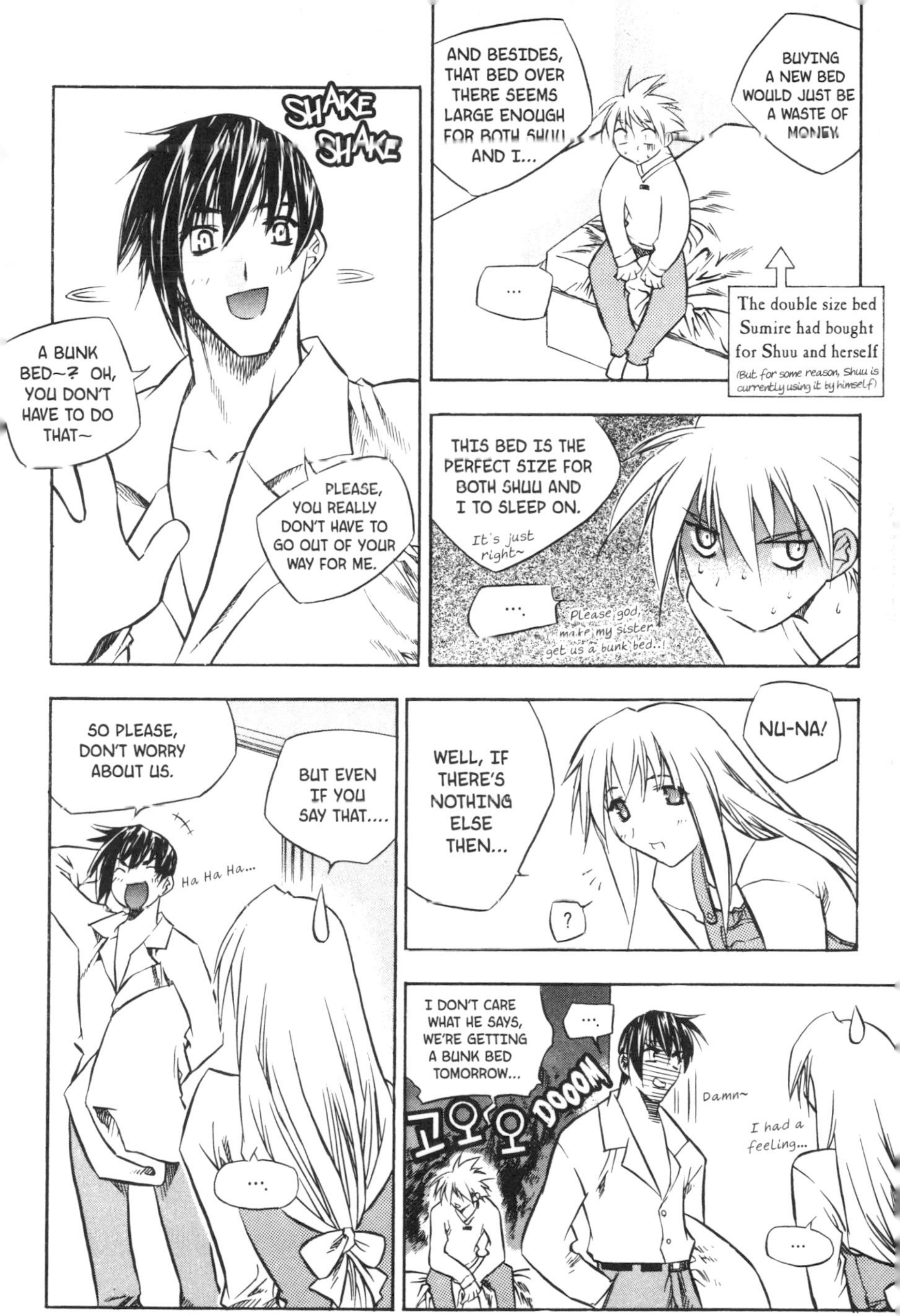
SHAKE SHAKE
A BUNK BED~? OH, YOU DON'T HAVE TO DO THAT~
PLEASE, YOU REALLY DON'T HAVE TO GO OUT OF YOUR WAY FOR ME.
AND BESIDES, THAT BED OVER THERE SEEMS LARGE ENOUGH FOR BOTH SHUU AND I...
BUYING A NEW BED WOULD JUST BE A WASTE OF MONEY.
...
The double size bed Sumire had bought for Shuu and herself
(But for some reason, Shuu is currently using it by himself)
THIS BED IS THE PERFECT SIZE FOR BOTH SHUU AND I TO SLEEP ON.
It's just right~
....
Please god, make my sister get us a bunk bed...!
SO PLEASE, DON'T WORRY ABOUT US.
BUT EVEN IF YOU SAY THAT....
Ha Ha Ha...
....
NU-NA!
WELL, IF THERE'S NOTHING ELSE THEN...
?
I DON'T CARE WHAT HE SAYS, WE'RE GETTING A BUNK BED TOMORROW...
....
고오오 DOOOM
Damn~
I had a feeling...
...

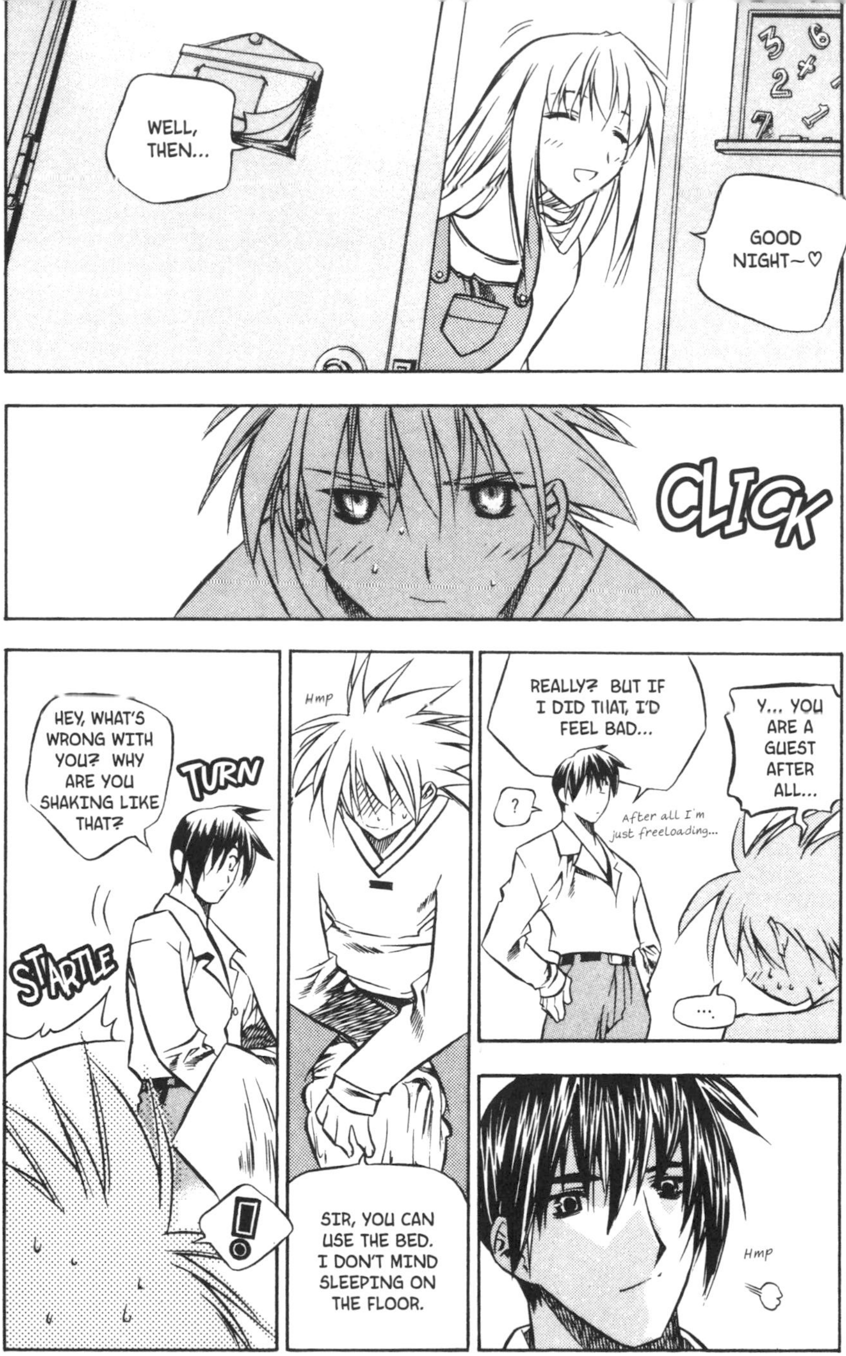
WELL, THEN...
GOOD NIGHT~♡
CLICK
HEY, WHAT'S WRONG WITH YOU? WHY ARE YOU SHAKING LIKE THAT?
TURN
STARTLE
!
Hmp
SIR, YOU CAN USE THE BED. I DON'T MIND SLEEPING ON THE FLOOR.
REALLY? BUT IF I DID THAT, I'D FEEL BAD...
?
After all I'm just freeloading...
Y... YOU ARE A GUEST AFTER ALL...
...
Hmp

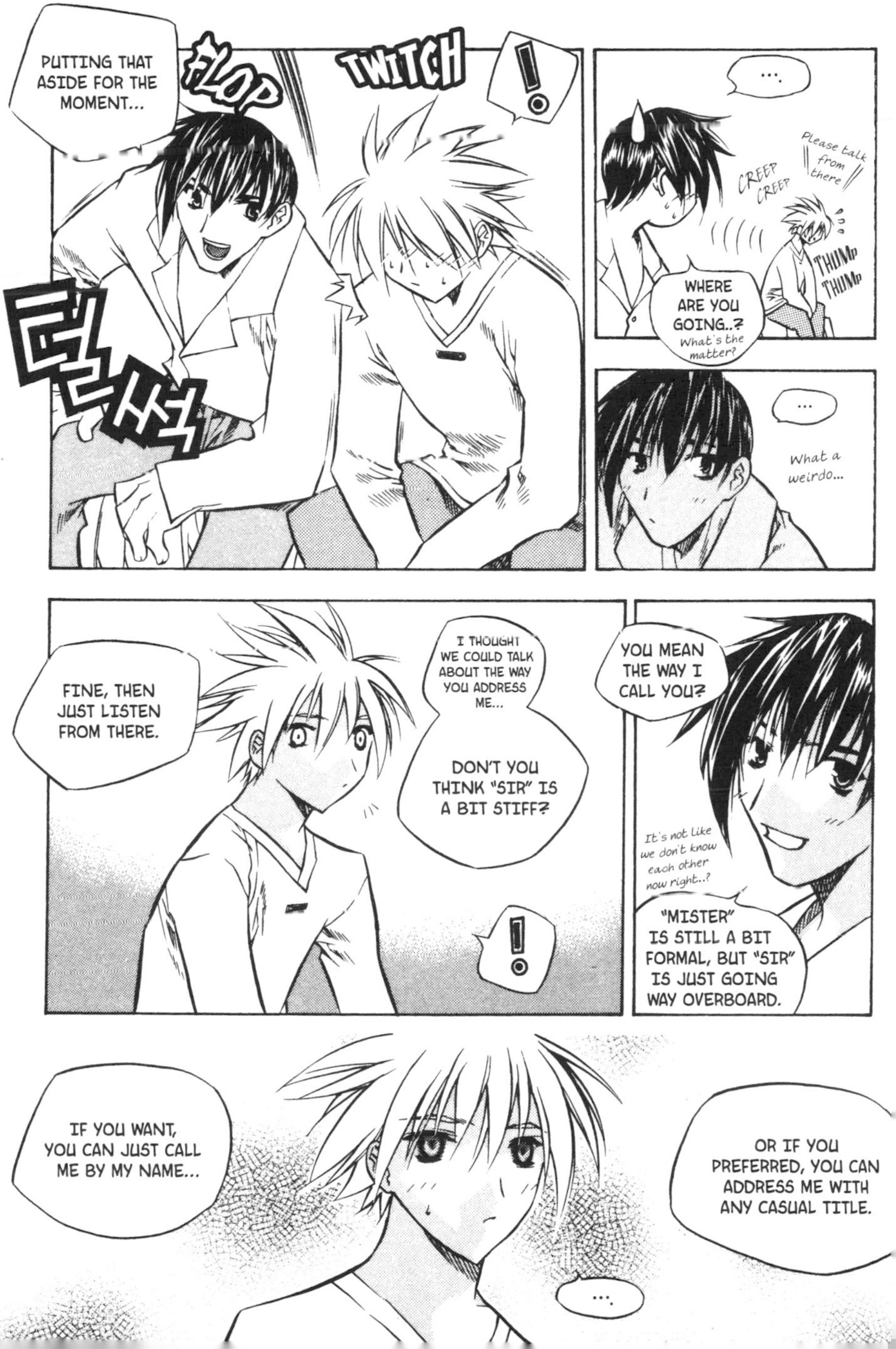

PUTTING THAT ASIDE FOR THE MOMENT...
FLOP
TWITCH
!
...
CREEP CREEP
Please talk from there
THUMP THUMP
WHERE ARE YOU GOING..?
What's the matter?
...
What a weirdo...
FINE, THEN JUST LISTEN FROM THERE.
I THOUGHT WE COULD TALK ABOUT THE WAY YOU ADDRESS ME...
DON'T YOU THINK "SIR" IS A BIT STIFF?
!
YOU MEAN THE WAY I CALL YOU?
It's not like we don't know each other now right..?
"MISTER" IS STILL A BIT FORMAL, BUT "SIR" IS JUST GOING WAY OVERBOARD.
IF YOU WANT, YOU CAN JUST CALL ME BY MY NAME...
OR IF YOU PREFERRED, YOU CAN ADDRESS ME WITH ANY CASUAL TITLE.
...

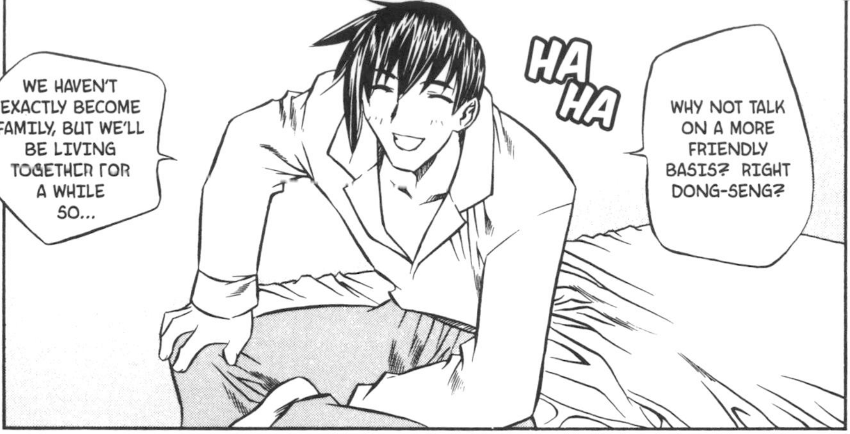
WE HAVEN'T EXACTLY BECOME FAMILY, BUT WE'LL BE LIVING TOGETHER FOR A WHILE SO...
HA HA
WHY NOT TALK ON A MORE FRIENDLY BASIS? RIGHT DONG-SENG?

Note : Dong-seng literally means "younger sibling" but it can also be casually used between two people not related by family. Use of this word implies a certain degree of affection.

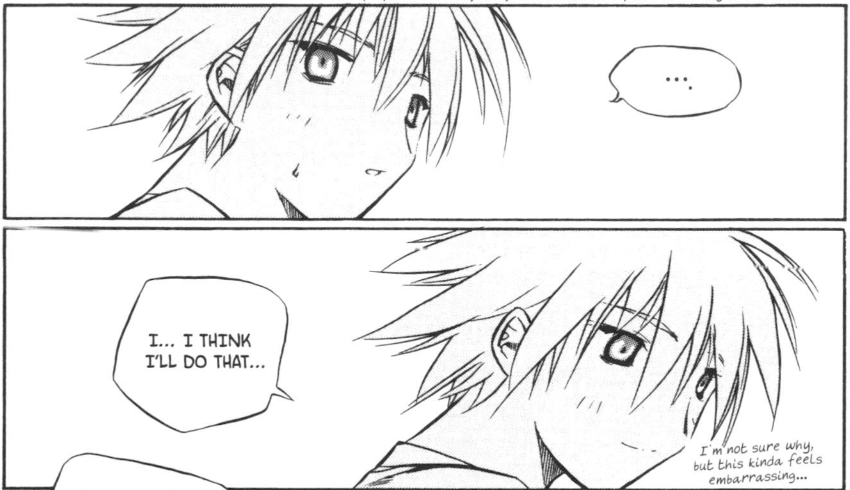
...
I... I THINK I'LL DO THAT...
I'm not sure why, but this kinda feels embarrassing...

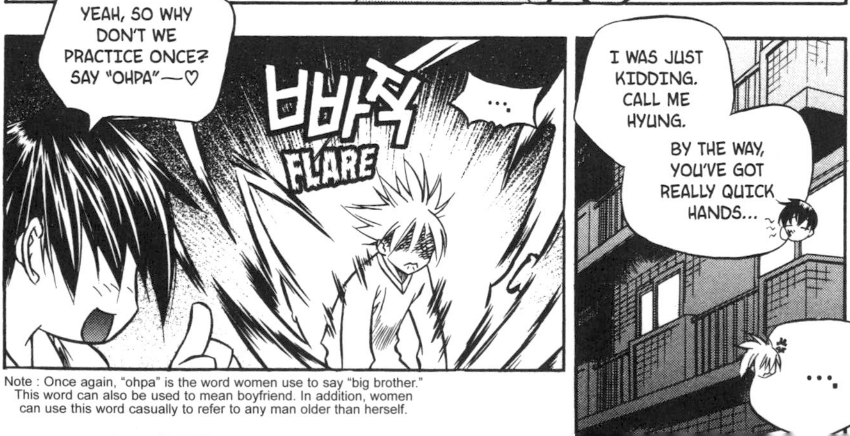
YEAH, SO WHY DON'T WE PRACTICE ONCE? SAY "OHPA"—♡
빠직
FLARE
...
I WAS JUST KIDDING. CALL ME HYUNG.
BY THE WAY, YOU'VE GOT REALLY QUICK HANDS...
...

Note : Once again, "ohpa" is the word women use to say "big brother." This word can also be used to mean boyfriend. In addition, women can use this word casually to refer to any man older than herself.

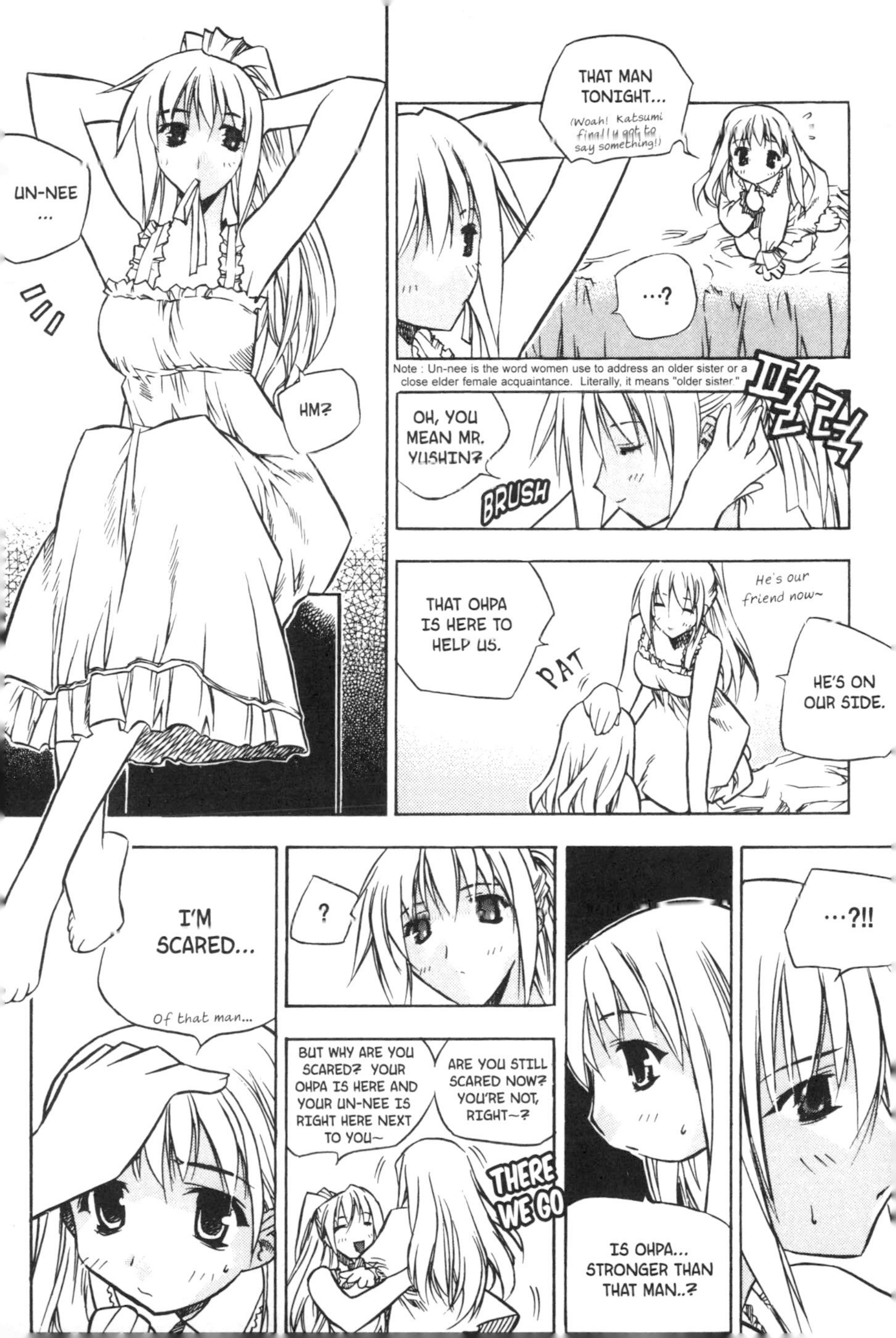
UN-NEE ...
HM?
THAT MAN TONIGHT...
(Woah! Katsumi finally got to say something!)
...?
펄럭
OH, YOU MEAN MR. YUSHIN?
BRUSH
THAT OHPA IS HERE TO HELP US.
PAT
He's our friend now~
HE'S ON OUR SIDE.
I'M SCARED...
Of that man...
?
BUT WHY ARE YOU SCARED? YOUR OHPA IS HERE AND YOUR UN-NEE IS RIGHT HERE NEXT TO YOU~
ARE YOU STILL SCARED NOW? YOU'RE NOT, RIGHT~?
THERE WE GO
IS OHPA... STRONGER THAN THAT MAN..?
...?!!

Note : Un-nee is the word women use to address an older sister or a close elder female acquaintance. Literally, it means "older sister."

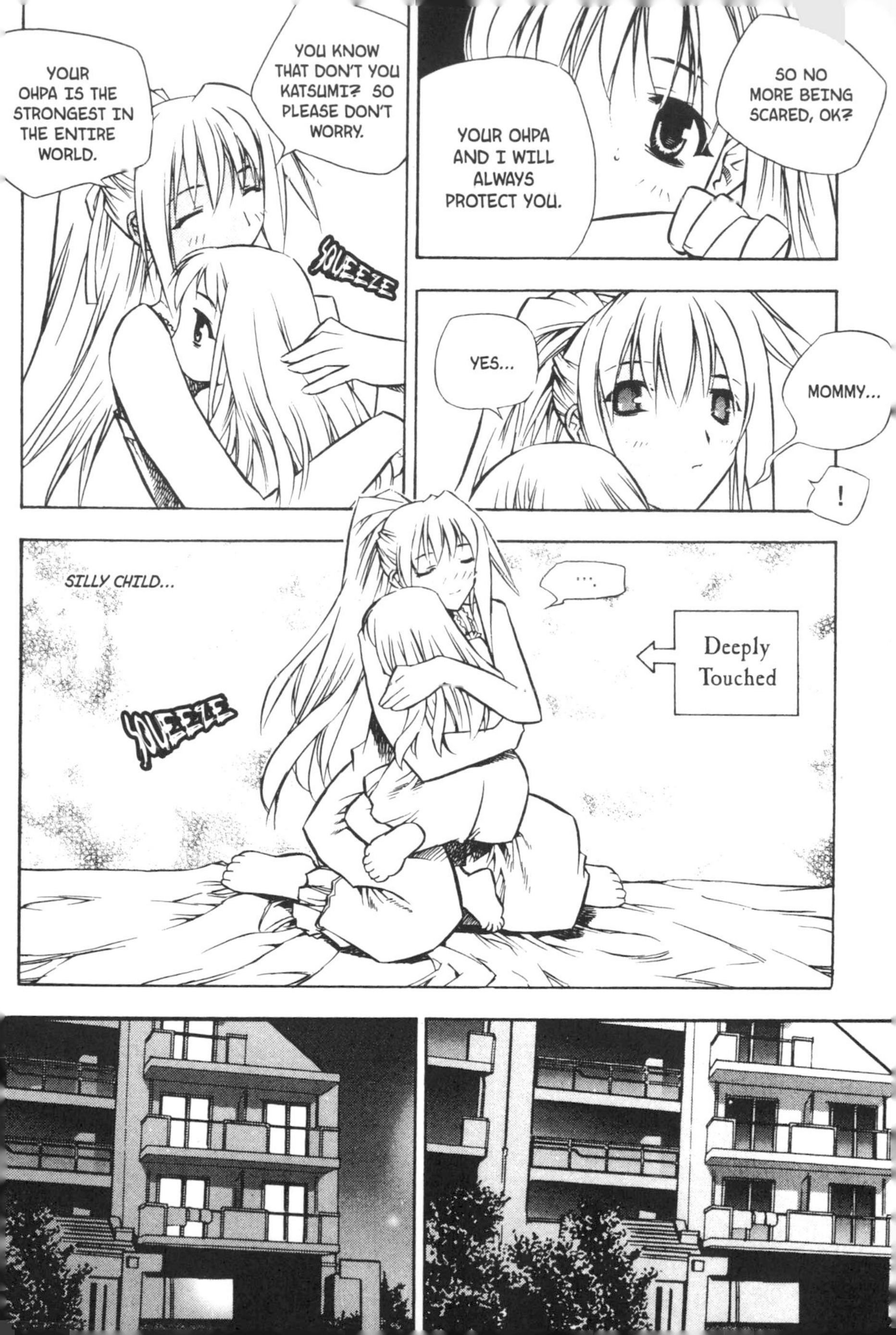

YOUR OHPA IS THE STRONGEST IN THE ENTIRE WORLD.
YOU KNOW THAT DON'T YOU KATSUMI? SO PLEASE DON'T WORRY.
SQUEEZE
YOUR OHPA AND I WILL ALWAYS PROTECT YOU.
SO NO MORE BEING SCARED, OK?
YES...
MOMMY...
!
SILLY CHILD...
...
Deeply Touched
SQUEEZE

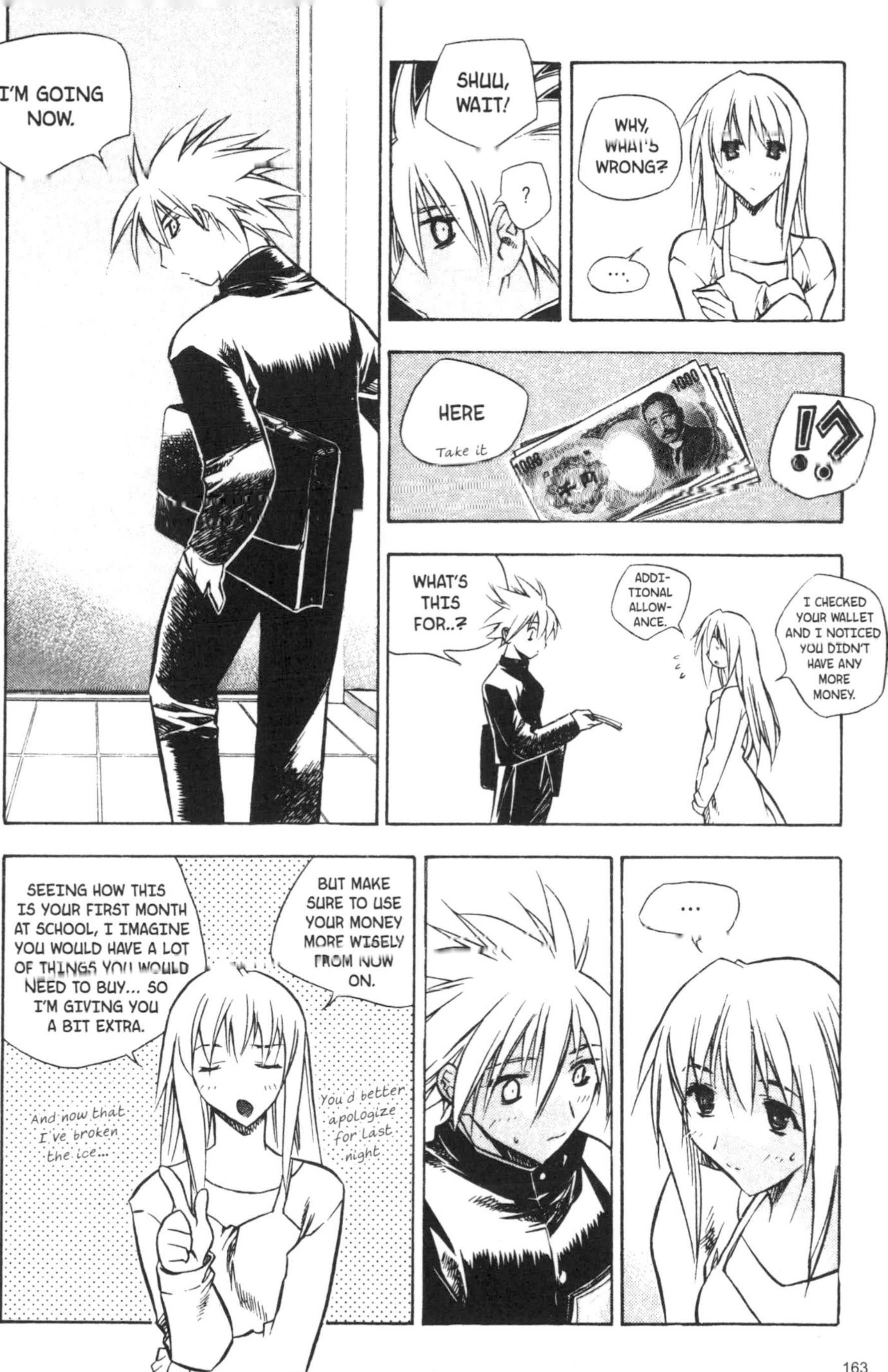

I'M GOING NOW.
SHUU, WAIT!
?
WHY, WHAT'S WRONG?
...
HERE
Take it
!?
WHAT'S THIS FOR..?
ADDITIONAL ALLOWANCE.
I CHECKED YOUR WALLET AND I NOTICED YOU DIDN'T HAVE ANY MORE MONEY.
SEEING HOW THIS IS YOUR FIRST MONTH AT SCHOOL, I IMAGINE YOU WOULD HAVE A LOT OF THINGS YOU WOULD NEED TO BUY... SO I'M GIVING YOU A BIT EXTRA.
BUT MAKE SURE TO USE YOUR MONEY MORE WISELY FROM NOW ON.
And now that I've broken the ice...
You'd better apologize for last night
...

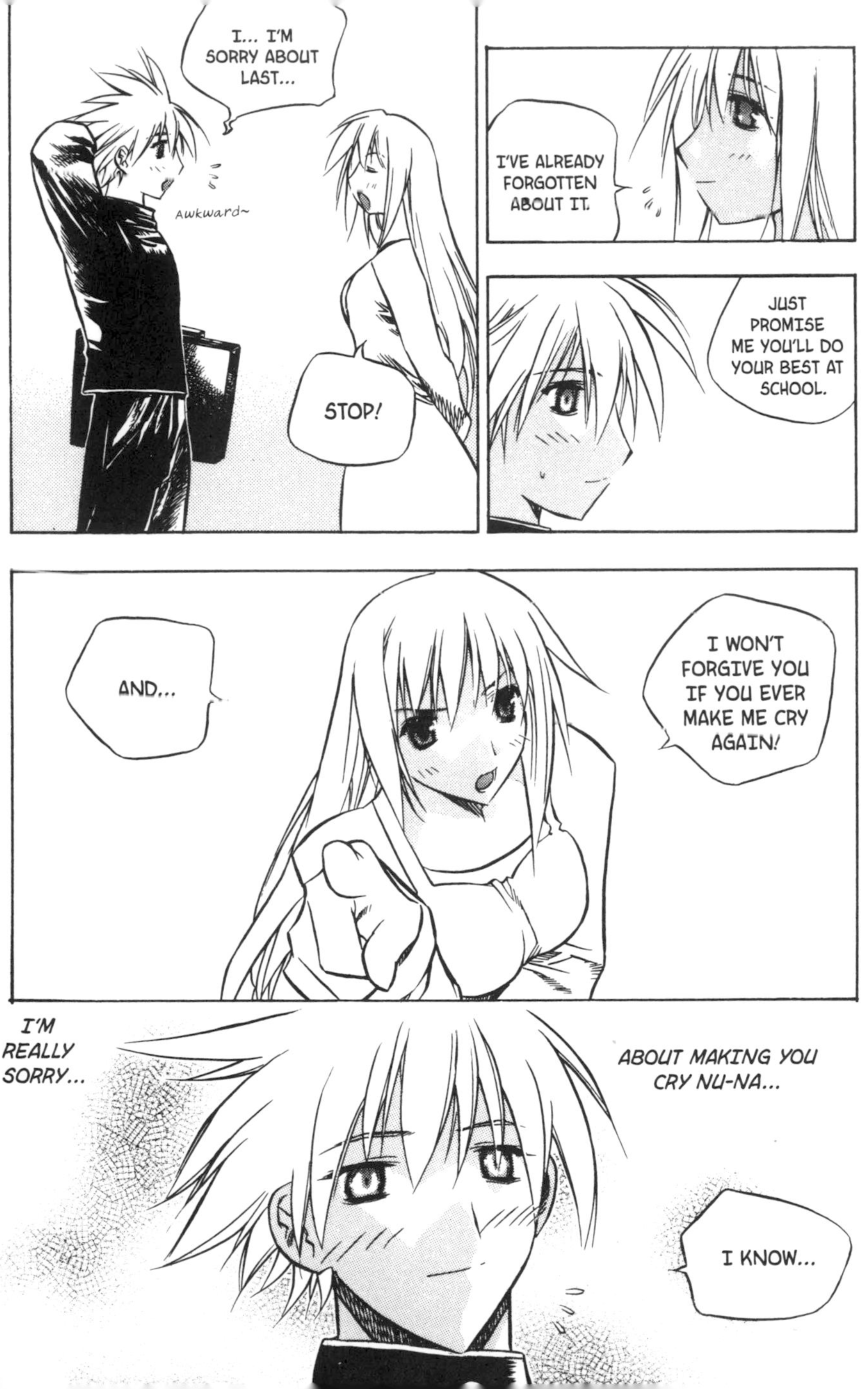

I... I'M SORRY ABOUT LAST...
Awkward~
STOP!
I'VE ALREADY FORGOTTEN ABOUT IT.
JUST PROMISE ME YOU'LL DO YOUR BEST AT SCHOOL.
AND...
I WON'T FORGIVE YOU IF YOU EVER MAKE ME CRY AGAIN!
I'M REALLY SORRY...
ABOUT MAKING YOU CRY NU-NA...
I KNOW...

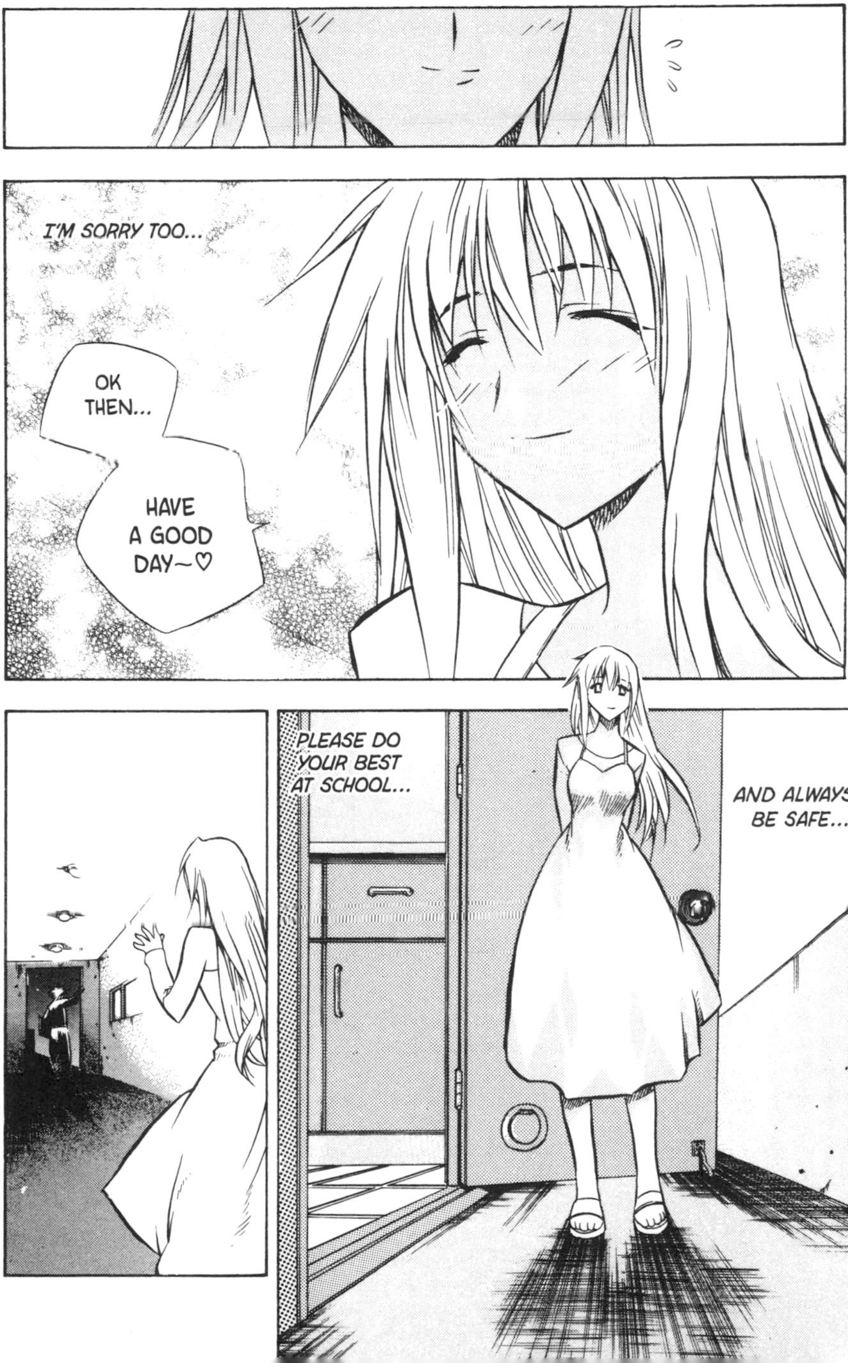
I'M SORRY TOO...
OK THEN...
HAVE A GOOD DAY~♡
PLEASE DO YOUR BEST AT SCHOOL...
AND ALWAYS BE SAFE...

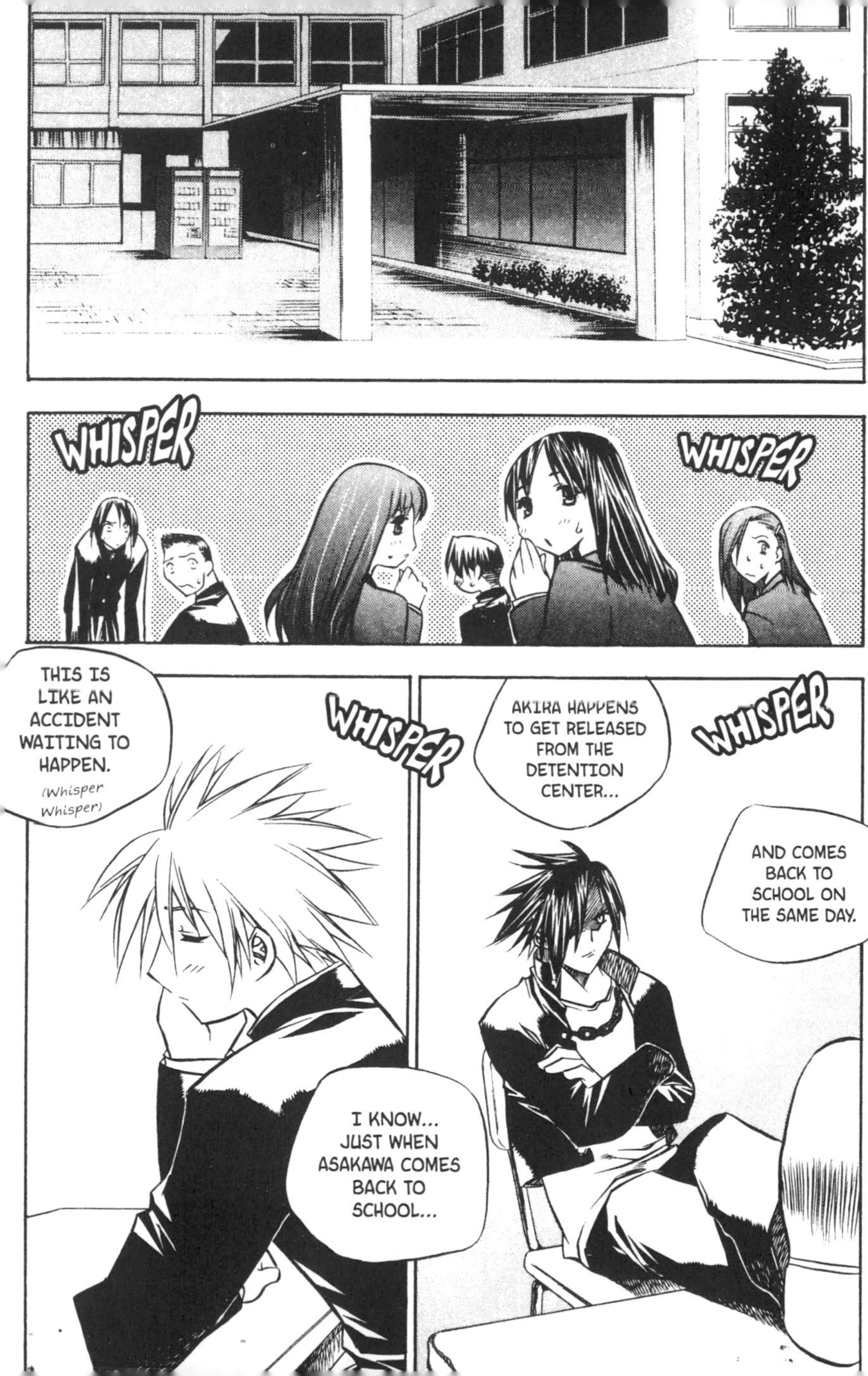
WHISPER
WHISPER
WHISPER
AKIRA HAPPENS TO GET RELEASED FROM THE DETENTION CENTER...
AND COMES BACK TO SCHOOL ON THE SAME DAY.
WHISPER
THIS IS LIKE AN ACCIDENT WAITING TO HAPPEN.
(Whisper Whisper)
I KNOW... JUST WHEN ASAKAWA COMES BACK TO SCHOOL...

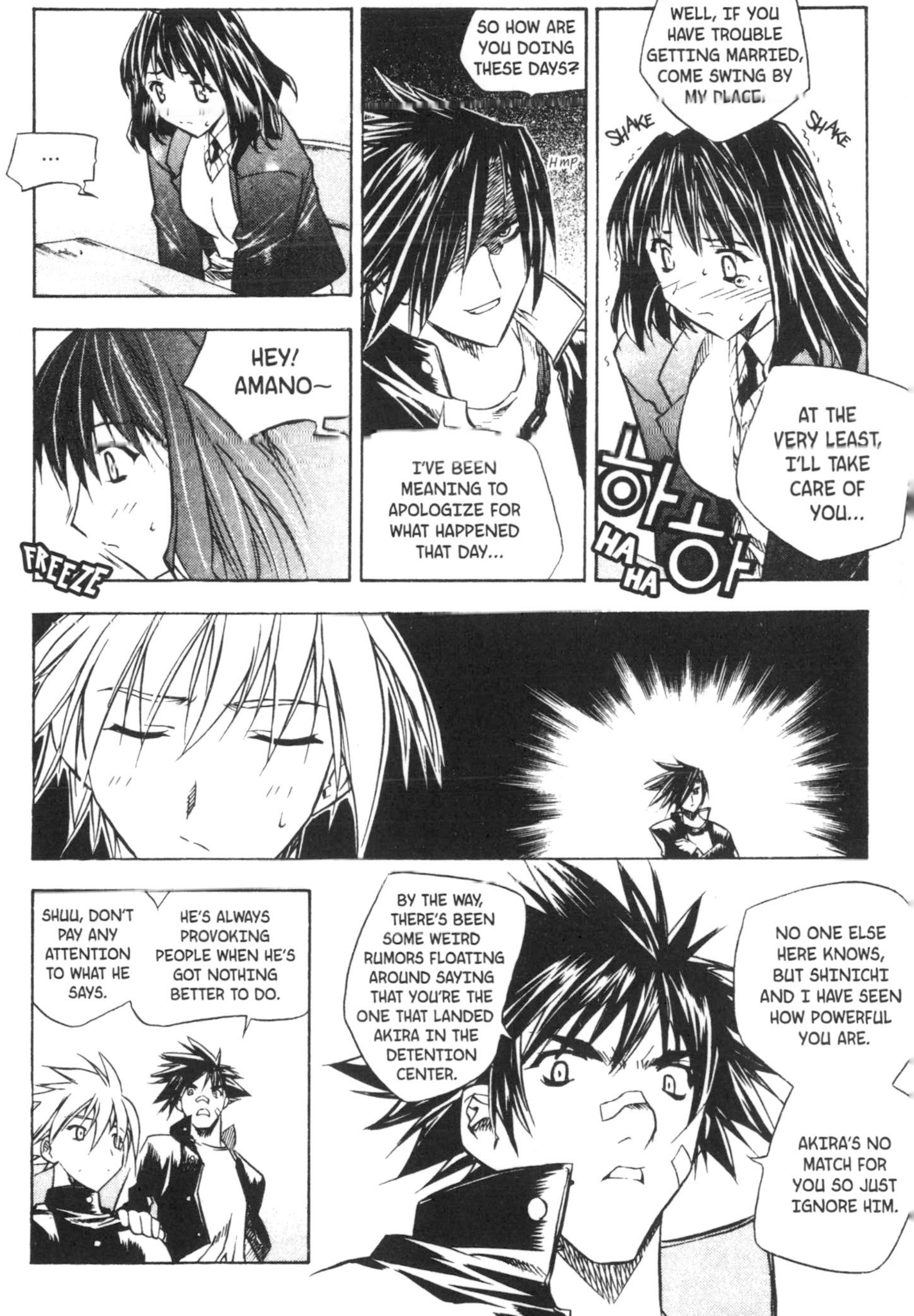
...
HEY! AMANO~
FREEZE
SO HOW ARE YOU DOING THESE DAYS?
Hmp
I'VE BEEN MEANING TO APOLOGIZE FOR WHAT HAPPENED THAT DAY...
WELL, IF YOU HAVE TROUBLE GETTING MARRIED, COME SWING BY MY PLACE.
SHAKE
SHAKE
AT THE VERY LEAST, I'LL TAKE CARE OF YOU...
하하
HA HA
SHUU, DON'T PAY ANY ATTENTION TO WHAT HE SAYS.
HE'S ALWAYS PROVOKING PEOPLE WHEN HE'S GOT NOTHING BETTER TO DO.
BY THE WAY, THERE'S BEEN SOME WEIRD RUMORS FLOATING AROUND SAYING THAT YOU'RE THE ONE THAT LANDED AKIRA IN THE DETENTION CENTER.
NO ONE ELSE HERE KNOWS, BUT SHINICHI AND I HAVE SEEN HOW POWERFUL YOU ARE.
AKIRA'S NO MATCH FOR YOU SO JUST IGNORE HIM.

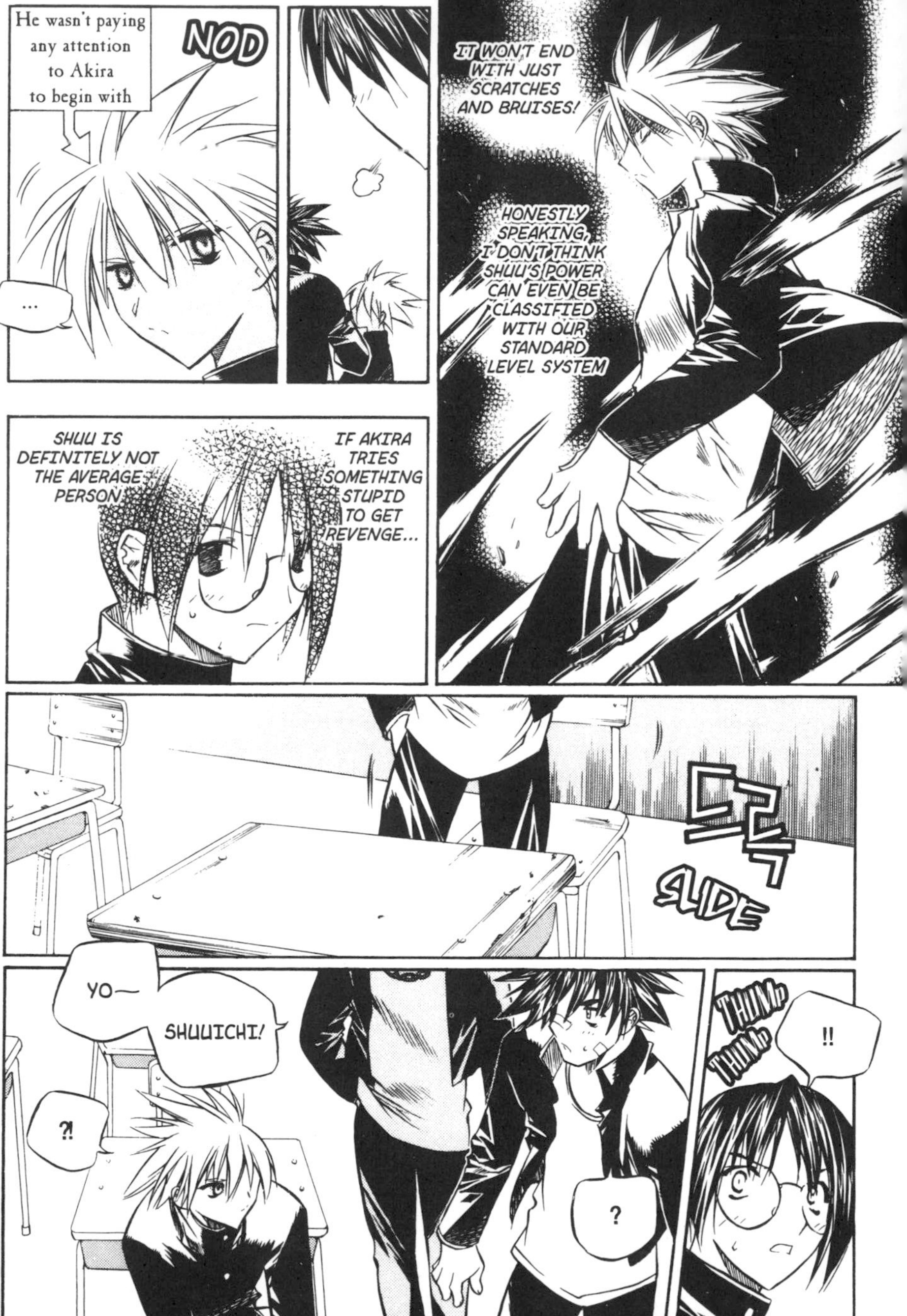

He wasn't paying any attention to Akira to begin with
NOD
...
SHUU IS DEFINITELY NOT THE AVERAGE PERSON
IF AKIRA TRIES SOMETHING STUPID TO GET REVENGE...
IT WON'T END WITH JUST SCRATCHES AND BRUISES!
HONESTLY SPEAKING, I DON'T THINK SHUU'S POWER CAN EVEN BE CLASSIFIED WITH OUR STANDARD LEVEL SYSTEM
SLIDE
THUMP THUMP
!!
YO—
SHUUICHI!
?!
?

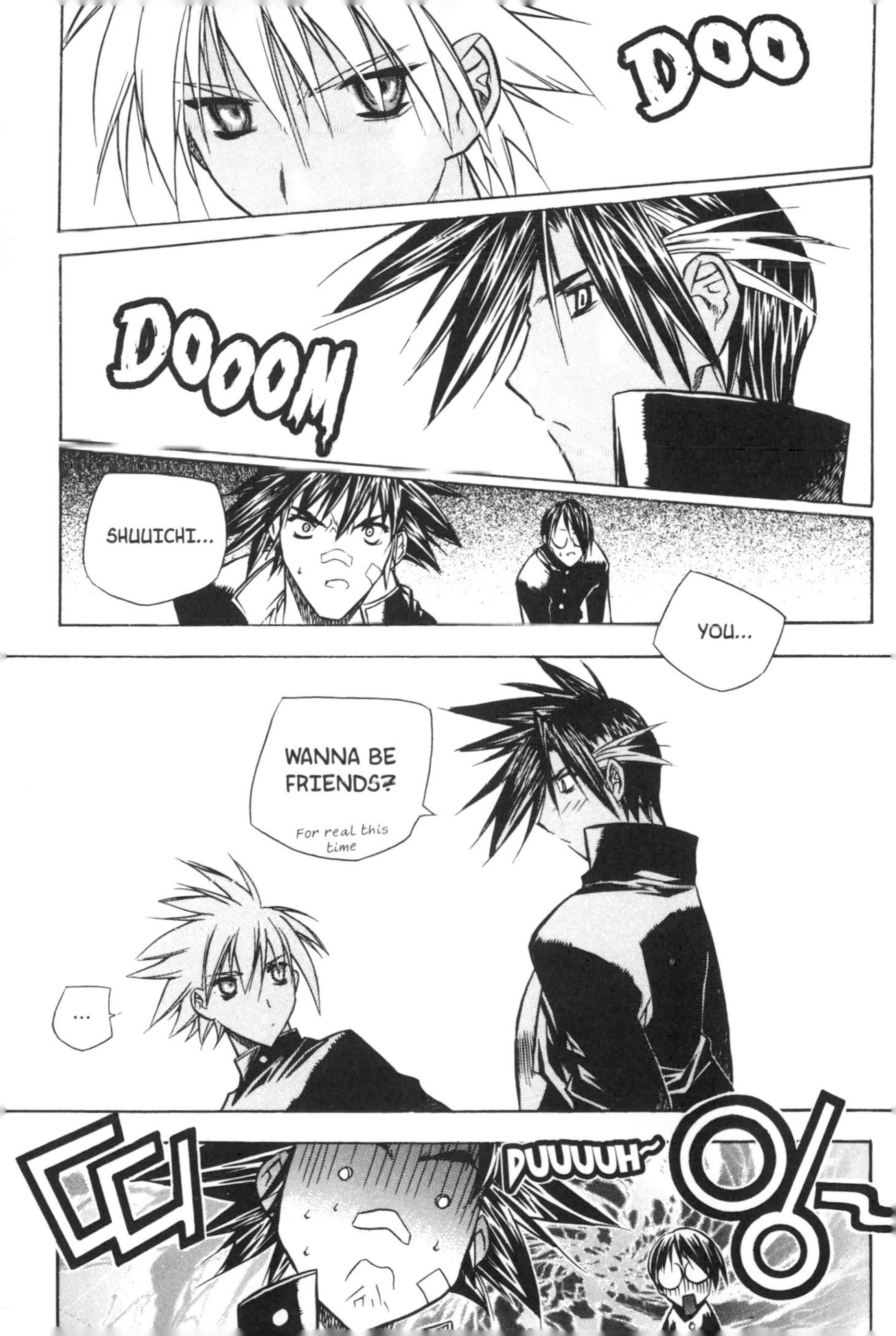
DOO
DOOOM
SHUUICHI...
YOU...
WANNA BE FRIENDS?
For real this time
...
DUUUUH~

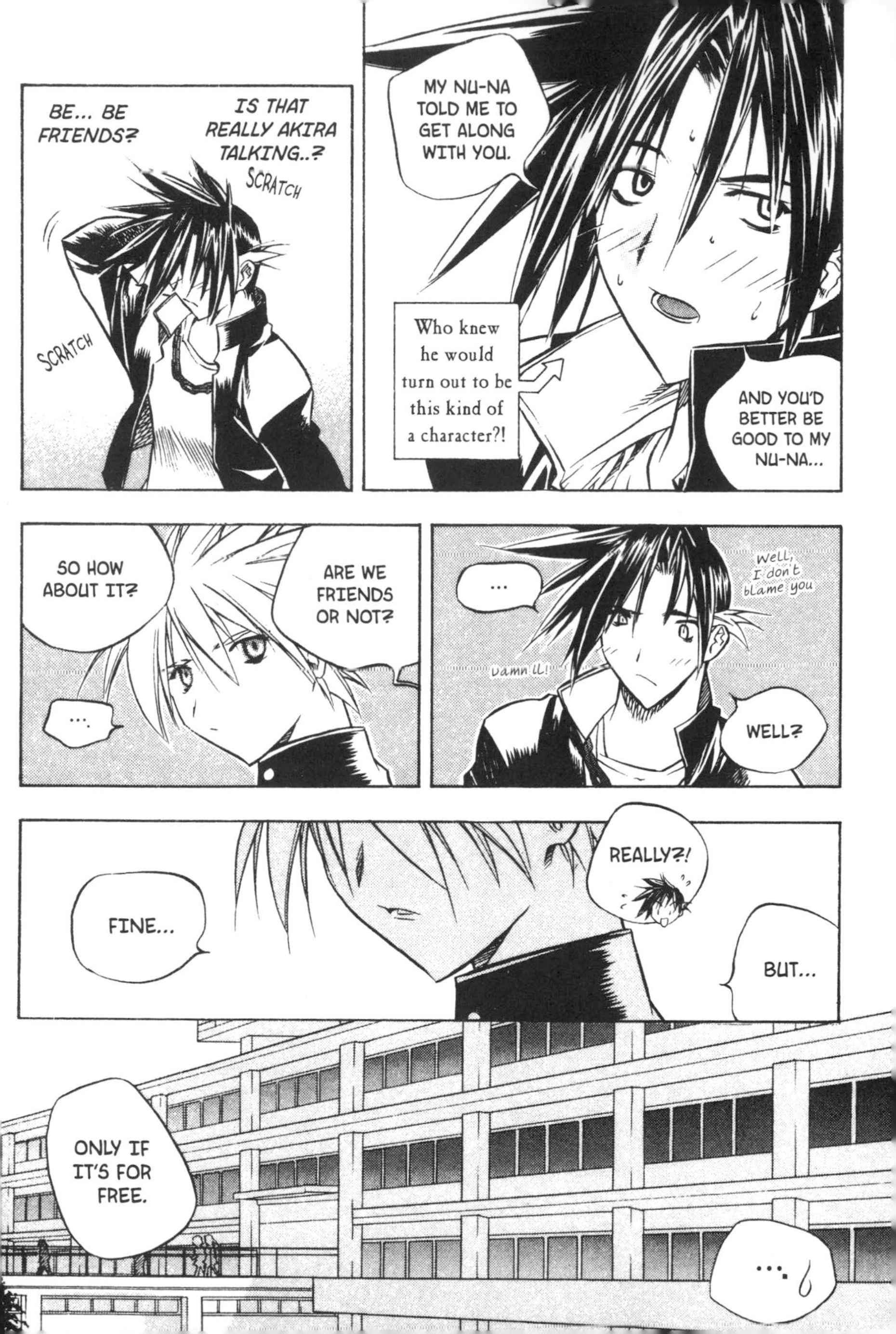
BE... BE FRIENDS?
IS THAT REALLY AKIRA TALKING..?
SCRATCH
SCRATCH
MY NU-NA TOLD ME TO GET ALONG WITH YOU.
Who knew he would turn out to be this kind of a character?!
AND YOU'D BETTER BE GOOD TO MY NU-NA...
SO HOW ABOUT IT?
ARE WE FRIENDS OR NOT?
...
...
Well, I don't blame you
Damn it!
WELL?
FINE...
REALLY?!
BUT...
ONLY IF IT'S FOR FREE.
...

CIRCLE 13 part I
The Time For Awakening

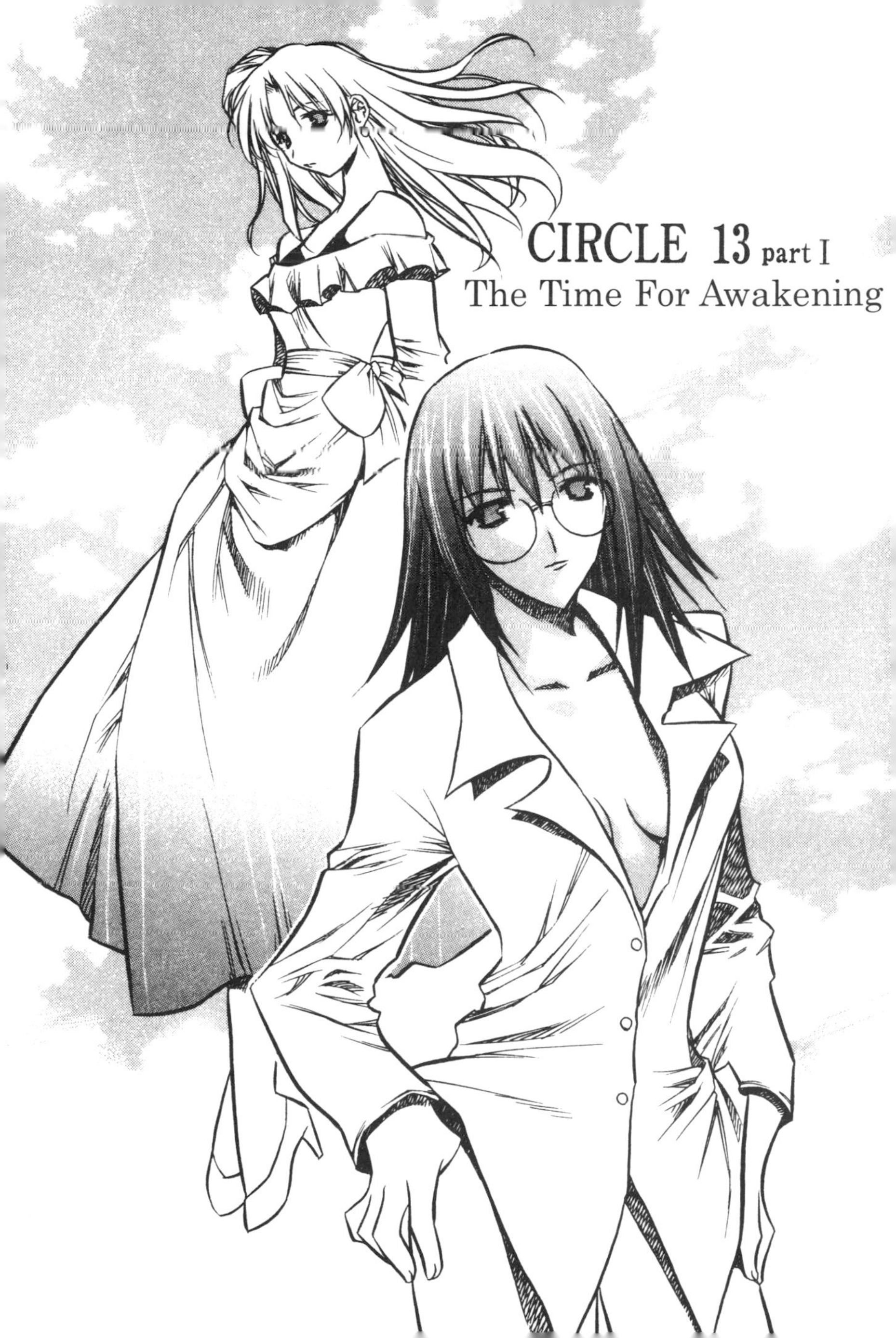

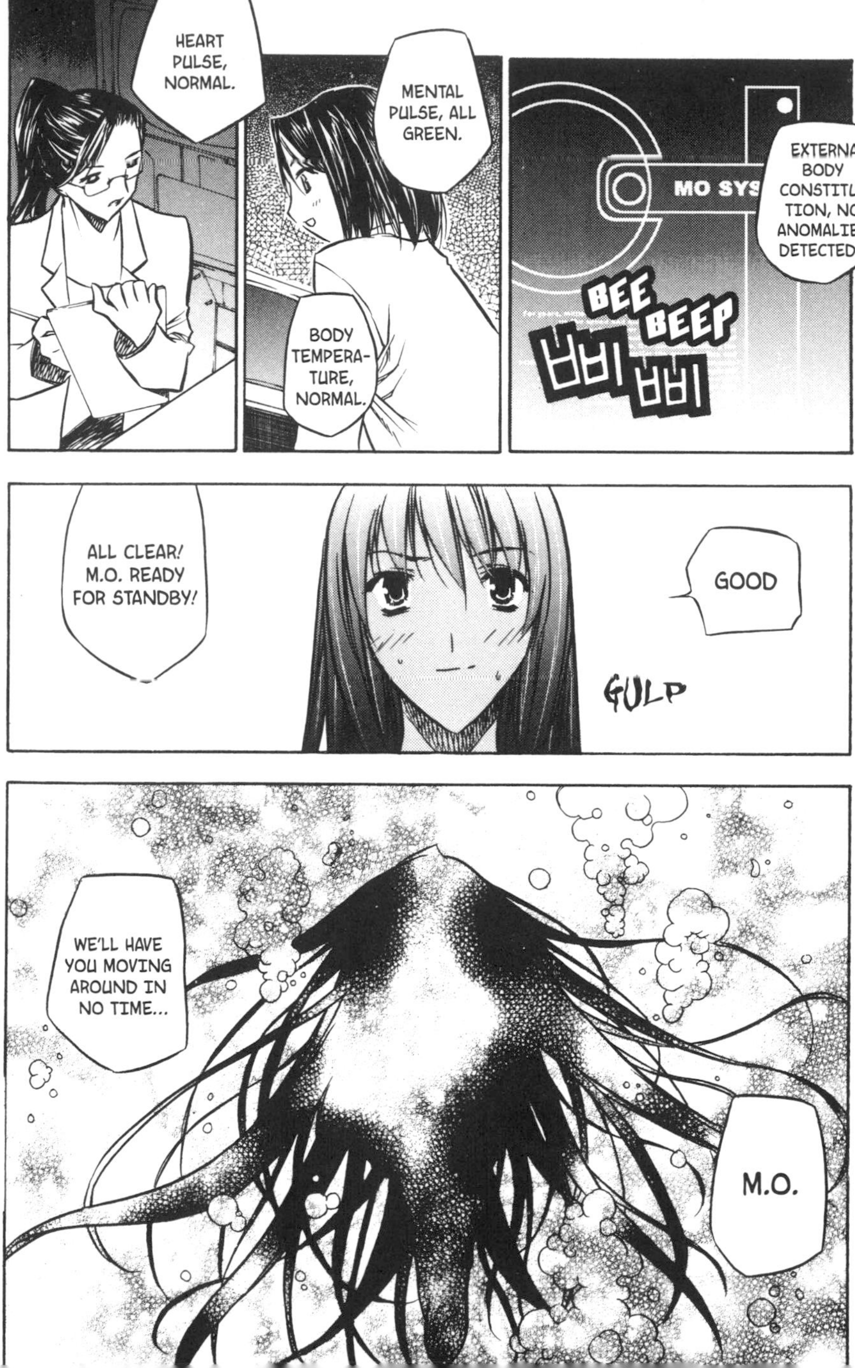
HEART PULSE, NORMAL.
MENTAL PULSE, ALL GREEN.
BODY TEMPERATURE, NORMAL.
MO SYS
EXTERNAL BODY CONSTITUTION, NO ANOMALIES DETECTED.
BEE BEEP
ALL CLEAR! M.O. READY FOR STANDBY!
GOOD
GULP
WE'LL HAVE YOU MOVING AROUND IN NO TIME...
M.O.

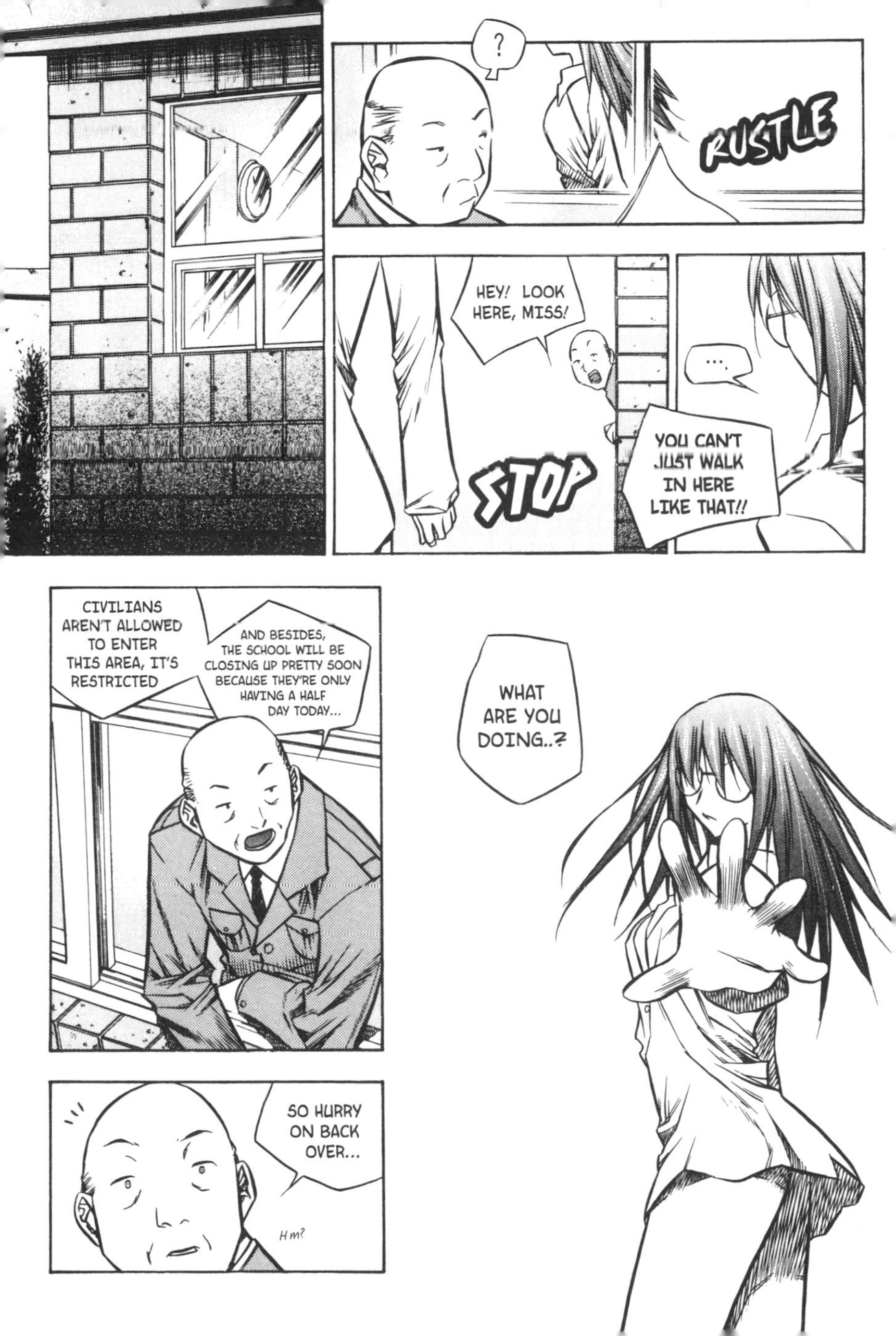
?
RUSTLE
HEY! LOOK HERE, MISS!
STOP
...
YOU CAN'T JUST WALK IN HERE LIKE THAT!!
CIVILIANS AREN'T ALLOWED TO ENTER THIS AREA, IT'S RESTRICTED
AND BESIDES, THE SCHOOL WILL BE CLOSING UP PRETTY SOON BECAUSE THEY'RE ONLY HAVING A HALF DAY TODAY...
SO HURRY ON BACK OVER...
Hm?
WHAT ARE YOU DOING..?

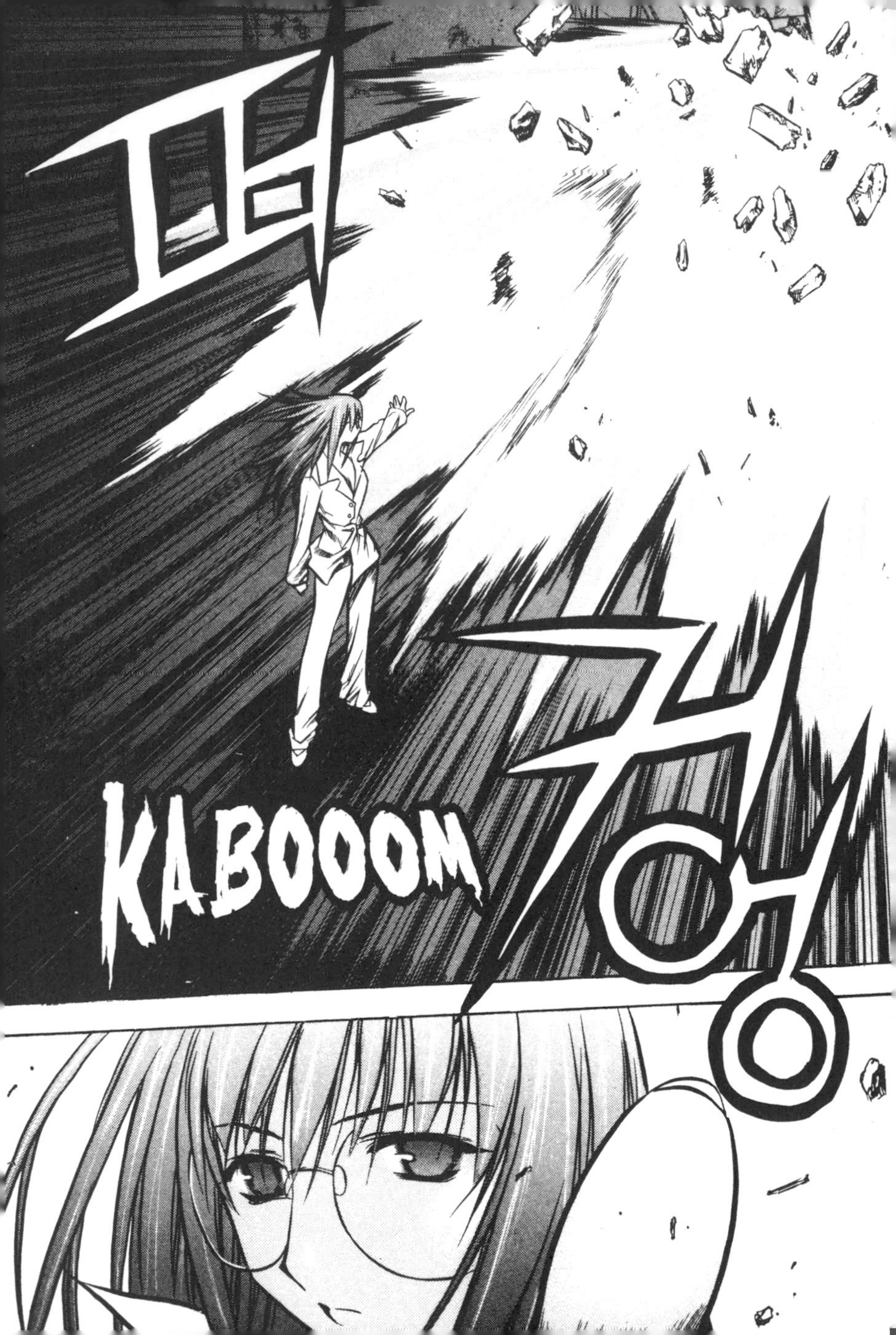
KABOOOM

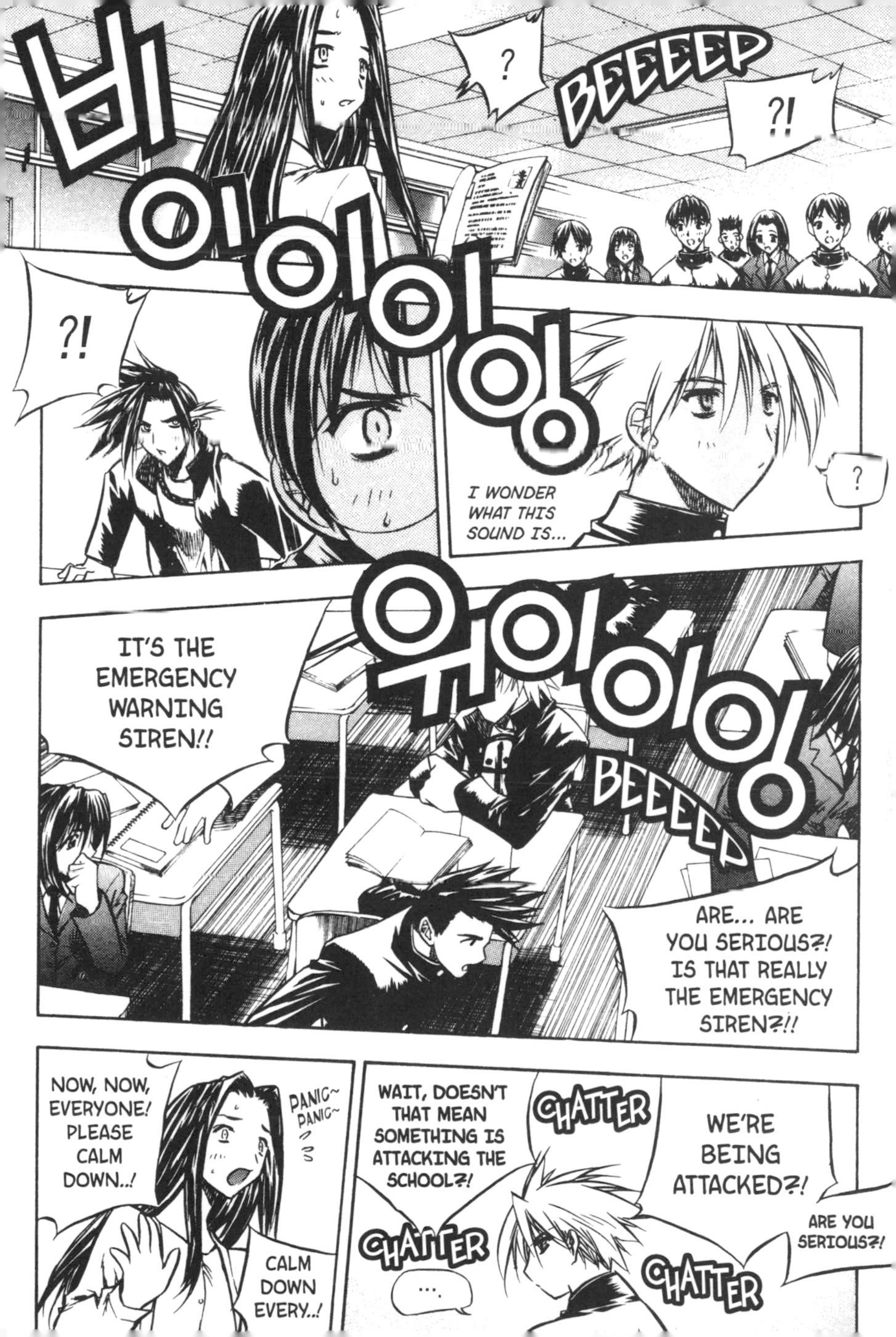
삐이이이잉
?
BEEEEP
?!
?!
I WONDER WHAT THIS SOUND IS...
?
우이이이잉
IT'S THE EMERGENCY WARNING SIREN!!
BEEEEP
ARE... ARE YOU SERIOUS?! IS THAT REALLY THE EMERGENCY SIREN?!!
NOW, NOW, EVERYONE! PLEASE CALM DOWN..!
PANIC~ PANIC~
CALM DOWN EVERY..!
WAIT, DOESN'T THAT MEAN SOMETHING IS ATTACKING THE SCHOOL?!
CHATTER
WE'RE BEING ATTACKED?!
CHATTER
...
CHATTER
ARE YOU SERIOUS?!

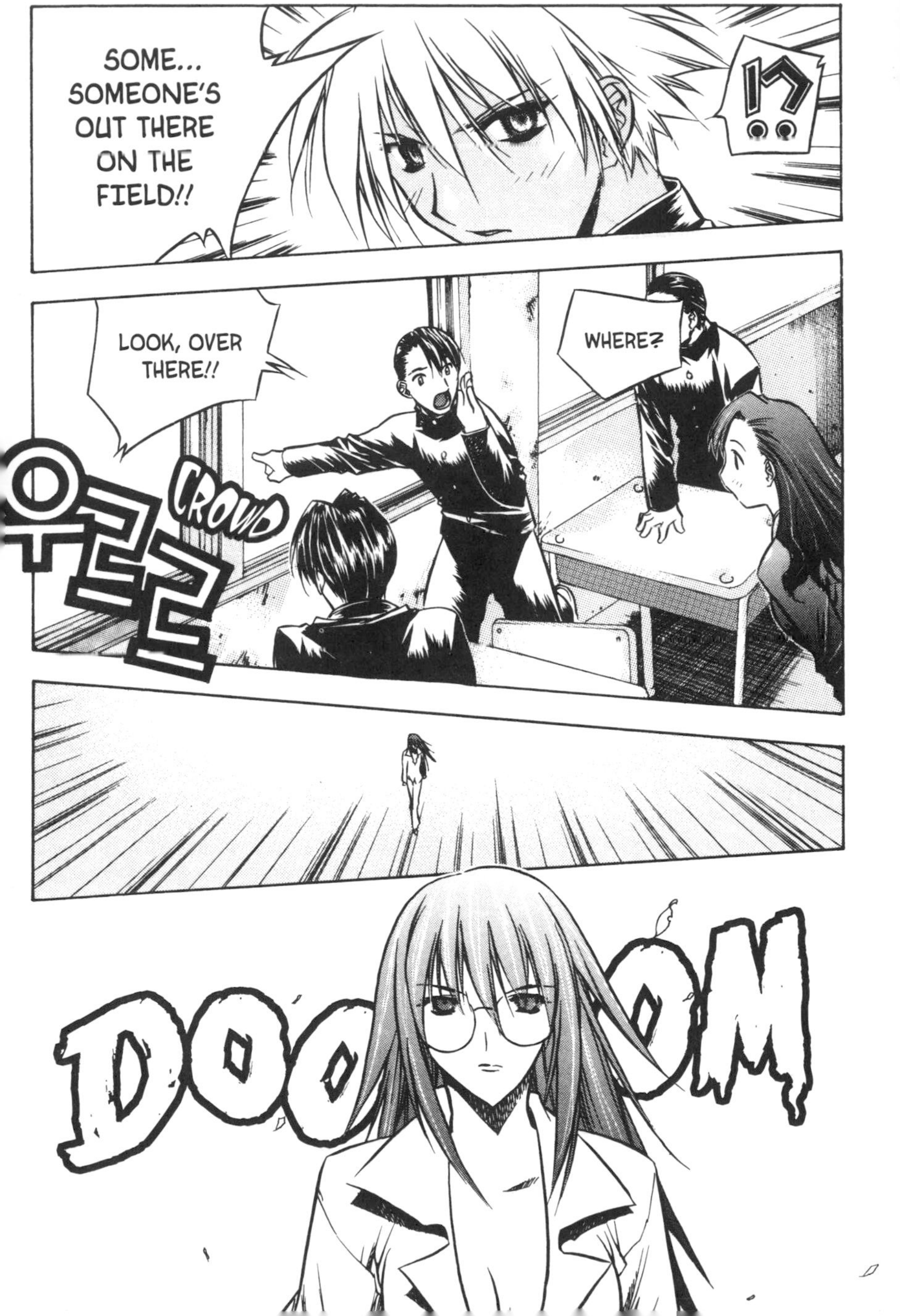
SOME... SOMEONE'S OUT THERE ON THE FIELD!!
!!
WHERE?
LOOK, OVER THERE!!
우글글
CROWD
DOOOM

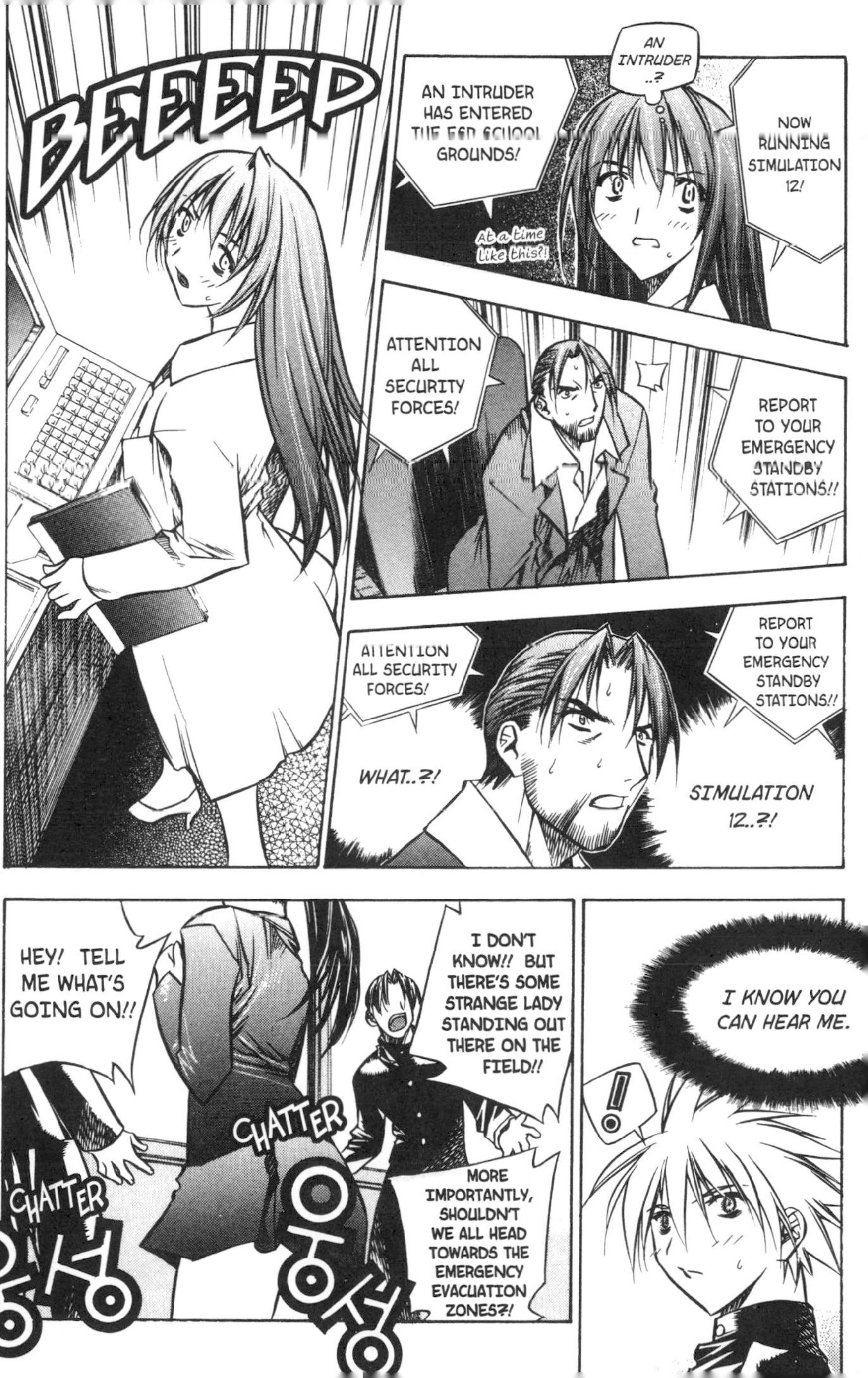
BEEEEP
AN INTRUDER HAS ENTERED THE ESP SCHOOL GROUNDS!
At a time like this?!
AN INTRUDER ..?
NOW RUNNING SIMULATION 12!
ATTENTION ALL SECURITY FORCES!
REPORT TO YOUR EMERGENCY STANDBY STATIONS!!
ATTENTION ALL SECURITY FORCES!
REPORT TO YOUR EMERGENCY STANDBY STATIONS!!
WHAT..?!
SIMULATION 12..?!
HEY! TELL ME WHAT'S GOING ON!!
I DON'T KNOW!! BUT THERE'S SOME STRANGE LADY STANDING OUT THERE ON THE FIELD!!
MORE IMPORTANTLY, SHOULDN'T WE ALL HEAD TOWARDS THE EMERGENCY EVACUATION ZONES?!
CHATTER
웅성
CHATTER
웅성
I KNOW YOU CAN HEAR ME.
!

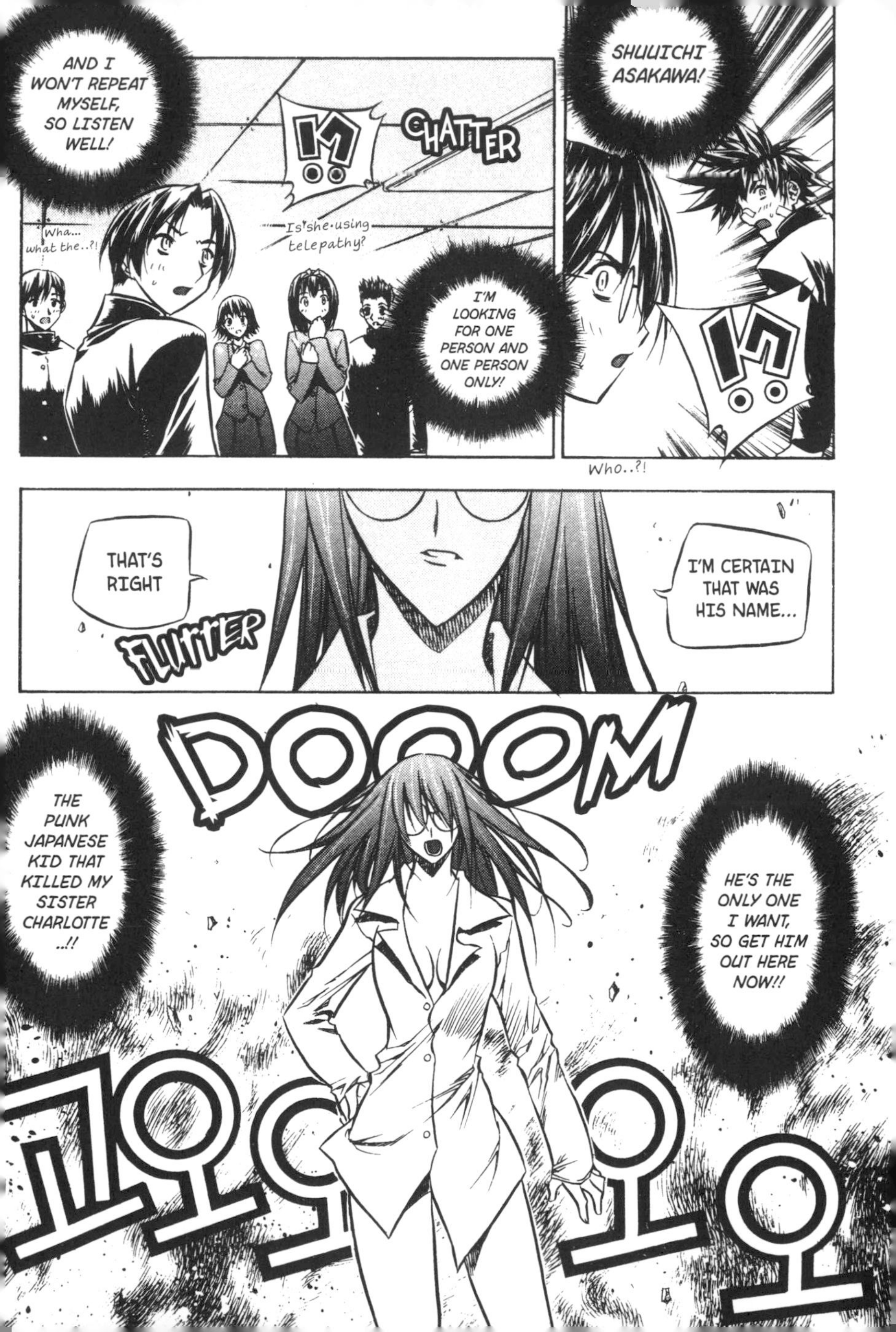
AND I WON'T REPEAT MYSELF, SO LISTEN WELL!
!?
CHATTER
Wha... what the..?!
Is she using telepathy?
I'M LOOKING FOR ONE PERSON AND ONE PERSON ONLY!
SHUUICHI ASAKAWA!
!?
Who..?!
I'M CERTAIN THAT WAS HIS NAME...
THAT'S RIGHT
FLUTTER
DOOOM
THE PUNK JAPANESE KID THAT KILLED MY SISTER CHARLOTTE ..!!
HE'S THE ONLY ONE I WANT, SO GET HIM OUT HERE NOW!!

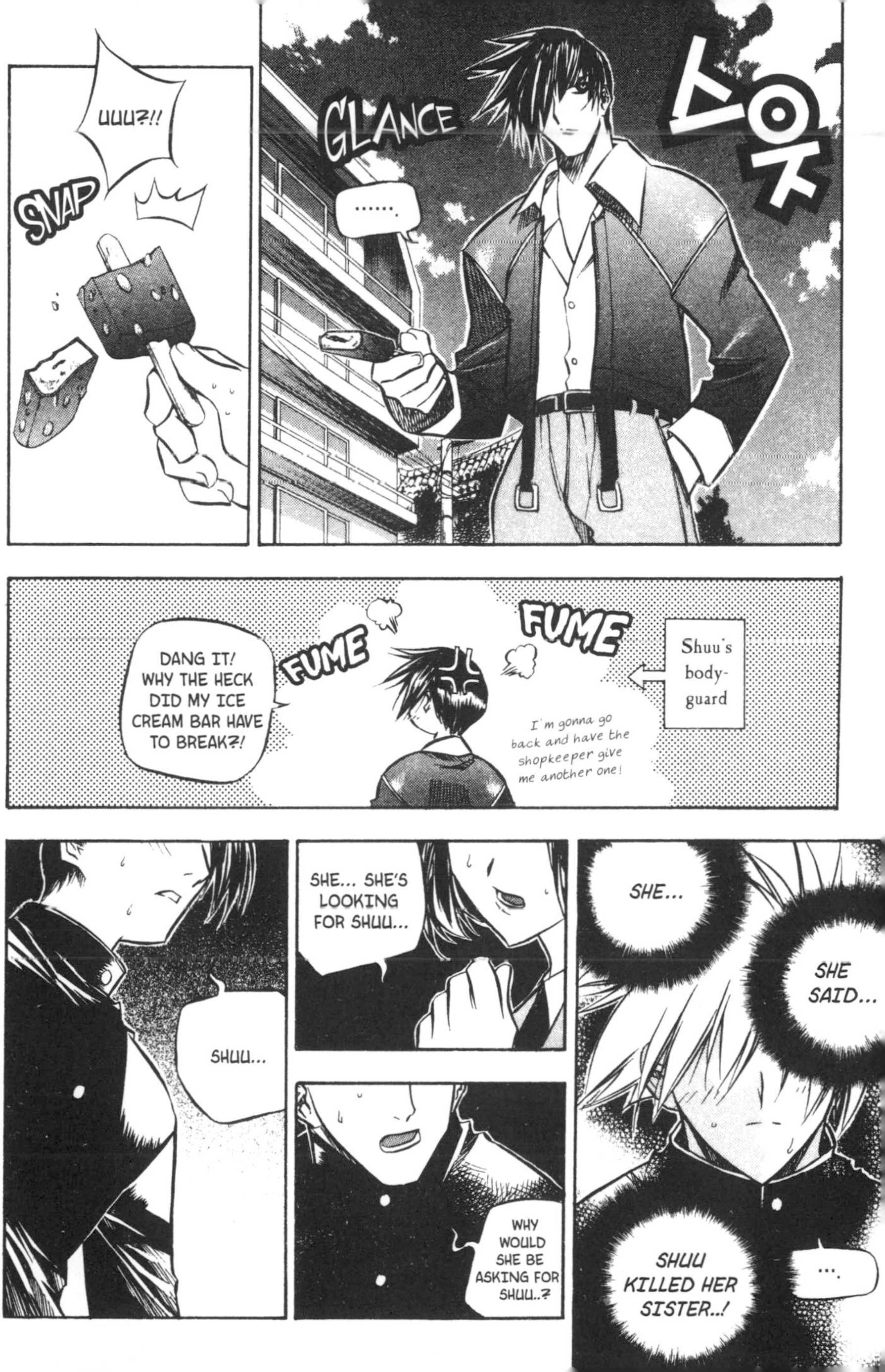

TOK
GLANCE
....
SNAP
UUU?!!
FUME
FUME
Shuu's bodyguard
I'm gonna go back and have the shopkeeper give me another one!
DANG IT! WHY THE HECK DID MY ICE CREAM BAR HAVE TO BREAK?!
SHE...
SHE SAID...
SHUU KILLED HER SISTER..!
....
SHE... SHE'S LOOKING FOR SHUU...
WHY WOULD SHE BE ASKING FOR SHUU..?
SHUU...

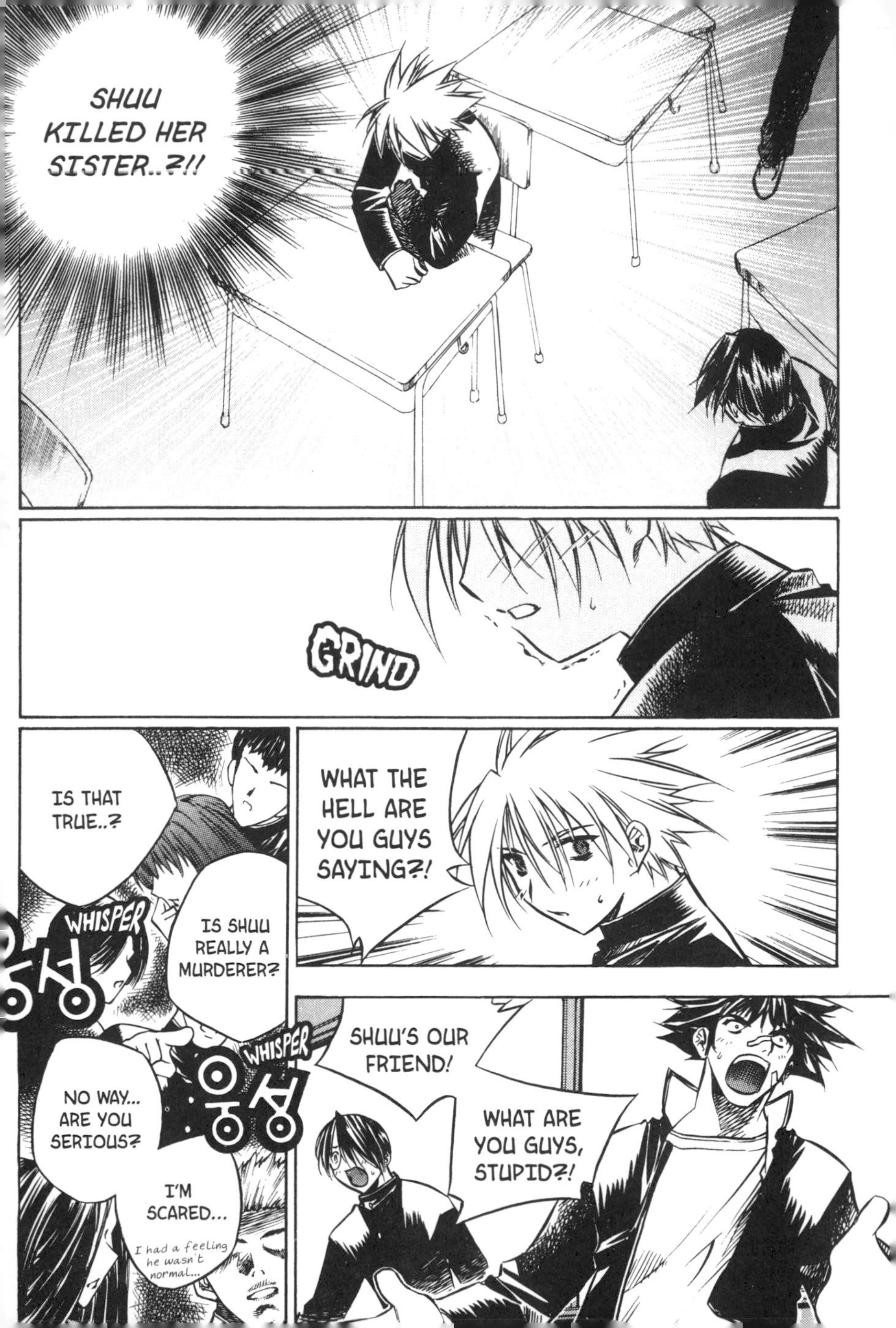
SHUU KILLED HER SISTER..?!!
GRIND
WHAT THE HELL ARE YOU GUYS SAYING?!
IS THAT TRUE..?
WHISPER
IS SHUU REALLY A MURDERER?
웅성
WHISPER
웅성
NO WAY... ARE YOU SERIOUS?
I'M SCARED...
I had a feeling he wasn't normal...
SHUU'S OUR FRIEND!
WHAT ARE YOU GUYS, STUPID?!

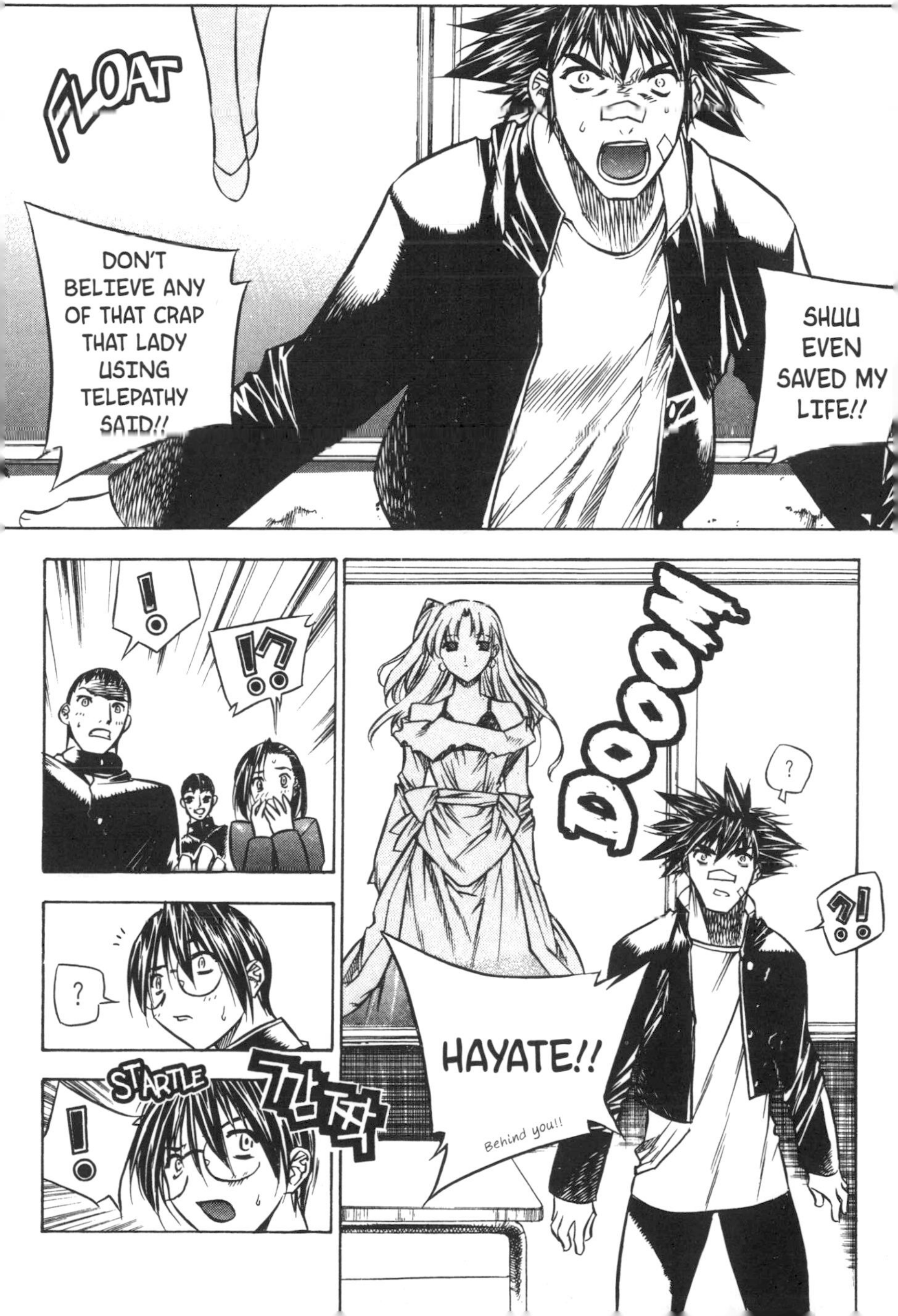
FLOAT
SHUU EVEN SAVED MY LIFE!!
DON'T BELIEVE ANY OF THAT CRAP THAT LADY USING TELEPATHY SAID!!
DOOOM
?
?!
!
!?
HAYATE!!
Behind you!!
?
STARTLE
깜짝
!

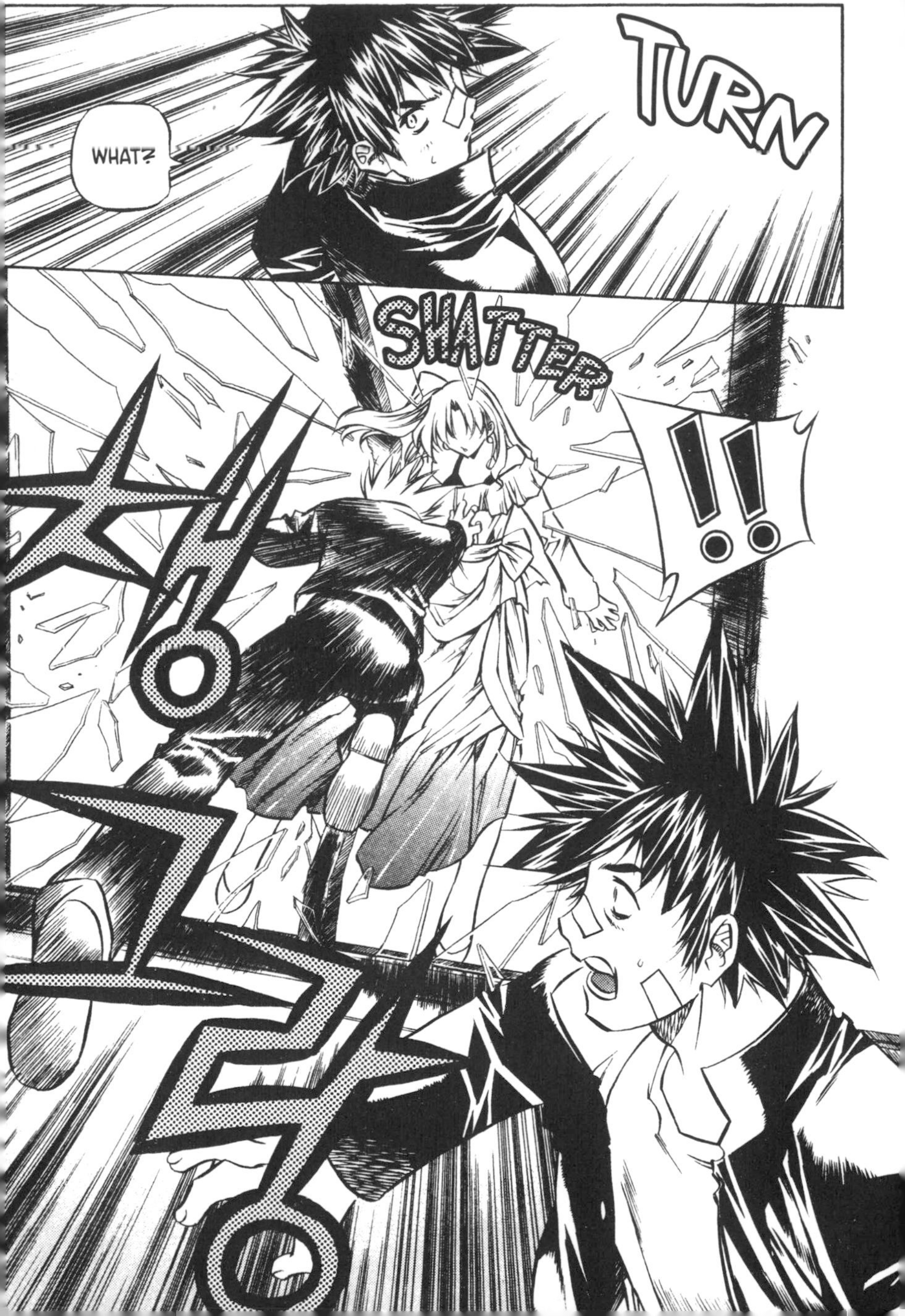
TURN
WHAT?
SHATTER
!!

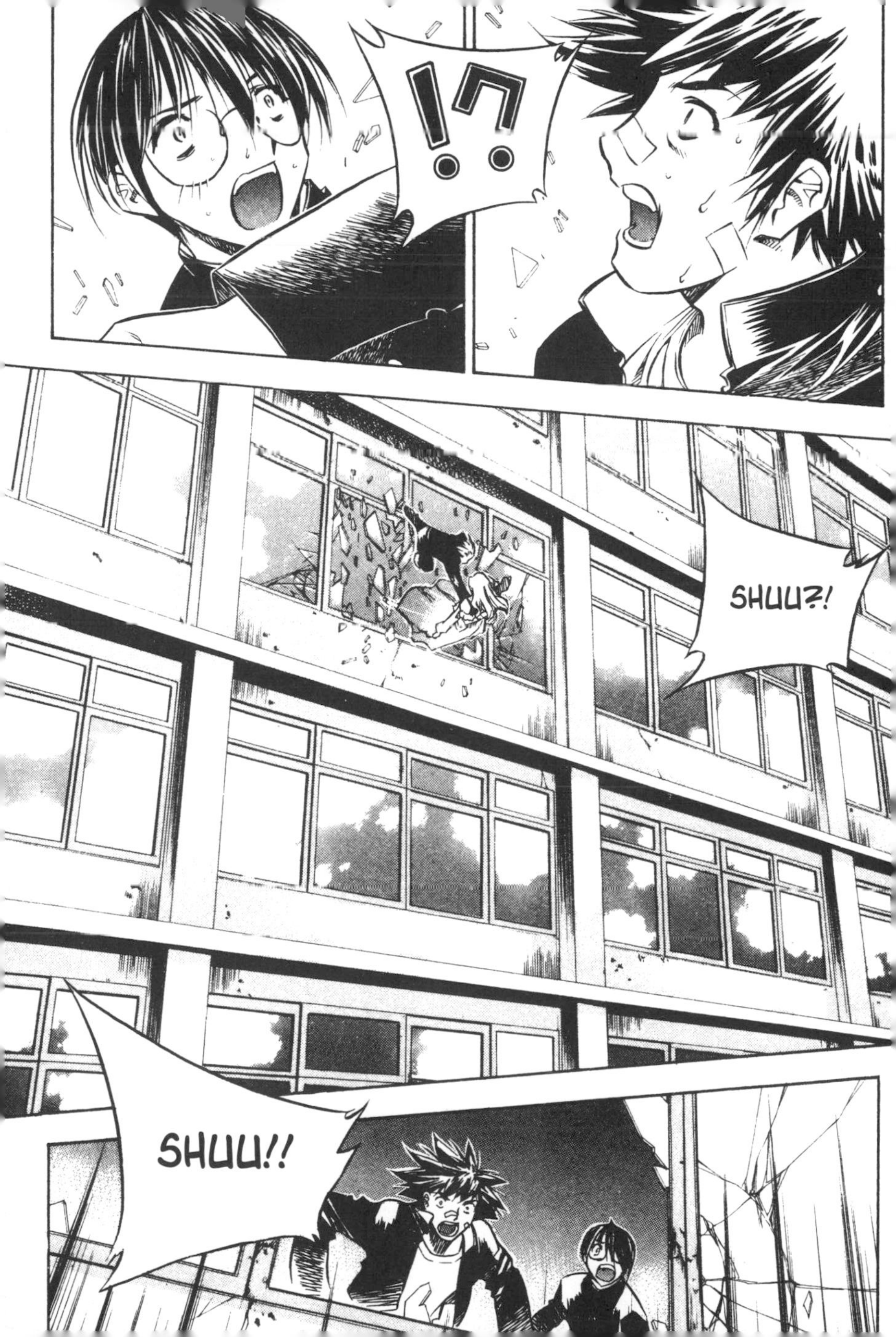
!?
SHUU?!
SHUU!!

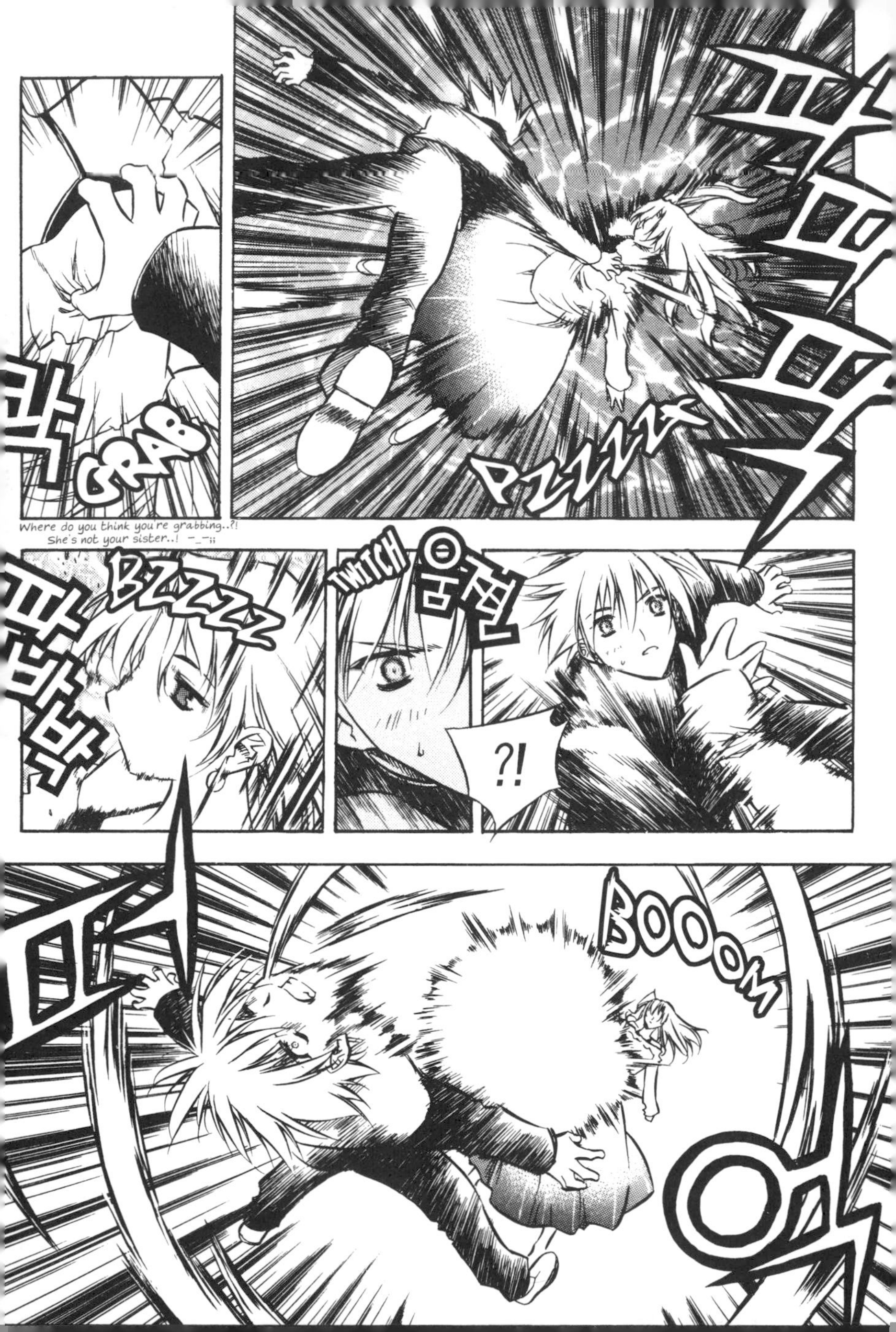

GRAB
PZZZZT
Where do you think you're grabbing..?!
She's not your sister..! -_-;;
BZZZZZ
TWITCH 움찔
?!
BOOOOM

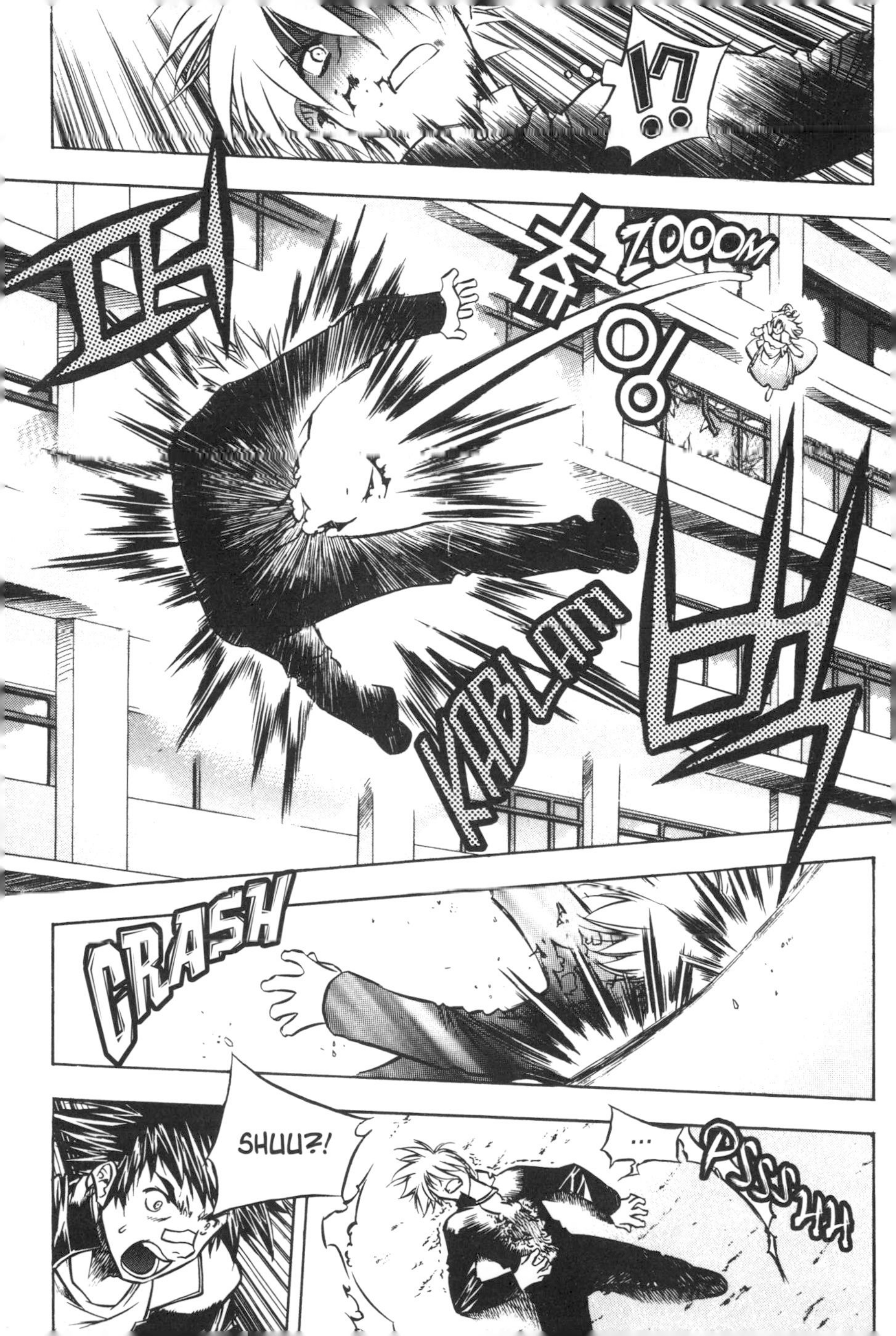
!?
ZOOOM
KABLAM
CRASH
SHUU?!
...
PSSSHH

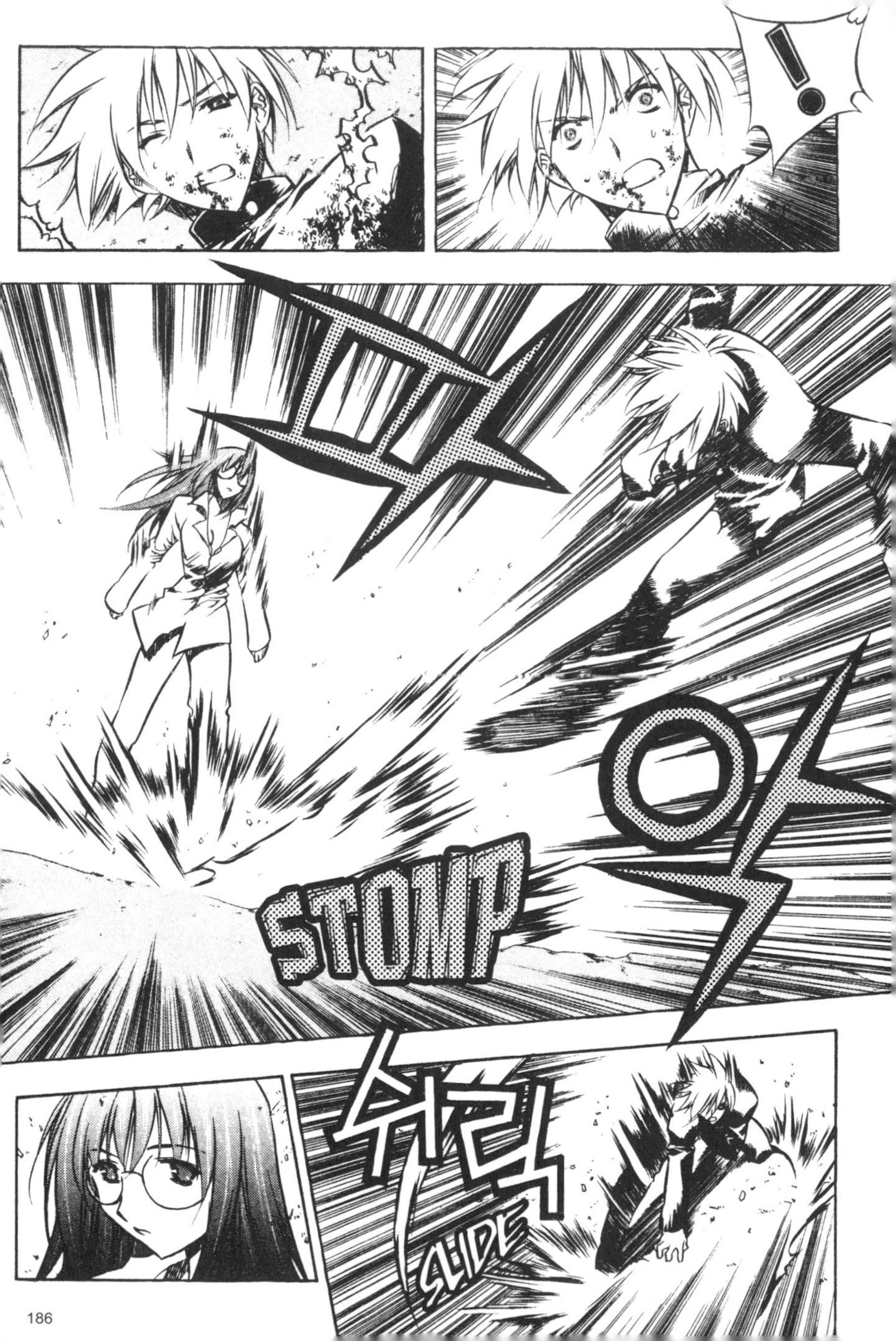
!
STOMP
SLIDE

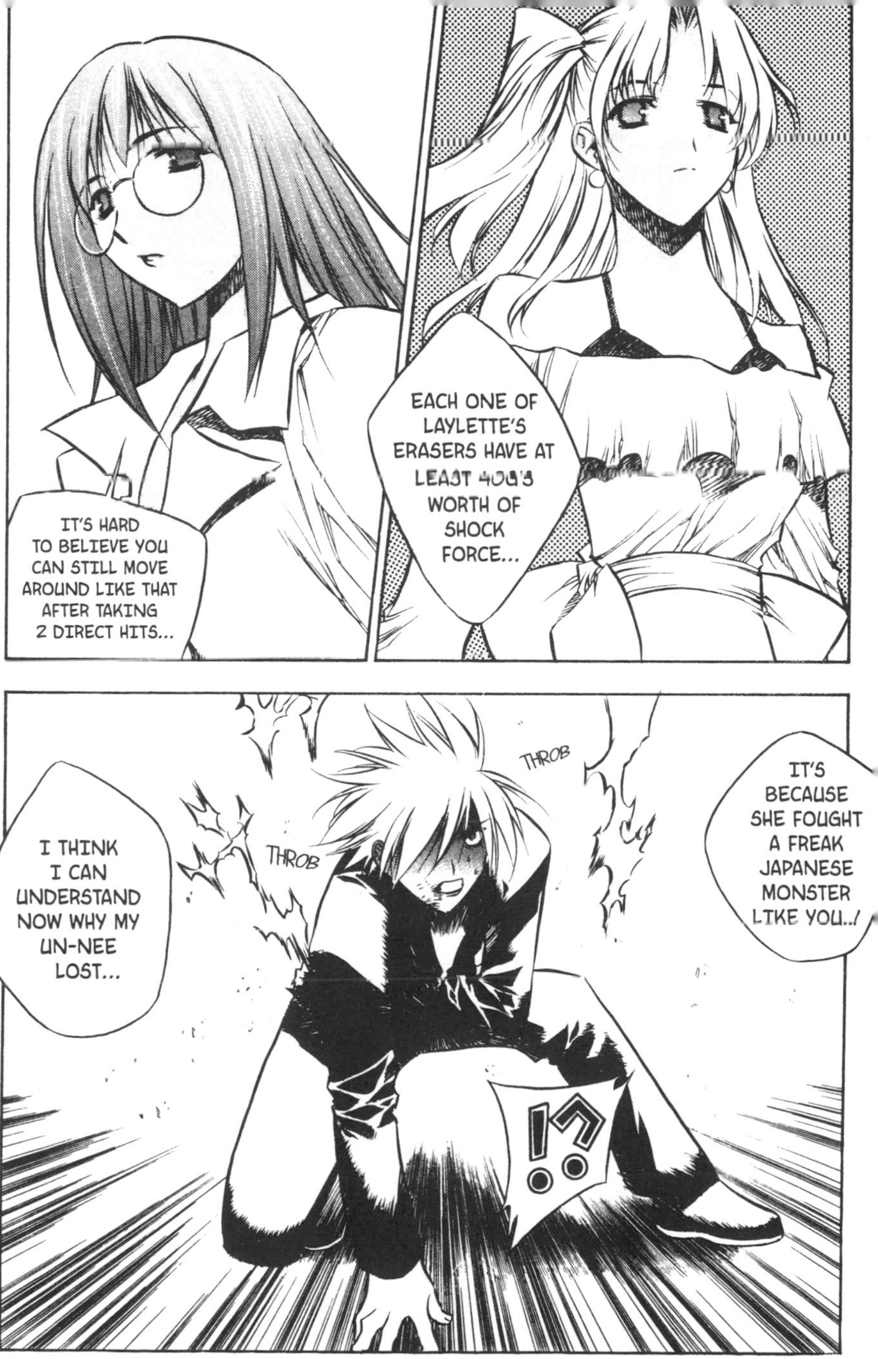
EACH ONE OF LAYLETTE'S ERASERS HAVE AT LEAST 40G'S WORTH OF SHOCK FORCE...
IT'S HARD TO BELIEVE YOU CAN STILL MOVE AROUND LIKE THAT AFTER TAKING 2 DIRECT HITS...
IT'S BECAUSE SHE FOUGHT A FREAK JAPANESE MONSTER LIKE YOU..!
THROB
THROB
I THINK I CAN UNDERSTAND NOW WHY MY UN-NEE LOST...
!?

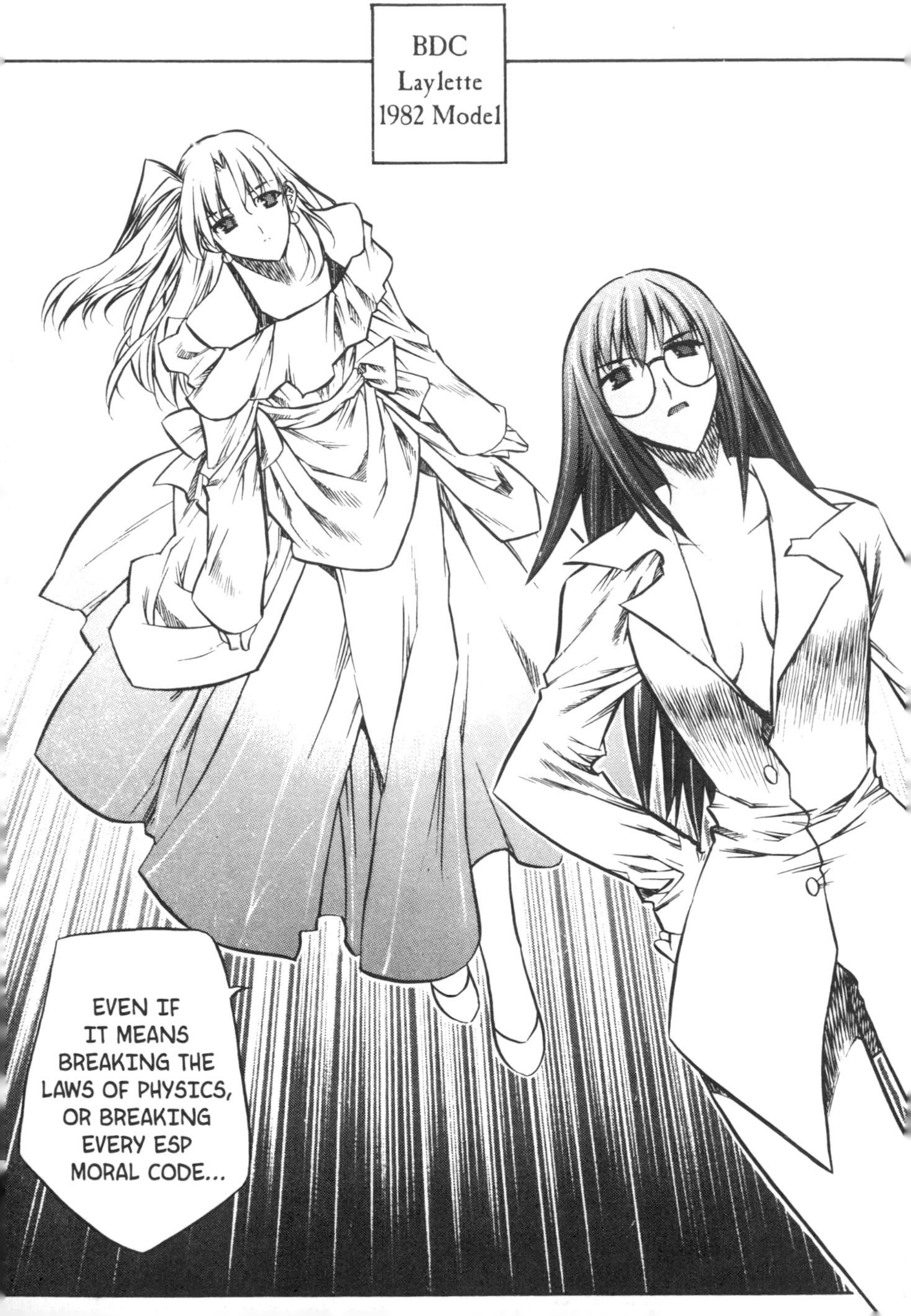
BDC
Laylette
1982 Model
EVEN IF IT MEANS BREAKING THE LAWS OF PHYSICS, OR BREAKING EVERY ESP MORAL CODE...

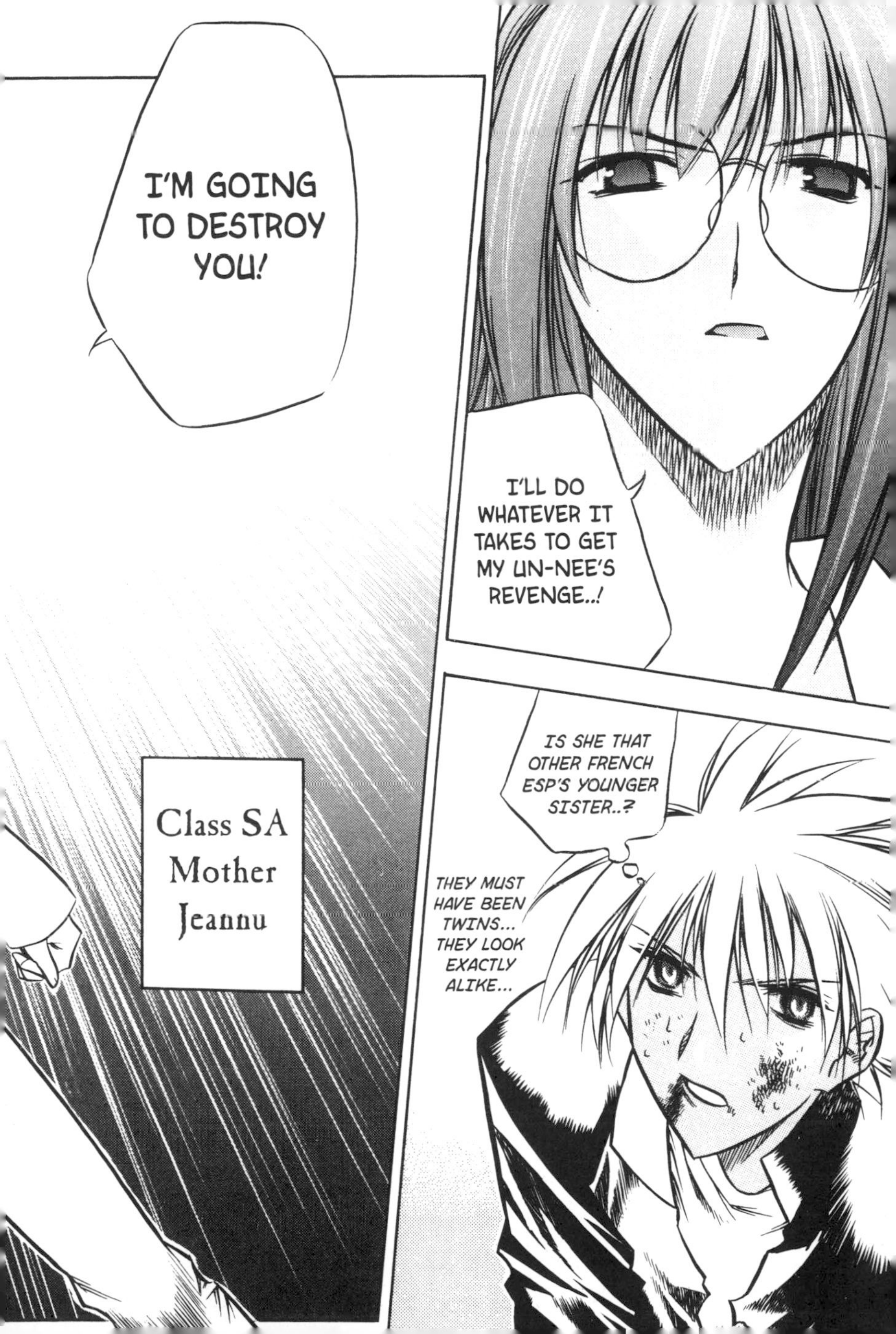
I'LL DO WHATEVER IT TAKES TO GET MY UN-NEE'S REVENGE..!
I'M GOING TO DESTROY YOU!
IS SHE THAT OTHER FRENCH ESP'S YOUNGER SISTER..?
THEY MUST HAVE BEEN TWINS... THEY LOOK EXACTLY ALIKE...
Class SA Mother Jeannu

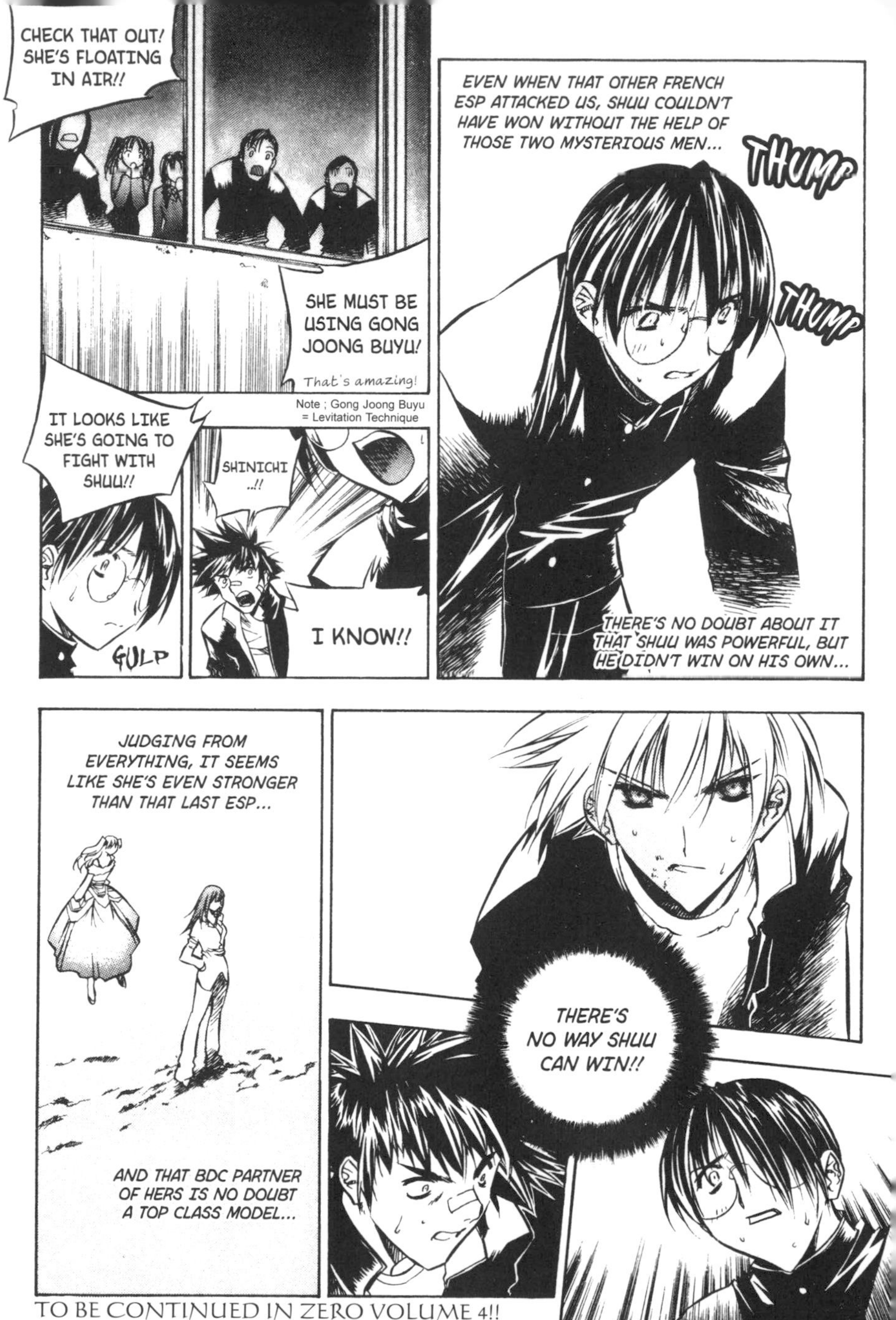
CHECK THAT OUT! SHE'S FLOATING IN AIR!!
SHE MUST BE USING GONG JOONG BUYU!
That's amazing!
Note ; Gong Joong Buyu = Levitation Technique
IT LOOKS LIKE SHE'S GOING TO FIGHT WITH SHUU!!
GULP
SHINICHI ..!!
I KNOW!!
EVEN WHEN THAT OTHER FRENCH ESP ATTACKED US, SHUU COULDN'T HAVE WON WITHOUT THE HELP OF THOSE TWO MYSTERIOUS MEN...
THUMP
THUMP
THERE'S NO DOUBT ABOUT IT THAT SHUU WAS POWERFUL, BUT HE DIDN'T WIN ON HIS OWN...
JUDGING FROM EVERYTHING, IT SEEMS LIKE SHE'S EVEN STRONGER THAN THAT LAST ESP...
AND THAT BDC PARTNER OF HERS IS NO DOUBT A TOP CLASS MODEL...
THERE'S NO WAY SHUU CAN WIN!!

TO BE CONTINUED IN ZERO VOLUME 4!!

ZERO
THE BEGINNING
OF THE COFFIN

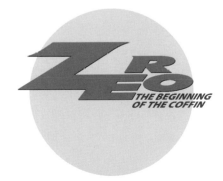

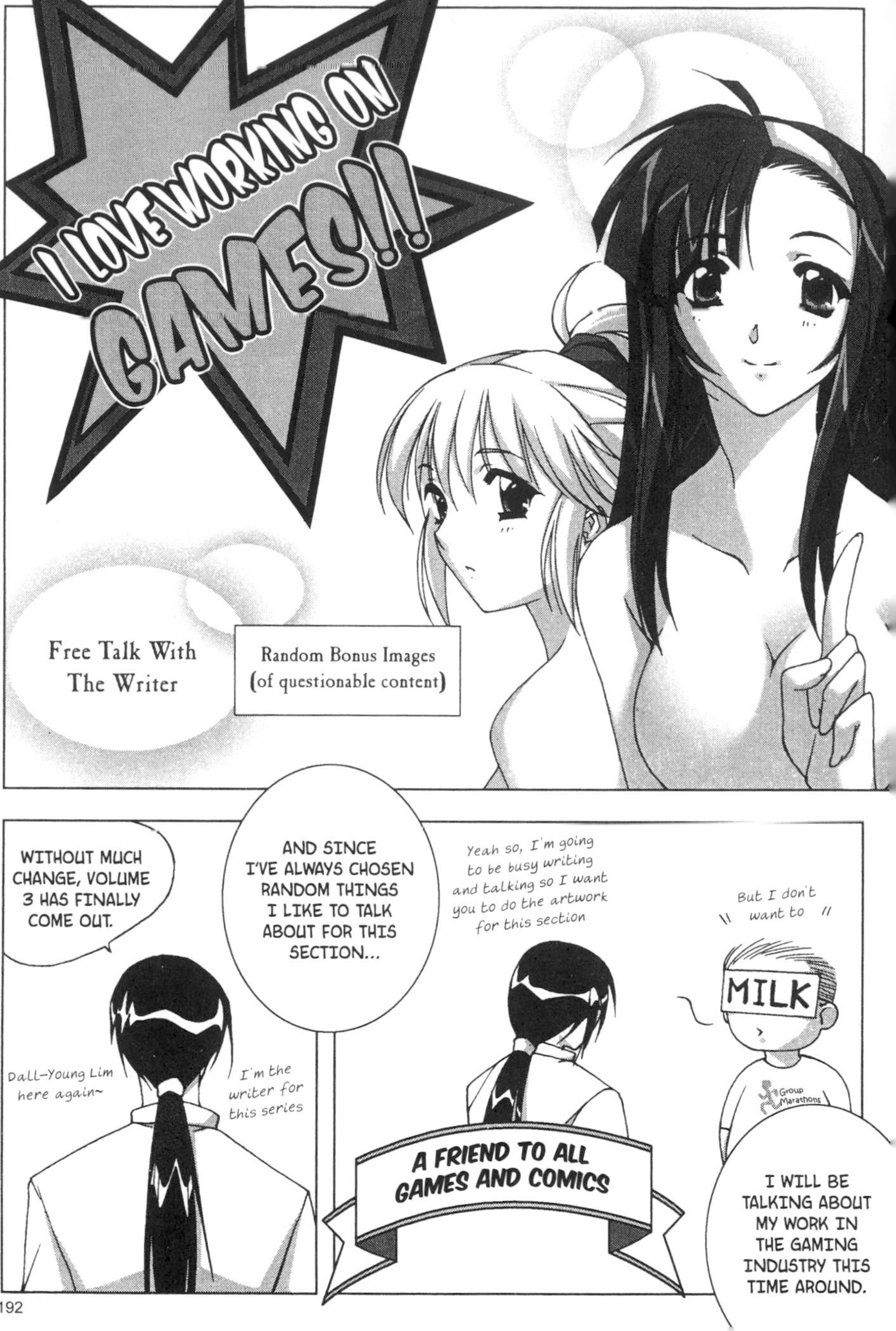
I LOVE WORKING ON GAMES!!
Free Talk With The Writer
Random Bonus Images (of questionable content)
WITHOUT MUCH CHANGE, VOLUME 3 HAS FINALLY COME OUT.
Dall-Young Lim here again~
I'm the writer for this series
AND SINCE I'VE ALWAYS CHOSEN RANDOM THINGS I LIKE TO TALK ABOUT FOR THIS SECTION...
Yeah so, I'm going to be busy writing and talking so I want you to do the artwork for this section
But I don't want to
MILK
Group Marathons
A FRIEND TO ALL GAMES AND COMICS
I WILL BE TALKING ABOUT MY WORK IN THE GAMING INDUSTRY THIS TIME AROUND.

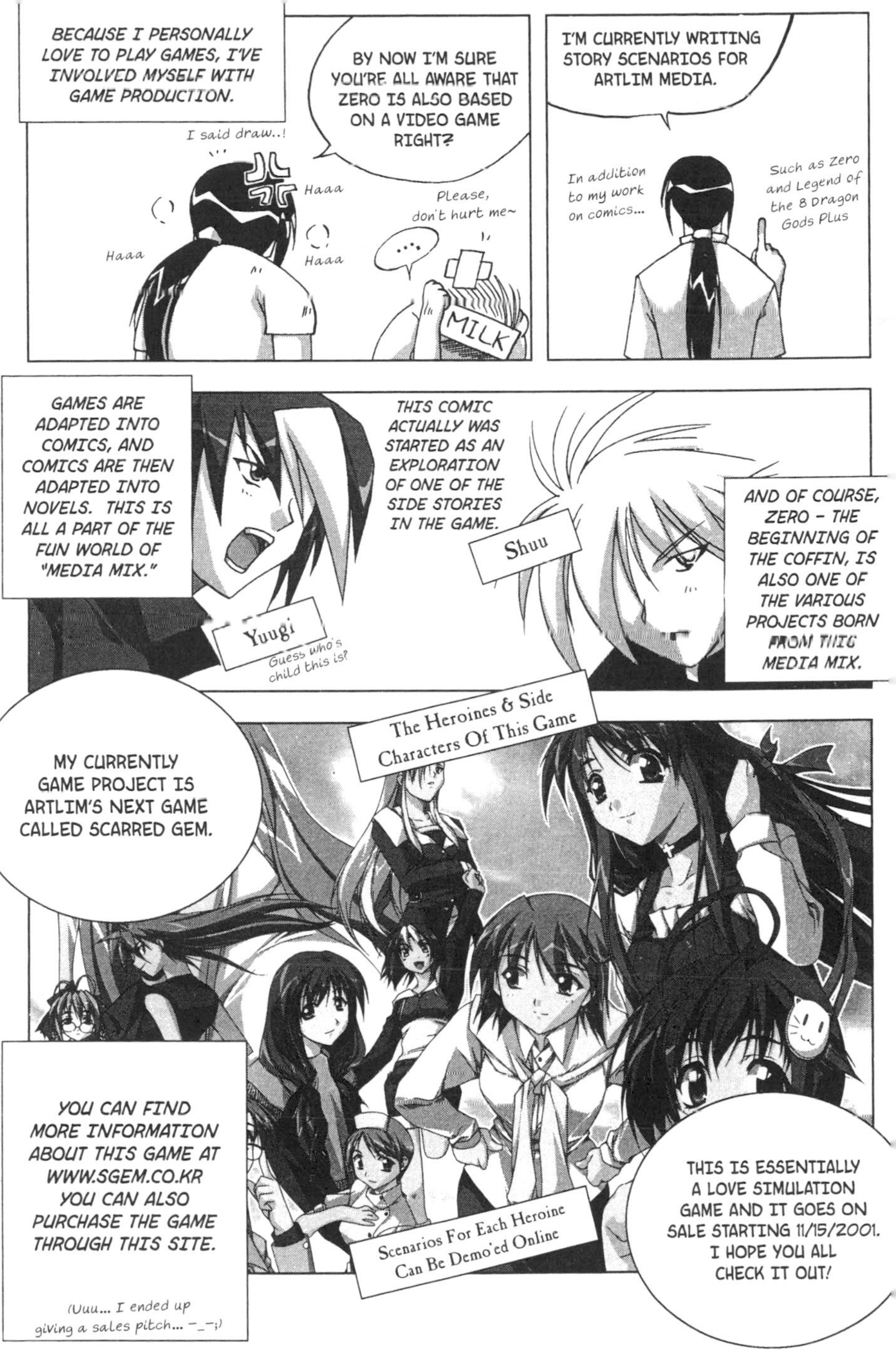
BECAUSE I PERSONALLY LOVE TO PLAY GAMES, I'VE INVOLVED MYSELF WITH GAME PRODUCTION.
BY NOW I'M SURE YOU'RE ALL AWARE THAT ZERO IS ALSO BASED ON A VIDEO GAME RIGHT?
I said draw..!
Haaa
Haaa
Haaa
Please, don't hurt me~
...
MILK
I'M CURRENTLY WRITING STORY SCENARIOS FOR ARTLIM MEDIA.
In addition to my work on comics...
Such as Zero and Legend of the 8 Dragon Gods Plus
GAMES ARE ADAPTED INTO COMICS, AND COMICS ARE THEN ADAPTED INTO NOVELS. THIS IS ALL A PART OF THE FUN WORLD OF "MEDIA MIX."
THIS COMIC ACTUALLY WAS STARTED AS AN EXPLORATION OF ONE OF THE SIDE STORIES IN THE GAME.
Shuu
Yuugi
Guess who's child this is?
AND OF COURSE, ZERO – THE BEGINNING OF THE COFFIN, IS ALSO ONE OF THE VARIOUS PROJECTS BORN FROM THIS MEDIA MIX.
MY CURRENTLY GAME PROJECT IS ARTLIM'S NEXT GAME CALLED SCARRED GEM.
The Heroines & Side Characters Of This Game
YOU CAN FIND MORE INFORMATION ABOUT THIS GAME AT WWW.SGEM.CO.KR YOU CAN ALSO PURCHASE THE GAME THROUGH THIS SITE.
(Uuu... I ended up giving a sales pitch... -_-;)
Scenarios For Each Heroine Can Be Demo'ed Online
THIS IS ESSENTIALLY A LOVE SIMULATION GAME AND IT GOES ON SALE STARTING 11/15/2001. I HOPE YOU ALL CHECK IT OUT!

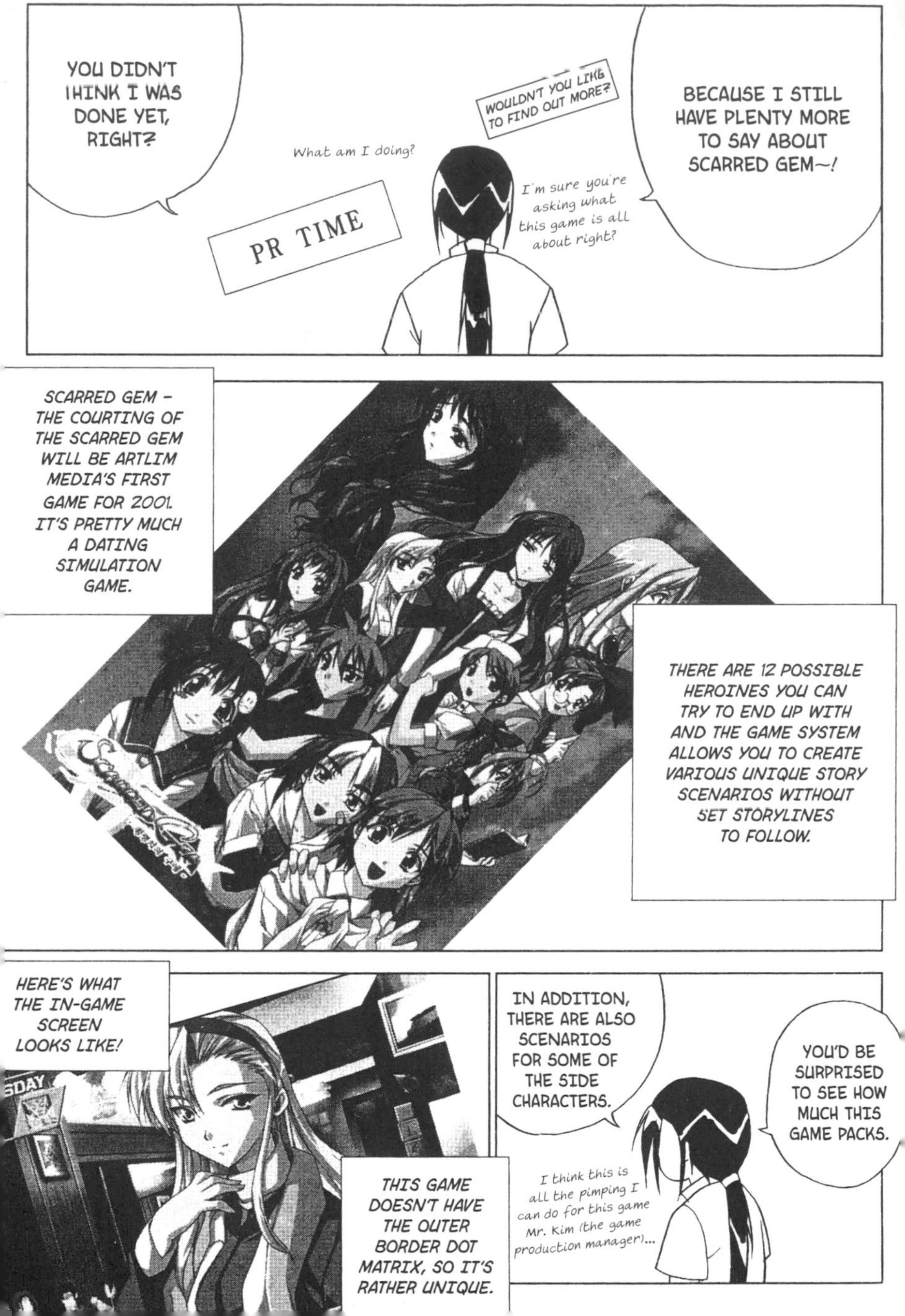

YOU DIDN'T THINK I WAS DONE YET, RIGHT?
WOULDN'T YOU LIKE TO FIND OUT MORE?
What am I doing?
PR TIME
BECAUSE I STILL HAVE PLENTY MORE TO SAY ABOUT SCARRED GEM~!
I'm sure you're asking what this game is all about right?
SCARRED GEM – THE COURTING OF THE SCARRED GEM WILL BE ARTLIM MEDIA'S FIRST GAME FOR 2001. IT'S PRETTY MUCH A DATING SIMULATION GAME.
THERE ARE 12 POSSIBLE HEROINES YOU CAN TRY TO END UP WITH AND THE GAME SYSTEM ALLOWS YOU TO CREATE VARIOUS UNIQUE STORY SCENARIOS WITHOUT SET STORYLINES TO FOLLOW.
HERE'S WHAT THE IN-GAME SCREEN LOOKS LIKE!
THIS GAME DOESN'T HAVE THE OUTER BORDER DOT MATRIX, SO IT'S RATHER UNIQUE.
IN ADDITION, THERE ARE ALSO SCENARIOS FOR SOME OF THE SIDE CHARACTERS.
YOU'D BE SURPRISED TO SEE HOW MUCH THIS GAME PACKS.
I think this is all the pimping I can do for this game Mr. Kim (the game production manager)...

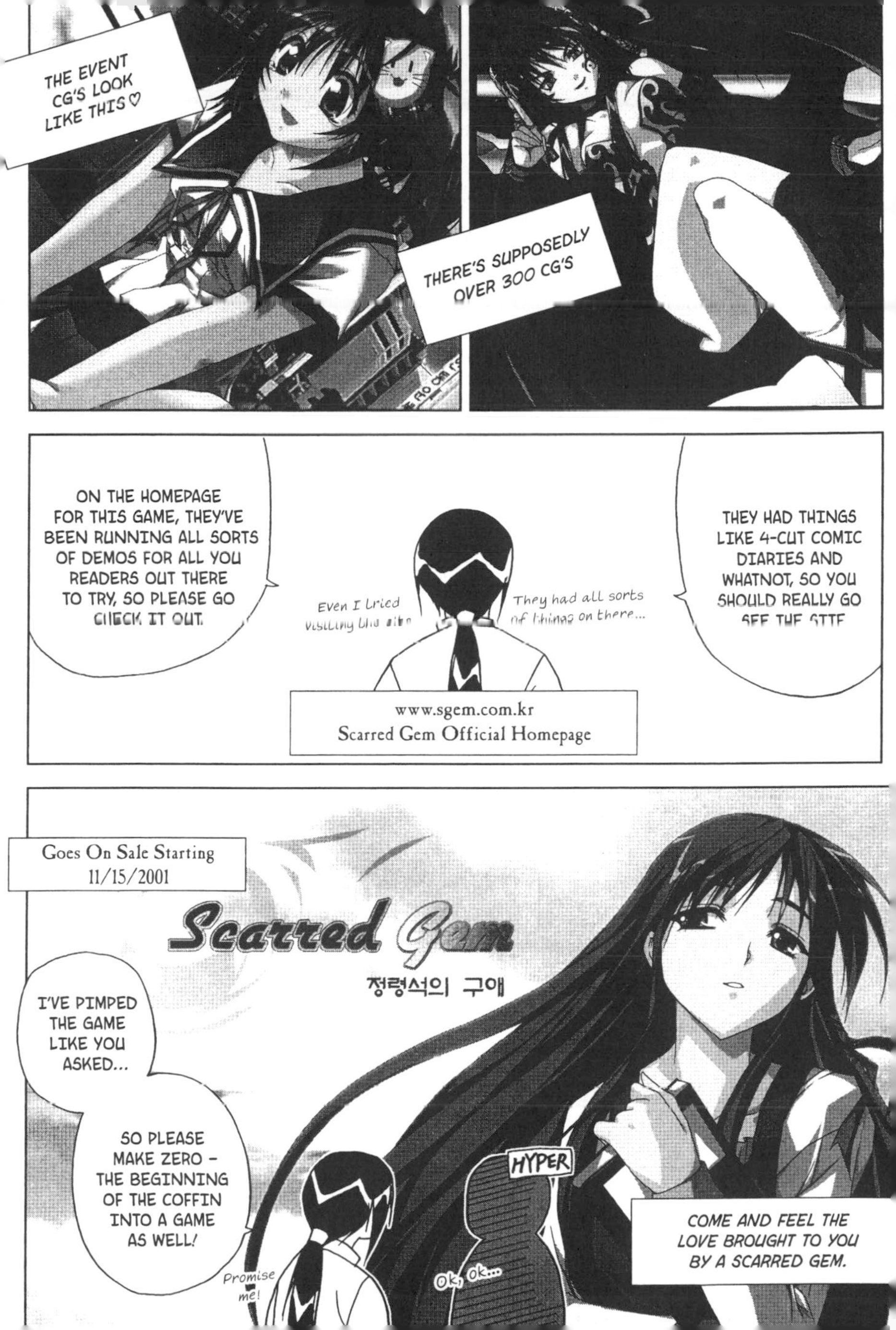

THE EVENT CG'S LOOK LIKE THIS♡
THERE'S SUPPOSEDLY OVER 300 CG'S
ON THE HOMEPAGE FOR THIS GAME, THEY'VE BEEN RUNNING ALL SORTS OF DEMOS FOR ALL YOU READERS OUT THERE TO TRY, SO PLEASE GO CHECK IT OUT.
Even I tried
They had all sorts of things on there...
THEY HAD THINGS LIKE 4-CUT COMIC DIARIES AND WHATNOT, SO YOU SHOULD REALLY GO SEE THE SITE
www.sgem.com.kr
Scarred Gem Official Homepage
Goes On Sale Starting
11/15/2001
Scarred Gem
정령석의 구애
I'VE PIMPED THE GAME LIKE YOU ASKED...
SO PLEASE MAKE ZERO - THE BEGINNING OF THE COFFIN INTO A GAME AS WELL!
HYPER
Promise me!
Ok, ok...
COME AND FEEL THE LOVE BROUGHT TO YOU BY A SCARRED GEM.

CHARACTER DESIGNS

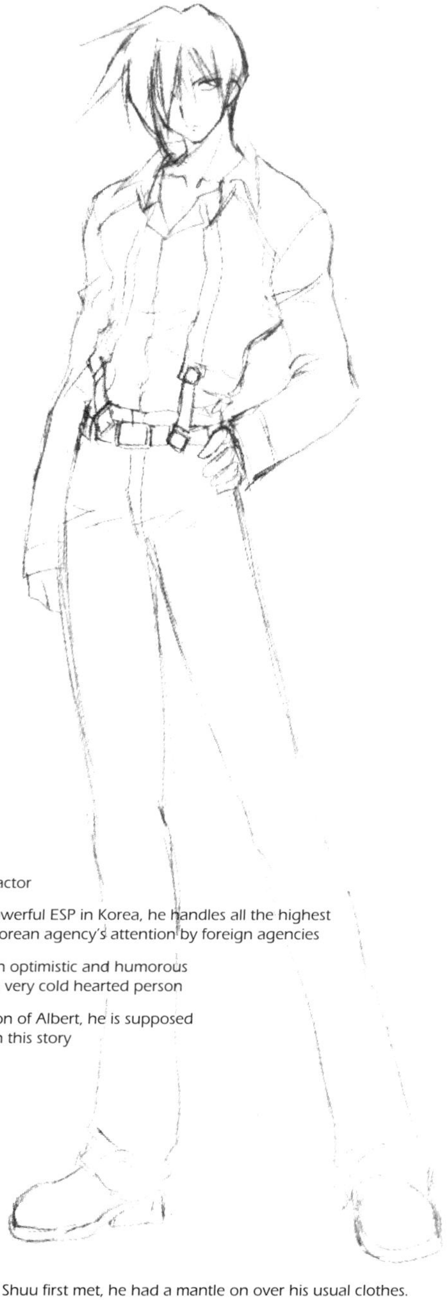

YUSHIN

- A Pro Level Korean ESP Contractor
- Acknowledged as the most powerful ESP in Korea, he handles all the highest priority cases brought to the Korean agency's attention by foreign agencies
- At first glance, he seems like an optimistic and humorous type of guy, but he's actually a very cold hearted person
- Power rank : With the exception of Albert, he is supposed to be the most powerful ESP in this story

When he and Shuu first met, he had a mantle on over his usual clothes.

JEANNU (MOTHER)

- She's a Class SA rank ESP from France
- She's the younger sister of Charlotte, the ESP who is killed by Shuu and the two mysterious ESP's
- She comes looking for Shuu at his school to get revenge for her sister.

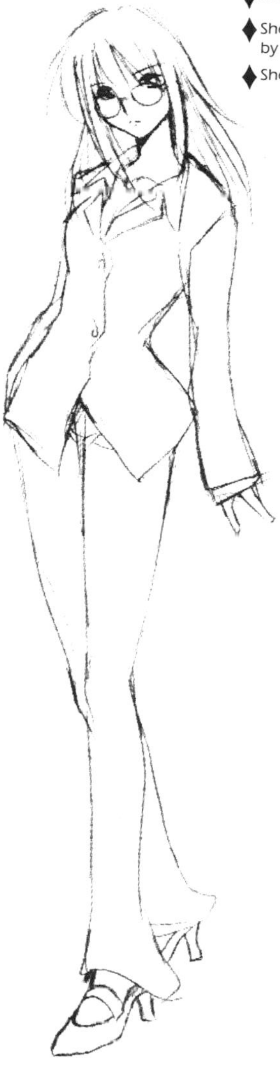

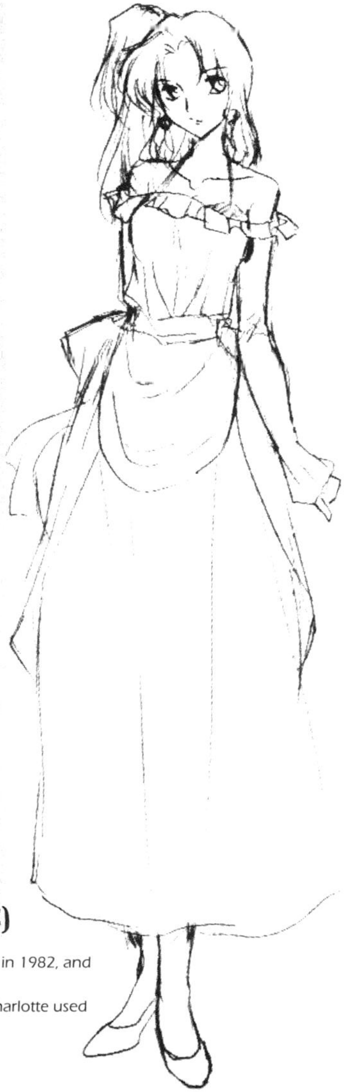

LAYLETTE (BDC)

- She's an elite model of BDC's created in 1982, and her "mother" ESP is Jeannu
- She is much more powerful than the BDC model Charlotte used

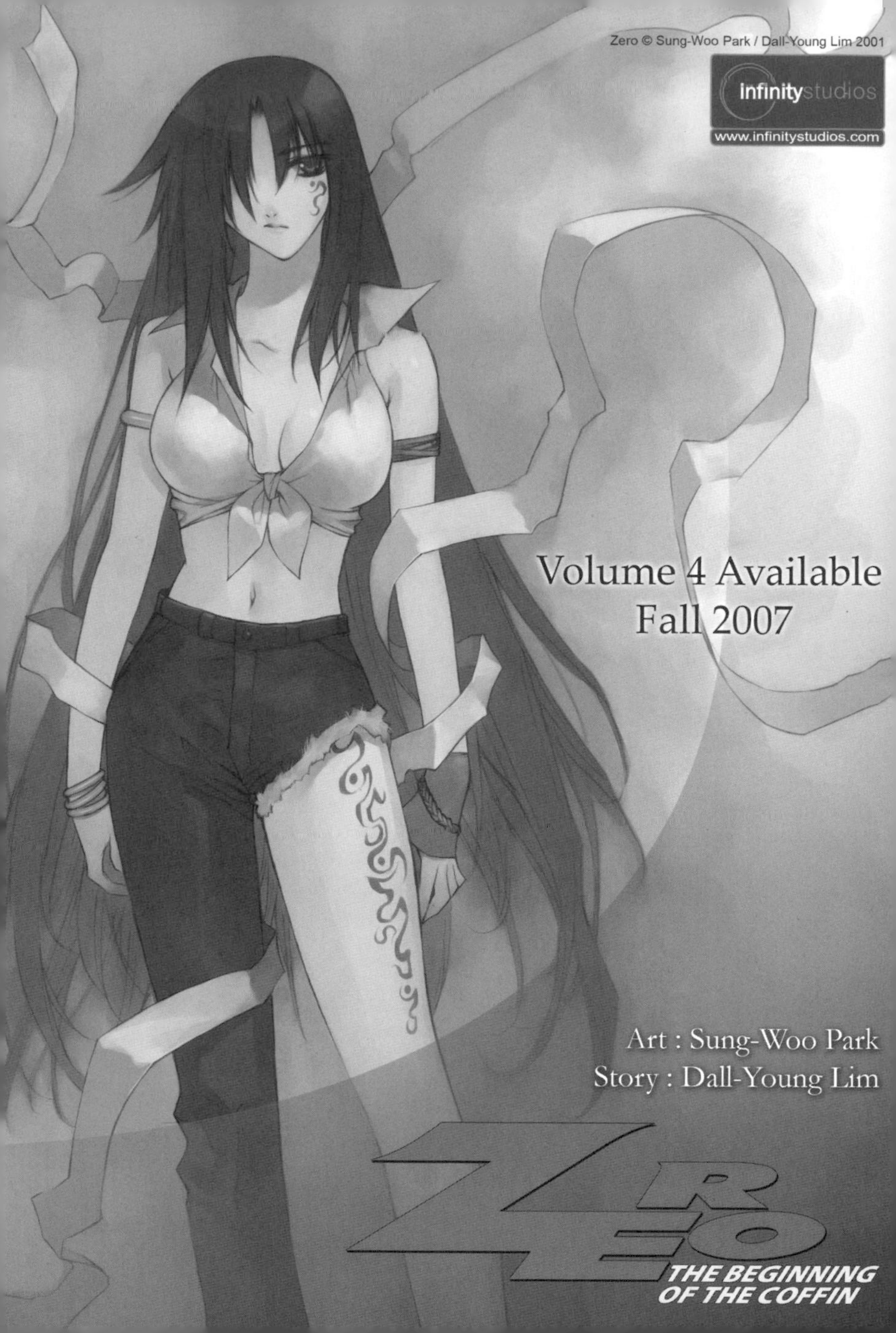
Zero © Sung-Woo Park / Dall-Young Lim 2001
infinitystudios
www.infinitystudios.com
Volume 4 Available
Fall 2007
Art : Sung-Woo Park
Story : Dall-Young Lim
ZERO
THE BEGINNING OF THE COFFIN

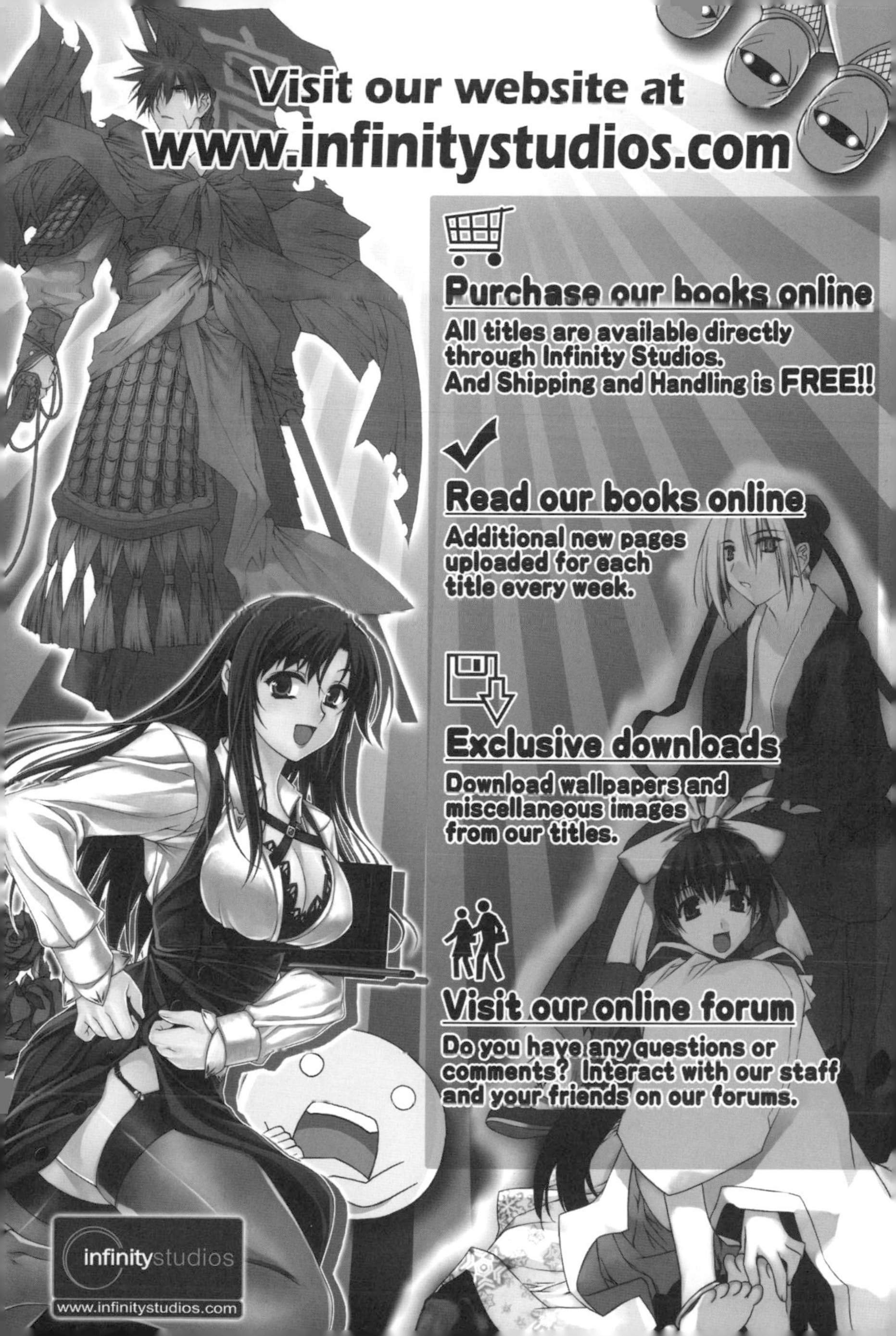

Visit our website at
www.infinitystudios.com
Purchase our books online
All titles are available directly through Infinity Studios. And Shipping and Handling is FREE!!
Read our books online
Additional new pages uploaded for each title every week.
Exclusive downloads
Download wallpapers and miscellaneous images from our titles.
Visit our online forum
Do you have any questions or comments? Interact with our staff and your friends on our forums.
infinitystudios
www.infinitystudios.com

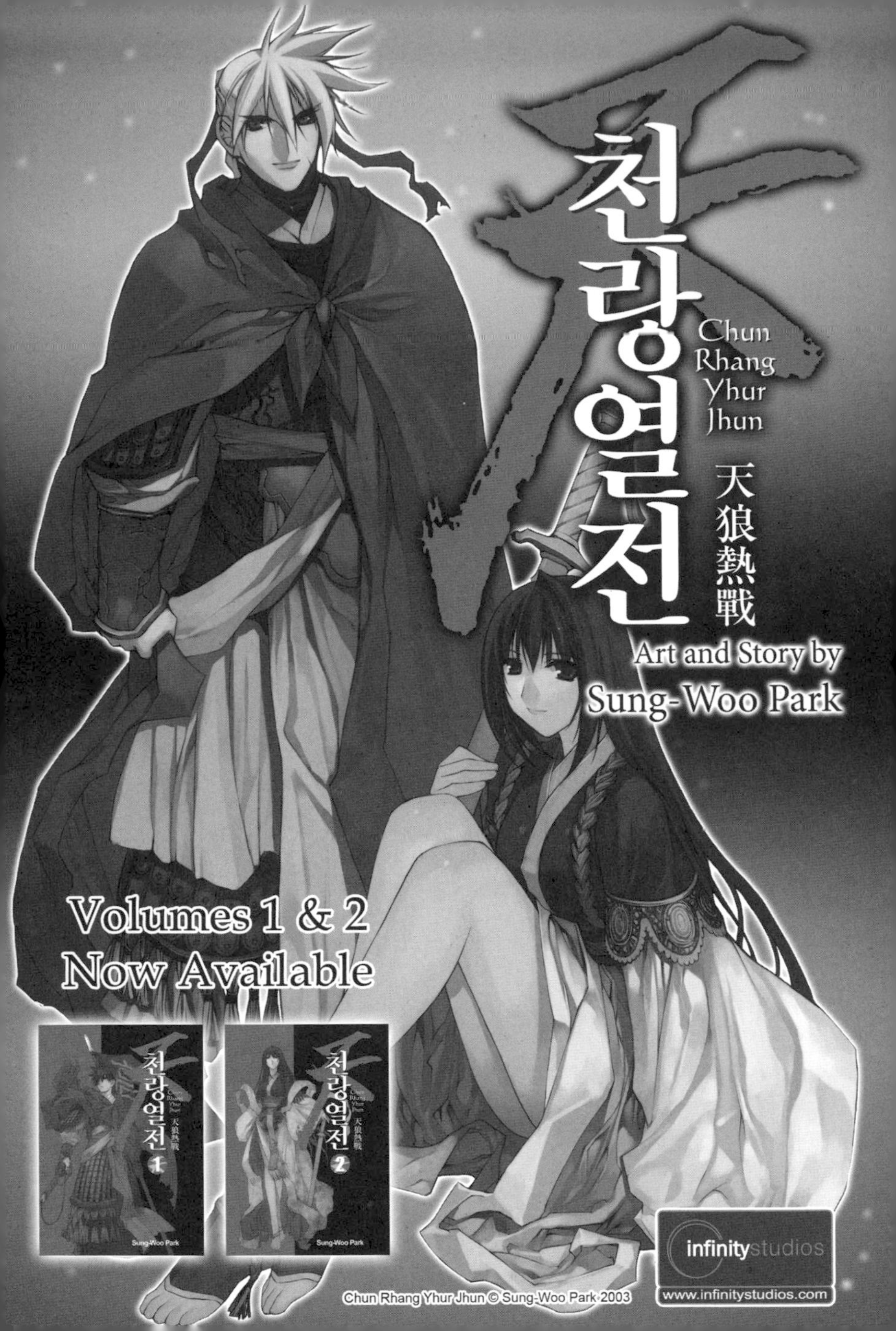

천랑열전
Chun Rhang Yhur Jhun
天狼熱戰
Art and Story by
Sung-Woo Park
Volumes 1 & 2
Now Available
infinitystudios
www.infinitystudios.com
Chun Rhang Yhur Jhun © Sung-Woo Park 2003

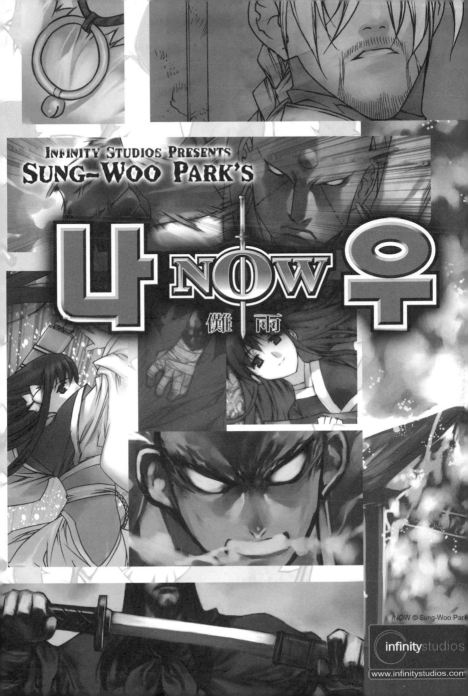

INFINITY STUDIOS PRESENTS
SUNG-WOO PARK'S

나 NOW 우

僕 雨

infinitystudios
www.infinitystudios.com

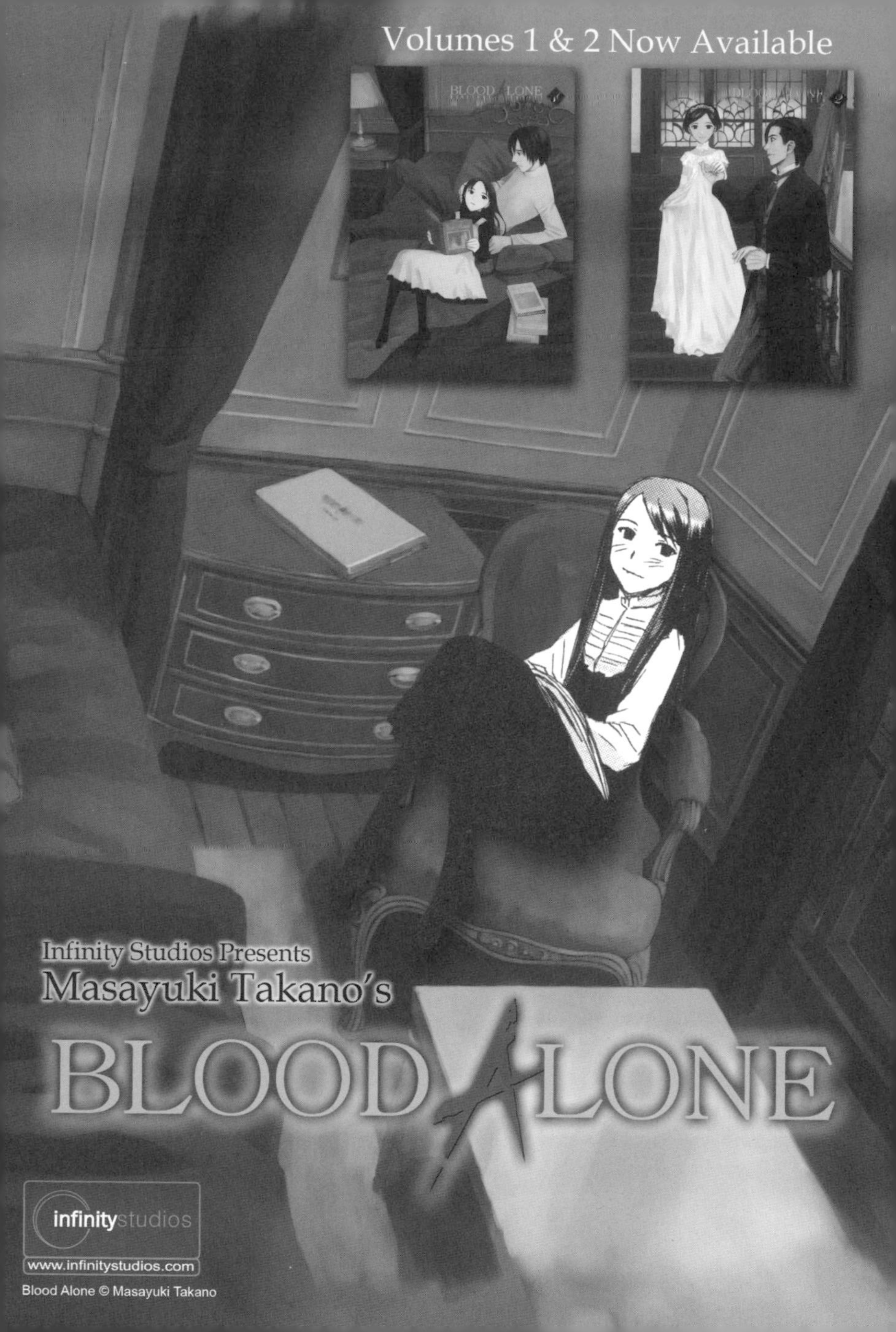

Volumes 1 & 2 Now Available
Infinity Studios Presents
Masayuki Takano's
BLOOD ALONE
infinitystudios
www.infinitystudios.com
Blood Alone © Masayuki Takano

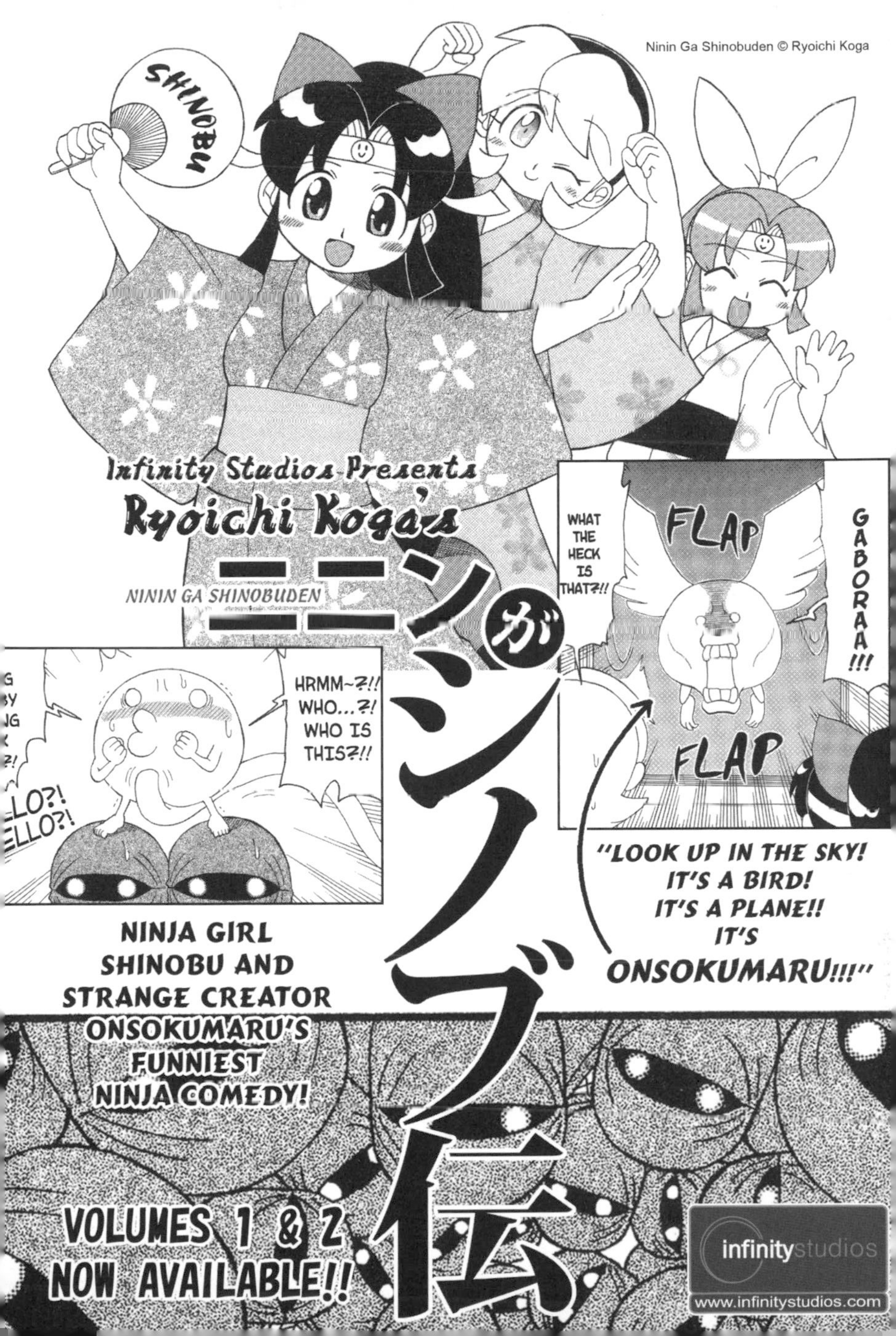

Ninin Ga Shinobuden © Ryoichi Koga
SHINOBU
Infinity Studios Presents
Ryoichi Koga's
NININ GA SHINOBUDEN
WHAT THE HECK IS THAT?!!
FLAP
GABORAA!!!
FLAP
HRMM~?!! WHO...?! WHO IS THIS?!!
"LOOK UP IN THE SKY! IT'S A BIRD! IT'S A PLANE!! IT'S ONSOKUMARU!!!"
NINJA GIRL SHINOBU AND STRANGE CREATOR ONSOKUMARU'S FUNNIEST NINJA COMEDY!
VOLUMES 1 & 2 NOW AVAILABLE!!
infinitystudios
www.infinitystudios.com

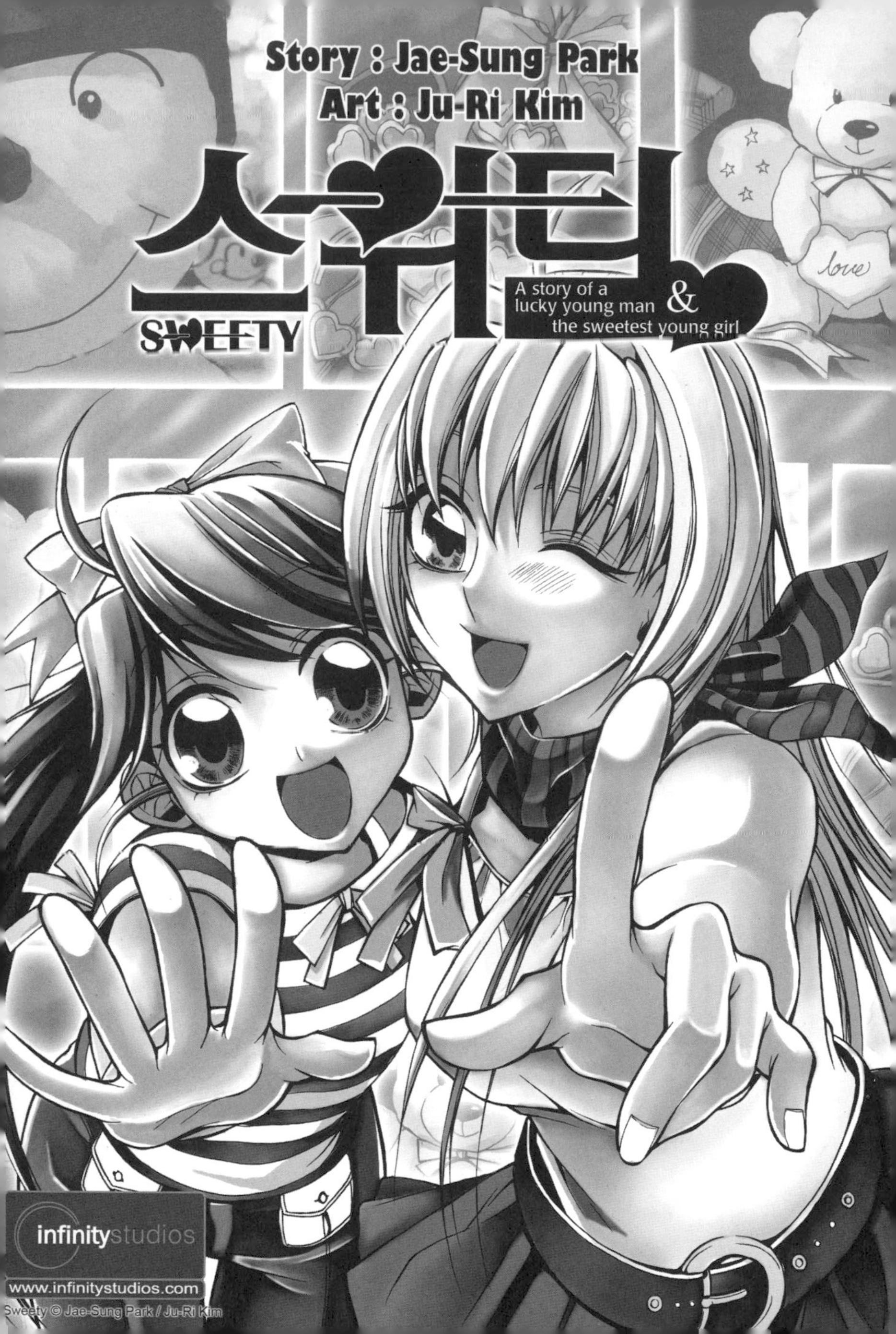
Story : Jae-Sung Park
Art : Ju-Ri Kim
스위티
SWEETY
A story of a lucky young man & the sweetest young girl
love
infinitystudios
www.infinitystudios.com
Sweety © Jae-Sung Park / Ju-Ri Kim

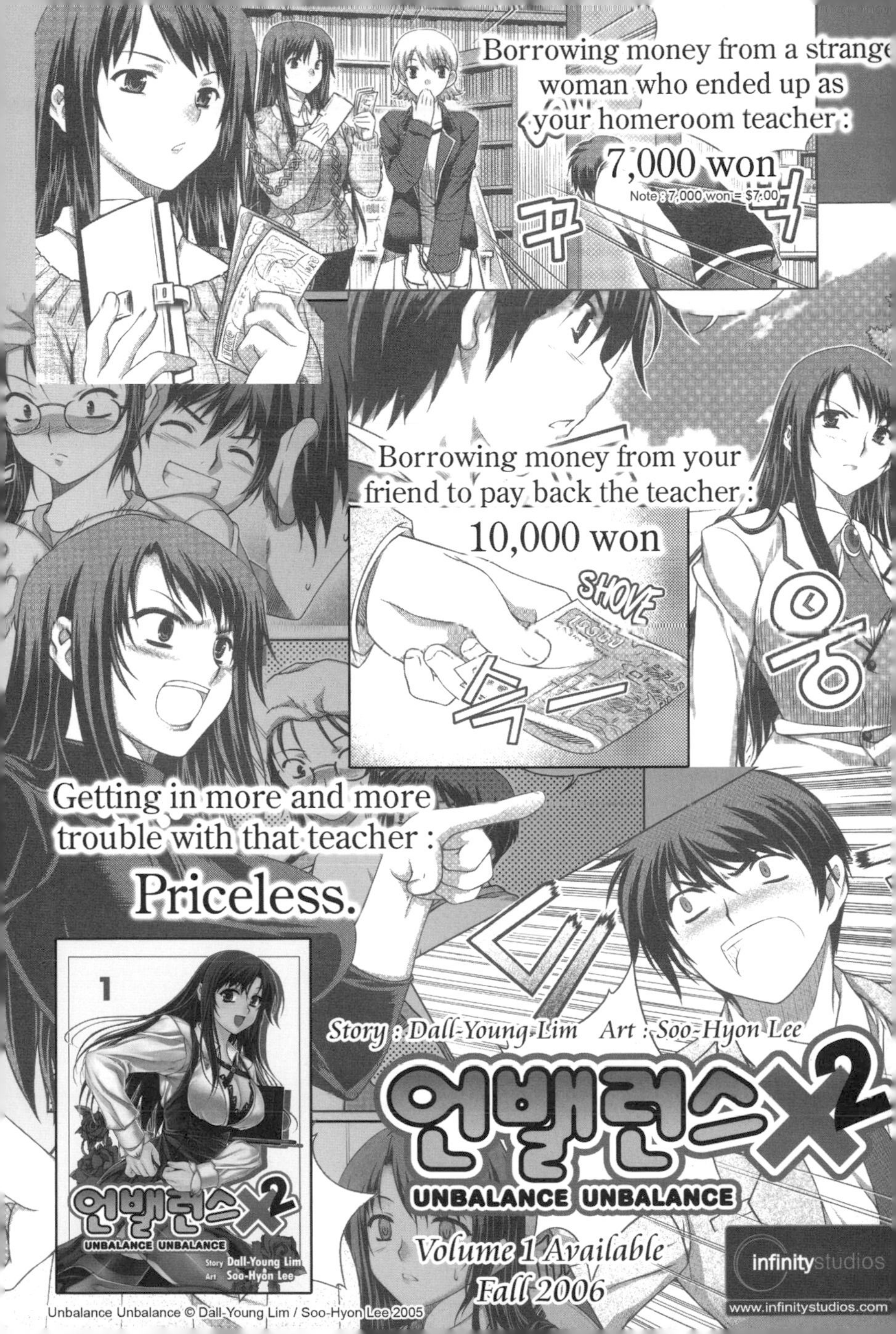
Borrowing money from a strange woman who ended up as your homeroom teacher :
7,000 won
Note : 7,000 won = $7.00
Borrowing money from your friend to pay back the teacher :
10,000 won
SHOVE
응
Getting in more and more trouble with that teacher :
Priceless.
Story : Dall-Young Lim Art : Soo-Hyon Lee
언밸런스×2
UNBALANCE UNBALANCE
Volume 1 Available Fall 2006
infinitystudios
www.infinitystudios.com
1
언밸런스×2
UNBALANCE UNBALANCE
Story Dall-Young Lim
Art Soo-Hyon Lee
Unbalance Unbalance © Dall-Young Lim / Soo-Hyon Lee 2005

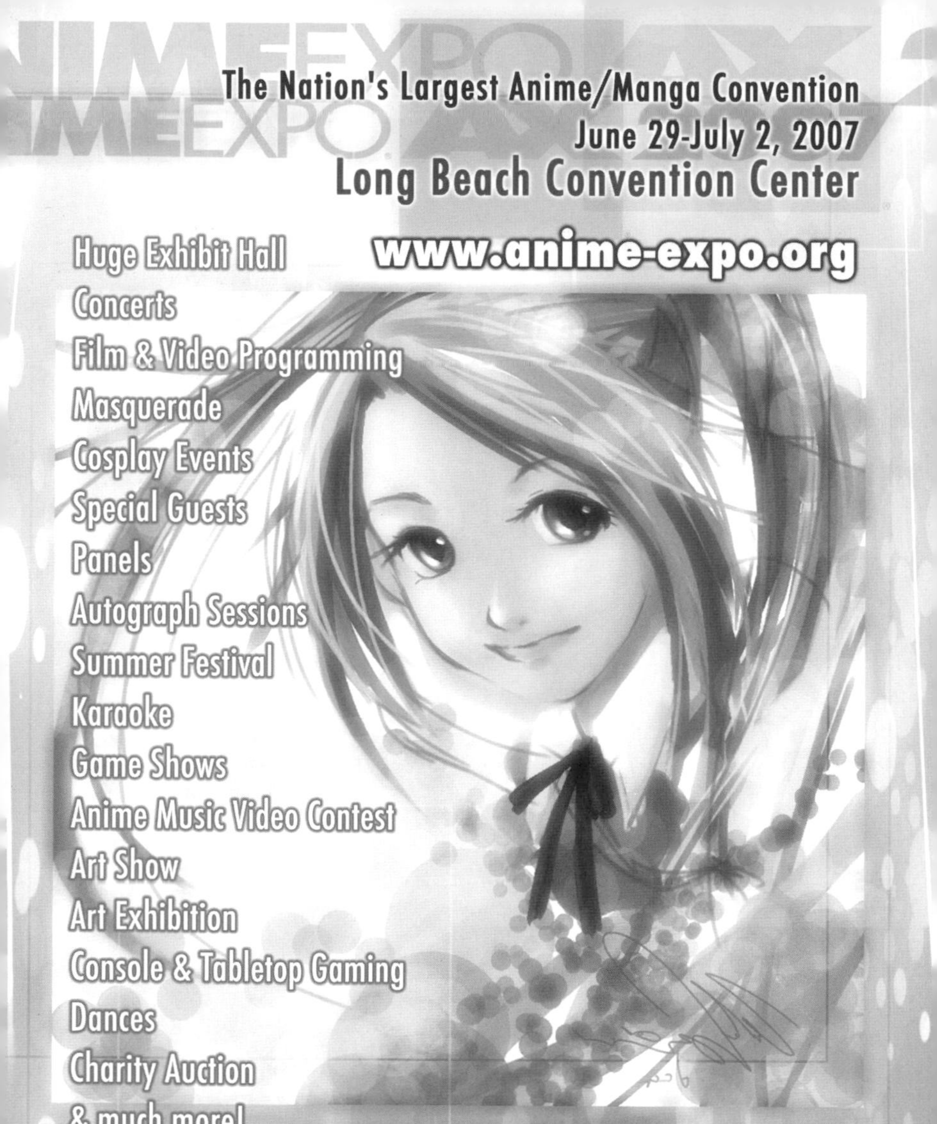
ANIME EXPO AX 2007
The Nation's Largest Anime/Manga Convention
June 29-July 2, 2007
Long Beach Convention Center
www.anime-expo.org
Huge Exhibit Hall
Concerts
Film & Video Programming
Masquerade
Cosplay Events
Special Guests
Panels
Autograph Sessions
Summer Festival
Karaoke
Game Shows
Anime Music Video Contest
Art Show
Art Exhibition
Console & Tabletop Gaming
Dances
Charity Auction
& much more!
ANIMEEXPO AX 2007

illustrated by Zelda C. Wang